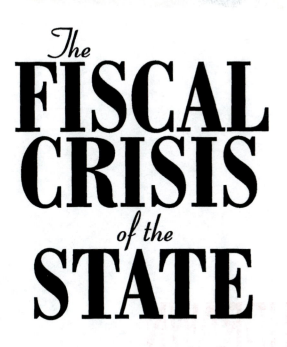

# The FISCAL CRISIS of the STATE

*The*
# FISCAL CRISIS
*of the*
# STATE

## James O'Connor

**With a new introduction by the author**

**Transaction Publishers**
New Brunswick (U.S.A.) and London (U.K.)

New material this edition copyright © 2002 by Transaction Publishers, New Brunswick, New Jersey. Originally published in 1973 by St. Martin's Press.

This book is printed on acid-free paper that meets the American National Standard for Permanence of Paper for Printed Library Materials.

Library of Congress Catalog Number: 2001018906
ISBN: 0-7658-0860-9
Printed in the United States of America

Library of Congress Cataloging-in-Publication Data

O'Connor, James (James R.)
The fiscal crisis of the state / James O'Connor ; with a new introduction by the author.
        p. cm.
Originally  published: New York : St. Martin's Press, 1973.
Includes bibliographical references and index.
ISBN 0-7658-0860-9 (pbk : alk. paper)
    1. Finance, Public—United States.  2. Budget—United States.
3. Taxation—United States.  I. Title.

HJ257.2 .O26  2001
352.4'.213'0973—dc21                                    2001018906

:

# ACKNOWLEDGMENTS

This work springs from two articles—"The Fiscal Crisis of the State" and "Inflation, Fiscal Crisis, and the Working Class"— that were published in the journal *Socialist Revolution*. I wish to thank the editors for letting me use the pages of *Socialist Revolution* to experiment with the ideas developed in this book, as well as for their encouragement and many helpful criticisms. I am indebted to Doug Dowd, Joan Robinson, and Lynn Turgeon for their useful criticisms of the original article, "The Fiscal Crisis of the State." I especially appreciate the criticisms of the entire manuscript made by Stephan Liebfried, David Gold, and members of the Max-Planck-Institute in Starnberg, Germany, during my visit in the fall of 1972— in particular, Claus Offe and Ulrich Rödel. Thanks also are due to Dan Feshbach, who has made me aware of the importance of recent developments in regional planning and regional government. In addition, I wish to thank Ellen Estrin, whose critical research was important during the formative stage of this work. Last but not least, I want to stress that studies such as this one owe a great deal to the general upsurge in Marxist and critical economic studies, which in turn is attributable to the current crisis of the capitalist system at home and on a worldwide scale. Specifically, I want to express my gratitude to the many audiences who have heard me present the fiscal crisis thesis in various stages of its development and whose questions and comments were extremely important in helping me work out many of the particular ideas set out in this book.

James O'Connor

For the workers, the unemployed, the poor,
the students, and others whose struggles
against the state have made this work possible

# CONTENTS

# INTRODUCTION
# TO THE TRANSACTION EDITION

*Fiscal Crisis of the State* (1973), written in the late 1960s and early 1970s, was the product of a unique combination of personal, intellectual and political experiences:

(1) My background in public finance comes from my experience as a graduate student at Columbia University in the late 1950s, when I was an assistant to Carl Shoup, then dean of public finance studies in the United States This work made me dimly aware that what I would later come to think of as bourgeois economics had no theory of the state budget, defined as a coherent explanation of the size of the budget and its main expenditures, of the amount and type of taxation, and of the distributive impact of the budget as a whole. As an economist-in-training who held some leftist political opinions, I was unaware at the time that such a theory would have to be both political economic and political sociological. About the former, I knew little at the time; about the latter, I knew less.

(2) My study of Paul Baran's and Paul Sweezy's *Monopoly Capital* (1966).[1] My attention was drawn to the authors' unproblematic treatment of state expenditures—all of which were defined as "economic surplus" (i.e., not even indirectly productive of value and surplus value). My studies indicated that some types of expenditures had the effect of raising the productivity of labor (directly or indirectly) hence *ceteris paribus* increasing surplus value. But, other types of state spending, for example, welfare payments, could not be so regarded, which created a puzzle. At this point I realized that there wasn't a satisfactory theory of the state budget in either bourgeois or Marxist economics. I came to believe that there was something very wrong about theoretically treating military spending in the same way that one would interpret, say, the education budget.

On the other hand, the U.S. military trained a lot of future workers and the U.S. education system was organized in partly militaristic ways, hence budget items can't always be neatly catalogued in ways pleasing to theorists. More problematically, the social and economic functions of any given expenditure category may carry one or another meaning according to the historical conjuncture of a particular capitalist country or social formation.

On the tax side, both bourgeois and Marxist theory also seemed to be unnecessarily weak. In theorizing tax cuts, for example, neither type of economics made a distinction between cutting taxes on the poor because "people needed more money to spend" versus reducing taxes on the middle class because "the economic system needed people to spend more money." The first is a social welfare approach to tax cuts, the second a simple Keynesian macroeconomic approach. Both approaches competed with still another rationale for cutting taxes, namely, reducing the tax burden on the rich because "the economic system needed more savings and investment." The class struggle seemed to be embedded in the language of tax policy in other ways. While it was assumed that the rich would invest more of their incomes only if they received more money from the state via a tax cut, it was thought that the poor would supply more laborpower to the labor market only if they received *less* money from the state via (for example) a cut in welfare benefits  The class analysis angle (which I failed to fully exploit in *Fiscal Crisis*) yielded more results of interest with respect to the sociological meaning of the various types of taxes imposed. Value added taxes were important in Europe, where the class struggle was relatively developed, because they helped to conceal the fact that the burden fell mainly on working people. In the U.S., individual income taxes yielded most federal government revenue: income taxes were (and are) deducted from wages directly by the government and most workers soon got used to figuring their wage income "after taxes." Over the years, the U.S. income tax became increasingly less progressive because (among other reasons) the rich opened up literally thousands of loopholes for themselves. Instead of fighting to open up loopholes for labor and the poor, unions and popular organizations wasted lots of time and energy trying to close loopholes for the rich.

(3) I recall reading the paper one morning in 1967, and noting that the first page was filled with stories all of a piece: a welfare struggle, a teachers' strike, a new government subsidy to business, a conflict over taxes. This was when I first realized that the class struggle had been displaced (in part) onto the state and its budget[2]—a fact that had important implications for both Marxist theory and social movements.

(4) When a few of us revived the old *Studies on the Left*[3] in the form of the new *Socialist Revolution* (now *Socialist Review*), I published my first attempt to theorize the budget in the first issue (1970). Claus Offe, the political sociologist, visited Berkeley shortly after and he invited me to work at Jürgen Habermas' new think tank in Starnberg (West Germany) for four months, where I found a sympathetic and upbeat critical ear. Habermas was working on the administrative contradictions (or steering problems) of the capitalist state while Offe focused on problems of political legitimation. Both types of studies complemented my own work

on the state's fiscal contradiction (or crisis), so this was a fruitful period for us and for social theory in this field generally.

(5) Between the *Socialist Revolution* article (1970) and the Starnberg visit (1973), during a vacation in Hawaii, I finally grasped the main thesis of *Fiscal Crisis,* or what I wanted the main thesis to be. This was simply that the "the state grows because it grows." For me a eureka moment, I realized that I was theorizing the expansion of the state budget (and state functions) in terms of the growing budget and state themselves (see below).

Since 1980 or so, however, two world historic and closely related phenomena clearly demanded amendments to my theory of the budget. Under an international regime with the U.S. as the imperial hegemon, the globalization of capital reestablished (and then some) capital's power over labor and the imposition of neoliberal theory and practice regained power for the U.S. (and the North generally) over the South. More, with hindsight we can see that neoliberalism was (and is) the political form of globalization of capital while the latter was (and is) the economic form of neoliberalism. Neoliberalism and global capital were (and are) both context and content of one another: the growth of globalism stimulated (and stimulates) more neoliberalism and the widening and deepening of the neoliberal project stimulates more global capital. An inner, not external, connection thus exists between neoliberalism and globalism. As global capital seeks more global investment chances, markets and easily exploitable laborpower, governments and international agencies forced ever more neoliberalism on the South and in somewhat different forms on the North itself. These developments put an end to what some call the "golden age" of capitalism (social democracy in Europe, laborism in Britain, New Dealism in the U.S., and nationalist development in the South).

Putting all this aside for a moment, today I would still defend *Fiscal Crisis*'s thesis that the "state grows because it grows" (although certainly not all the specific analyses found in the book) and it should be emphasized that I was careful to include a disclaimer that the book was a study of *one particular historical conjuncture of the U.S. economy and society, and the U.S. state and state budget.* Yet one can find many "fiscal-crisis type" phenomena in other countries in the same era and also in today's globalist era.

*FCS* had a number of consequences. I met other social scientists, state worker unionists, and others in different countries, who were working on the same general problem of the capitalist state in the political context of Rudi Deutsche's lament of the early 1970s. This line of thought was basically that the New Left was stalled because its leaders relied on "time-honored formulae and time-worn slogans" with respect to the nature of the modern state and state power, and the meaning of the state budget. This lack or absence inspired me, with the help of a German political scientist, to launch the journal *Kapitalistate*, which lasted eight years, and which was devoted to what came to be called "state theory." In the States, I organized an editorial group with Clarence Lo, Erik Olin Wright, Margaret Fay, David Gold and half a dozen other younger left scholars who later made names for themselves in academia, in the world of movement research and policy-making, and in activism. *Kapitalistate* didn't *cause* the explosion of research and writing on the capitalist state and the state in capitalist society from the mid-1970s until the last half of the 1980s, but it definitely was an influence. The cause was the utter confusion within activist circles, unions, and other groups, about what could be expected from the state (stick or carrot); how to go about struggling within and against the state to defend gains which even then were starting to erode; and, among many other questions and issues, how and why the state budget and administration generally had the effects that they did on the national macro-economy. Other works on state finance appeared, some following the methods and theory of *FCS*, others developing more orthodox Marxist theories, still others forging new paths. New types of debates sprang up; many historical studies of state budgets and programs were completed; international comparative research on state spending in relation to GDP (and so on) was carried out. Finally, there developed by the mid-1980s a big academic industry of state theory and research. New left-of-center journals were launched that focused on the state and related problems, and journals that hitherto had failed to publish in this area began to print articles of the *Kapitalistate* type. By the mid-1980s, half a dozen years after I accepted a position at the University of California (Santa Cruz), "state theory" generally and the state finances in specific had become central and respectable subjects—especially in political sociology and among "left-Weberians." Symbolic politics; the problem of "no-cost claims" and state policy; the growth of theories of the state and human, natural and communal capital; and a host of other issues and questions appeared in many leftist scholarly journals and popular leftist magazines, as well as in mainstream journals.

By then I was deep into a new study of the development of the U.S. (and by extension) Western working classes; the U.S. national ideology of individualism; and the connection between changes in class composition, ideology in the Gramscian sense, and the macro-economics of U.S. capitalism.[4] When I reached a level of understanding that I thought was adequate to the problem of theorizing the labor and social movements in the States, I turned away from "state theory." Two short works are significant exceptions: one is the seventh chapter of *Accumulation Crisis* (1984), treating the state and the reproduction costs of laborpower; the other is an essay titled "The Conditions of Production and the Production of Conditions," in which I deployed "state theory" to help to explain the relationship between environmental and social conflicts and the role or "functions" of the state therein.[5]

As for my own politics, I became a defender of a kind of neo-or-quasi-Leninist strategy of democratizing the state bureaucracy (or administration) through struggles "within and against the state." I believed (and still believe) that this is a winning radical strategy, in that it overcomes the weakness of Rousseau-type state theorizing and also of the standard anarchist view of the state (in both theories a specifically democratic state administration is rejected). It also meshed nicely with the new movement for "radical democracy," that is, the demand to democratize *all* institutions in society, the state bureaucracy (as contrasted with the elected or representative bodies) being the key to radical political change. Co-workers produced new terms, for example, "popular bureaucracies." These were based on the idea that bureaucracies as Weber defined them (a perfect form for doing routine business) were increasingly inadequate as the capitalist state began to change more rapidly in various ways during the U.S.-led push to globalize the capitalist system, and that looser definitions of administration (or bureaucracy) that placed more emphasis on individual initiatives, horizontal sharing of information and decision-making, and the porosity of the state from the standpoint of social movements, made sense theoretically and practically.

In the States, today, almost every struggle around the conditions of production has at least implicitly a political goal—to democratize state decision-making—without, however, the participants being really aware of what they're doing! In Santa Cruz, to take a local example, while the homeless activists and the women's movement against domestic abuse and violence both struggle within and against City Hall and the police department for changes in the way police work is defined and with respect to the division of labor and reward system within the police forces, neither group is aware that they have the same *political goal* (even though both are aware that they are using *political means* to struggle for specific social goals). At the national and world level, the current struggle to democratize (or abolish) the International Monetary Fund (IMF), World Bank, and (most recently) the World Trade Organization, indicates the importance of the "democratize the state" line today. My writings on this subject were published in *Kapitalistate*, *Natural Causes*, and the journal I helped found in 1988, *Capitalism, Nature, Socialism*.

*   *   *

Perhaps the first question present-day readers of *Fiscal Crisis* would ask is, what happened to the fiscal crisis? Hasn't it disappeared, at least in the U.S.? Hasn't the IMF been forcing balanced budgets on the South as part of its neoliberal Structural Adjustment Programs (SAPs) from the late 1970s to the present? The "New Democrats" (e.g., Clinton) and defenders of the "Third Way" (Blair) are adopting a kind of social supply-side economic policy which conceptualizes education and heath spending, for example, as social or human capital, in a way similar to that defined in *FCS*. On the other hand, doesn't the dominant ideology of neoliberalism reject the idea that state spending has any productive role to play and that state taxation should be hugely reduced to lower interest rates and free money up for private capital investment, as well as to strengthen private incentives to accumulate capital (thus rejecting or qualifying the Keynesian line that state spending is needed to shore up aggregate demand and the social democratic view that taxation on working people should be reduced)?

It's true that the U.S. federal budget for the time being is showing a surplus, that some federal debt is being retired, and that most State-level governments are running fiscal surpluses or balanced budgets. Yet these surpluses have arisen in part because of a four-fold growth of U.S. State and local spending—mainly on social capital—in the 1990s (after fluctuating around a zero growth trend line in the 1970s and 1980s). The supply of (indirectly productive) educated laborpower, of port, airport, and freeway capacity, of agricultural research in both bioengineering crops and organic farming, and of other capitalist social investments helped to create the 1990s boom (which from the standpoint of per capita GDP growth was more a "modest expansion" than an "economic boom" in any case).

The fact remains that *Fiscal Crisis* failed to anticipate the rise of neoliberalism and globalization and the reestablishment of U.S. political hegemony after the fall of the Soviet empire. These revolutionary (or counter-revolutionary) changes have important implications for the way that the U.S. economy works, which in turn have important effects on fiscal politics and the budget. While I was perfectly aware of the role of imperialism and neocolonialism in world economy in the 1950s and 1960s,[6] I wasn't able to integrate my studies of international political economic relations into *FCS* (see below).

The main reason why *Fiscal Crisis* didn't anticipate the U.S. budget surplus of the late 1990s, nor cast its theses in terms of the context of world capitalist economy as a whole, pertained to the method I used in working on the book, which was to develop my own thinking in the form of a critique of bourgeois economic accounts of state expenditures and taxation. Bourgeois economics adopted one of two points of view toward the budget: the first is a normative account of what an economically efficient and socially equitable spending and tax structure would look like—in the mirror of neoclassical welfare economics[7] (which by the way is one of the pathetically weak edifices on which globalist capitalism is being developed today). The second is a practical account of macroeconomic stabilization.[8]

In the macroeconomics of the 1960s, the budget was treated as an exogenous variable in economic growth models, as a way that the government could regulate aggregate demand to avoid or control both recession and inflation (an approach that was blown apart in the U.S. by the stagflation of the 1970s). My goal was to produce a sociological, political sociological, and political economic explanation of how and why various expenditures found their way into the budget in the first place, and why these items were more or less costly. Put another way, I rejected the normative (wish-thinking) view that what the economist sought as economically *desirable* state policy in fact *explained* the major budgetary items and their changes over time.

Whatever validity a purely macroeconomic-type argument might have in particular circumstances, it isn't interesting from the point of view of political economy and political sociology. More important, it doesn't require a Marxist-type class analysis (which in my view is indispensable in a class society). The thesis of *Fiscal Crisis* therefore is not basically a macroeconomic argument. It's a theory that depends on two kinds of observations, the first political-economic, the second political-sociological.

First, given the increasingly social nature of capitalist production and exchange, the state has to build, for example, more or better freeways as physical inputs into road freight and into work commutes. Failure to expand or modernize roadways (and airports, seaports and so on) would drive up the cost of the commute (or freight) and hence increase the cost of wages (or transport costs). This argument pertains to the "physicality" of capitalism as well as to the workings of the market. This type of spending I called social capital because it increases (or prevents a decrease in) labor productivity. Human capital as a form of social capital is another example: an expansion of human mental capacities relevant to producing and realizing value also reduces labor costs and increases productivity in various ways. The result: countries that permit workers to acquire more years of education are typically more economically and productive and better-paid. In the U.S., workers with a college education on the average earn twice as much as workers with only a high school education.

Increased quantity and quality of physical and human social capital pertain to the input side of private capitalist production. The second part of the argument pertains to the output side. Social capital is an input into *private* production and roughly measures how much private capital appropriates free-of-charge or with minimal outlay what it needs from the social product as a whole. *Private* production in turn results not only in marketable commodities but also unmarketable *social* costs and, more generally, unwanted *social* consequences. These costs and consequences are a rough measure of how much damage private capital can wreak without paying the harmed party or parties (which in some cases includes society as a whole) any compensation. Social capital and social costs defined in the broadest sense together measure the power that private capital exercises in the political system. Large uncompensated social costs, for example, indicate how little power labor unions, consumer groups, and community organizations have in the polity.

"Externalized" costs or damages are many and varied: environmental and ecological destruction, urban pollution and congestion, high rents, unsafe or unhealthy water and foods, leached out soils and dry water tables, depleted forests and fisheries, worker and community malhealth, unemployment and poverty, and, at a more systemic level, social disorder and political delegitimation. State budget funds allocated to mitigate or compensate for these kinds of externalities can be carrots or sticks (for example, more welfare spending or more police and prisons, more funds for organic agriculture or more funds for repressing social movements against agribusiness, more money for drug rehabilitation or more money for drug wars). State monies expended on these kinds of carrots and sticks I called *social expenses*

In short, state outlays on social capital make private capital grow or accumulate. Private capital growth results in many kinds of "negative externalities" or harm to workers, communities, and environments. Historically, there arose (first in the West, today everywhere on the globe) labor and other social movements which demanded that either private capital prevent the damage it causes or mitigate this damage in different ways. Or what is more typical, social movements demand that the state pay for capital's systemic harm to the "losers" in the growth game. These have included small business and farmers whose livelihood is threatened by big business; unemployed workers and the working poor; environmental spending to clean up projects such as toxic dump sites when it is impossible to attribute damage to any particular guilty capital(s), for example, Superfund sites. Social movements including labor movements place these demands on the guilty party(ies) or the state budget or both. Social movements can be leftist or rightist in orientation and the demand may be for more government jobs and welfare payments or more police and tougher prison sentences. Whatever the case, the state tends to spend more on social expenses to mitigate the bad effects of private capitalist accumulation.

According to the *Fiscal Crisis* thesis, social capital spending fulfills the state's "accumulation function" while social expenses meet the state's "legitimation function" (which may pertain to governments in power, a political party, or the political system as such). These terms were perhaps unfortunate because some reviewers of *FCS* concluded that my work was "functionalist." This means that they believed that I assumed that the system generates certain needs and *also* the political, administrative, and fiscal means by which these needs can be met or fulfilled. In fact, I didn't argue this line, believing that capitalism is a highly contradictory system in which social movements, corporate power in the state, and state policies typically have many kinds of unintended or unforeseen consequences. To illustrate, take just one contradiction, that between the functional needs of capital as a whole (defined by the political party in power) and the interests of individual capitals (or businesses). This contradiction still ratchets up government spending. In May of 2000, it was revealed that Medicare spending for home care nursing which the government had planned to reduce by a percentage point or two, in fact had fallen by ten to twenty percent. Disabled and elderly people were unable to get Medicare authorization for home care and so had to stay in more expensive nursing homes and hospitals longer than would otherwise be the case. Many who couldn't afford nursing homes died before their time (the ultimate "externality"). The attempt to find a less expensive general solution to the problem of rising health care costs (a systemic need) was thwarted by the politically well-organized drug companies and other "special interests." Medicare's bill thus went up, not down, and it is expected to increase further if and when funds are restored for home nursing care.

In terms of economic theory, it's clear that in *Fiscal Crisis* I tried to explain macroeconomic changes in the economy in terms of the state budget (social capital at once adding productive capacity and demand to the economy), not vice versa, which was the standard approach of economists at the time. Then and only then did I seek to explain changes in the growth and composition of the budget—social expenses—in terms of the mal-effects of macroeconomic changes (undergirded in the first place by social capital).

I was at the time not fully conscious of the "missing link" in my theory of the fiscal crisis, namely, the effect of the expansion of social expenses on the macroeconomic behavior of the economy. One answer could have been: Social expenses not being a (social) form of capital are basically a drain on surplus value hence on accumulation. This is the line developed by Paul Mattick, but concerning state spending as a whole and not just social expenses. Others tried to study the effects of the growth of welfare and police functions on labor discipline or morale, and the growth of ghettos and redlining of investments. I should have perhaps played up more the warfare side of what I called the American welfare/warfare state. Interestingly, Bristow Hardin, one of my Ph.D. students, wrote a thesis showing that in terms of education subsidies, housing allowances, health care and child care, insurance and retirement benefits—the U.S. military *was* the U.S. welfare state, or a large part of same.[9] This is one of many studies that developed in critical ways the themes of *FCS*. Perhaps if I had carried out the full line of reasoning inherent in the *FCS*'s accumulation model, I could have better anticipated certain neoliberal reforms—for example, the abolition of welfare. But I didn't. What I did was to work out the logic of the situation not for the macro economy but for the future of the budget itself. I noted the structural gap between state spending and state revenues (taxes), which I termed a "fiscal crisis," and posed a series of questions as to how this could be overcome. Here I was pretty much on the mark: my notion of a "social-industrial complex"[10] to lower average social capital costs (e.g., mass transit over cars, HMOs in the health field) and also to lower the costs of social expenses (e.g., prison labor, welfare "reform") captured fairly accurately the actual turn of events in the 1980s and 1990s. However, my "predictions" would have been more soundly based had I completed the circle of reasoning to include the effects of a growth of social expenses on macroeconomic growth and, even more so, if I had anticipated the sea of changes coming up in the South, beginning with the 1980's debt crisis and the IMF and World Bank SAPs, and continuing into the 1990's debt and foreign exchange crises in Latin America, Southeast Asia, and Russia.

I should add however that in the late 1970s and 1980s, research in Southern countries such as Brazil and Mexico and some others, some of it inspired by *FCS*, theorized fiscal economics and politics in light of the overriding phenomena of the time—the 1980s debt crisis and growth of neoliberalism and SAPs in the South. On the other hand, the pillars of neoliberalism—privatization, liberalization of foreign exchange markets and investments, deregulation, and harmonization—are all consistent with the analysis in *FCS*, although as noted above a proper *explanation* of neoliberalism would have required a more global theory than the one I provided in *FCS*.

If I were to take into account the workings of globalization today, I would have to modify the basic model of American capitalism that I developed for the study of the fiscal crisis. Put simply, in the original model there were three economic sectors: the monopoly sector, the competitive sector, and the state sector. I showed how capital accumulation in the monopoly sector was typically labor-saving and often labor-spurning; hence accumulation tended to increase the supply of laborpower offered to the labor-intensive competitive and state sectors. The reader will find much more than this simple relationship in the book itself; however, the idea of a displacement of labor from the monopoly to the competitive sector is sufficient to underline how globalization today dictates that the original model needs to be made more realistic in order to retain its validity. It's the monopoly sector, of course, that's being globalized (in the form of foreign direct investment, outsourcing, downsizing, increased competition joint ventures across borders, mergers and acquisitions across borders, the establishment of a single world market price for many commodities, etc.). While production in heavy manufacturing (the heart of the monopoly sector) as a percentage of GDP hasn't changed much in the past 20 years or so, the ratio of manufacturing employment to manufacturing output has taken a big nose dive. Given the neoliberalist slowdown of the expansion of government employment, the effect has been to flood the competitive sector with "cheap" labor. This has revived all kinds of small business ventures hitherto dormant or that were merely extensions of big capital and reproduced the poor conditions of existence of African-Americans and other oppressed minorities.

The expansion of labor supply in the low-wage competitive sector (which I believe was the single most important factor increasing employment in the U S. in the 1990s, without stimulating inflation) and the concomitant weakening of the unions in the monopoly sector (hence the sluggish growth of money wages and lower labor costs per worker in that sector) were intensified by the growth of legal foreign workers and undocumented workers from Mexico, Central America, Asia, and other countries and regions, which tended to push money wages down still further. Also, the decline in wage income in the competitive sector forced families to increase labor force participation rates to maintain established levels of family income, thus tending to reduce wages paid by small business still further. In some parts of the U.S., this would become a downward cycle of falling wages, increasing hours of work by the typical family, further declines in wages, higher rents, and finally, out-migration of the growing class of the "working poor" to regions and cities with relatively fast economic growth.

Thus the birth of the new low-inflationary, "full employment," low-wage U.S. economy of 2000, in the U.S.-led economically globalized world of hyper-competition disciplined by financial markets and IMF/World Bank SAPs. Combined with the centralization of capital (i.e., capital expansion by acquisition not via new investment), this became a formula for an increase in riches for the few, poverty for the many, and until 1996, stagnant wages for the majority. The monopoly sector itself came under increasing attack by big foreign capital, hence money wage increases failed to keep pace with productivity advances. This was partly offset by new investments from foreign corporations in the U.S., which, however, were most often difficult or impossible to unionize. Meanwhile, as noted, the neo-liberalizing federal state sector failed to absorb its "normal" or historical share of displaced workers, which further expanded labor supplies in the competitive sector. One could complicate this model in various ways, but its essence is obvious: the contradictions of the system are no longer displaced as frequently into the state and state finances as they are into the sector of small or competitive capital. The result: the lower one-third or one-half of the U.S. working class suffers impaired conditions of life and real incomes. In other words, the state's "legitimation function" no longer requires "pay offs" to economic losers (e.g., small business or its work force), as was true of the Cold War era when political parties and the state administration had to do whatever it took to maintain the Cold War political consensus. The problem of legitimation has been transformed into the problem of "competitiveness in the global marketplace." This has become the first task of the state—a first in the U.S. which in the past enjoyed a well-integrated national economy. Only Social Security and Medicare have survived more or less intact in the world of 21st century global capitalism, but the privatization of retirement and health care insurance (as well as water, power, education and other facilities that may be privatized under new WTO rules) may destroy those redoubts of traditional social democracy, too.

One of the most important changes since the late 1960s and early 1970s is the central role of fiscal discipline in the evolution of neoliberalism at home and overseas. This has been manifested in many ways:

(1) the replacement of fiscal policy by a variety of monetarism;

(2) the attempt to free monies from their employment by the state for the private capital market (hence avoiding increases in interest rates);

(3) privatization, which reduces state functions and money-losing businesses and disciplines state workers;

(4) a tax revolt that never became generalized to include most of the wage and salary working population, or to include the individual income tax itself (the main source of federal revenues). Property taxes were reduced in numerous states and localities but payroll taxes (financing Social Security and Medicare) have increased sharply since the early 1970s. Why the tax revolt didn't spread beyond property income (real estate, capital gains, wealth, and inheritance taxes) to the heart of the fiscal system (payroll and personal income taxes) has never been studied. Such a study would have to contain a strong class analysis;

(5) in the South, SAPs that focus on reducing state budget deficits and taxes and expenditures generally;

(6) the reduction of social services and welfare.

These and other changes both caused and were caused by the rising power of global capital, and finance capital and financial markets (at the expense of the working class the world over) All these changes are most pronounced in the U.S. and in U.S.-dominated international institutions such as the IMF. With lower interest rates and plenty of money capital available for business borrowing and investment, stock market speculation, and mortgage and consumer credit; with a high-flying stock market and real estate markets that generated higher consumption spending via the "wealth effect;" with a strong dollar (despite a growing import surplus) which cheapened imports and kept inflation down, on the one hand, and attracted huge sums of money from crisis-struck Asian, Latin American and some European countries, on the other; and with Japan in the doldrums and the euro weak and European Union growing only slowly; and finally with the U.S. getting back its monopoly on high tech innovation and export markets—all these came together to produce the export-led boom of the early 1990s and the faster-growing consumer-led and high-tech-led investment boom of the late 1990s This rapidly increased tax revenues (while expenditures rose relatively little) such that by 1999 the federal deficit had turned into a budgetary surplus. (As noted above, this process was significantly aided by the growth of State-level and local social capital spending.)

It should be stressed, however, that the new era of fiscal surpluses (or the "end of the fiscal crisis") was confined mainly to the U.S. In Japan, Italy, and dozens of economies in the South, increasing fiscal deficits were the rule during the 1990s. If in most of Europe deficits were too small to be worrisome, it was because the German state and central bank imposed low deficit/GDP ratios on the European states joining the European Monetary Union. In sum, the U.S. fiscal crisis at the federal level was "solved" primarily because of the longish boom of the 1990s, especially the fast-growing late 1990s, hence the big increase in income tax revenues by the national government. But U.S. growth generally would have been impossible without globalization (or the "Americanization" of the world), which funneled huge sums of money to the U.S. from abroad and had other effects favoring low inflation, growth, and larger tax collections.

\* \* \*

To conclude, a few words on the reception by reviewers of *FCS* might be in order. General interest in the book is indicated by its sales figures (35,000 of the English language edition over 25 years); by the number of translations (German, Italian, Spanish, Greek, Portuguese, Japanese, and Korean); and by the number of invitations to lecture at universities here and abroad on various subjects covered by the book (lots). The reviews of the book in scholarly journals and popular periodicals, however, were mixed. Some (Marxist economist) reviewers didn't like the book because it departed too much from the orthodox Marxist treatment of the state and state budget. The Marxist *Monthly Review* gave *FCS* to a hostile reviewer. Some (mainstream economist) reviewers panned the book because it "wasn't economics" (*FCS* was a study in political economy and political sociology). Both sets of reviewers were right, in their own ways, although neither had enough confidence in their own methods and theories to suspend disbelief in their own paradigms long enough to appreciate what I was trying to do. Both Marxist and straight economists still have trouble theorizing a relatively new concept of "social capital," broken down into human capital, natural capital, and communal capital (goods or services treated as if they are commodities even though they aren't produced as commodities). There were also reviews that were in effect debates on the method I used in *FCS*: as noted, some reviewers and commentators have said that *FCS* is flawed by its "functionalism;" others that it is marred by its voluntaristic (class struggle) theory of the budget. This was one of those cases where some reviewers were condemning not so much my book but other reviewers with different methodological perspectives. All of them, however, commended me for tackling the sociology of public finance, which Joseph Schumpeter long ago said held great promise, but which until *FCS* remained one of the most undeveloped field of study in social theory and social science.

By and large, political sociologists liked the book, as did radical political economists who hadn't tied themselves down to any particular method of studying and theorizing modern capitalism. As much as social theoretical books are read at all in the labor movement, *FCS* had a appreciative readership. This was especially true of leaders and staff in organizations of state workers and clients, e.g., teachers' unions and welfare rights groups. *FCS* had its best reaction among left Weberians of various kinds, political sociologists who read Weber's master texts on bureaucracy and politics in ways that kept their minds open. As noted above, *FCS* went over best among those working on problems of administrative rationality (crisis) and political legitimation (crisis) of the modern state, as the theory of the fiscal crisis complemented these works very well.

I conclude by noting that until I finished *Accumulation Crisis* and *The Meaning of Crisis* I was unable theoretically to integrate the ideological nature of everyday life in U.S. capitalism into theories of political economy and political sociology. Reviewers of the former book who were knowledgeable about the critique of ideology in the Marxist tradition (especially that of Antonio Gramsci) praised this work. Reviews of the *Meaning of Crisis* were few and far between and failed to grasp the taxonomy of crisis theory developed therein (at one extreme I noted that market theories of crisis were the most abstract, at the other extreme that psychological theories of personality crisis were the least abstract, and indicated that social theorists could move between different levels of crisis theory in ways that would enhance their own work on economic, social, political, and psychological crises in late 20th century U.S. capitalism). Finally, my latest work, *Natural Causes*, based on a combination of methods derived from environmental history, Marxism, and the work of Karl Polanyi, was greatly appreciated by economic sociologists and sociological economists, as well as by some environmental historians and scholars working in the general field of political ecology, and also by many environmental activists, but ignored or trivialized by orthodox Marxists and orthodox economists. The circle was thus closed, as *Natural Causes* was received in the same poor way as *Fiscal Crisis* by both of these groups of hidebound academics.

James O'Connor
May 15, 2000

## NOTES AND REFERENCES

**1.** Paul A Baran and Paul M Sweezy, *Monopoly Capital: An Essay on the American Economic and Social Order*, New York: Monthly Review Press, 1966; James O'Connor, "Monopoly Capital," *New Left Review* 40, November-December, 1966

**2.** The seeming triumph of neoliberalism in the recent past has to some unknown degree pushed the class struggle out of the state budget and back into the labor market and point of production

**3.** For a selection of representative articles first published in this journal, see James Weinstein and David W Eakins, eds , *For a New America: Essays in History and Politics from 'Studies on the Left' 1959 – 1967*, New York: Random House, 1970

**4.** See James O'Connor, *Accumulation Crisis*, New York and Oxford: Basil Blackwell, 1984; *The Meaning of Crisis: A Theoretical Introduction*, New York and Oxford: Basil Blackwell, 1987

**5.** See James O'Connor, *Natural Causes: Essays in Ecological Marxism*, New York: Guilford Press, 1998

**6.** Most important, the "age of neoliberalism" didn't really begin until c 1980, more than ten years after I started writing *FCS* See, for example, "The Meaning of Economic Imperialism," in my *The Corporations and the State: Essays in the Theory of Capitalism and Imperialism*, New York, Harper and Row, 1974

**7.** *Fiscal Crisis*, op cit , pp 3-5

**8.** "Scientific and Ideological Elements in the Economic Theory of Government Policy," *The Corporations and the State*, op cit

**9.** Bristow Hardin, "The Militarized Social Democracy and Racism: The Relationship Between Militarism, Racism and Social Welfare Policy in the United States " Ph D dissertation, University of California at Santa Cruz, 1991

**10.** The social-industrial complex I saw as an attempt to reduce outlays on the commute to work, health care, and education In the 1960s, Hubert Humphrey, last of the great Cold War social democrats in the U S , noted that in his state urban dwellers commuted to the suburbs to work, and that suburbanites commuted to the city for employment, hence that a reorganization of workers' housing could save "society" (capitalism) a significant amount of social capital outlays Today this tradition is in the hands of the "new democrats" and "third wayers " For example, the HMO movement seeks to lower health care costs by partly socializing health care; the anti-urban sprawl movement aims to lower the costs of transportation and economize on energy and other resources via regional planning. In *Accumulation Crisis* I would interpret changes or movements such as these in terms of the cost of reproducing laborpower (or the value content of the consumption basket). This has become a more complicated subject due to the effects of globalization, that is, the abundance of cheap consumer articles produced in export platforms, e g , China, which tend to raise real wages in the U.S without the necessity of increasing money wages Education, health care, public recreation, environmental amenities, and the like can't be globalized without creating political opposition, hence the importance of the social-industrial complex or of planning to reduce the cost of reproducing laborpower as a complement to globalization This theme, needless to say, I missed in *Fiscal Crisis*

# INTRODUCTION

"Lockheed Gets Loan Guarantees," "President Says, 'No Vietnam Dividend,'" "New $50 Million BART Issue," "Medicare Spending Up 20%," "30% City Budget Increase," "Teachers' Strike Begins Third Week," "Violence Mars Welfare Rights Demonstration" —these were some of the typical headlines of the 1960s and early 1970s. Each is a variation on the same theme: Corporations want government to build more freeways; bankers and investors want government to underwrite more loans and investments; small businessmen and farmers want more subsidies; organized labor wants more social insurance; welfare rights groups want higher income allowances, more housing, and better public health services; government employees want higher wages and salaries; and government agencies want more appropriations.

Other familiar headlines—"School Bond Issue Voted Down," "Gallup Poll: Tax Relief Top Worry," "Unified School District Referendum Defeated," "Commuter Tax Declared Unconstitutional," "Homeowners Vote to Shift Tax to Downtown Business," "Reagan Supports State Withholding Tax"—tell a similar story. Large corporations and wealthy investors want working people and small businessmen to foot the bill for airport modernization, freeway expansion, rapid transit, water investment projects, and pollution control. Small businessmen and homeowners want property tax relief. Middle-income wage and salary earners want income tax relief. Poor people want tax relief, period. Suburbanites don't want to pay taxes in the central city where they work, and they don't want central-city residents to get any of the taxes that they pay in the suburbs.

Every economic and social class and group wants government to spend more and more money on more and more things. But no one wants to pay new taxes or higher rates on old taxes. Indeed, nearly everyone wants lower taxes, and many groups have agitated successfully for tax relief. Society's demands on local and state budgets seemingly are unlimited, but people's willingness and capacity to pay for these demands appear to be narrowly limited. And at the federal level expenditures have increased significantly faster than the growth of total production. In the words of the head of the Federal Reserve System,

1

We stand at a crossroads in our fiscal arrangements. Many of our citizens are alarmed by the increasing share of their incomes that is taken away by Federal, State, and local taxes. . . . The propensity to spend more than we are prepared to finance through taxes is becoming deep-seated and ominous. An early end to Federal deficits is not now in sight. Numerous Federal programs have a huge growth of expenditures built into them, and there are proposals presently before the Congress that would raise expenditures by vast amounts in coming years.[1]

We have termed this tendency for government expenditures to outrace revenues the "fiscal crisis of the state." There is no iron law that expenditures must always rise more rapidly than revenues, but it is a fact that growing needs which only the state can meet create ever greater claims on the state budget. Several factors, singly or in combination, may offset the crisis. People who need government-provided services may be ignored and their needs neglected, as happened in New York's welfare cutback during the 1970–1971 recession. Corporations that want loans and subsidies from the government may not get them, as happened in the Congressional defeat of proposed subsidies for the development of the SST. Government-employee income may fall behind private sector income or below the cost of living, but this does not mean that these workers get automatic pay increases. In fact, the government may even freeze wages and salaries in an attempt to ameliorate the fiscal crisis. Furthermore, people can be forced to pay higher taxes. Should they be unwilling to pay taxes directly because large numbers oppose particular spending programs, the government can force them to pay taxes indirectly by financing increased expenditures via inflation or credit expansion —as the Johnson Administration did during the peak years of American aggression in Southeast Asia.

A combination of some of these countertendencies resulted in budgetary surpluses in many state and local governments in 1972. According to one "optimistic" estimate, state and local governments will be able to meet their normal needs through 1975 by increasing tax rates by not more than 5 percent.[2]

The volume and composition of government expenditures and the distribution of the tax burden are not determined by the laws of the market but rather reflect and are structurally determined by social and economic conflicts between classes and groups. The English Prime Minister Gladstone once said that "budgets are not merely matters of arithmetic, but in a thousand ways go to the root of prosperity of individuals, and relations of classes, and the strength of Kingdoms." The "relations of classes" were then expressed

INTRODUCTION

in many ways that today are of only historical interest. In modern America individual well-being, class relationships, and national wealth and power are bound up in the agony of the cities, poverty and racism, profits of big and small business, inflation, unemployment, the balance-of-payments problem, imperialism and war, and other crises that seem a permanent part of daily life. No one is exempt from the fiscal crisis and the underlying social crises which it aggravates. We need a way to think about and ultimately act on this fiscal crisis that clarifies the contradictory processes which find both their reflection and cause in the government budget. We need a theory of government budget and a method for discovering the meaning for the political economy and society as a whole.

Perhaps then we will be able to answer such questions as: Who will pay for rising government expenditures? Will some kinds of spending rise while others are cut back? Can the government deliver more services for less taxes? Why don't Americans want to pay for services that presumably benefit the "people"? Can the fiscal system survive in its present form? Political-economic analysis is needed to answer these and dozens of other equally important related questions.

## THE THEORETICAL BANKRUPTCY OF
## TRADITIONAL ECONOMICS

The theory of government budget put forth in this work is based on the study of fiscal politics, an investigation of the sociological foundations of government or state finances.[3] The main concerns of fiscal politics are to discover the principles governing the volume and allocation of state finances and expenditures and the distribution of the tax burden among various economic classes. The major work of the German Marxist Rudolph Goldscheid, founder of the contemporary science of fiscal politics, appeared in the second decade of this century.[4] A few years thereafter Joseph Schumpeter wrote glowingly of the promise of fiscal politics:

> The public finances are one of the best starting points for an investigation of society, especially though not exclusively of its political life. The full fruitfulness of this approach is seen particularly at those turning points, or better epochs, during which existing forms begin to die off and to change into something new. This is true both of the causal significance of fiscal policy (insofar as fiscal events are an important element in the causation of all change) and of the symptomatic significance (insofar

as everything that happens has its fiscal reflection). Notwithstanding all the qualifications which always have to be made . . . we may surely speak of . . . a special field: fiscal sociology, of which much may be expected.[5]

Schumpeter's optimism proved to be premature. The budget remains, in his words, a "collection of hard, naked facts" not yet "drawn into the realm of sociology." "Unfortunately," one scholar confesses, "there exists no integrated theory of the economics and politics of public finance which would serve as a framework for analyzing [state] finance." [6] No blunter admission of theoretical bankruptcy can be found than the declaration that within the mainstream of Western economic thought,

> public finance, traditionally, has neither contained a theory of demand nor one of supply. . . . The scholar from outer space, coming to earth in the post-Marshallian era, might have concluded on perusing the English-language literature that governments exist wholly apart from their citizens, that these units impose taxes on individuals and firms primarily to nourish the state; and he might have thought that positive public finance consists in predicting the effects of these taxes.[7]

The "scholar from outer space" would have been only partly right. Orthodox public finance theorists are concerned not only with the economic effects of taxation (and expenditures), but also with the problem of what the government should take away in taxes (and provide in expenditures). For example, in his study of state enterprise Ralph Turvey writes that "because it is public, what interests us about public enterprise is how it ought to behave. . . . [W]e are not so much concerned with understanding its behavior and making predictions as with criticizing and making recommendations." [8] Turvey's interest lies in how the behavior of state enterprise can be made to conform to a preconceived notion of economic optimum. This is the focus of the best known treatise on public finance, Richard Musgrave's *The Theory of Public Finance*. Musgrave tries to synthesize the entire modern literature on government finance and, in particular, "to state the rules and principles that make for an efficient conduct of the public economy." Musgrave devises an "optimal budget plan on the basis of initially defined conditions" and then tries to "see how it can be achieved." He calls it "a normative or optimal theory of the public household." [9]

The effect of this emphasis on normative theory has been to ignore the application of the theory of economic growth. The

INTRODUCTION

absence of an "integrated theory of the economics and politics of public finance" (or "a theory of demand and supply of public goods and services") has compelled economists to adopt an almost metaphysical attitude toward government spending. For example, the Keynesian Evsey Domar theorized that government expenditures can be dealt with (1) by assuming that they are exogenous, or determined by forces outside the economic system; (2) by merging them with consumption expenditures; or (3) by assuming them away altogether. The last alternative is obviously completely unsatisfactory, and to assume that government spending is determined by undefinable outside forces is to beg the question. And merging all government spending with private consumption is merely a convenient fiction. Methods of analysis such as this have led two public finance specialists to write that "growth models in their present form cannot be treated as anything more than exercises in a technique of arrangement." [10]

As government expenditures come to constitute a larger and larger share of total spending in advanced capitalist countries, economic theorists who ignore the impact of the state budget do so at their own (and capitalism's) peril. Currently, economists do not consider actual determinants in their theoretical models but rather restrict themselves to estimates of the volume of state spending necessary to effect desired changes such as high employment or more rapid accumulation and growth. Their premise is that the government budget should and can be increased or lowered to compensate for reduced or increased private spending. Many orthodox economists believe that the volume of federal spending (if not its composition) is determined by and inversely related to the volume of private spending.

As will be seen in the course of this study, the orthodox approach is at best simplistic. Although changes in tax rates and the tax structure have been increasingly used to regulate private economic activity, the growth of federal spending over the past two or three decades has not resulted from the government's adopting compensatory fiscal policies, "except perhaps to a very limited degree." [11] Particular expenditures and programs and the budget as a whole are explicable only in terms of power relationships within the private economy.

## SUMMATION OF THE THEORY OF THE FISCAL CRISIS

To avoid "exercises in a technique of arrangement," we have attempted to develop a theory of economic growth that is rooted in the basic economic and political facts of late capitalist society. We hope to elucidate the relationship between the private and state sectors and between private and state spending. Although we believe that many of the ideas presented can be adapted to the experience of other advanced capitalist countries, the focus is on the post–World War II United States. Basically an interpretation of the period's economic development and crisis tendencies, this study does not offer a comprehensive analysis of state budgetary planning and policy or a comprehensive guide to state finance. Many of the data presented have been chosen more to illustrate a line of theoretical argument than to verify a set of hypotheses.

The categories that make up this theoretical framework are drawn from Marxist economics and adapted to the problem of budgetary analysis. Our first premise is that the capitalistic state must try to fulfill two basic and often mutually contradictory functions—*accumulation* and *legitimization*. (See Chapter 3.) This means that the state must try to maintain or create the conditions in which profitable capital accumulation is possible. However, the state also must try to maintain or create the conditions for social harmony. A capitalist state that openly uses its coercive forces to help one class accumulate capital at the expense of other classes loses its legitimacy and hence undermines the basis of its loyalty and support. But a state that ignores the necessity of assisting the process of capital accumulation risks drying up the source of its own power, the economy's surplus production capacity and the taxes drawn from this surplus (and other forms of capital). This contradiction explains why President Nixon calls a legislated increase in profit rates a "job development credit," why the government announces that new fiscal policies are aimed at "stability and growth" when in fact their purpose is to keep profits high and growing, why the tax system is nominally progressive and theoretically based on "ability to pay" when in fact the system is regressive. The state must involve itself in the accumulation process, but it must either mystify its policies by calling them something that they are not, or it must try to conceal them (e.g., by making them into administrative, not political, issues).

Our second premise is that the fiscal crisis can be understood only in terms of the basic Marxist economic categories (adapted to the problems taken up here). State expenditures have a twofold character corresponding to the capitalist state's two basic functions: social capital and social expenses. *Social capital* is expenditures required for profitable private accumulation; it is indirectly productive (in Marxist terms, social capital indirectly expands surplus value). There are two kinds of social capital: social investment and social consumption (in Marxist terms, social constant capital and social variable capital). (See Chapters 4 and 5.) *Social investment* consists of projects and services that increase the productivity of a given amount of laborpower and, other factors being equal, increase the rate of profit. A good example is state-financed industrial-development parks. *Social consumption* consists of projects and services that lower the reproduction costs of labor and, other factors being equal, increase the rate of profit. An example of this is social insurance, which expands the reproductive powers of the work force while simultaneously lowering labor costs. The second category, *social expenses,* consists of projects and services which are required to maintain social harmony—to fulfill the state's "legitimization" function. They are not even indirectly productive. (See Chapter 6.) The best example is the welfare system, which is designed chiefly to keep social peace among unemployed workers. (The costs of politically repressed populations in revolt would also constitute a part of social expenses.)

Because of the dual and contradictory character of the capitalist state, nearly every state agency is involved in the accumulation and legitimization functions, and nearly every state expenditure has this twofold character. For example, some education spending constitutes social capital (e.g., teachers and equipment needed to reproduce and expand work-force technical and skill levels), whereas other outlays constitute social expenses (e.g., salaries of campus policemen). To take another example, the main purpose of some transfer payments (e.g., social insurance) is to reproduce the work force, whereas the purpose of others (e.g., income subsidies to the poor) is to pacify and control the surplus population. The national income accounts lump the various categories of state spending together. (The state does not analyze its budget in class terms ) Clearly, the different categories cannot be separated if each budget item is not examined.

Furthermore, precisely because of the social character of social capital and social expenses, nearly every state expenditure serves these two (or more) purposes simultaneously, so that few state outlays can be classified unambiguously. For example, freeways move workers to and from work and are therefore items of social consumption, but they also transport commercial freight and are therefore a form of social investment. And, when used for either purpose, they may be considered forms of social capital. However, the Pentagon also needs freeways; therefore they in part constitute social expenses. Despite this complex social character of state outlays we can determine the political-economic forces served by any budgetary decision, and thus the main purpose (or purposes) of each budgetary item. (See Chapters 4 through 6.)

The first basic thesis presented here is that the growth of

the state sector and state spending is functioning increasingly as the basis for the growth of the monopoly sector and total production. Conversely, it is argued that the growth of state spending and state programs is the result of the growth of the monopoly industries. In other words, the growth of the state is both a cause and effect of the expansion of monopoly capital. (See Chapter 1.)

More specifically, the socialization of the costs of social investment and social consumption capital increases over time and increasingly is needed for profitable accumulation by monopoly capital. The general reason is that the increase in the social character of production (specialization, division of labor, interdependency, the growth of new social forms of capital such as education, etc.) either prohibits or renders unprofitable the private accumulation of constant and variable capital. The growth of the monopoly sector is irrational in the sense that it is accompanied by unemployment, poverty, economic stagnation, and so on. To insure mass loyalty and maintain its legitimacy, the state must meet various demands of those who suffer the "costs" of economic growth. (See Chapter 1.)

It might help to compare our approach with traditional economic theory. Bourgeois economists have shown that increases in private consumption beget increases in private investment via the accelerator effect. In turn, increases in private investment beget increases in private consumption via the multiplier effect. Similarly, we argue that greater social investment and social consumption spending generate greater private investment and private consumption spending, which in turn generate surplus capital (surplus productive capacity and a surplus population) and a larger volume of social expenses. Briefly, the supply of social capital creates the demand for social expenses. In effect, we work with a model of expanded reproduction (or a model of the economy as a whole) which is generalized to take into account the socialization of constant and variable capital costs and the costs of social expenses.[12] The impact of the budget depends on the volume and indirect productivity of social capital and the volume of social expenses. On the one hand, social capital outlays indirectly increase productive capacity and simultaneously increase aggregate demand. On the other hand, social expense outlays do not increase productive capacity, although they do expand aggregate demand. Whether the growth of productive capacity runs ahead or behind the growth of demand thus depends on the composition of the state budget. In this way, we can see that the theory of economic growth depends on class and political analyses of the determinants of the budget.

This view contrasts sharply with modern conservative

INTRODUCTION

thought, which asserts that the state sector grows at the expense of private industry. We argue that the growth of the state sector is indispensable to the expansion of private industry, particularly monopoly industries. Our thesis also contrasts sharply with a basic tenet of modern liberal thought—that the expansion of monopoly industries inhibits the growth of the state sector.[13] The fact of the matter is that the growth of monopoly capital generates increased expansion of social expenses. In sum, the greater the growth of social capital, the greater the growth of the monopoly sector. And the greater the growth of the monopoly sector, the greater the state's expenditures on social expenses of production.

The second basic thesis in this study is that the accumulation of social capital and social expenses is a contradictory process which creates tendencies toward economic, social, and political crises. (See Chapter 2.) Two separate but related lines of analysis are explored.

First, we argue that although the state has socialized more and more capital costs, the social surplus (including profits) continues to be appropriated privately. (See Chapters 7 and 8.) The socialization of costs and the private appropriation of profits creates a fiscal crisis, or "structural gap," between state expenditures and state revenues. The result is a tendency for state expenditures to increase more rapidly than the means of financing them.[14] While the accumulation of social capital indirectly increases total production and society's surplus and thus in principle appears to underwrite the expansion of social expenses, large monopoly-sector corporations and unions strongly resist the appropriation of this surplus for new social capital or social expense outlays. (See Chapter 1.)

Second, we argue that the fiscal crisis is exacerbated by the private appropriation of state power for particularistic ends. A host of "special interests"—corporations, industries, regional and other business interests—make claims on the budget for various kinds of social investment. (See Chapter 3.) (These claims are politically processed in ways that must either be legitimated or obscured from public view.) Organized labor and workers generally make various claims for different kinds of social consumption, and the unemployed and poor (together with businessmen in financial trouble) stake their claims for expanded social expenses. Few if any claims are coordinated by the market. Most are processed by the political system and are won or lost as a result of political struggle. Precisely because the accumulation of social capital and social expenses occurs within a political framework, there is a great deal of waste, duplication, and overlapping of state projects and services. Some claims conflict and cancel one another out. Others are mutually contradictory in a variety of ways. The accumulation of social capital and social expenses is a highly irrational process from the standpoint of administrative coherence, fiscal stability, and potentially profitable private capital accumulation. In Chapter 9, we discuss the ways in which struggles around the control of the budget have developed in recent years and the ways in which these struggles impair the fiscal capacity of the system and potentially threaten the capacity of the system to produce surplus.

## NOTES AND REFERENCES

**1.** Arthur F Burns, statement to the Joint Economic Committee, July 26, 1972, *Federal Reserve Bulletin,* August 1972, p. 699 Burns concludes that "the fundamental problem . . is how to regain control over Federal expenditures " As this study will attempt to show, the lack of control of federal expenditures is merely a symptom of a much more deep-rooted problem.

**2.** Richard Musgrave and A. Mitchell Polinsky: cited by Edward C Banfield, "Revenue Sharing in Theory and Practice," *The Public Interest,* 33 (Spring 1971), 35.

**3.** The conventional phrase "public finance" reveals the ideological content of orthodox economic thought by prejudging the question of the real purposes of the budget. The phrase "state finance" is preferable to "public finance" (and "state sector" to "public sector," etc) precisely because it remains to be investigated how "public" are the real and financial transcations that take place in the state sector. For example, many so-called public investments are merely special forms of private investments

**4.** Rudolf Goldscheid, "A Sociological Approach to the Problem of Public Finance," reprinted in translation in Richard Musgrave and Alan T Peacock, eds., *Classics in the Theory of Public Finance* (New York: 1958); *Staatssocialismus oder Staatskapitalismus* (Wien-Leipzig, 1917); *Socialisierung der Wirtschaff oder Staatsbankeroff* (Leipzig-Wien, 1919).

**5.** Joseph Schumpeter, "The Crisis of the Tax State," reprinted in *International Economic Papers,* No. 4 (1954), p. 7 Schumpeter was expecting much of the mainstream of economic thought (the orthodox or bourgeois economists) Fiscal sociology has always been central to the Marxist tradition. Marx himself wrote extensively on the subject For example, compare Marx's conclusion that "tax struggle is the oldest form of class struggle" with the contemporary English Marxist John Eaton's statement that "state expenditure is . . . unceasingly the battleground of class interests."

**6.** Glenn W. Fisher, *Taxes and Politics, A Study of Illinois Public Finance* (Urbana, Ill.: 1969), p. 3.

**7.** James M. Buchanan, *The Demand and Supply of Public Goods*

(Chicago: 1968), p. v. Political scientists also have tended to take the state and political order for granted in their analyses of politics and administration as natural phenomena. See Theodore Lowi, "Decision Making vs. Policy Making: Toward an Antidote for Technocracy," *Public Administration Review*, 30:3 (May/June 1970).

**8.** Ralph Turvey, *Public Enterprise* (Baltimore: 1968)

**9.** Richard A. Musgrave, *The Theory of Public Finance* (New York: 1959), p 4 Musgrave's treatise is a perfect example of what Paul Baran was talking about years ago when he wrote that "in our time .   . faith in the manipulative omnipotence of the State has all but displaced analysis of its social structure and understanding of its political and economic functions " Paul A Baran, *The Longer View* (New York: 1969), p. 262.

**10.** Evsey Domar, *Essays in the Theory of Economic Growth* (New York: 1957), p. 6; Alan T. Peacock and Jack Wiseman, *The Growth of Public Expenditures in the United Kingdom* (Princeton, N.J : 1961), p 10

**11.** Herbert Stein, *The Fiscal Revolution in America* (Chicago: 1969), p. 69 Stein is an establishment economist who participated in many crucial corporate and government decisions in the 1950s and 1960s He was associated for a long time with the corporate-dominated Committee for Economic Development and was chief economic advisor to President Nixon in 1971–1972 "[A] very limited degree" means that Congress is more receptive to new spending bills during periods of recession Three other exceptions to the general rule should be noted: (1) In 1958, the federal government began extending unemployment insurance programs to give workers additional purchasing power and thus offset expected declines in private spending (the policy has been applied fitfully since 1958) (2) Federal highway expenditures have been adjusted to smooth out fluctuations in the economy. However, fiscal policy probably has affected the timing of government outlays much more than the total volume of highway spending (3) The President has tried to regulate spending by impounding funds (impounded funds rose from about 3 5 percent of total appropriations in 1964 to roughly 5 5 percent in 1971).

**12.** We have not presented a theory of the relationship between private investment and private consumption in either the short run or long run Nor have we worked out in detail the dialectical movements between the different kinds of state expenditures Consider, briefly, education expenditures Education spending does double-duty as both constant and variable capital. The education system also temporarily takes surplus population off the labor market. In other words, the growth of education simultaneously absorbs surplus labor and expands productivity (and thus creates more surplus labor). In short, education spending creates and eliminates surplus capital simultaneously. Any detailed study of the education system would have to take this basic contradiction into account. A further complication arises to the degree that the growth of the education establishment and the growth of militarism are inseparable processes (as they seem to have been in the United States) It is probably true that one of the reasons that state-financed higher education in Europe is relatively undeveloped is that military and related spending is comparatively small.

Finally, it might be added that both Marx's notion of realization crises and Keynesian notions of crises of effective demand require emendation. The reason is that "supply creates its own demand" in ways that neoclassical economics never dreamed of.

**13.** The standard conservative work is Milton Friedman's *Capitalism and Freedom* (Chicago: 1962). The standard liberal work is John Kenneth Galbraith's *The Affluent Society* (Boston: 1958).

# INTRODUCTION

**14.** The socialization of profits consists of the redistribution of productive wealth from capital to labor, or the confiscation of the owning classes by the working class. Although wealth and profits as a whole have not been socialized, a portion of surplus value is appropriated by the state and used to finance expanded social capital and social expense outlays. Instead of private capital "plowing back" a portion of surplus value into expanded reproduction (net capital formation) in a particular corporation or industry, the state "plows back" that part of the pool of surplus value that it appropriated into expanded social reproduction (new social capital formation) in industry as a whole How-ever, the state also appropriates part of constant and variable capital. Because capital's and labor's claims on budgetary resources are processed by the political mechanism, there is rarely a one-to-one correspondence between sources of financing and the uses of tax monies On the one hand, taxes must appear to conform to bourgeois democratic norms of "equity" and "ability to pay." On the other hand, the mixed character of social capital and social expense outlays makes it difficult to develop clearly defined criteria for identifying state expenditures empirically. Perhaps the closest correspondence between private and social forms of capital is the tax on payrolls (levied on private variable capital or wages) which is used to finance social insurance (a form of social variable capital).

# CHAPTER 1
# AN ANATOMY OF AMERICAN STATE CAPITALISM

## INTRODUCTION

Economic activities in modern American society may be classified into two broad groups: industries organized by private capital and those organized by the state.[1] Production and distribution in the private sector fall into two subgroups: competitive industries organized by small business and monopolistic industries organized by large-scale capital. The three groups of industries overlap considerably, and each sector depends on the others in various ways. Nevertheless, each has its own distinguishing features.

## THE COMPETITIVE SECTOR

In the competitive sector the physical capital-to-labor ratio and output per worker, or productivity, are low, and growth of production depends less on physical capital investment and technical progress than on growth of employment. Production is typically small scale, and markets are normally local or regional in scope. Familiar examples include restaurants, drug and grocery stores, service stations, and other branches of trade; garages, appliance repair shops, and other services; clothing and accessories, commercial displays, and other manufacturing industries. Competitive industries employ roughly one-third of the U.S. labor force, with the largest proportion in services and distribution.

What is the significance of low ratios of capital to labor and low productivity? First, competitive sector wages are relatively low, and second, there is a tendency toward overcrowding because it is relatively easy to set up business. Further, many competitive industries produce for (or sell in) markets that are seasonal, subject to sudden change in fashion or style, or otherwise irregular or unstable. Small businessmen whose product markets are irregular have little opportunity to stabilize production and employment. Nor is there much incentive to do so even when the opportunity arises:

they have invested very little capital per worker and thus business losses from excess physical capacity and time in set-up and shut-down operations are relatively small.

Unstable and irregular product markets and unstable and irregular labor markets go together in competitive industries. Employment in the competitive sector tends to be relatively low paid and casual, temporary, or seasonal. Workers who want and are unable to find full-time, year-round, well-paid work in the monopolistic or state sectors will accept employment in the competitive sector on almost any terms. In the United States the chief examples are black and other minority workers who are cut off from "mainstream" opportunities by racism and discrimination, women who are excluded by sexism from good jobs and good pay, and older workers who are retired involuntarily from high-wage industries (which dictate most compulsory retirement rules).[2] The supply of labor in competitive industries is further inflated by workers (e.g., married women, students, retired workers) who want, and will accept lower wages to obtain, irregular work; they make up about one-half of the non-agricultural labor force working less than thirty-five hours weekly.[3] It has been estimated that about 45 percent of the U.S. work force is "peripheral," or marginal, either by choice or necessity.[4]

The labor movement in the competitive sector is relatively underdeveloped, in part because the social characteristics of the work force, the multitude of firms in a particular industry, and the small-scale, localized nature of production obstruct the organization of strong unions. Further, highly competitive product markets, rapid business turnover, and small profit margins make it costly for employers to recognize unions. Thus it is not unusual for union negotiators to sign "sweetheart" contracts, and established unions often are unable to influence wage rates significantly. There are partial or full exceptions—for example, the foundry industry, with about 5000 small plants, where the trend is toward industry-wide bargaining; and branches of the garment industry concentrated in a few square blocks of mid-Manhattan, where unions and contractors have enormous influence in local and state government, and which employ skilled workers.

Still, the dominant feature of the competitive sector is that workers are condemned to relative material impoverishment. In 1968, over 10 million workers earned less than $1.60 per hour, including 3.5 million paid less than $1.00 per hour. Two-thirds of these workers were employed in retail trade and service industries, and more than one-tenth were employed in agriculture, forestry, and

THE FISCAL CRISIS OF THE STATE

fishing—all highly competitive and relatively low-wage industries.[5]

Working conditions in competitive industries tend to be poor and unemployment and underemployment high. Normally, workers do not earn enough to save for times of unemployment, indebtedness, sickness, or death. Weak or corrupt labor organizations do not secure adequate company-paid health, retirement, and other fringe benefits.

Historically, incomes have been supplemented in this sector by subsistence production, extended family systems, and community-help programs (e.g., "mom and pop" grocery stores, small-scale manufacturing and related facilities which provide employment for family members independent of their productivity, subsistence farming, artisan labor, "taking in the neighbor's wash," etc.). However, in modern capitalism the increasing "proletarianization" (or increase in percent of workforce with nothing to sell but labor power) of the entire population, the decline in subsistence and artisan production, and the weakening and destruction of traditional community bonds increasingly compel workers to look to the state for means of subsistence. Thus they are condemned to be full or partial dependents of the state, the recipients of income supplements in the form of public hospital services and health care, subsidized housing, welfare and relief, old age assistance, food stamps, transportation subsidies, and the like.

## THE MONOPOLY SECTOR

At one time most if not all industries now in the monopoly sector were organized along competitive lines. The process of monopolization involved a rapid growth in the physical capital-to-labor ratio and output per worker (physical productivity). Today, the growth of production depends less on growth of employment than on increases in physical capital per worker and technical progress.[6] Production is typically large scale and markets are normally national or international in scope—for example, capital goods such as steel, copper, aluminum, and electrical equipment; consumer goods such as automobiles, appliances, soap products, and various food products; transportation industries such as railroads, airlines, and branches of shipping. About one-third of the U.S. work force is employed in monopolistic industries, the largest proportion in manufacturing and mining.[7]

Wages are relatively high, even in the smaller "fringe"

firms that coexist with the giants in some monopoly industries.[8] However, low-seniority workers and many in unskilled and semi-skilled jobs are frequently little better off than their counterparts in competitive industries. For example, steelworkers with less than two years' service are ineligible for supplementary unemployment benefits, and a 1971 Equal Employment Opportunity Commission report condemned "Ma Bell" for confining women workers to "the most stifling and repetitive (and low-paid) jobs."

Barriers to the entry of new capital in monopoly industries (e.g., state regulatory agencies, high capital requirements, high overhead costs, advertising and brand loyalty, and product differentiation) create relatively stable industrial structures. Moreover, the large amounts of fixed capital invested per worker compel management to regularize production and employment to avoid losses attributable to unused productive capacity. The complexity of modern technology and work processes and the enormous task of coordinating disparate elements in the production process also compel management to minimize arbitrary or unexpected elements in production and distribution. Planning is extended downward to insure the availability of raw materials and other supplies at stable prices and upward into wholesale and retail operations in order to control demand.

For these reasons, the demand for labor is relatively stable and work is available on a full-time, year-round basis. There are two broad layers of monopoly sector workers in the monopoly sector (in addition to the bottom layer mentioned previously): (1) blue-collar production, maintenance, and similar workers and (2) a so-called middle class of white-collar, technical, administrative workers (the great majority white adult males, excluding women who hold typing, filing, and other unskilled and semiskilled white-collar jobs). The typical competitive firm is small and its technology is less complex; thus the demand for bureaucratic-administrative and technical-scientific workers in this sector is relatively low.

The social makeup of the work force, the relatively inelastic demand for labor, and the physical and geographic concentration of production units facilitate the growth of powerful labor unions in monopolistic industries. And monopolistic product markets, stable industrial structures, and large profit margins make it comparatively inexpensive for corporations to recognize unions. Thus since the 1930s and early 1940s, when workers in most monopolistic industries forced employers to recognize and bargain with their unions, the labor movement in this sector has been relatively well developed.

THE FISCAL CRISIS OF THE STATE

# THE STATE SECTOR

The third major sector of the economy, state industry, falls into two categories: production of goods and services organized by the state itself and production organized by industries under contract with the state. Examples of the first are mail service, education, public health, welfare, and other social services, and military service (excluding arms production). Examples of the second are military equipment and supplies, capital construction, and highway construction. (In Europe many manufacturing activities are included in this group.) About one-eighth of the U.S. civilian labor force is engaged in the first type of activity, and perhaps as much as one-third is employed in both activities combined.[9]

In state-organized activities the ratio of capital to labor and productivity is relatively low (and increases slowly), and production growth depends mainly on increased employment. National-income accountants assume that productivity in these activities never changes, although economists estimate that it increases by 1 or 1.5 percent yearly.[10] In the second category the ratio of capital to labor is relatively high, and the production growth depends on capital investment and technical progress and the number of workers employed. Nevertheless, productivity here also tends to be low and to increase sluggishly. First, the outputs of many state contractors are original, one-of-a-kind products—for example, new weapons systems, research and development (R & D), airbases on unfamiliar terrain—and hence it is difficult to make sectoral or temporal comparisons of labor's physical productivity and to regularize production planning and coordination and other aspects of the work process. And second, neither the market nor the drive for profit maximization discipline state contractors because they are producing under government contract (this is particularly true under cost-plus contracts). Thus production in both categories of state industries depends on the state's budgetary priorities and its ability to mobilize tax revenues. Taxpayers bear costs in both sets of activities (including state contractors' profits), except for those wholly or partially organized on the benefit principle (e.g., postal services).

The demand for labor in the state sector, although relatively stable, is subject to political shifts that affect budgetary priorities. In general, state subsidization of production insures stability. Management of demand reduces or eliminates the unpredictable ups and downs of competitive markets. White males who seek job security and relatively high wages (see below) practically monopolize the better-paid state sector positions. At the same time, the political norms that govern hiring, promotion, transfer, and other personnel decisions (e.g., equality of opportunity, equal pay for equal work, etc.) compel state enterprises and contractors to open doors to oppressed minorities and women. For example, although black workers are underrepresented in the monopoly sector (especially in the secure blue-collar and white-collar jobs) and over-represented in the competitive sector (excluding the construction industry), the percentage of blacks employed in the state sector is roughly equivalent to the percentage of blacks in the work force.[11]

Stability of employment, labor immobility, and the large size of production units foster the organization and growth of labor unions in state industries. But the social heterogeneity of the work force (old and young, whites, minority-group members, and women in sex-typed jobs) inhibits unions. Professionalism, part-time work, and status distinctions based on bureaucratic hierarchies also play an inhibiting role. Perhaps of more significance in the long run, because it is difficult for state administrators and contractors to raise labor productivity, wage increases tend to force up unit labor costs (and hence, taxes). For this reason, among others, government agencies normally attempt to discourage the development of unions. Nonetheless, in recent years state industries have become better organized than competitive sector industries, but are still more poorly organized than those in the monopoly sector.

## WAGE AND PRICE DETERMINATION
## IN THE PRIVATE SECTOR

Competitive sector wages, prices, and profits are determined chiefly by market forces. The essence of the competitive market mechanism is the process by which productivity increases are transformed into higher standards of living via changes in prices and profits. Assume, for example, that a group of farmers introduces hybrid corn that doubles land yields and hence (ignoring other costs) reduces costs by one-half. Clearly, given the market price of corn, they will make a profit over and above the usual margin in the industry. Three consequences are likely: first, the innovating farmers will be tempted to expand production to make even greater profits; second, other corn farmers will be compelled to introduce the hybrid, or risk being driven out of business; third, farmers growing other crops will be tempted to plant corn. In any (or all) of these events, total corn production and supply increase, and more corn is sold, but at lower prices. With demand constant, the expansion of supply

THE FISCAL CRISIS OF THE STATE

will drive down prices and sooner or later eliminate the original larger-than-normal profit margins. The final effect is that the consumer (i.e., society as a whole) benefits from the innovation and cost reductions in the form of lower prices for things needed for survival.

If consumers buy the entire crop for immediate use, there is a direct link between the technical innovation (hybrid corn) and a higher material standard of life (lower prices). If manufacturers buy the corn to process it, the effect on material well-being is indirect: Fresh corn prices fall, pushing down production costs in the canneries, thus increasing profits in this branch of industry. In turn, a mechanism similar to the one just described is touched off. Cannery owners will expand production to take advantage of higher profit margins, and other businessmen will enter the corn-canning industry to make a higher return on their capital. The effect will be to increase the supply of processed corn, lower prices, eliminate excessive profits, and indirectly spread the gains from technical progress to society.[12]

To summarize: All other things being equal, prices in competitive industries fall more or less in proportion to increases in productivity. The gains from technical progress are not monopolized by any one group of capitalists and workers in the form of permanently higher prices, profits, and wages, but rather are distributed more or less evenly among the population as a whole. "The basic principle of the market system," Joan Robinson writes, summarizing the whole issue, "is that the benefits of progress are passed on to the community as a whole, not bottled up in the industries where they happen to arise." [13]

If prices are determined by productivity in the competitive sector, what determines wages? Total demand in the economy as a whole. Upward surges of competitive-sector money wages are attributable to inflation, not to technical progress and improvements in productivity.[14] During periods of high labor demand and general inflation, wages in unorganized industries (mainly competitive industries) increase faster than wages in organized industries (mainly monopoly industries). During periods of sluggish labor demand, union–nonunion wage differentials shift in favor of organized workers.[15]

In the monopoly sector market forces are not the main determinants of wages, prices, and profits. Monopolistic corporations have substantial market power. Prices are administered, and in comparative terms price movements are sealed off from market forces.[16] Most corporations operate on the basis of an after-tax profit target (normally between 10 and 15 percent). If labor costs rise, monopolistic corporations will attempt to protect planned profit targets by increasing prices. Assuming that labor productivity remains unchanged, money wages are thus the main determinants of monopoly sector prices.

What forces determine the level of money wages? The process of wage determination in the monopoly sector will be simplified in order to highlight its essential features. First assume that the economy is expanding. In an economic boom the demand for labor increases (as well as demand for nearly everything else) in both competitive and monopoly sectors.

The supply of labor available to competitive industries is relatively inelastic and hence a sizable increase in demand will raise wages in this sector. If businessmen fail to raise wages they will not be able to attract enough workers to expand production and fill orders, nor will they be able to retain some workers already employed in competitive industry. Workers in the competitive sector (and the unemployed, as well) will seek employment in the generally more desirable monopoly sectors. Will monopoly capital be forced to offer higher wages to attract the workers it requires to expand production in the short run and meet the higher level of demand? Except during periods of extreme boom (e.g., the peak years of the Korean War), the supply of labor available to monopoly capital is relatively elastic. Thus it can attract all the workers it needs from the competitive sector at the going wage rate. Put another way, monopoly capital is able to draw on the pool of underemployed competitive sector labor (or the "invisible" reserve army of the unemployed).

Although the market forces tending to drive up monopoly sector wages normally are relatively weak, the political forces at work are very powerful. In a nutshell, during a boom the production relations alter in favor of labor. Profit margins grow at precisely the same time that unemployment falls, and union bargaining strength is enhanced at the same time that there is a larger surplus (profits) to bargain over. In the last analysis it is the collective power of organized labor that wrests higher wages from monopolistic corporations, not the normal forces of supply and demand.[17]

What are the specific principles governing the administration of wages in monopoly industries? First, labor productivity; second, cost of living. Again the process will be simplified in order to focus on basic elements. The sequence of wage changes starts in monopoly sector industries in which productivity is advancing most rapidly. Unions bargain for wage increases at least commensurate with productivity increases. Subsequently, unions representing workers in other monopolistic industries seek wage increases as great as those won by their brethren in the high-productivity industries. This is called *pattern bargaining.* One of its results is that average wages tend to rise somewhat faster than average productivity (and, of course, considerably faster than productivity throughout the economy).

Several empirical studies support these theses. According to one of the most thorough, "productivity gains are more likely to go to the workers the more unionized and concentrated [i.e., monopolized] the industry, although the union elasticity carries the greater weight." [18] Another scholar concludes that wage increases in one monopoly sector industry spill over to others.[19] However, pattern bargaining and uniformity of wage increases do not "trickle down" into the competitive sector. "Changes in the union–nonunion [wage] differential," Livernash writes, summing up available evidence, "and changes in relative earnings among industries do not support the existence of strong pattern influences operating broadly across industry lines throughout the economy as a whole." [20]

The final result of the process of administered prices and wages, productivity wage increases, and pattern bargaining is that many or most gains from productivity increases arising from technical progress (and other factors such as scale of production and degree of capacity utilization) are not distributed evenly throughout the population, but rather are "bottled up" in the monopoly sector by corporations and organized labor.[21] One side-effect is the drift toward permanent inflation—that is, the continuous upward movement of wages and prices.[22] In effect, the classic competitive market mechanism breaks down and the dominant production relations (monopoly capital and organized labor), not impersonal market forces, determine the allocation of economic resources, the wage structure and distribution of income within the working class and capitalist class.

At this point, an anomaly in the political economy of modern America must be emphasized. The determination of wages and prices in the competitive sector was analyzed without reference to the actual production or power relationships because wages and prices in these industries are determined by market forces—that is, they are determined independently of the intentions of businessmen and workers. For example, as indicated above, capitalists attempting to increase profits by expanding production lower prices and thus reduce all capitalists' profits—clearly an unintended effect.

Comparatively speaking, the situation is different in the monopoly sector: Production is planned and wages and prices are administered. Because there is more conscious human control over income and income distribution, market theory per se can throw only a limited light on the determinants of wages, prices, and profits. Precisely because wages are relatively insensitive to changes in the demand for labor and because productivity gains tend to be monopolized, we must look behind the market categories and discover the historical, social, and political forces shaping wages, prices, and income distribution.

This excursion into history begins at the close of World War II. The inseparable link between productivity and cost of living and wages in the monopoly sector and the bifurcation of wage-price determination in the monopoly and competitive sectors is rooted in an agreement imposed on organized labor during the last half of the 1940s.[23] At the end of the war the large industrial unions entered into permanent collective bargaining relationships (for the first time under normal conditions) with large corporations that exercised monopolistic control over prices. The unions could win higher wages in two ways. The first was to demand higher wages at the expense of profits. However, because the corporations controlled prices, they could (and can) easily raise prices and pass on wage increases not "justified" by rising productivity to consumers—and thus protect their profit margins. The unions could have countered this move only by adopting a working-class perspective (in contrast to an industrial-union perspective) and agitating politically for a return to price controls without a revival of wage controls. Obviously, such a course would have been unrealistic in the context of early cold war America.

The alternative for the industrial unions was to demand that the workers share in the benefits accruing from increased productivity. In theory, two courses were available to union leaders. First, they could try to force the monopolistic corporations to lower prices when increased productivity led to lower production costs. Thus the benefits of technical progress would have been distributed more or less evenly among all consumers. But the unions recognized that they had (and have) no control over prices and chose the second course: They demanded that wages increase with productivity (and demanded cost-of-living wage adjustments, as well), with the inevitable (and clearly unintended) effect of bifurcating the working class still further. Competitive sector workers suffered. On the one hand, their wages were (and are) relatively low; on the other, they had (and have) to buy at relatively high monopolistic prices.[24]

Needless to say, big business did not begin to grant annual wage increases, cost-of-living adjustments,[25] additional fringe benefits, and so on without a quid pro quo. In return for wage scales

THE FISCAL CRISIS OF THE STATE

pegged to productivity plus, the unions agreed not only to abstain from fighting mechanization but also to collaborate actively when major innovations required large-scale reorganization of the work process. There have been exceptions, mainly in declining industries such as railroading where featherbedding has been a major issue.[26] From the standpoint of monopoly capital the main function of unions was (and is) to inhibit disruptive, spontaneous rank-and-file activity (e.g., wildcat strikes and slowdowns) and to maintain labor discipline in general. In other words, unions were (and are) the guarantors of "managerial prerogatives." Union leaders have long recognized that demands for both increased wages and more control over production are contradictory because wage demands are based on rising productivity which requires that management be free to fire redundant workers. At times, union leaders have been hard pressed to maintain labor discipline, especially over the issue of labor-saving technological changes. As will be seen, the number of jobs (and employed workers) in the monopoly sector tends to rise slowly, in some cases to decrease absolutely. Hence unions are one agent of technical progress and rational (in terms of profits) laborpower planning by monopoly capital.[27]

## INTERRELATIONSHIPS BETWEEN PRIVATE AND STATE SECTORS

In all capitalist economies the creative powers of the producing class are harnessed to (and the source of) private profit. Without actual or expected profits, production is cut back or halted. Because state industries are not organized for direct profit the private sector plays the preeminent role in economic expansion. Within the private sector monopoly industries are the "engine" of capital accumulation and economic growth. Their markets expand on the basis of new product development, product model and style changes, product differentiation, and so on, and (excepting the short run) production expands on the basis of increased productivity (not increased employment). It should be emphasized that both market expansion and growth of productivity and production (i.e., demand and supply) depend on the advancement of science and technology and their exploitation by monopoly capital.

What forces determine scientific and technical progress and product development and increases in productivity? The growth of social capital and the state sector. It will be argued here that the general cause of monopoly sector growth has been the expansion of the state sector.[28] We will also argue that the general effect of monopoly sector growth has been the growth of the state sector. In other words, the growth of monopoly and state sectors is a single process.

Both bourgeois and Marxist economists agree that economic growth depends on the expansion of investment and consumption (or constant and variable capital, in Marxist terms). But both groups still tend to focus on the growth of private investment and consumption. There have been few if any investigations of the role of social investment and social consumption (capital not subject to direct private ownership) in the accumulation of capital and economic growth.

What has, in fact, happened over the past century or so? Capitalist production has become more interdependent—more dependent on science and technology, labor functions more specialized, and the division of labor more extensive. Consequently, the monopoly sector (and to a much lesser degree the competitive sector) requires increasing numbers of technical and administrative workers. It also requires increasing amounts of infrastructure (physical overhead capital)—transportation, communication, R&D, education, and other facilities. In short, the monopoly sector requires more and more social investment in relation to private capital. (It was estimated in 1967 that the U.S. economy would require an annual investment of $50 billion in physical social capital between 1966 and 1975.[29]) The costs of social investment (or social constant capital) are not borne by monopoly capital but rather are socialized and fall on the state.

Increasing interdependency in production also dictates greater outlays on social consumption (or social variable capital)—for example, insurance against sickness, old age, economic insecurity; public housing; state-financed suburban development; recreational facilities. Unquestionably, monopoly sector growth depends on the continuous expansion of social investment and social consumption projects that in part or in whole indirectly increase productivity from the standpoint of monopoly capital. In short, monopoly capital socializes more and more costs of production.

What are the general effects of monopoly sector growth (which, in turn, is increasingly based on the growth of the state sector)? Monopoly sector markets normally do not expand fast enough to maintain a "full-employment" volume of production. In other words, productive capacity tends to grow faster than demand for output.

Two factors acount for the more rapid expansion of capacity.[30] First, monopoly sector money wages increase in rough proportion to increases in productivity and the cost of living (i.e.,

THE FISCAL CRISIS OF THE STATE

inflation). Thus, real wages normally grow in proportion to productivity. The problem arises when we consider the movement of competitive sector wages. Real wages in this sector are low and increase relatively slowly. It follows that real wages throughout the economy rise more slowly than monopoly sector productivity and productive capacity. The absence of effective unions in the competitive sector and the bifurcation of the wage- and price-determination process in the competitive and monopoly sectors keep consumer demand (in terms of average wage increases) from advancing as rapidly as productive capacity in monopoly industries.

It might be objected that there would not be a drag on the growth of monopoly sector markets if this sector were to appropriate a disproportionate share of the total demand. In other words, if *all* workers (competitive and state as well as monopoly) were to expend a relatively large share of income on monopoly sector output, then total demand in this sector would rise as fast as or even faster than its productive capacity. In fact, the monopoly sector receives a smaller than proportional share of total demand because competitive sector productivity (especially in services and trade) and in the state sector increases relatively slowly, and thus costs of production rise relatively rapidly. Competitive and state sectors absorb an ever-larger share of total demand, thus depriving the monopoly sector of markets. We spend so much on taxes, services, interest charges, and the expenses of distribution (trade) that we do not have much left for the products of monopolistic industry, and job opportunities for new workers tend to be few and far between.

The lag between increases in output and employment has become greater and greater and the impact of increases in output on employment has become smaller and smaller. Between 1957 and 1969, employment gains averaged over 4 percent annually in only four of thirty-six major American industries. By contrast, productivity rose by more than 4 percent in seventeen industries (and declined in none). And in thirteen industries—notably coal mining, railroads, petroleum refining, and flour milling, in which small increases in production and large increases in productivity went hand in hand—employment actually declined.[31]


## SURPLUS CAPACITY AND SURPLUS POPULATION

Monopoly sector growth tends to generate surplus capital in the form of surplus goods (or surplus productive capacity) and surplus population (or technological unemployment). Workers employed in the monopoly sector who become redundant constitute the relative surplus population. Black and other minority workers who are "last hired, first fired" make up a comparatively large part of the relative surplus population. It also becomes difficult for job seekers entering the labor force the first time to find employment in the monopoly sector. Those so affected, primarily youth and women, constitute the absolute surplus population.[32]

With the growth of both absolute and relative surplus populations more and more workers are compelled to seek employment in the competitive and state sectors. Jobs in retail trade, services, small-scale manufacturing, and government have absorbed most of the slack, and the "reserve army of the unemployed" has become largely "invisible."[33] Workers who have been pushed out of or cannot find monopoly sector jobs range from unskilled and semiskilled laborers to professionals. For example, wives of technologically unemployed Appalachian coal miners provide a pool of cheap labor for small manufacturers who establish "runaway" shops in labor surplus areas. That this is a general phenomenon is suggested by studies showing that women whose husbands are unemployed are more likely to enter the labor force than women with husbands at work.[34] At the other extreme, one Department of Labor study projects that by 1982 there will be twice as many applicants as openings for workers with the Ph.D. degree. Programs have been set up to find state jobs for many unemployed (or underemployed) professional and technical workers. Certainly of particular importance is the role of the state in absorbing black and other minority workers. It has been estimated that from the late 1950s to the mid-1960s the number of black workers hired by the state equaled the number of blacks who were either technologically unemployed or first entering the labor force.[35] And in 1971, the federal government launched nine programs intended to create 120,000 temporary jobs in state and local government; 50 percent were to be allotted to blacks and other minorities.[36] The situation is especially critical because the federal government attempts to maintain high employment in the monopoly sector, thus keeping up wages and encouraging the more rapid introduction of labor-saving innovations, which in turn creates more unemployment in the competitive sector.

Growth of monopoly sector production also indirectly increases state sector employment. Competitive sector workers become increasingly impoverished in terms of the relation between their wage income and their needs. First, the increased supply of labor (the growing relative and absolute surplus population) tends to reduce wages or at least to prevent wages from rising as fast as they

THE FISCAL CRISIS OF THE STATE

would otherwise. Second, the availability of cheap labor power tends to discourage technical progress and thus tends to depress wages in the long run.

Why is the disparity between wages in the monopoly and competitive sectors not offset by movements of workers from low-paid, competitive industries to relatively high-paid monopolistic industries? Why are there two major and distinct labor markets in modern America? The short-run demand for labor power in the monopoly sector is highly inelastic because production coefficients are fixed. And the long-run demand for labor increases relatively slowly because productivity tends to grow faster than demand for products (or markets). Several studies support this general thesis. A work cited earlier indicates that the allocation of labor between industries is determined more by job vacancies than by wage differentials and wage movements.[37] Another study indicates that labor force participation of younger males is positively related to wages in retail trade (a large branch of the competitive sector). But where institutional factors (i.e., monopoly) create artificially high wage levels and excess labor supply, high wages connote limited job availability, which in turn discourages labor force participation.[38]

The result of the bifurcation of the work force and the expansion of the supply of competitive sector labor is that both unemployed and underemployed *and* fully employed workers in this sector are increasingly impoverished. According to a government study published in 1968, "The employed poor—with earnings below the poverty-line even for full-time work—now represents a larger problem, at least in terms of numbers, than the unemployed." These workers depend more and more on the state to meet their needs and supplement their incomes, either directly in the form of minimum wage laws or indirectly in the form of social welfare and social services. The surplus population today is eligible for a wide range of social programs, including emergency and general assistance benefits, welfare benefits, food stamps and commodity distribution, Medicaid and Medicare, public housing, and supplementary education pro grams. Each such program requires a new or expanded state agency, and thus an expansion of state employment.[39] To summarize, monopoly sector growth indirectly leads to the expansion of the state sector, particularly social expenses of production.

But this is only one side of the story. The other is the tendency of the monopoly sector to generate surplus goods (surplus productive capacity). Monopoly capital must create expanding markets (which it can control) in order to utilize productive capacity that otherwise would be idle. The historical solution has been the rapid expansion of overseas investment and trade, which tend to take up the slack between actual and potential output and thus help prevent the weakening of monopolistic market structures at home. In turn, the growth of U.S. controlled world markets and investment networks has required a worldwide military establishment, foreign aid and loan programs, and other imperial expenditures. Military and related spending also constitute social expenses of production to the degree that they are the effect of the process of capital accumulation in the monopoly industries. (This relationship is analyzed in greater detail in Chapter 6.)

We believe that the growth of the surplus population and surplus productive capacity is a single process (or two sides of the same process). Thus, the growth of state expenditures in the form of welfare expenses and warfare expenses is also a single process (or two sides of the same process). In other words the growth of the welfare state is integrally related to the growth of the warfare state— so much so that the modern state can be described as the welfare-warfare state.[40]

We have seen that long-run monopoly sector growth tends to generate surplus industrial capacity and surplus labor, or surplus capital. In the short run, economic expansion temporarily can liquidate all or a part of surplus capital. During World War II, for example, the demand for labor rose sharply and large numbers of women and black and other minority workers crossed from the competitive sector into the monopoly sector. However, during periods of economic recession or depression, when the demand for monopoly sector labor is weak, there is a general movement of workers in the opposite direction.

If surplus capacity and surplus labor appear and disappear together during times of economic recession and boom, respectively, then why do both warfare and welfare expenditures tend to increase in the long run? Rephrasing the question, if the "expenses of empire" expand in direct proportion to the growth of surplus capital, why do the "expenses of welfare" also expand (or vice versa)? The answer appears to be that there is no necessary reason (or reason generic to capitalist production) for this to be so. At one extreme, Nazi Germany dealt with the problem of surplus labor by militarism alone. At the other extreme, Sweden deals with its surplus capital problem by welfare alone. Clearly, the specific historical development of a country or region is the crucial factor determining the "mix" between warfare and welfare spending.

Indisputably, U.S. warfare and welfare expenditures have increased hand in hand in the long run. The general reason is that during past periods of overseas and military expansion, the state welfare apparatus has not been dismantled. And when the welfare budget has expanded (e.g., during the period 1965–1970), the military establishment has not been dismantled. Until 1937–1938, the New Deal greatly expanded welfare but not military expenses. During and directly after World War II, the relationship was reversed, but during the 1950s, and especially in the 1960s, with the accelerated growth of surplus capital, both the welfare and warfare establishments were strengthened. Indeed, since 1965 military and welfare spending have increased very rapidly. The present situation thus is attributable to growing unemployment and poverty and the further development of the welfare state, on the one hand, and growing surplus productive capacity, the drive to expand, protect, and control foreign markets, and the growth of the warfare state, on the other. But whatever the specific conjuncture of forces at any time and in any society, the underlying dynamic of the expansion of welfare and warfare expenses is the process of capital accumulation in monopoly industries.

## SURPLUS CAPITALISTS

As we have seen, the growth of monopoly sector production tends to increase employment in the competitive sector. But there is another mechanism at work, which contracts competitive industries: the tendency for monopoly capital to take over and dominate competitive capital. The extensive (as contrasted with intensive) character of monopoly capital growth not only generates more unemployment in competitive industries (surplus labor) but also liquidates large numbers of small businessmen (surplus capitalists). Consider U.S. agricultural production, for example. Farming is increasingly dominated by large-scale capital employing modern technology. Thus farm output expanded by 45 percent between 1950 and 1965, whereas farm employment (workers and owners) fell by 45 percent. In the mid-1960s, almost 30 percent of the farm population (3.9 million people; an unknown number were previously farm owners) and over 23 percent of the rural nonfarm population (almost 10 million people) lived in poverty.[41] This high incidence of poverty is attributable more to unemployment (unemployment and under-employment rates in the mid-1960s were about 20 and 40 percent, respectively) and the displacement of the small farm operator than to low wages.

The take-over by monopoly capital of traditional competitive industries such as agriculture, construction, trade, and services, together with the long-run expansion of labor supply, tends to depress profits of competitive capital. Profits also are depressed when small business must compete with large-scale capital and when a superabundance of cheap labor encourages the setting up of small business, and thus produces "overcrowding" in the competitive sector. Moreover, the relative decline in wages in competitive industries that have resisted union organization tends to keep prices down, and under certain circumstances can decrease profits.[42] Finally, because of the economically depressed condition of competitive industries, small businessmen and farmers (as well as workers) are forced to depend more and more on the state for material survival, indirectly in the form of fair-trade laws and similar protective legislation, directly in the form of loan guarantees, farm subsidies, and similar programs. Outlays on such indirect and direct state programs are also forms of social expense.

## WAGE INFLATION IN THE STATE SECTOR

The state sector expands because state agencies and contractors must supply social capital to the monopoly sector and because monopoly sector growth in turn requires that the state devote even more funds to social expenses. Costs of expanding state agencies and programs increase rapidly for two reasons: First, productivity increases are relatively small, and thus a rising portion of the total productive forces must flow into the state sector to maintain a constant level of state services per unit of growing outputs.[43] Second, wages are relatively high and increase relatively rapidly. Wages are high because many if not most state services (especially in construction) require a skilled and experienced labor force. And wages increase rapidly because state sector rates tend to be tied to monopoly sector productivity.

Monopoly sector money wages are pegged to productivity and cost of living. This fact has important consequences for wages, costs, and production in state industries. There is a general tendency for state sector wages to be driven up to the level prevailing in the monopoly sector. First, one provision of the general agreement between monopoly capital and labor is that workers employed by state contractors (e.g., aerospace workers represented by unions such as the UAW) and state agencies (e.g., construction workers hired by highway departments) will receive union pay scales. Second, many state and local government employee associations exert considerable political clout and the bargaining power of many state worker unions is growing. The associations and unions attempt to enforce wage and salary scales commensurate with those in the monopoly sector.[44] Third, although the supply of labor in the state sector is highly elastic (for the same reason that it is elastic in monopoly industries), market forces do not determine wages as in the competitive sector. Wages are determined politically (rather than by the necessity of surplus value production, as in the private sector), thus placing a floor on average pay scales, a floor absent in the competitive sector.[45]

The effect of linking wages in state industries to productivity in the monopoly sector is clearly to drive up costs in the state sector. According to Baumol, "the very progress of the technologically progressive sectors inevitably adds to the costs of the technologically-unchanging sectors of the economy, unless somehow the labor markets in these areas can be sealed off and wages held absolutely constant." [46] However, to the degree that monopolistic industries pass on productivity increases and cost reductions in the form of lower prices (or better quality goods), costs of production in the state sector tend to decline. But this is a weak tendency, first, because monopolistic prices are inflexible in the downward direction, and second, because for the most part the state produces services and hence purchases relatively few monopoly sector outputs. Thus, costs in monopolistic industries can decrease substantially with little or no positive spill-over into the state sector.

Whether the rise in unit costs in state sector activities results in a decline in state production (and hence employment) depends on the elasticity of product demand. In turn, demand elasticity depends on the balance of political forces. For example, the state's demand for the outputs of the military-industrial complex during the 1960s was highly inelastic; by contrast, its demand for welfare services and low-income housing was relatively elastic. By and large, however, government expenditures are difficult to reduce, and so is state employment. Baumol's conclusion that "since there is no reason to anticipate a cessation of capital accumulation or innovation in the progressive sectors of the economy, the upward trend in the real costs of services cannot be expected to halt" [47] undoubtedly applies to state industries.

The monopoly and state sectors are interrelated in an asymmetric way. Unions and corporations in monopolistic industries have agreed that workers will be forced to accept labor-saving innovation in return for wages pegged to productivity and cost of living, even at the price of long-run technological unemployment (which is absorbed in part or in whole by the state and competitive sectors).

Without this agreement technical progress would be highly uneven and irregular. Thus the increase in output per worker is merely the proximate cause of rising wages and unit labor costs in state industries. The underlying cause resides in the harmonious relations of production in the monopolistic sector. Therefore, to the degree that rising costs in the state sector inhibit state production, and to the degree that productivity increases in the monopoly sector depend on the growth of indirectly productive state industries such as education, any reduction in the growth of monopoly sector production and productivity can be attributed to the relations of production in the monopoly sector. Put another way, if and when rising costs force education expenditures, for example, and ultimately productivity to contract, it will be because education outlays have raised monopoly sector productivity, profits, and wages, thus forcing up state sector costs. This process may be described in Marxist terms as one way in which capitalist relations of production inhibit the development of the forces of production. Productivity is inhibited by the relations of production indirectly, not directly at the point of production (as, e.g., on the railroads).

## NOTES AND REFERENCES

1. This definition excludes both household and other labor that produces use values but not exchange values and petty commodity production (i.e., individuals who "work for themselves").

2. There are no comprehensive empirical studies of the relationship between employment stability and security and degree of market competition in the U.S. economy. We do know that the inferior conditions of blacks are attributable in significant part to white monopoly power in labor and product markets [Lester Thurow, *Poverty and Discrimination* (New York: 1969)]. We also know that it is "easier" for black workers to find jobs in industries that depend on unskilled labor [Raymond Franklin and Michael Tanzer, "Traditional Microeconomic Analysis of Racial Discrimination: A Critical View and Alternative Approach," in David Mermelstein, ed., *Economics: Mainstream Readings and Radical Critiques* (New York: 1970), p. 120, n. 10]. Many of these industries are in the monopolistic sector where the introduction of capital-intensive production techniques creates semiskilled and unskilled jobs. For example, the southern tobacco industry sells in monopolistic product markets but single-handedly accounts for nearly all black female employment in southern monopolistic industries (ibid, p. 121). Further, there are southern competitive industries—in silk and rayon and woolen and worsted manufactures, knit goods—in which white workers hold a near monopoly on jobs. However, over time there is a tendency for monopolistic industries to become automated. When this occurs, average skill levels are higher in the monopolistic than in the competitive sector.

Franklin and Tanzer could find no correlation between the proportion of black to total workers and the degree of monopoly in southern manu-

THE FISCAL CRISIS OF THE STATE

facturing industries. But their data were drawn from the 1940 census, which was taken at a time when blacks were barred from manufacturing industries and forced into competitive, labor-intensive, and low-paid activities such as lumbering, farm employment, and domestic service. They also report that blacks are, to a large degree, confined to labor-intensive manufacturing industries that have relatively unstructured labor markets—i.e., assignment, promotion, hiring and firing, etc., are irregular. Our guess is that most of these are, in fact, competitive industries by the definition given above.

A recent Federal Reserve study estimated that in 1970 black workers held about 9.9 percent of manufacturing jobs—by a small margin, less than the proportion of blacks in the work force. "In several industries, their share of the jobs was considerably higher For example . . . in 1971 their shares were: tobacco, 32.5 percent; lumber and wood products, 20 percent; primary metals, 14.4 percent; apparel, 13.2 percent; food processing, 12.4 percent; stone, clay, and glass, 11 9 percent; transportation equipment, 11.6 percent; and furniture, 11.5 percent" (Andrew F. Brimmer, "Economic Situation of Blacks in the United States," *Federal Reserve Bulletin* (March 1972), 262).

Branches of the tobacco industry and lumber and wood products, food processing, stone, clay, and glass, apparel, and furniture are all relatively competitive. Primary metals and transportation equipment are comparatively monopolistic. But, as Brimmer points out, "to a considerable extent, the industries with large numbers of black employees are those in which numerous jobs are unpleasant and routine or which require much physical strength or long endurance. Moreover, blacks are typically found in the lower-paid blue-collar occupations requiring only limited skills" (ibid.).

Brimmer reports (and corroborates our model) that "blacks were overly represented in services (29.1 percent of employed blacks vs. 20.1 percent of the total [number of workers]" (ibid.). However, "a sizable divergence is evident in the trade field, in which 14.2 percent of blacks—in contrast to 20.1 percent of the total—had found jobs" (ibid , p. 261) These findings are not consistent with our model; racism probably keeps retail stores from hiring blacks to serve customers. A breakdown of job categories would probably show a relatively large number of black workers in such positions as clean-up and material-handling jobs in the trade field.

An abundance of specific historical data indicates that racial minorities and women are condemned by racism and sexism to the competitive sector or to low-paid, dead-end jobs in the monopolistic sector. For example, in the 1920s, women workers in manufacturing were concentrated in three competitive industries—cigar making, textiles, and garments. In the garment trades there was a 100 percent turnover every five years, pointing up the irregular nature of employment in this industry [Theresa Wolfson, *The Woman Worker and the Trade Unions* (New York: 1926), cited in *American Labor History*, Critical Summaries Written for an Interdisciplinary Seminar at the University of Wisconsin, February–August 1970, June 1971].

We might add that the oppression of ethnic minorities and women also tends to force them as capitalists into the competitive sector (dress shops, hairdressers, junk jewelry stores. European Protestants own and manage most of the large-scale capital organized in the monopolistic sector; the garment and construction industries are dominated by Jews and Irishmen and Italians, respectively. In America racism and sexism and the dominant relations of production are inseparably linked.

3. It probably does not need to be stressed that the political-

economic importance of a large number of workers who voluntarily seek employment in the competitive sector is one thing, and that of large numbers of people who involuntarily are forced into the competitive sector is another. As will be seen, the latter group is made up of the absolute and relative surplus population.

**4.** Dean Morse, *The Peripheral Worker* (New York: 1969).

**5.** U.S. Department of Labor, *Manpower Report of the President, 1968* (Washington, D C, 1968), pp. 83–84. The remaining workers earning less than $1.60 hourly were employed in manufacturing, mining, and other industries. These workers constitute about one-fourth of the total Our guess is that most of them worked in the competitive sector. See also, Steven Sternlieb and Alvin Bauman, "Employment Characteristics of Low-Wage Workers," *Monthly Labor Review* (July 1972), passim.

That low competitive sector wages are essential for profitable operation is underlined by a Cost of Living Council decision in June 1972 denying over 40,000 hotel and restaurant workers an increase in minimum wages from $1.60 to $2.25 hourly on the grounds that such an increase would force small companies out of business.

**6.** Phillips has shown that industries with high concentration ratios (i.e., monopoly industries) experience greater technological change than unconcentrated (i.e, competitive) industries [Almarin Phillips, "Concentration, Scale and Technological Change in Selected Manufacturing Industries, 1899–1939," *The Journal of Industrial Economics,* 4 (June 1956)]. Borch established that high productivity is associated with large firms, although there were many exceptions [Karl Borch, "Productivity and Size of Firm," *Productivity Measurement Review,* 12 (February 1958)]. Palmerio has shown that in Italy productivity changes have depended primarily on economies of large-scale production and increasing returns, and only secondarily on technical progress This is a "learn by doing" theory of productivity, where productivity is made dependent on production (rather than vice versa), which in turn depends on absolute size of firm [G Palmerio, "Economies of Scale and Embodied Technical Progress in Italian Industry, 1951–1965," *L'industria* (July/September 1969), passim].

**7.** The 500 largest manufacturing and mining corporations employ about two-thirds of all workers in these industries. However, this is only a crude measure of the number of workers in the monopolistic sector. Many large corporations also sell in competitive markets, and many smaller corporations sell in monopolistic markets.

**8.** The general reason is that the AFL-CIO does not normally accept a low-wage policy for small business [Seymour Brandwein, "Are the Charges True?" *AFL-CIO American Federationist,* 65 (October 1958), passim]. In 1971, average hourly wages in the steel and automobile industries were $3.98 and $4 54, respectively. Fringe benefits and overtime premiums increase these rates by about one-third.

**9.** According to a Brookings Institution study by Victor K. Heyman [cited in John R. Bunting, *The Hidden Face of Free Enterprise* (New York: 1964, pp 145–146)], over one-fourth of the labor force was directly or indirectly supported by state payrolls and contracts a decade ago. The proportion undoubtedly has increased since then, perhaps to one-third. Whatever the case, we will assume that the competitive, monopolistic, and state sectors are of equal size, each employing one-third of the labor force

**10.** *Business Week,* October 17, 1970, p. 179. It has been estimated that between 1947 and 1957 the increase in state sector productivity was little more than one-half that in the private sector [Henry D. Lytton, "Public Sector Productivity in the Truman–Eisenhower Years," *Review of Economics and Statistics* (May 1961), passim].

11. As of May 31, 1970, black workers held about 15 percent of federal government jobs [U S Civil Service Commission, *Minority Group Employment in the Federal Government* (Washington, D.C., 1970), p. 3]. In the state-owned transit industries, the proportion of black workers rose from 6.4 percent in 1950 to about 30 percent in 1970 [Darold T. Barnum, "From Private to Public: Labor Relations in Urban Transit," *Industrial and Labor Relations Review,* 25:1 (October 1971), 97].

12. Reductions in costs and prices of commodities that are not themselves means of production (i e , do not enter into the production of other commodities) will not have an effect on general well-being. For example, if the price of steel falls, production costs of all commodities that require steel fall. Under conditions of competition the prices of these commodities will fall. But if the price of race horses falls, production costs in other industries are not affected because there is no demand for race horses in other industries

13. Joan Robinson, *Economics: An Awkward Corner* (New York: 1968), p. 14.

14. E Robert Livernash, "Wages and Benefits," in *A Review of Industrial Relations Research,* pp. 111–12.

15. According to a well-known study by H. G. Lewis (cited in ibid., p. 98).

16. For example, see Gardiner C. Means, "The Administered Price Theory Reconfirmed," *American Economic Review* (June 1972).

17. For example, according to one authority, "what has apparently happened in the 1947–1955 period is that a more powerful force, collective bargaining, has dwarfed and all but obliterated .   market forces" [Robert Ozanne, "The Impact of Unions on Wage Trends and Income Distribution," in Richard Perlman, ed , *Wage Determination: Market or Power Forces?* (Boston: 1964, p. 121)]

18. Sara Behman, "Wage Changes, Institutions, and Relative Factor Prices in Manufacturing," *Review of Economics and Statistics,* 51 (August 1969), 236.

19. "Similarity in wage changes has been particularly noted among a group of highly concentrated highly organized industries as found by Harold M Levinson. John E. Maher demonstrated a high degree of uniformity in wage change in 23 large key-bargain situations. . . . Lloyd Ulman found a strong correlation of wage change with wage level from 1948–1962" ("Wages and Benefits," op. cit , p. 110). Summarizing the findings of other studies, this economist writes that "the high and low-wage industries .   correspond in large measure to well and poorly organized and to higher and lower degrees of concentration [i.e , monopoly])" (ibid , p. 100). The key study is Albert Rees and Mary T. Hamilton, "Postwar Movements of Wage Levels and Unit Labor Costs," *Journal of Law and Economics,* 6 (October 1963).

20. "Wages and Benefits," op. cit., p. 100.

21. As will be seen, the benefits from technical progress are also shared by the state, which claims a large proportion in the form of taxes and distributes them to certain sections of the population in the form of programs and expenditures.

22. To prevent depression, the government has monetized wage and price increases (i.e , increased money supply commensurate with higher wages and prices) via monetary and fiscal policy. Monetization has been an important

element in forcing up costs and the price level. Inflation also is caused by an excess of total demand. The model developed above abstracts from the phenomenon of generalized demand-pull inflation in order to highlight the central social and political forces at work in the economy.

**23.** The revolutionary idea that corporations should not cut wages during recessions (and periods of high unemployment) goes back at least to Herbert Hoover [Herbert Stein, *The Fiscal Revolution in America* (Chicago: 1969, p. 8)]. Previously, Andrew Mellon's classic advice on how to respond to a recession—"liquidate labor"—had dominated the views of monopoly capital. But, as Hoover pointed out, if wage rates were not cut consumer purchasing power would be maintained and thus economic activity would be stimulated. In fact, a high-wage philosophy was briefly popular during the 1920s. In 1929, Hoover requested that corporate chieftains not cut wages. At first, most agreed, but later they changed their minds (ibid., p. 9). President Roosevelt made a similar appeal during the New Deal. Thus, it was not until the post-World War II period that large corporations ceased cutting wages during recessions, partly because they had learned the errors of their ways, but mainly because the big industrial unions were by then strong enough to prevent wage cuts.

**24.** It bears repeating that the cold war fostered interest-group as opposed to class consciousness. Still, in the late 1940s the possibility of a unified working-class movement and/or political party was so remote that union leaders had no alternative. Again, in theory, the unions could have attempted to forge an alliance with farmers and small businessmen and seek to re-create industrial conditions favorable to the competitive mechanism through which productivity gains are transformed into lower prices and higher real incomes for all consumers. But the unions understood that large-scale capital, mass production, and monopolistic corporations were necessary to maintain the high productivity and standard of living already achieved.

It is interesting to note that even before the war, in 1939, although it agitated politically for larger relief appropriations, and thus could claim to speak for all workers, the CIO was primarily concerned with organizing employed workers in the monopoly sector (and to a lesser degree the competitive sector) and getting wage increases for its members.

**25.** Monopoly sector workers sought cost-of-living wage increases to ensure that inflation would not erode their purchasing power. From August 1945 to November 1946, straight-time hourly earnings in U.S. industry rose 18.5 percent, but consumer prices rose by almost the same degree (17.9 percent). By 1948 the United Auto Workers had won a contract that included a cost-of-living escalator. Quickly the escalator clause spread to other industries.

**26.** Unions also have fought for reductions in work-time. Since World War II workers have gained more paid vacations and holidays and earlier retirement (not a shorter work day). Because reduced work-time (like higher wages) depends on increased productivity and lower unit wage costs, unions have been all the more willing to help management expand productivity.

**27.** At times, the "pact" between labor and capital has had to be enforced by strikes or lockouts or both. Normally, however, if the monopoly sector (and the economy as a whole) is expanding, at however slow a pace, unions call a strike and employers shut down plants only under extreme pressure.

**28.** Some bourgeois economists now admit that government spending, not private investment, has been the main cause of economic growth in the United States since World War II. But most believe that the sole importance of government spending has been the maintenance of aggregate demand. The argument developed in these pages is that the government also provides essential supplies for the monopoly sector.

**29.** U.S. Congress, Subcommittee on Economic Progress, Joint Economic Committee, *Financing Municipal Facilities* (Washington, D.C., 1968). If investment in "human capital" was added to investment in physical capital, and if the volume of social capital in relation to total capital were calculated, social investment no doubt would prove to be considerably greater than private investment.

**30.** We are concerned only with consumption demand. The reasons that investment demand in the monopoly sector is sluggish in the long-run have been analyzed by Paul Baran and Paul Sweezy, Maurice Dobb, Joseph Gillman, and others, and are summarized in James O'Connor, "The Meaning of Economic Imperialism," in Robert Rhodes, ed., *Imperialism and Underdevelopment* (New York: 1970, pp. 123–124). The discussion here suggests two other reasons for the sluggishness of investment demand: First, the slow growth of consumption demand weakens the accelerator effect and discourages induced investment; second, the state pays for a larger share of total investment.

**31.** U.S. Department of Labor, Bureau of Labor Statistics, *Indexes of Output Per Man-Hour, Selected Industries, 1939 and 1957–1969,* Bulletin No 1680 (Washington, D.C.: 1970), pp. 1–2.

**32.** Marx showed how factory production created an absolute surplus population by outcompeting traditional handicraft and artisan production, cottage industries, etc. Today, this process works somewhat differently. To take perhaps the most important example, women are "freed" from housework by labor-saving appliances, frozen foods, etc., supplied by monopoly capital. In effect, they are "liberated" from the traditional (oppressive) man–woman familial relationships. However, precisely because monopoly capital cannot end the general social oppression of women, most are not able to find good jobs in the monopoly sector, but rather are confined to the competitive sector.

**33.** We put "reserve army" in quotes because in the original Marxist model its economic role was to regulate the wage rate, more precisely, to prevent wages from rising too fast, making accumulation unprofitable But today the market does not regulate money wages in the monopoly sector; rather, wages are subject to collective bargaining.

**34.** Herbert S. Parnes, "Labor Force and Labor Markets," in *A Review of Industrial Relations Research,* vol. 1 (Madison, Wisc.: Industrial Relations Research Association, University of Wisconsin, 1970).

**35.** Courtesy of Ray Brown.

**36.** James Hodgson, "Any Cure for Big Strikes?" *U.S. News and World Report,* November 29, 1971, p. 72.

**37.** "Wages and Benefits," op. cit., p. 106.

**38.** "Labor Force and Labor Markets," op. cit., p. 10. Authorities cited are William G. Bowen and T. Aldrich Finegan, *The Economics of Labor Force Participation* (Princeton: 1969), p. 440. Between 1953 and 1960, money wages in industries organized by strong unions rose faster than in industries organized by weaker unions ("Wages and Benefits," op. cit., p. 92). The researcher was Gail Pierson.

**39.** Not surprisingly, the best-known older study of the expansion of the state sector shows that the main reason for the growth of government employment is the expansion of government services [Solomon Fabricant, *The Rising Trend of Government Employment* (New York: National Bureau of Economic

Research, 1949)]. It should be added that the growth of government services is due to the expansion of both social costs and social expenses.

**40.** As will be seen in the Appendix to Chapter 6, the expansion of the monopoly sector also creates the need for another kind of social expense—that of protecting and reconstructing the physical environment which is being destroyed by the uncritical utilization of modern technology in the accumulation process. Outlays on economic regulation and the administration of the effects of economic growth also constitute social expenses

In Marxist theoretical terms social expense outlays do not enlarge capitalist production relations because they do not expand capital—i.e, surplus value However, social consumption and social investment spending indirectly enlarge capitalist production relations. Thus, the distinction between social capital and social expenses is indispensable for any understanding of modern class relationships.

**41.** National Advisory Commission on Rural Poverty, *The People Left Behind* (Washington, D.C., 1968), p. 3 In the suburbs 3.3 million people were poor (by official standards), representing only 6.7 percent of all suburban residents In the small cities and central cities the figures were 36.6 and 17 4 percent, respectively (6.4 and 10 2 million individuals).

**42.** In pure theory surplus value (the money form of which is profits) is pumped out of the competitive and into the monopoly sector. Because the money value of output per labor hour is relatively low, the market transmits surplus value from competitive to monopoly industries via the price mechanism. Because it is difficult for competitive industries to pass taxes back to workers and/or other capitalists or forward to consumers or both (and because it is relatively easy for monopoly industries to do so), more surplus value is transmitted to the state—and hence to monopoly capital in the form of social investment and social consumption. Mathematically, $p = rk + wl$, where $p$ = price, $r$ = rate of profit, $k$ = capital per unit of output, $w$ = wages, and $l$ = labor With low $r$, low $k/l$, and low $w$, the money value of output is low per labor hour (formulation courtesy of Steve Hymer).

**43.** These are the findings of the Kuznets-Clark studies of sectoral productivity as reported and analyzed by Jeffrey G. Williamson, "Public Expenditures and Revenue: An International Comparison," *The Manchester School of Economic and Social Sciences* (January 1961).

**44.** A good study documenting the bilateral determination of pay at the local level is David T. Stanley, *Managing Local Government Under Pressure* (Washington, D.C.: The Brookings Institution, 1972), pp 136–137. The positive effect of state sector collective bargaining on wage rates is documented in Robert N Baird and John H. Landon, "The Effects of Collective Bargaining on Public School Teachers' Salaries," *Industrial and Labor Relations Review*, 25:3 (April 1972); Orley Ashenfelter, "The Effect of Unionization on Wages in the Public Sector: The Case of Fire Fighters," *Industrial and Labor Relations Review*, 24:2 (January 1971). Another recent study suggests that teachers' salaries are determined in a particular area by the level of per capita income (implying that well-to-do communities pay high salaries to recruit and keep good teachers) and by the level of salaries paid in competing occupations (implying that high pay in the monopoly sector "supports" salaries in the state sector) [John D Owen, "Toward a Public Employment Wage Theory: Some Econometric Evidence on Teacher Quality," *Industrial and Labor Relations Review*, 25:2 (January 1972)].

**45.** The fact that state employment is sealed off from normal market pressures is stressed in Darold T. Barnum, "From Private to Public: Labor

Relations in Urban Transit," *Industrial and Labor Relations Review,* 25:1 (October 1971) Barnum points to the following differences between the private and state sectors. First, private transit systems cannot afford the kind of pension plan that a large city such as New York can afford. Second, "the present movement toward subsidization of operating losses increasingly will remove the public systems from market pressures, making possible wage raises which probably would not have occurred under strict market conditions" (p 114). Third, "as with public employees in general, public transit workers only recently are beginning to test their power, especially their political power As they become more adept at using this power, their wage rates may increase at a more rapid pace" (ibid ).

**46.** William J Baumol, "Macroeconomics of Unbalanced Growth: The Anatomy of Urban Crisis," in Robert L Heilbroner and Arthur M Ford, eds , *Is Economics Relevant?: A Reader in Political Economics* (Pacific Palisades, Cal.: 1971), p. 111. According to Baumol, the unrelenting rise in costs in technologically backward sectors "drives outputs from the market"—examples are hand-made or craft objects. However, if demand is inelastic and production is maintained even in the face of sharply rising costs, technologically backward sectors will require more workers to maintain production Baumol argues that this is why there is a rising number of workers in retailing and why a rising proportion of costs is accounted for by outlays on marketing As we have seen, however, wages in nonunionized "technologically backward sectors" do not rise as fast as wages in "progressive sectors." Further, craft objects were "driven from the market" not primarily because they were costly in an absolute sense, but rather because they were expensive in relation to mass-produced objects and because of the general debasement of capitalist culture. Finally, marketing costs have risen also because of the need to keep up aggregate demand in an epoch in which capitalism tends to stagnate.

**47.** Ibid.

# CHAPTER 2
# DIMENSIONS OF THE CRISIS

## INTRODUCTION

The relationship between the monopoly sector and the state sector is examined in greater detail in this chapter. Our purpose is to show that the simultaneous growth of these sectors generates an increasingly severe social crisis and fiscal (or budgetary) crisis.

The basic cause of the fiscal crisis is the contradiction of capitalist production itself—the fact that production is social whereas the means of production are owned privately. And its severity today is attributable to the confluence of tendencies in modern capitalist society, particularly in the United States. These tendencies may be summarized as follows:

First, in the long run, monopoly capital socializes more and more capital costs and social expenses of production. However, profits are not socialized (in fact, the point of socializing costs and expenses is to raise profits). This contradiction is especially blatant in industries in which production is organized by private individuals under contract with the state, and which use state-supplied inputs. Such private contractors appropriate profits as a condition for supplying the state with goods and services (e.g., privately delivered medical care, state construction work, and military production).

Second, in the medium run, state sector wage costs become increasingly inflated because wage increases tend to outrace productivity increases. This contradiction also is pronounced in activities organized by private individuals under state contracts, which are implicitly or explicitly cost-plus contracts.

These factors have merged with the more general (and worldwide) tendency for a larger proportion of the population to become dependents of the state. Capitalist production increasingly replaces subsistence production on the farm, in family-centered crafts and cottage industries, and in other spheres of noncapitalist production. Over time, more and more people are proletarianized: Their material well-being depends on their ability to sell labor power in the market. And with the decline of family, community, ethnic, and other primary groups, comes a huge increase in the aggregate of social needs. Thus they must look to the state for material necessities which private capital will not supply and which people cannot provide for themselves.

Throughout the 1960s, especially the late 1960s, the fiscal (and social) crisis was particularly acute. Advanced capitalist economies were hard put to cope with growing excess capacity and a static tax base. Increased international competition and economic stagnation exacerbated conflict over budget control—the distribution of state expenditures and the burden of taxation. Between 1970 and 1971, the federal government tried every weapon in the arsenal of national policy in a desperate attempt to ameliorate the crisis—for example, international monetary reform, managed recession, wage and price controls.

The proximate source of the medium and long-run tendencies is the relationship between labor and capital in the monopoly sector. Monopoly capital and organized labor have, in effect, "exported" their conflicts to the competitive and state sectors.

First, monopoly capital and organized labor have supported the growth of state-financed social investments. For more than two decades, "labor and the academic liberals joined with downtown business interests in sponsoring urban renewal; with auto manufacturers and highway contractors in supporting vast road projects; with suburban legislators in promoting state-supported higher education." [1] From the standpoint of monoply capital the greater the socialization of social investment costs, the greater the profits. From the standpoint of organized labor the greater the socialization of these outlays, the greater the rise in productivity and wages.

Second, monopoly capital and labor also have favored socializing social consumption expenditures such as medical costs and workers' retirement income. Thus they have supported national health insurance, the expansion of old age and survivors' insurance, and similar programs. Monopoly industries have been willing to socialize variable capital costs because of the burden of expensive pension, health, and medical insurance plans won by unions through collective bargaining. Unions have supported socializing these costs because of membership needs and demands for better and more comprehensive medical care, higher and more liberalized pensions, and so forth.

Third, monopoly capital and labor have advocated increased social expense outlays. Both have been ardent defenders of the military budget and the development of new military programs. Both have favored (albeit grudgingly) the existence of the welfare system—the union leaders because they have feared that the relative surplus population otherwise might turn against the unions, and corporate leaders because they have feared that the absolute and relative surplus populations otherwise might turn against the capitalist system itself. Further, monopoly capital and labor have combined to socialize the expenses of reconstructing the environment—the costs of ameliorating urban decay, reducing pollution, and so on. Shifting these expenses to the taxpayers has permitted profits *and* wages in monopoly industries to expand more rapidly.

Finally, monopoly capital and the unions have collaborated in the introduction of labor-saving technology, which has led to an expansion of employment not only in the competitive sector (and thus indirectly to an expansion of welfare expenses) but also in the state sector. And, of course, when the slack is taken up by expanding state employment (as opposed to increasing welfare) wage costs in state industries tend to increase.[2]

There is one crucial difference between the attitudes of capital and labor toward state-organized economic activity. Capital normally opposes the establishment of state industry that competes with monopoly capital—that is, it opposes any program that socializes profits. Thus, it supports national health insurance but not socialized medicine, or favors federal highway programs but not state-managed construction companies. In other words, it urges that capital costs be socialized and that profits be contractually guaranteed by the state. Organized labor, however, has no vested interest in "ripping off" production facilities for the benefit of private capital: The growth of the state contract system does not lead directly to increases in physical productivity and hence to potential increases in wages.

## TAXATION AND INFLATION
## AND WORKING CLASS SOLIDARITY

State outlays in the form of social investment and social consumption have contributed to the growth of total production and income throughout the economy and particularly in the monopoly sector. The significance of this is that state spending (insofar as it has expanded social capital) has increased the tax base (by indirectly increasing production and income) and thus has been in part self-financing. However, as more and more capital costs are socialized, as social expenses mount, and as state sector wage costs rise out of proportion to productivity, it becomes increasingly difficult for the state to finance its activities from the "growth dividend" indirectly produced by outlays on social capital. Because state expenditures normally are financed by advanced capitalist countries in a noninflationary way,[3] tax rates (and state expenditures as a percentage of

THE FISCAL CRISIS OF THE STATE

GNP) have risen more or less steadily since the last decade of the nineteenth century.[4] Increases in tax rates and/or inflationary finance ("forced taxation") thus have been necessary to finance an enlarged state economy.[5] The power of monopoly capital prohibits the third mode of state finance—the establishment of state industry and the socialization of profits.

In abnormal periods, when state expenditures (e.g., for the war in Southeast Asia) are especially unpopular among the general public and particularly the working class, the state resorts to inflationary finance: It foregoes real borrowing and monetizes the state debt. In general, the higher the rate of interest, the more likely that the state will finance expenditures by "borrowing from itself"—that is, by arbitrarily increasing its deposits with banks and thus bank liabilities. But when state expenditures are politically advantageous (e.g., increased spending on public education) the state is not reluctant to increase taxes directly. Finally, when state expenditures are widely unpopular and also are considered useless or destructive by monopoly capital the pressure to retrench is irresistible.

Whatever the particular combination of tax and inflation finance, the effect is to reduce the rate of increase of real wages. For example, assume that monopoly sector productivity and money wages increase by 3 percent annually and that money wages in state and competitive industries increase by 3 and 1 percent, respectively. Next, assume that inflation and/or taxation reduce money wages in all three sectors by 2 percent (under the condition that inflation and the tax load fall proportionately on working-class income).[6] *Ceteris paribus,* the rise in real wages (wages adjusted for higher prices and taxes) in the monopoly and state sectors will be confined to 1 percent anually and to lower real wages in competitive industries. Now recall the assumptions that the work force is divided evenly among the three sectors and that productivity in the state and competitive sectors rises by a mere 1 percent per year. It follows that real wages in monopoly and state industries rise slightly less than average productivity throughout the economy, whereas real wages in the competitive sector fall below average productivity increases.

It is important to stress that this process is triggered by the agreement forced by capital on organized labor in the monopoly industries to keep money wages in line with productivity and the agreement between organized labor, state workers, and the state administration to keep money wages in line with monopoly sector wages. In this way the relations of production in the monopoly and state sectors work to the absolute disadvantage of competitive sector workers. The majority are not only the direct victims of social oppression (and therefore economic discrimination) because they are confined to low-income jobs which do not share equally in the benefits of technical progress and increased productivity, but they are also indirect victims because they are forced to pay a share of the costs of monopoly production—that is, the costs of social capital.

In the last analysis most competitive sector workers are materially impoverished because they are socially oppressed, the victims of racism and sexism. But the causal relationship between oppression and impoverishment runs both ways. The relative or absolute decline in real wages reduces material standards of living and limits upward mobility. Declining material standards force competitive sector workers to rely even more on state services for bare survival (thus increasing state expenditures and triggering the mechanism described above), and constricted upward mobility and increased dependency on the state reinforce race-typing and sex-typing of jobs. The effect is to aggravate antagonisms between "mainstream" workers in the monopoly and state sectors and peripheral competitive sector workers. Finally, the issue of taxes and budgetary priorities further divides the working class. Monopoly and state workers call for budgetary priorities favoring these two sectors and reductions in the tax load. Workers in competitive industries increasingly require a change in budgetary priorities in their favor. The only way for the working class to get what it wants and needs is to establish an alliance against monopoly capital. But this is impractical precisely because of the collaboration between big business and organized labor: Monopoly sector workers are guaranteed their "fair share" of productivity, big business is guaranteed more than a modicum of labor peace.

## CHANGES IN PRODUCTION RELATIONS
## IN MONOPOLY INDUSTRIES

Sooner or later, the fiscal crisis begins to threaten the traditional conditions for "labor peace" in the monopoly industries. The fiscal crisis is at root a social crisis: Economic and political antagonisms divide not only labor and capital but also the working class. This social crisis and the fiscal crisis, which mirrors and enlarges it, finally work their way back into the arena where the decisive conflicts and compromises between labor and capital occur—the monopoly industries.

Despite increases in money wages, real wages of monopoly sector workers tend to fall behind productivity gains. Between 1965 and 1970, productivity in U.S. manufacturing industries increased by about 13 percent, but real wages did not rise.[7] This fact has stupendous potential implications for the functioning of the economy (and capitalist society). Union leaders increasingly become unable and/or unwilling to discipline rank-and-file workers whose standard of living is threatened by inflation and taxation. In brief, they become unwilling to watch union membership stagnate or decline (and to collaborate with employers in the introduction of labor-saving innovation) because they are no longer confident that the real wages of members who keep their jobs will rise with productivity—or even be maintained at a given level. Inflation and heavy taxation thus encourage militancy on the part of union leaders as well as rank-and-file workers.

The result is that monopoly sector labor-management relations begin to deteriorate as the unions organize defensive strikes to keep real wages in line with productivity. As one economist noted, "unionists pointed to the rising costs of medical services, interest, and other items [including taxes] and insisted on wage adjustments that would compensate for these higher costs as well as provide a share in rising national productivity."[8] In 1970–1971, increases of 10 percent annually were common in many monopoly industries (and some organized competitive industries).[9] For example, the construction trades negotiated wage and fringe increases amounting to between 10 and 20 percent (as they had done throughout the 1960s).

If money wages increase more rapidly than productivity, unit labor costs are pushed up, which forces monopoly industries to raise prices to protect profit margins. Needless to say, across-the-board price increases are inflationary (unless, e.g., increased price is offset by improved quality). They are especially inflationary (at least in the short run) to the degree that employment and production expand in the less efficient competitive and state sectors; increases in these sectors pull down average productivity for the economy as a whole. They are even more inflationary when social consumption and social expense outlays are increased to protect the standard of living of workers dependent on the state (e.g., the more than 10 percent cost-of-living increase in social security passed by Congress in March 1971).[10] Thus, in one limited sense, the cost-push theory of inflation is correct: The erosion of living standards by inflation forces workers to demand higher wages, which, in turn, generate more inflationary pressure.

The effect of these struggles is to trigger the process of inflation, fiscal crisis, and social crisis. Wage increases in the monopoly sector spread to the state sector, increasing unit labor costs there as well. If monopoly capital protects profit margins by introducing labor-saving methods, additional workers are pushed into the competitive sector (unless monopoly workers agree to forego wage increases to keep their jobs, as they did occasionally in 1971 and 1972). More and more workers thus come to depend on the state budget to maintain their living standards. If monopoly capital depends solely on price increases to maintain profits, inflation worsens, burdening the state with higher expenditures and/or encouraging workers to demand higher money wages. In either case taxes and/or inflation tend to continue to rise, the social crisis tends to deepen, and monopoly sector production relations tend to worsen.

## STABILITY OF THE SYSTEM:
## STATE CAPITALISM'S THREE OPTIONS

In the post-World War II period the stability of U.S. capitalist society has depended on three factors: Economic expansion overseas and worldwide economic hegemony; [11] the maintenance of harmonious production relations in the monopoly sector; and the socialization of monopoly sector production costs and expenses, together with the private appropriation of profits and the absence of the socialization of wage payments. All of these conditions are closely related, and each has proven to be inflationary. In a nutshell, stability has required continuing inflation and a continuing fiscal crisis (or "inflation" of the state budget).

Inflation (and fiscal strains on the state budget) has been acceptable to monopoly labor to the degree that workers' real living standards have been protected by cost-of-living adjustments. It has been acceptable to monopoly capital because government deficits have underwritten profits [12] and because prices have been administered and wage bargains based on productivity and cost of living. Capital's historic fear that inflation pushes the economy close to full employment, thus strengthening labor's bargaining position (and subverting working-class discipline), has lessened in recent decades. To be sure, inflation complicates rational corporate planning by distorting company accounts and giving the illusion of profits when in fact capital is being consumed. For the giant monopolistic corporations, however, the danger that runaway prices will spark wild speculation and hyper-inflation is minimized because capital accumulation tends to outrace demand.

Monopoly labor and capital are not the only classes (or groups) that have found inflation acceptable. It sometimes is argued that inflation is opposed by banks, wealthy individuals, and other creditors because it undermines the credit structure. Many small banks

THE FISCAL CRISIS OF THE STATE

and financial intermediaries do fear inflationary policies for this reason. Larger banks, however, are linked in ownership and control with manufacturing and other nonfinancial corporations—the main authors and beneficiaries of controlled inflation. Furthermore, financial and other institutions that own federal, state, and local government bonds and securities have a vested interest in an expanding economy (the best collateral for state loans). In addition, banks have used their monopoly power to maintain high interest rates in order to profit from inflation.

Finally, the federal government has supported a policy of moderate, controlled inflation in order to preserve stability. The government also has used inflation to repudiate part of the federal debt and to finance the war in Southeast Asia. And until 1969 or 1970, the federal government did not worry excessively about the effects of inflation on the U.S. balance of payments because the central banks of the advanced capitalist powers had agreed to buy up excess dollars and protect the dollar as the world's reserve currency. In sum, until recently, the political balance favored moderate inflation—even though people on fixed incomes, many state employees and state clients, many small businessmen, and others were victimized by inflation.

Today, inflation and fiscal crisis are anathema to monopoly capital and the state. Reducing inflation and ameliorating the fiscal crisis have become the basic conditions of stability.[13] Monopoly capital and the state must face up to a critical dilemma. On the one hand, monopoly industries must grant increases in money wages to avoid a rupture in relations with labor, even though unit labor costs and prices continuously rise. On the other, domestic inflation worsens the fiscal crisis and tends to reduce foreign demand for U.S. products, cutting into exports and worsening the balance of trade.[14] In addition, inflation pushes up the interest rate, which, in turn, tends to choke off credit-financed spending on housing and consumer durable goods—two mainstays of the private economy. In brief, if monopoly capital keeps prices firm, rising costs cut into profit margins; if it increases prices, falling demand reduces sales and profits (demand will decline even more if inflation is accompanied by unemployment).

From a theoretical point of view there are three ways for the state to keep costs down and ameliorate the fiscal crisis and inflation. The first is to deflate the economy as a whole by engineering a managed recession. The second is to introduce and enforce wage and price controls. And the third is to cooperate with monopoly capital to increase productivity in the private and state sectors (in order to lower costs and relieve the fiscal crisis within the state sector).[15] The successful application of each measure requires more or less deep-going changes in the relations of production throughout the society. Each of these measures has been used to a greater or lesser extent in nearly all of the advanced capitalist countries. Let us now consider each in turn.[15]

## MANAGED RECESSION AND WAGE AND PRICE CONTROLS

The first option open to the state is to use fiscal and monetary policy to reduce aggregate demand, increase unemployment, and weaken unions in the monopoly and state sectors.[16] Assuming that labor's bargaining power is effectively reduced, the positive result of managed recession from the standpoint of capital and the government is to reduce the rate of increase of money wages (and potentially unit labor costs) and interest rates, and indirectly to slow down the growth of price inflation. But there are negative effects. One is the reduction of aggregate demand and sales, which creates unused productive capacity. This tends to reduce labor productivity and raise unit labor costs, which produces a special kind of cost-push inflation.[17] Another negative effect is to increase unemployment and underemployment and thus the number of people dependent on the state budget. Managed recession simultaneously reduces aggregate wage and profit income, lowers the tax base, and cuts into tax receipts, which squeezes the budget from the revenue side. In other words, recession creates demands on the state budget at precisely the time when the state's fiscal ability to meet these demands without recourse to large-scale deficit financing is relatively weak.[18]

Whatever the combination of positive and negative effects of managed recession, the question still remains, how realistic a policy is it? Since the late 1940s, the relation of production in the monopoly sector clearly has been one of annual wage increases and the elimination of wage decreases during recessions.[19] Similarly, since the Korean War interest rates have risen during expansionary periods, and have not declined significantly during recessions. Because monopoly capital and labor favor administered interest rates, prices, and wages it is not surprising that "despite the planned but painful recession in the United States in 1969–1970, and the moderation of inflation which it produced, wage rates continued to escalate." [20] In brief, far from loosening the monopoly labor market, managed recession has increased the absolute surplus population and

THE FISCAL CRISIS OF THE STATE

unemployment in the competitive sector. The reason is that planned recession and the growing impoverishment of competitive sector workers have led to changes in the composition of the work force—particularly a big influx of so-called secondary workers (teenagers and married women).[21]

The second option is to impose wage and price controls on the monopoly sector (or any sector in which money wages advance significantly faster than productivity—e.g., the construction industry). From the standpoint of monopoly capital, controls have the same advantage as managed recession: Responsibility for keeping money wages down is shifted to the government. Such controls also reduce the risk of a downward spiral of employment, income, production, and profits—a latent risk in managed recessions. When the state decides that a particular volume of investment (and savings) is needed for high employment or balance-of-payments equilibrium, and establishes wages and prices accordingly, it effectively controls the distributive shares of income and guarantees a certain level of profits.[22]

From the standpoint of the state, controls have the advantage of easing wage inflation in the state sector, which helps keep the fiscal crisis from getting out of hand. Controls also can slow wage inflation indirectly by putting ceilings on monopoly sector wages (and thus on wage spillovers into the state society). For example, New Deal legislation insuring that wages of construction workers on government jobs are commensurate with union scale in private industry was repealed in 1971. In January 1972, the Pay Board rejected as inflationary contract settlements between 200,000 workers and five major aerospace corporations (operating under federal contract), and in the summer of 1972, the Board began to tighten up on wages of state and local government workers.

Organized labor in the monopoly sector typically abhors wage controls, particularly during periods of unemployment and stagnation. One reason is that the unions are forced to bargain away their right to improve labor's share of income in return for policies designed to maintain stable prices and high employment. And wage controls inhibit collective bargaining to reduce inequities in the wage structure and to win comparable pay scales for comparable occupations. Monopoly capital and the state administration also have reservations about wage and price controls. For monopoly capital, controls introduce an element of inflexibility in management's ability to mobilize, allocate, and accumulate capital profitably. Obviously, it is extremely difficult for the state to enforce controls. A few examples will indicate the complexity of the task: Thousands of wage rates are determined not by collective bargaining at the national level but by local management; it is difficult to define productivity and to win agreement on measures of productivity; [23] fringe costs are not subject to controls.

A final problem of wage and price controls is that they transform antagonisms between labor and capital at the point of direct production into conflicts between labor and the state. Controls thus create possibilities for the development of alliances between workers within the monopoly sector and between workers in the monopoly and competitive sectors. Perhaps this is the basic danger of wage controls from the standpoint of monopoly capital and the state—the potential growth of a class-conscious and unified working class. How dangerous this can be for the stability of the system was emphasized by the May 1968 general strike in France, where state management of the peacetime economy has reached unprecedented levels: Government control of wages was undermined by one massive action of the working class.[24]

For all of these reasons, wage and price controls have worked poorly when they have worked at all in advanced capitalist countries. In Europe temporary reductions in real wages and/or wage freezes have not been followed by "gradual wage thaws" but rather by "explosive 'dam breaks.' " [25] Nor have price controls fared any better. Kidron writes, "while blanket price and profit controls have been imposed at one time or another in peace-time in most countries . . . they have quickly eroded in practice." [26] The record in the United States is, if anything, even worse. In the middle of LBJ's wage-price "guidelines" policy, Council of Economic Advisors Chairman Gardner C. Ackley announced that the guideposts "recently suffered some stunning defeats." [27] Summing up the policy, another economist writes, "economists and others who have been closest to union-management negotiations tend to regard guideposts wage restraint as nonexistent or very minimal." [28] Nixon's New Economic Policy (1971–1972) tightened up the wage control mechanism by substituting formal control machinery for informal guidelines and indirect pressure on unions and corporations. However, the new policy failed to change any of the basic rules of the game. The relations between capital and labor that have evolved in the monopoly sector and that are the dominant force in the American political economy were reflected in the policies of Nixon's Pay Board. Five and one-half percent annually was established as the standard wage increase—a figure that allows for both productivity gains and moderate inflation. Wage increases in 1971 came to 8.1 percent (and 7.8 percent yearly during the first quarter of 1972).[29] Wholesale prices rose at an annual rate of 5.2 percent during the first six months following the end of the Nixon administration's wage-price freeze in November 1971.

THE FISCAL CRISIS OF THE STATE

## A SOCIAL-INDUSTRIAL COMPLEX?

The third and only practical long-run option available to the state is to encourage productivity in the monopoly sector (to restrain costs and prices and increase production and profits) and in the state sector (to ameliorate the fiscal crisis). Raising productivity in competitive industries is impractical because of the large number of firms, the small scale of production, and the relative absence of economic integration. Direct intervention by the state in the monopoly sector (direct planning by state authorities of technological priorities, new investments, industrial location, pricing, etc.) is impractical except in wartime. The state is thus compelled to increase efficiency in the state sector (including facilities owned by state contractors) and help raise monopoly sector productivity indirectly.

Federal, state and local governments have realized some economies of large-scale production in transportation, education, and other activities. Data-handling processes have been mechanized and state employee qualifications have been upgraded. Centralized purchasing, a basic element of efficient management, has been introduced in every large city and most state governments and federal agencies. In 1962, the federal government began to use systematic measures of input-output relationships in such agencies as the Veterans Administration, Treasury Department, and Post Office.[30] By 1972, Nixon's Productivity Commission was developing techniques to measure the productivity of up to three-quarters of federal workers. The federal government also has introduced techniques such as systems analysis and program budgeting, which it now offers to state and local governments. Since World War II, but particularly since 1960, the federal government has become preoccupied with "efficiency" in military purchases and programs. In the Department of Defense "a buyer-seller scheme [attempts] to impose on a sprawling network of military units a coordination and constraint that controls economic units under private property in the market."[31] Cost-benefit analysis is now used by most federal departments and agencies. And at the level of administration, the most recent move to improve productivity was Nixon's reorganization plan of 1970, which was partly inspired by the need "to increase the efficiency of the operations of the Government to the fullest extent possible."[32]

Such techniques can cut some of the fat from the state budget, but not very much. The very meaning of "efficiency" outside of the marketplace and the test of profitability (i.e., when there are no independent buyers and sellers) is uncertain and continues to be debated by government officials and economists. As for services (whether provided by the state or by private capital), it is difficult both to measure productivity and to increase it. Consider for example, the problem of measuring productivity in education. The use of rating scales to assess "input factors" such as teaching quality, cooperation with other teachers, and related criteria is rapidly being phased out by school administrators.[33] But the use of "output factors" may be even more complex and confusing. According to Frank Ackerman,

> A teacher's "output" may simply be defined as the number of pupil-hours of teaching done in a day. In this case "productivity" increases could come about only through longer hours and/or larger classes. [Or] a teacher's output might be measured by his/her student's achievement on standardized tests. "Productivity" increases would then mean teaching to the test. In either case productivity standards would be an obvious educational disaster, providing new incentives to bad teaching as the only route to higher salaries.[34]

As for goods, most state investment is in one-of-a-kind infrastructure (freeways, school buildings, airports, etc.) and military projects (new weapons systems, etc.). For these and related reasons, monopoly capital's central educational and policy-making body, the Committee for Economic Development, once claimed that "no satisfactory measure of output-per-man-hour of government employees can be computed. . . ."[35]

More significantly, conflicting private interests and irrationalities within the state administration limit the state's ability to develop programs characterized by overall efficiency. State, local, and federal river valley development and transportation programs must satisfy the demands of diverse farm, power, auto industry and other interests. Industries that supply military goods are freed from economic risk: The state underwrites capital investments, guarantees orders, and provides needed technical help, thus eliminating the traditional entrepreneurial function and virtually "dictating" gross inefficiency.[36] Unquestionably, government programs that seek to stabilize the social order by providing regular employment for unskilled or unemployed competitive sector workers do not minimize costs and maximize output. The political consequences of adding significantly to unemployment probably accounts for the federal government's failure to automate postal services; thus productivity increases at a snail's pace (less than .05 percent yearly between 1965 and 1970).[37] Finally, until the United States and the Soviet Union agree on a "permissible" number, type, and deployment of weapons, and in the context of on-going national liberation struggles in the Third World, the Department of Defense must concentrate mainly on new weapons development, not on improving the efficiency of weapons production and distribution. All in all, although "review of some factors affecting the trend of government productivity—the use of improved technology and equipment, the spread of the merit system, the introduction of centralized purchasing, and various other advances in public administration—leaves the strong impression that the savings effected by their means have been far from negligible," [38] the prospect of improving productivity further in established state activities is still relatively dim.

However, the prospect of using the state budget to improve productivity (and profitability) in the private sector—particularly the monopoly industries—potentially is bright. It will be recalled that many state expenditures constitute social capital outlays and thus are indirectly productive from the standpoint of monopoly capital. In contrast to the situation in the state sector, there are many (and largely untried) opportunities to lower unit labor costs in the monopoly sector. Our main point here is that "increased productivity" means less increasing efficiency in current state activities than it does adjusting budgetary priorities to favor the monopoly sector. In turn, this requires centralized administrative control and budgetary planning.

Consider education and laborpower development. Federal and state education and job training programs are being designed to tap laborpower reserves, create fresh reserves, upgrade labor skills, and so forth. Reform of the education system around the theme of "career education"—a euphemism for the revival of vocational education—was introduced by the Nixon Administration in 1970–1971. In Los Angeles, according to official policy, many academic courses (and personnel) are scheduled to be dropped and graduates will be awarded certificates of "minimum standards of skill performance exportable to and acceptable for gaining employment." [39] The New Career Program, established in 1966 under the Equal Opportunity Act, finances training programs for paraprofessional workers in the health, education, social work, and related fields; the goal of this reform is to lower unit labor costs in the state sector.

The state is also trying both to eliminate "inefficiency" from the public housing budget and to attract monopoly capital investment by putting construction on a subsidized, mass-production basis. Other sources of "inefficiency" are being rooted out in highway and other transportation programs. For example, the Bay Area Council, monopoly capital's central agency in the San Francisco Bay Area, has developed and partly implemented plans to modernize and eliminate duplication in port facilities and to reduce costs in the state and private sectors by locating new housing and industrial development on the periphery of the Bay Area where land and construction costs are relatively low. In transportation, a number of experiments to gear supply to demand have been financed by the federal government—for example, community involvement in routing, grants to finance modernization of local bus lines under the auspices of new transit authorities, and so on. In addition, "new capital and up-to-date technology for systems like [the Bay Area Rapid Transit in California] can do much to automate public transportation, reduce operating and maintenance costs, thus lessening the impact of inflation. . . ." [40]

The state and monopoly capital hope to ensure additional savings by developing vast "halfway house" programs for mental patients and criminal offenders. Local government and non-profit hospitals turn increasingly to private corporations to operate hospitals and nursing homes. And private capital now manages whole cities on a contract basis. The list of new budgetary priorities and state programs that can improve productivity and/or profitability in the private and/or state sector is close to endless.

Programs such as these may lead to the development of a full-scale "social-industrial complex" under the auspices of the state and monopoly industries.[41] The military-industrial complex has seized some opportunities to convert from military to civilian production (when the federal government has provided handsome subsidies).[42] Yet military contractors still have a large vested interest in the cold war and the expansion of American imperialism and hence in the growth of the military establishment. Summarizing a report (1970) by the Senate Subcommittee on Executive Reorganization, Senator Abraham Ribicoff noted,

> In general, the responses [of military-industrial firms] indicated that private industry is not interested in initiating any major attempts at meeting critical public needs. Most industries have no plans or projects designed to apply their resources to civilian production. . . . [T]hey indicated an unwillingness to initiate such actions without a firm commitment from the Government that their efforts will quickly reap the financial rewards to which they are accustomed. Otherwise, they appear eager to pursue greater defense contracts or stick to proven commercial products within the private sector. . . .[43]

Further, monopoly capital could reap enormous benefits from the development of a large-scale social-industrial complex. Social and related programs geared to expanding productivity throughout the economy and financed in whole or in part by the state would provide new investment opportunities for monopoly industries. "Companies from AT&T to Xerox have been urged to—and in many cases have willingly accepted—the challenges to educate our children, police our streets, clean up our polluted air and water, teach our disadvantaged citizens how to earn a living, rebuild our slums, and even tell us how to run our cities more efficiently." [44] According to one Wall Street firm, "the education area is the last remaining capital-investment industry" with "significant long-term thrust." [45] But the "significant long-term thrust" depends on massive state subsidies and contracts, as the President's Council on Private Enterprise made crystal clear. "Companies could be induced to participate (in social programs)," the Council declared, "only if appropriate monetary incentives are provided by the Federal government to defray the unusual costs of participation." [46] Assuming that "monetary incentives" are forthcoming in sufficient quantities, the social-industrial complex would have additional benefits. Social tensions in the competitive sector (especially among oppressed minorities) might be reduced by creating jobs for the unemployed and underemployed. Further, to the degree that social outlays were organized by the complex directly (e.g., the new teaching systems sold by private corporations to local school districts under performance contracts), the fiscal crisis of the state might be partially relieved in a direct and immediate way.

Whether monopoly capital can develop fully the social-industrial complex is in the last analysis, a political question. Marx showed how new class and political relationships necessarily evolve with the development of new forms of capital, and the social-industrial complex is no exception. Three political changes will be required by the full development of the complex. First, monopoly capital will have to develop new and closer (and strengthen existing) ties with the state. This has been widely recognized by political leaders and corporate spokesmen. For example, *Fortune* magazine has written that

> implicit in the governmental appeals for help at all levels is an acknowledgement that large corporations are the major repository of some rather special capabilities that are now required. Business executives are increasingly identified as the most likely organizers of community-action programs, like the Urban Co-

alition and its local counterparts. Corporate managers often have the special close-quarters knowledge that enables them to visualize opportunities for getting at particular urban problems —e.g., the insurance companies' plans for investments in the slums. Finally, the new "systems engineering" capabilities of many corporations has opened up some large possibilities for dealing with just about any complex social problems.[47]

But corporate organization of community-action programs and corporate initiatives in urban development require formal changes in monopoly capital-state relationships. At the national level, for example, the Department of Housing and Urban Development (HUD) reports that it "has sought and found ways to bring about a fusion of private and public resources—each helping the other in meeting urgent housing needs." [48] As for state and local levels, the political leaders who dominate the Advisory Commission on Intergovernmental Relations have recommended "that each of the industrial or highly urbanized States remove existing constitutional and statutory barriers to involvement of private enterprise in efforts directed toward enlarging and revitalizing the economic and fiscal base of their major cities, and that after such action take positive steps to enhance private-public cooperation in these endeavors.[49]

Second, the success of the social-industrial complex depends not only on strengthening the combined power of the state and monopoly capital, but also on weakening competitive capital, particularly its influence and power in local and state government and in Congress. Competitive sector capital has everything to lose and little to gain from the growth of the social-industrial complex. Goods-producing industries, for example, require cheap labor and a flexible and often transient labor force. Distribution and trade thrives on slum housing, high rent housing, and high retail prices. And small and highly exploitative credit and loan companies also have a strong interest in maintaining the status quo, as do small-scale construction and related firms.

In addition to weakening small-scale capital in the marketplace and in local and state politics, class as opposed to special-interest political-economic priorities will have to be developed within the monopoly industries. This is particularly important in fields such as transportation in which client agencies within the executive branch function to protect special interests, not to develop overall "rational" national policies. Thus, for example, Senator William Proxmire has endorsed abolishing the Highway Trust Fund (the special preserve of the automobile companies and the highway lobby).[50] Certainly the whole area of regional planning requires that the power of competitive capital in local government be reduced and that special-interest policies yield to monopoly-class priorities and planning.[51]

Finally, it is essential that monopoly capital forge new relationships with organized labor to ensure that workers will not be harmed by (and resist) the growth of the social-industrial complex. Much of the surplus generated within the monopoly sector, which now is distributed to workers in the form of increases in money wages commensurate with (or in excess of) productivity gains, would have to be appropriated by the state and plowed into the social-industrial complex. While social capital geared to expanding productivity in the medium-run or long-run may be successful, the growth of productivity in the monopoly and state sectors during the transition period will not be very rapid, and there will be little surplus available for wage increases. In short, the success of the social-industrial complex requires that gains from technical progress be redistributed; they must devolve to monopoly capital and competitive sector workers, not to monopoly and state sector workers.

In Britain the state has begun to remodel the industrial relations system by encouraging labor and capital to accept "productivity agreements" which give management more control over labor costs. There is a similar trend in the United States. For example, the current three-year contract in the steel industry provides for a joint labor-management Committee on Productivity in every mill.

Productivity bargaining is rapidly becoming the official policy of the federal government. The purpose, of course, is to keep wages somewhat behind or at the most in line with productivity increases in monopoly industries (and construction). The next step may be to introduce a national value-added tax (VAT) to appropriate a larger share of the surplus in the monopoly sector for use by the social-industrial complex. The final step is to use the federal budget and the social-industrial complex to raise productivity. Thus the state could control monopoly sector unit labor costs, first, by keeping wages down, and second, by raising physical productivity by plowing a larger share of the monopoly sector surplus into the social-industrial complex. In short, although organized labor has traditionally supported a wide range of "human services," [52] unions probably will not support the kinds of changes in the process of wage determination and in the tax structure needed to finance the social-industrial complex.

It will be helpful at this point to summarize some of the implications of attempting to create a social-industrial complex: (1) Basic changes will be required in the relations between monopoly capital and organized labor—changes labor may feel obliged to resist. (2) The interests of competitive capital and particular industries within the monopoly sector will be challenged. (3) Closer and friendlier relations between competitive sector workers (especially the oppressed minorities) and monopoly capital will be essential. (4) There will be changes in the tax system designed to strengthen monopoly capital and competitive sector impoverished workers (e.g., via negative income taxation) at the expense of workers in the monopoly and state sectors. (5) Profound changes in the political relationships between and within social classes will be required. In Chapter 9, we will attempt to determine whether these political changes (and thus the social-industrial complex) are possible or practical in present-day American society.[53]

## NOTES AND REFERENCES

**1.** Leonard Ross, "The Myth That Things Are Getting Better," *New York Review of Books,* August 12, 1971.

**2.** Wage inflation in the state sector has increased the volume of surplus capital: Because taxes must be increased (to pay wage costs) there is a smaller volume of demand for monopoly sector products. Thus the fiscal crisis (in the sense of wage inflation) and surplus capital are different aspects of the same general phenomenon.

**3.** J. R. Lotz, "Some Economic Effects of Increasing Public Expenditures: An Empirical Study of Selected Developed Countries," *Public Finance,* 24:4 (1969).

**4.** Richard A. Musgrave, *Fiscal Systems* (New Haven, Conn.: 1969), pp. 96–98, tables 4–1, 4–2, and 4–3; pp. 102–104, tables 4–4, 4–5, and 4–6

**5.** Schultze estimates that about one-third of the rise in tax revenues at the state and local levels between 1955 and 1969 was attributable to increases in tax rates or the imposition of new taxes [Charles Schultz et al., *Setting National Priorities, 1972* (Washington, D.C.: The Brookings Institution, 1972), p. 140].

**6.** In fact inflation may fall less than porportionately on competitive sector workers because their wages rise relatively rapidly during inflationary periods. As will be seen in Chapter 8, low-income, middle-income, and high-income workers probably pay roughly the same proportion of their income in taxes.

**7.** Productivity growth was relatively slow (and thus unit labor cost relatively high) because of the large amount of excess physical capacity. The description here provides only a rough approximation of the relationship between productivity and real wages in the monopoly sector because many manufacturing industries are in the competitive sector Because monopoly sector wages probably increased more than competitive sector wages and because taxes fall more or less equally on workers in both sectors, our guess is that the disparity between monopoly sector productivity and real wages during this period was less than these data indicate.

**8.** Milton Derber, "The Wage-Price Freeze in Historical Perspective," *Illinois Business Review,* 28:8 (September 1971), 7 Otto Eckstein claims that "there is a kind of money-illusion 'threshold.' It will not be crossed if there are brief bursts of galloping inflation or a more or less permanent 'creeping inflation ' But it is crossed when we have an inflation rate of over 2.5 percent for more than two years; at that point workers begin to make demands that lead to a wage-price spiral     ." ["The Emerging Debate about Inflation," *Fortune* (March 1972), 153].

**9.** Ibid. In 1971, the railroad workers won a pay rise of 42 percent over a 42-month period. In containers, nonferrous metals, aluminum, and basic steel, the United Steel Workers won an advance of 31 percent spread over three years And many if not most of these and other long-term agreements contained the traditional cost-of-living escalator clauses

**10.** It seems likely that automatic cost-of-living adjustments will be included in social security in the near future.

**11.** The significance of the U S. role in the world economy for domestic society and the fiscal crisis is discussed in Chapter 6.

**12.** The optimism of some economists that the state can increase profits and private investment and expand the state budget at the expense of private consumption without upward pressures on prices via an expansionary monetary policy and an antiinflationary fiscal policy has been abandoned by and large. Easy money in the context of an "administrative inflation . . . would not only raise market prices by expanding demand, but would also, in part, validate the administrative inflation which has already taken place and lay the basis for further administrative inflation" [Gardiner C. Means, *The Corporate Revolution in America* (New York: 1964), pp. 145–146].

**13.** The problem is especially difficult because successive tax rate cuts at the federal level aimed at legislating increases in profits and investment have helped to reduce the "fiscal dividend" to zero or near-zero [*Fortune* (March 1972), 45].

**14.** This tendency is especially severe today because there exists excessive worldwide productive capacity.

**15.** Capitalist governments sometimes give lip service to another measure—breaking up industrial monopolies and "labor monopolies" to make the economy more competitive This is at best a remote possibility in the modern era. Finally, the state can cut back the budget (as Nixon did in October 1972); this may "save money," but it fails to ameliorate the fiscal crisis because it leaves specific needs unmet.

**16.** Monopoly sector capacity tends to increase more rapidly than product demand, which results in surplus capital (goods and labor). But the competitive and state sectors tend to absorb the surplus capital (which the state sector helps to produce), keeping up the level of aggregate demand. Part of the solution to the Keynesian problem of deficient aggregate demand thus lies in the matrix of the political economy. In effect, the economy tends to stabilize itself. But this fact does not rule out the use of managed recession policies, which were used by Nixon in 1970.

DIMENSIONS OF THE CRISIS                                                          59

**17.** Lynn Turgeon, "The Crisis of Post-Keynesian Economics: A Revisionist Interpretation of Recent Economic History" (unpublished manuscript). The Council of Economic Advisors warned against this kind of cost-push inflation in its annual report for 1968. The Council argued that rising prices in the United States from mid-1966 to mid-1967 were due to rising costs, not too much demand. Because of the harmful effect on productivity of managed recession this option also has been played down by European governments since the late 1950s.

**18.** Unemployment of labor and underutilization of productive capacity mean that state spending may raise not only aggregate demand but also real output and incomes and, finally, the tax base and tax receipts. In other words, in a recession state expenditures may help to pay for themselves and can be virtually costless in terms of real resources utilized.

**19.** E. Robert Livernash, "Wages and Benefits," in *A Review of Industrial Relations Research,* op. cit , p 82. Another study in this volume indicates, that compared with earlier periods real wages rose much faster from 1949 to 1960, undoubtedly because of the strength of organized labor in the monopoly sector.

**20.** Gaylord Freeman, "The International Economic Problem of the United States and Japan," The First National Bank of Chicago, September 21, 1971, p. 13.

**21.** Only the British economy has been adjusted via managed recession to the realities of inflation, fiscal crisis, and balance-of-payments crisis The reason is the dominant role of balance of payments in Britain. Thus, for example, faced with a balance-of-payments crisis and unable to devalue the pound because of commitments to the United States, the Labour Government introduced a set of moderate new taxes in 1965. The tax measures undermined the confidence of the business community and there was a run on the pound; in 1966, Labour was forced to deflate the economy [Richard Pryke, "The Predictable Crisis," *New Left Review* (September/October 1966), 39].

**22.** For a good discussion see, Domenico Mario Nuti, "On Incomes Policy," *Science and Society,* 33:4 (Fall/Winter 1969), 422.

**23.** Furthermore, "assuming we arrive at a definition [of productivity], operating rules can be daunting. Are wages to be cut when productivity falls? Or raised when it rises even if other conditions—say, the external balance—indicate restraint? . . . Besides, who is responsible for productivity—management or workers? And where management is clearly at fault, are some workers to forego rises accruing to others elsewhere. . . The difficulties are inexhaustible . . ." [Michael Kildron, *Western Capitalism Since the War* (Baltimore, Md.: 1970), p 85].

**24.** As Ernest Mandel foresaw, wage and price controls or incomes policy "tend to bring the crisis in the trade union movement to a head, rather than integrating it further into the State and eliminating conflict" [Ernest Mandel, "A Socialist Strategy for Western Europe," *International Socialist Journal,* 2:10 (August 1965), 433].

**25.** *Western Capitalism Since the War,* op. cit., p. 102 (quoting a study by Jean-Marie Vincent).

**26.** Ibid , p 100.

**27.** *St. Louis Post-Dispatch,* August 8, 1966.

**28.** "Wages and Benefits," op. cit., p 102.

**29.** *Business Week,* May 6, 1972, p. 16, citing a Bureau of Labor Statistics study. The failure of Nixon's Price Commission to change the basic relations of production in the monopoly sector is evidenced by its refusal to order price cuts when productivity increases rapidly. Some price cuts have been ordered

THE FISCAL CRISIS OF THE STATE

in cases where windfall profits have been made: "Officials talk publicly about ordering price cuts in such cases In practice, they say forced cuts would be impractical in most instances" (*U.S. News and World Report,* November 29, 1971, p. 56).

30. John W. Kendrick, "Exploring Productivity Measurement in Government," *Public Administration Review,* 23:2 (June 1963).

31. Norman V. Breckner, "Government Efficiency and the Military 'Buyer-Seller' Device," *Journal of Political Economy,* 68:5 (October 1960) In 1972,

> the Pentagon [made] a fundamental change in the way it sets profits for defense contractors The new profit yardstick will reduce profit opportunities for contractors who rely heavily on government-furnished plant and equipment, while increasing the profit potential for those who provide their own facilities and tooling

(*Business Week,* May 13, 1972, p. 102). Prior to 1969, the Pentagon had not made any detailed studies of military contractor profits.

32. U.S. Code, Chapter 9, Title 5.

33. Robert Bhaerman, " 'Merit'-Paid Teachers Tell How It Really Is," *American Teacher* (October 1971), 25.

34. Frank Ackerman, "Nixon's Wage-Price Freeze," *The Red Pencil,* 3:1 (October 1971), 13.

35. Committee for Economic Development, *Economic Growth in the U.S.: Its Past and Future* (February 1958), p. 17, n. 1.

36. It should be added that efficiency and mechanization are two different things. For example, the use of numerical control machine tools in the state sector (e g , by military contractors) is widespread However, from an economic point of view, if the machines are expensive relative to labor power (wages), the use of numerical machinery is inefficient economically. The classic study of noncontrolled costs in the military establishment is Joint Economic Committee, Subcommittee on Economy in Government, *The Economics of Military Procurement* (Washington, D.C , 1969).

37. *Business Week,* May 13, 1972, p. 160. However, the new Postal Service has negotiated an agreement with two newly combined postal worker unions that gives wide latitude in introducing automation and changing work rules. How much these opportunities are exploited remains to be seen.

38. Solomon Fabricant, *The Rising Trend of Government Employment,* National Bureau of Economic Research, Occasional Paper 29 (New York, June 1949), p. 24.

39. *San Francisco Examiner and Chronicle,* March 11, 1972.

40. "Attacking the Mass Transit Mess," *Business Week,* June 2, 1972, p. 60.

41. As early as 1966, IBM board member Lyle Spencer looked forward to the growth of what he called a "social-industrial complex" (Fred Cohen and Marc Weiss, "Big Business and Urban Stagnation," *Pacific Research and World Empire Telegram,* 1970, p 9. The most recent promoter of the social-industrial complex is industrialist Simon Ramos. At the White House Conference on the Industrial World Ahead held in February 1972, Ramos said, "the coming social-industrial complex will involve more jobs, more private investment, and more of the nation's resources." Reporting on the conference, Sterling Green wrote that "no conceivable combination of U S. corporations could amass the capital to finance depollution of the Great Lakes, even if the project would be profitable in the end. . . . The same goes for housing the poor and ending the transit jam" (*Ann Arbor News,* March 12, 1972).

42. Some progress toward conversion has been made in California

where the state government has subsidized several aerospace companies to develop ways to apply systems analysis in such areas as transportation, data handling, pollution control, and "social control problems" in the prisons and mental institutions The pioneers in urban systems studies are aerospace-computer-electronics companies such as Litton, Lockheed, IBM, and North American Aviation As Les Shipnuck writes,

> large defense contractors, shaken by the threat of peace, are eyeing urban redevelopment for its market potential. They are still waiting for the federal government to assure them sizeable profits through subsidies and handouts of land and equipment. Defense contractors currently moving into the industrialized housing field are General Electric, Alcoa, TRW, and Kaiser.

"BART, Regionalization, and Pacific Rim Strategy," unpublished manuscript, 1971, p. 14).

**43.** Quoted in Seymour Melman, ed., *The War Economy of the United States: Readings on Military Industry and Economy* (New York: 1971), p. 7. It should be noted that the barriers to the conversion of the military-industrial complex to social-industrial production differ from the factors keeping military contractors from converting to commercial business. Military contractors are "geared to the requirements of governmental rather than commercial markets, to high technology rather than to high volume, to high quality rather than low prices, and to a single or small group of customers rather than mass distribution" (Murray L. Wiedenbaum, *Federal Resources and Urban Needs,* unpublished manuscript, 1965).

**44.** "Should Business Tackle Society's Problems?" *Economic and Business News* (New York: Houghton Mifflin, 1972), p. 3.

**45.** *American Teacher* (October 1970), 10

**46.** Quoted in "Big Business and Urban Stagnation," op cit , p. 8. Corporate executives "doubt that business leaders will become deeply involved in providing jobs for the hard-core unemployed unless they are guaranteed a profit as is done with defense contracts . . . Private industry will attack society's problems if (1) there is a profit in doing so, (2) government awards a fair contract, (3) a partial government subsidy reduces the risk, and (4) actual losses through inaction, as in the case of boycotts and demonstrations, are sustained" ("Should Business Tackle Society's Problems, op cit , p. 8)

**47.** "What Business Can Do for the Cities," *Fortune,* January 1968, p. 128.

**48.** HUD, *Third Annual Report* (Washington, D C., 1967), p. 7. Thus, it is not surprising that HUD's Advisory Committee to Rebuild America's Slums in 1967 included the heads of several leading firms in construction and contraction material, such as Kaiser Industries, U S. Gypsum, Boise-Cascade, and Bechtel.

**49.** Advisory Commission on Intergovernmental Relations, *Fiscal Balance in the American Federal System,* vol. I (Washington, D C , 1967), p. xxvii

**50.** Proxmire clearly stated the need for overall transportation planning:

> It seems to me that a rational Federal policy would require that the public value of investment in different modes of transportation be estimated and that funds be allocated accordingly. In the past we have largely failed to make these needed comparisons among modes and to allocate funds to those uses promising the highest social return. . . . Rather our approach has been one under which expenditures on each mode of transportation would be separately administered and separately justified. . . . We allocate re-

gardless of the benefits and regardless of the costs those funds in the particular area where the user charges apply. . . . Inflexible financing arrangements, legal constraints on the Department of Transportation's authority to establish investment criteria, complicated intergovernmental relationships —all of these factors [i e., special interest politics] have caused us to overinvest in some forms of transportation and to underinvest in others

[*Hearings Before the Subcommittee on Economy in Government of the Joint Economic Committee*, "Economic Analysis and the Efficiency of Government," May 4, 1970 (Washington, D.C , 1971), p. 1031 ]

**51.** One of the leading (if not the leading) monopoly capitalist spokesman, David Rockefeller, chairman of the Chase Manhattan Bank, clearly understands the need for class priorities:

[T]he need now, as I see it, is for more massive collaboration by groups of corporations in diverse fields to tackle some of those major problems that surpass the resources of a single company. Businesses must learn to create consortiums to achieve social objectives . . Unless business and finance take the initiative in this area, government may decree that a businessman must be concerned not only to find the quantity of money he requires but also to obtain specific authorization to use the funds in the manner he proposes.

(*Wall Street Journal*, December 21, 1971 )

**52.** See, for example, Conference on Economic Progress, *Taxes and the Public Interest* (Washington, D.C., June 1963), p 9. The situation is somewhat more complicated than that described above  To stop inflationary wage demands, the state must stop inflation, thus keeping money wages in line with productivity. If the state tried to siphon off enough surplus to finance a social-industrial complex (i.e., subsidize monopoly capital and competitive sector workers) without halting the present decline in real wages due to inflation, the alliance between monopoly capital and labor would explode  However, stopping inflation means slowing down the rate of growth of aggregate demand. Because competitive sector wages depend closely on the growth of aggregate demand and inflation the state might end up taking away from competitive workers with one hand what it gives with the other.

**53.** Economically, the social-industrial complex implies vast new government-subsidized investments in social areas mentioned above  Sociologically, the complex implies the creation of new class alignments and a new class of "social workers" (e g., paraprofessionals, social service technicians, etc ) Politically, the complex implies a realignment of the political system.

# CHAPTER 3
# POLITICAL POWER AND
# BUDGETARY CONTROL
# IN THE UNITED STATES

## INTRODUCTION

The main premise of bourgeois economic theory is that the market mechanism (influenced and modified by the power of monopolistic corporations) determines the volume, composition, method, and distribution of private production. However, the market mechanism plays little or no direct role in the determination of the volume, composition, method, and distribution of state expenditures and programs. As we have argued, the development of the monopoly sector indirectly determines the state budget by generating needs that the state must satisfy. But the actual mechanisms that transform these needs into material production (including services) are very different from the mechanisms that dominate the private marketplace. Capital organizes production for the market and employs labor power only if there is a reasonable expectation of profit. The state administration organizes production as the result of a series of political decisions.

These political decisions are made within a definite framework of social relationships and as a consequence of social, economic, and political conflict. Two systems of social relationships must be considered: first, those between and within economic classes, and second, those between economic classes and state power (including the legislative and executive branches of government). We must analyze the general relationship between labor and capital and also that between capital and the state. There is no necessary and direct connection between the economic might and needs of monopoly capital and state budgetary priorities. Monopoly capital must .work within the political framework of the federal system. In other words, it is compelled to work within the framework of different political systems at different levels of government.[1]

The relationship between monopoly capital and organized labor is the dominant production relation or social relation of production in U.S. society. Less significant relationships include those between monopoly capital and competitive capital, competitive capital and competitive labor, and so on.

In this chapter we will describe the main relationships between private power and state power. We also will describe the centralizing tendencies that are at work in both the executive and legislative branches of the federal government. We will examine the relationship between the executive branch (which increasingly is under the dominance of class-conscious monopoly capital) and the legislative branch (which still is powerfully influenced by interest-conscious competitive capital and to a lesser degree by monopoly capital). Finally, we will review the politics of budgeting at the state and local levels.

## A POLITICAL FRAMEWORK
## FOR BUDGETARY ANALYSIS:
## THE FEDERAL GOVERNMENT

What are the channels through which economic class relationships find their political expression in the federal government? Whose interests does the national government serve? The large number of power centers within the national state, each with a measure of autonomy, mitigates against any simplistic analysis of federal power in budgetary matters. One political scientist notes:

> In Federal government alone, it may be necessary to consider the reactions of at least ten institutions to any major changes in taxing and spending: the Ways and Means Committee in the House of Representatives, the Finance Committee in the Senate, Appropriations Committees in both Houses of Congress, the Council of Economic Advisors, the Bureau of the Budget, the Treasury Department, the Internal Revenue Service, the General Accounting Office, and the Federal Reserve Board.[2]

A modern Marxist writer has expressed the same idea in more general theoretical terms:

> the power elite does not just guarantee a certain type of economic system and economic domination. It also intervenes in the sphere of such domination. By means of tax policy and budgets the power elite effects a redistribution of the national income. It thus intervenes in the distribution of values desired and fought for by the various classes. It is frequently difficult to

say which side the power elite supports in this area of everyday decisions. For the situation is very complicated.[3]

The first and most powerful influence in the national government is the capitalist class—owners and controllers of the monopoly corporations and state contractors. The members of this class have organized themselves along interest-group and class lines (competitive capital organizes itself mainly along interest-group lines).

Interest-group organization and participation in the national state have been studied by McConnell, Hamilton, Kolko, Engler, and many other social scientists and historians. In Hamilton's words:

> there are currently associations of manufacturers, of distributors, and of retailers; there are organizations which take all commerce as their province; and there are federations of local clubs of businessmen with tentacles which reach into the smaller urban centers and market towns. All such organizations are active instruments in the creation of attitudes, in the dissemination of sound opinion, and in the promotion of practices which may become widespread.[4]

An example is the national committee of the U.S. Chamber of Commerce, which is charged with reviewing the federal budget (state and local budgets too) and federal operations and recommending budgetary or operational changes.

These self-regulatory private associations normally are organized along industry not regional lines because of the national character of most commodity markets. More often than not, they use the state to mediate between their members (e.g., conduct elections to determine the form and extent of farm commodity price support programs) as well as to provide needed credits, subsidies, technical aid, and general support. Key industry groups include the highway lobby (automobiles, oil, rubber, glass, branches of construction, etc.), the military lobby, oil, cotton, textiles, railroads, airlines, radio and television, public utilities, and banking and brokerage. Wheat, cotton, sugar (among other growers), and cattle ranchers also are organized into associations.

Interest groups have appropriated many small pieces of state power through a "multiplicity of intimate contacts with the government."[5] They dominate most of the so-called regulatory agencies at the federal, state, and local levels, many bureaus within

THE FISCAL CRISIS OF THE STATE

the Departments of Agriculture and Interior (Agriculture was the first Department established to serve a special clientele), the Bureau of Highways, and a number of congressional committees. Their specific interests are reflected in the partial or full range of policies of hundreds of national and state government agencies—for example, the Interstate Commerce Commission and other regulatory bodies, the Department of Defense, the Corps of Engineers, the U.S. Tariff Commission, and the Federal Reserve System. In a summary of the politics of interest groups McConnell writes that

> What emerges as the most important political reality is an array of relatively separated political systems, each with a number of elements. These typically include: (1) a federal administrative agency within the executive branch; (2) a heavily committed group of Congressmen and Senators, usually members of a particular committee or subcommittee; (3) a private (or quasi-private) association representing the agency clientele; (4) a quite homogeneous constituency usually composed of local elites. Where dramatic conflicts over policy have occurred, they have appeared as rivalries among the public administrative agencies, but the conflicts are more conspicuous and less important than the agreements among these systems. The most frequent solution to conflict is jurisdictional demarcation and establishment of spheres of influence. Log-rolling, rather than compromise, is the normal pattern of relationship.[6]

In other words, the interpenetration of private economy and the state and the growth of the federal bureaucracy have transformed political economic issues and conflicts into problems of administration. Historically, pressure-group activity and conflict have characterized not only the legislative branch but also the executive branch of government.

By itself, however, interest-group politics is inconsistent with the survival and expansion of capitalism. For one thing, "the interests which keep the interest groups going are too disparate, and the least common denominator of action is too passive to bring into being a completely cohesive union." [7] For another, interest consciousness obviously leads to contradictory policies, making it difficult or impossible to plan the economy as a whole. Thus, a class-conscious political directorate is needed to coordinate the activities of nominally independent government agencies. Paradoxically, enduring interest groups require a sense of "responsibility"—that is, class consciousness. For example, the attempt by regulatory agencies to maintain profitable conditions in a particular industry tends to freeze the pattern of resource allocation and establish monopoly conditions, which, in turn, retard capital accumulation and expansion throughout the economy. Another example is planning for overseas expansion which clearly requires a class-conscious political directorate.

The class organization of monopoly sector capital—both its private activity and participation in the state—have been studied by Williams, Weinstein, Kolko, Domhoff, Eakins, and others.[8] These writers have shown that the instability and inefficiency attendant upon capitalist production in the past increased investment risk and uncertainty, contributed to crises and depressions and deficiencies of aggregate demand, and created other economic problems. By the turn of the century, and especially during the New Deal, it was apparent to vanguard corporate leaders that some form of rationalization of the economy was necessary.[9] And as the twentieth century wore on, the owners of corporate capital generated the financial ability, learned the organizational skills, and developed the ideas necessary for their self-regulation as a class.

Thus, it was a class-conscious political directorate that controlled the War Industry Board during World War I, parts of the National Recovery Administration and the Agricultural Adjustment Administration, and the Office of War Mobilization, the last of the World War II planning agencies. Class-conscious politicians and administrators today influence or control the Department of Defense, agencies within HUD, HEW, and the Departments of Commerce, Transportation, Treasury, and State, the Council of Economic Advisors (CEA), and the Bureau of the Budget. Because conflicts within the corporate ruling class must be reconciled and compromised and because of the complex and wide-ranging nature of the interests of this class, policy is dictated not by a single directorate but by a multitude of private, quasipublic, and public agencies. Policy is formulated within the highly influential Business Council, in key universities and policy-planning agencies such as the Foreign Policy Association and the Committee for Economic Development (CED), and by the corporate-dominated political parties. This policy is a key input in the formulation of legislation initiated by the executive branch. But the President and his key aides must remain independent; they must interpret class (as opposed to particular economic) corporate interests and translate these interests into action, not only in terms of immediate economic and political needs, but also in terms of the relations between monopoly capital and competitive sector labor and capital. Monopoly capitalist class interests (as a social force rather than as an abstraction) are not the aggregate of the particular interest of this class but rather emerge within the state administration "unintentionally." In this important sense, the capitalist state is not an "instrument" but a "structure."

The second way production relations are expressed politically is in the regulation of interclass social relations to ensure that the technical level of the work force will be reproduced and expanded (social capital) and the social order as a whole maintained (social expenses). Around the turn of the century, populist, labor, and socialist forces posed a potentially serious threat to American capitalism. In a series of political steps designed to prevent popular movements from (in Marx's words) "removing the extremes of society" (capital and wage labor), corporate leaders and the political directorate sought "to weaken their antagonisms and transform them into a harmonious whole." The state must try to integrate all elements of the population into a coherent system, win mass loyalty, and legitimate itself and society. Far and away the most important element is monopoly sector organized labor, which gradually was taught to adopt responsible attitudes and behavior toward monopoly capital and capitalist society. This required regular cooperation between the leaders of organized labor, the corporations, and the state to head off mass social movements, transform collective bargaining into an instrument of corporate planning, strive for a high level of employment and wages commensurate with productivity advances, and maintain labor's reproductive powers, with regard not only to the level of private consumption but also to social consumption (social insurance, health, housing, etc.).

The need to develop and maintain a "responsible" social order also has led to the creation of agencies and programs designed to control the surplus population politically and to fend off the tendency toward a legitimization crisis. The government attempts to administer and bureaucratize (encapsulate) not only monopoly sector labor-management conflict but also social-political conflict emerging from competitive sector workers and the surplus population. The specific agencies for regulating the relations between capital and organized labor and unorganized workers are many and varied—for example, agencies within HUD and HEW, the Department of Labor, the National Labor Relations Board (NLRB), the National Mediation Board and Federal Mediation and Conciliation Service, the Social Security Administration, various congressional committees, state employment agencies (or human resource development agencies), and so on. Some of these agencies were established primarily to maintain social control of the surplus population (e.g., HEW's Bureau of Family Services); others serve mainly to attempt to maintain harmony between labor and capital within the monopoly sector (e.g., the Bureau of Old Age and Survivors Insurance). In both cases the state must remain independent or "distant" from the particular interests of capital (which are very different from the politically organized interests of capital as the ruling class). The basic problem is to win mass loyalty to insure legitimacy; too intimate a relation between capital and state normally is unacceptable or inadmissible to the ordinary person.

The state also regulates the relations between big and small capital (e.g., the Small Business Administration, various farm agencies, etc.), between capital based in different regions (e.g., TVA), and between capital in expanding and contracting sectors of the economy (e.g., the Maritime Administration within the Department of Commerce). Relations between small-scale capital and the working class also must be regulated (e.g., Department of Agriculture programs designed to protect consumers). Because it requires their political support for national and international programs, monopoly capital cannot afford to antagonize local and regional capital needlessly. Subsidies must be granted to declining industries (e.g., fishing) and to capital in underdeveloped regions (e.g., Appalachia). The Department of Agriculture, Department of Commerce agencies, many congressional committees, and federal grant-in-aid programs are deeply involved in managing relations within the business classes, and permanently engaged in financing small-scale capital's political support for large-scale capital's programs.[10]

Finally, the state administration itself has its own logic or rationality. As we know, the state has two major functions—"accumulation" and "loyalty." These two functions are contradictory, and it is the task of administrative rationality in every state agency to try to reconcile them.

## BUDGETARY PRINCIPLES OF THE FEUDAL AND EARLY CAPITALIST STATE

These functions of the national state, which are not unique to modern capitalism, but which have taken new forms during the twentieth century, are extremely expensive. Further, these functions require effective central executive control over the federal budget and administrative machinery. The exception is interest-group economic needs, to which the legislative branch and many executive agencies are highly responsive. Modern capitalism, a system of highly specialized and interdependent production, also requires central co-

THE FISCAL CRISIS OF THE STATE

ordination and control. Finally, in the context of the conflict between capitalism and world revolution and socialism, the leading capitalist powers (chiefly the United States) require a highly centralized system of military production and distribution—a military-industrial complex that functions more or less independently of the legislative branch.

The growth of the executive branch, the development of class politics within both the executive and legislature, and the decline of "particularism" in Congress, is a familiar story. Less familiar, but important for understanding the fiscal crisis, are the corresponding changes in budgetary control and policy.

Before the rise of capitalism and modern democracy, public property was a special form of private property, which was owned by the ruling groups. In the feudal state's budget, for example, "under liabilities we find a mixture of private and public expenditures. Indeed, no distinction is made between the two. Keeping guards on an estate to protect it from any depredation is exactly the same thing as possessing an army to defend the territory." [11] With the development of mercantile and industrial capitalism, public property increasingly came under public control, and private property established itself as autonomous. This separation of the state and the economy was completed in the nineteenth century, which ushered in the political triumph of the middle classes.

The triumph of liberalism and middle-class democracy inaugurated new budgetary principles, which were generally applied throughout the nineteenth century in the developing capitalist economies of western Europe and North America. First, ordinary expenditures were kept to an absolute minimum to prevent the state's reextending its sway over the economy and to insure that funds would be available to pay the state's new creditors—the bourgeoisie. Second, taxation was mainly indirect, both to conceal tax exploitation and to prevent the state from encroaching on private interests by making independent inquiries into, and thus potentially controlling, personal income and wealth. Third, loan finance was limited to exceptional circumstances, chiefly warfare. The bourgeoisie further restricted the state by adopting the principle that the state could borrow only on the same terms as private debtors, and only to cover nonperiodic expenses. In this way the state could remain solvent and guarantee debts incurred in the past. Fourth, money could be created only as a temporary expedient or if the money supply was under the ruling classes' absolute control. Last, a balanced budget was maintained in order to restrict state economic activity to expenditures that could be financed by tax revenues. "Respect for private property, belief in the superiority of the individual initiative and in the malfeasance of the state in the economic field," Jean Marchal has written, "all this necessarily leads to moderate budgets." [12]


## STATE CAPITALIST BUDGETARY PRINCIPLES
## AND CONTROL

As state capitalism and monopolistic industry developed, the budgetary principles of the liberal state were gradually discarded. One change was the substitution of direct for indirect taxation; another was the surrender of the principle of balanced budgets; a third was the acceptance of an inconvertible paper monetary standard and a new role for loan finance. But most important, there was a steady expansion of state expenditures and an increase in the number and variety of state economic functions. The evolution of the state budget as a crucial factor in economic life has gone hand in hand with the development of a permanent state bureaucracy. State capitalism is no temporary phenomenon which will be dismantled once capitalism returns to "normalcy," but rather is the integrating principle of the modern economic era. [13]

A brief review of the changing relationships between and within the legislative and executive branches of the federal government is needed to appreciate the significance of the revolutionary developments in the budgetary principles of modern capitalism. In Britain the rising middle classes transformed the budget into an instrument of financial control over the crown during their struggle for political representation. In the United States a revolution eliminated the crown, removing any analogous development. From the very beginning there existed a relatively close harmony between Congress and the executive because both closely represented the interests of local and regional capital. The budget was from the beginning the expression of the particular interests of the farmer, planter, and merchant classes (and later the industrialists), and was always a source of private profit. By the early twentieth century, the ascendancy of national capital and the regional interest groups began to drive a wedge between the power of local or particular interests and the legislative and executive branches. The latter finally became the representative of national capital. The former still largely represents regional and local capital (and branches of or-

THE FISCAL CRISIS OF THE STATE

ganized labor). Congress became increasingly unable or unwilling to exercise its prerogatives and voluntarily or involuntarily helped transfer them to the executive and to class-conscious congressional leaders. Since the turn of the century congressional control over appropriations has become increasingly weak. Congress has disabled itself in several ways—for example, by establishing revolving funds, creating government corporations, refusing to prohibit transfers between appropriations, authorizing the use of departmental receipts without limitation of amount, and voting lump-sum appropriations.[14] Attempts to reestablish control by voting specific appropriations "far from securing to Congress that completeness of financial control which is . . . its constitutional birthright, has served only to make the law less certain and to satisfy Congress with the name, rather than the substance of power." [15] Congressional control after funds have been appropriated has been equally weak, especially in comparison with Britain, where the House of Commons is able to ensure that its policies are carried out "accurately, faithfully, and efficiently." [16]

Meanwhile, class-conscious elements within the executive (and to a lesser degree the legislative) branch have been eager to transform the budget into an instrument of national economic planning. The executive branch has consolidated its own financial powers by mingling appropriations, bringing forward the unexpended balance of former appropriations and backward the anticipated balance of future appropriations, and impounding appropriations it does not want to spend.[17]

However, the executive branch has long recognized that securing financial control requires changes in the formal character of the budget. Between 1912 and 1956, four presidential commissions made essentially the same recommendations for budgetary reform. A key figure was Frederick Cleveland, chairman of President Taft's Commission on Economy and Efficiency, whose work subsequently became extremely influential in higher corporate circles. Summarizing the ideas of these commissions, Sharkansky writes,

The Cleveland-Buck school of reformers would have the agencies present their budget requests to the President, together with detailed information about past accomplishments of each program and the accomplishments to be expected from a given level of expenditures. The President and his Bureau of the Budget would edit these requests for the purpose of developing a budget coinciding with their policy intentions. Then a single Executive Budget would go to a single Appropriations Committee in the House and Senate, together with supporting data about agency accomplishments and expectations.[18]

Finally, the unified Appropriations Committee and Congress as a whole would review and act on these requests. Cabinet members would be given the privileges of the floor in Congress to explain and defend their past actions and present proposals.

The thrust of these proposals is to force congressmen to act "responsibly" in budgetary matters—that is, to act in the interests of the society as a whole (meaning monopoly capital). Behind-the-scene deals would be eliminated, congressmen would be forced out into the open, and the special interests they represent would be exposed to public view. Needless to say, these proposals have not been implemented because they would eliminate the raison d'être for Congress—the game of give and take it plays.

However at least three major budgetary changes have been made—each a step in the direction of centralized executive budgetary control. The first was the creation of the Bureau of the Budget by the Budget and Accounting Act of 1920 and the introduction of the administrative budget, which coordinates expenditures proposed by the executive. Coordinated executive expenditures were recommended by Alexander Hamilton, the first Secretary of the Treasury, but individual executive departments and agencies dealt directly with congressional committees until 1920. In effect, there was no federal budget, but rather a series of "congressional budgets" which were developed by particular economic and political interest groups and combined into a budget bill which was then signed by the President.

What enabled the executive branch to make this change? Dave Eakins has established that the origins of the federal administrative budget can be found in the municipal reform movement which began in the 1890s and reached its zenith in the 1920s. By 1890, as a result of immigration and industrialization, a large and growing proletariat was crowded into the urban centers. The urban working class was organized by political machines, which were by no means models of democracy, but which did "deliver the goods" to their constituents. Corporate liberal reformers (lawyers, businessmen, professionals, et al.) agitated against the corrupt machines and the ward system and working-class representation on school boards; in general they sought to give more authority to the city executive—the mayor or city council (or city managers). Established in 1905, the New York Bureau of Municipal Research pushed for city commission government, a strong mayor's office, and a centralized city budget. During the first three decades of the twentieth century, the Bureau exported some of its experience to other cities and the municipal reform movement was widely successful. Subsequently, the reformers turned their attention to the federal government. A new organization, the corporate-dominated and class-conscious Institute for Government Research (later to become the Brookings Institution which was set up and staffed by many who had been active in municipal reform) led the way in convincing businessmen, Congress, and the public that a national budget was indispensable for "efficient" national administration. One move was to reorganize and streamline the executive branch with the aim of trying to establish effective administrative control from the top. Another was to create an administrative budget, the basic instrument for coordinating congressional committees, which remained responsive to the needs of special interests within the owning classes.

The administrative budget has been described as the chief mode of "management and control by the Executive and Congress over activities financed with federal funds. . . . [W]hich (once approved) becomes a tool of Executive control over the spending of the various departments, agencies, and government corporations." [19] Although executive agencies continued to prepare their own estimates, the locus of responsibility was shifted by the 1920 act from Congress to the President, who was made formally responsible for initiating an annual budget through his new staff agency, the Bureau of the Budget (now the Office of Management and Budget—OBM). In sum, it was not until well into the twentieth century that monopoly capital was strong and well-organized enough for the state to try to impose the monopoly sector's class interests on society. And the working class could not resist successfully either the municipal reform movement in most cities or the centralization of national political power and budgetary control accomplished by the Budget and Accounting Act.

The second major step toward class-conscious and executive domination of the national budget has been the gradual shift from line-item budgets to program budgets. Line-item budgets classify expenditures in terms of the items to be purchased, whereas *program budgets* classify outlays in terms of the outputs that will be produced by a given program (or services provided). Program budgeting is a device for steering the economy as a whole and centralizing the allocation of budgetary resources—and for ameliorating the fiscal crisis. Beginning in 1961, program budgeting was introduced in the Department of Defense in the more elaborate program-performance-budgeting system (PPBS). By combining program budgeting with detailed measurement of costs and performance efficiency ("performance budgeting" was first introduced in 1951), PPBS permits expenditure decisions to be based on comparisons of the costs and effectiveness of alternative ways of achieving the objectives of "public policy." It assumes that public policy is already determined and thus that there are no political conflicts, or that political conflicts that do arise concern the allocation of scarce resources, which always can be rationalized.

In 1968, twenty-three major departments and agencies prepared program budgets, and many other departments were encouraged to do so.[20] The Bureau of the Budget, which was supposed to monitor PPBS programs, was in fact, the main user of PPBS. A few class-conscious senators (e.g., William Proxmire) have endorsed it but most congressmen and agency heads have been either hostile or indifferent to the system: The special interests of powerful agency constituencies would not be served, and might be undermined, by such policy analysis.[21]

Because of resistance to PPBS, contained specialization and incremental decision making remain the two main budgeting devices. *Contained specialization* refers to the take-over of budgetary decisions by specialists who are guided by professional and technical criteria. *Incremental decision making* means that budget experts accept programs and policies presently in force, and strive mightily to avoid political disputes or otherwise upset the status quo. With the widespread use of these devices political expertise and professional competence replace "partisan in-fighting"—in other words, budgetary decisions tend to be taken out of the realm of politics and become bureaucratized.[22]

Specialization and incremental decision making appeal to many economists in policy-making positions. For example, Arthur Smithies writes that "budgeting is essentially an economic problem in solving as it does the allocation of scarce resources among almost insatiable and competing demands."[23] This school of thought denies that budgetary issues are political in character and sees little or no difference between the allocation of resources by the household or business firm, on the one hand, and the state, on the other. Critical analysis of the state and the budget is replaced by an implicit acceptance of the given balance of private interests and relationships. "Certainly," writes another economist, "the most fruitful systems analyses have not indulged in argument about objectives for argument's sake, but have been forced to review existing objectives and priorities as inconsistencies among them have appeared or because

THE FISCAL CRISIS OF THE STATE

they proved to be inappropriate under changing conditions." [24]

Superficially, the whole purpose of PPBS (which sees process politics and incremental decision making as interferences in the planning process) is to reveal and rationalize conflicting or inconsistent objectives, but underlying this is the state-corporate planners' desire to serve state-corporate planning as a whole by forcing compromises when conflict arises within or between economic classes over particular issues. The real significance of program budgeting, however, is that it is a step toward strengthening the executive office, in relation not only to the federal agencies but also to special interests in the Congress. The program budget, Jesse Burkhead correctly states, "becomes a technique, not for management at the operating level, but for the centralization of administrative authority." [25]

As suggested above, the application of program budgeting has been limited. The basic reason is that PPBS by itself cannot challenge or change underlying power relations. Congress has insisted on maintaining the radical disjuncture between the legislation and the funding of new programs. Enabling or authorizing legislation is not handled by the appropriations committees in the two houses, but rather by substantive committees such as Public Works. The power of particular interests in the substantive committees and executive agencies is described by Wiedenbaum as

> institutional obstacles to improving the allocation of public resources. . . . The end result . . . is that the process of public resource allocation is hardly deliberate and systematic choice among alternatives that economists try to envision. Rather, it is a fragmented and compartmentalized affair. Many of the key decisions are not made during the budget process or within the budgetary framework at all.[26]

In a nutshell, as Wildavsky writes, at the highest level of government it is "difficult to get and find a national consensus" on priorities and goals. "The 'grand objectives'—how much health, how much education, how much welfare, and which groups in the population shall benefit—are questions of value judgment and politics. Yet [PPBS] analysis cannot make much contribution to their resolution." [27] In terms of budgetary priorities for social consumption and welfare (i.e., in areas where priorities are determined by the relations of production) there can be no consensus on national goals. In these spheres PPBS is particularly irrelevant. But it has also been difficult (although less so) to establish national goals for social investment and military spending. (Under the Nixon Administration systems analysis has suffered a decline even in the Defense Department.) The scope for the determination of budgetary priorities by special interests remains fairly wide, albeit not as wide as in the past. Thus, PPBS has had "limited application [because of] the inability of the (Budget) Bureau to significantly overhaul its own or the bureaucracy's budget traditions." [28]

In sum, even after widespread experimentation with program budgeting, budgetary priorities still are based on a mixture of class and special-interest needs. Overall budgetary planning based totally on monopoly capital's class needs is not an accomplished fact, but a future goal which will not be realized until administrative power is effectively centralized within the executive branch.[29]

There is one important exception to this conclusion—*aggregative fiscal policy*, or the determination of the total volume of spending and taxation. The federal budget is closely connected with general economic movements (revenue, e.g., is determined by ups and downs in the tax base). In turn, general economic conditions are determined in part by the federal budget (by changes in the tax rate and level of spending). As federal spending and taxation have grown in absolute and relative terms, the executive (the only branch structurally capable of fiscal planning) has had to take into account the two-way movements between total taxation and spending and total employment, income, and production. This has required even greater executive control over state finances—and a third step toward centralization of budgetary authority.

The budget contained the first analysis of expenditures and receipts on a national-income accounting basis. As early as 1947, the CED recommended the adoption of a cash-consolidated budget as a guide to fiscal planning and policy. But the national-income budget introduced in 1963 is a superior measure of the impact of federal spending on general economic activity because it excludes purely financial credit transactions and accounts for receipts and expenditures at the time of their economic impact rather than when cash receipts and payments occur. It explicitly recognizes the integral relation between the budget and the private sectors and is an essential tool of overall fiscal planning. In 1967, a presidential commission recommended a unified budget concept to eliminate the confusion that had arisen from the simultaneous use of the administrative budget, the consolidated-cash budget (which included trust funds), and the national income accounts budget. And in 1972, fiscal planning reached a new apex with the adoption of the full-employment budget—a guide to federal spending based not on revenues collected but on revenues that would be yielded by a full-employment economy.

## CONGRESS AND THE EXECUTIVE: CONTEMPORARY RELATIONSHIP

Special-interest elements within Congress by and large have not resisted the increasing centralization of power within the executive branch, mainly because there has been no immediate sense of loss of power. Until the fiscal crisis compelled Nixon to attempt to limit federal spending to $250 billion in 1972, the executive has been pushing for across-the-board budgetary expansion, which delights the typical representative and senator (the economy-minded House Appropriations Committee excepted). More, the executive has not sought to abolish any formal legislative procedures or functions, and attempts by class-conscious congressmen to reform the congressional committee structure and thus centralize authority within the legislative branch have been a near-total failure.[30]

Most congressmen still prefer the administrative budget concept to the unified format, and few members have accepted such Keynesian concepts as full-employment surplus and fiscal drag. Congress is still inclined to emphasize the fiscal or dollar-level aspect of the budget, at the expense of its program orientation.[31] And Congress has developed its own specialized committees and its own bureaucracy (e.g., the General Accounting Office), and its appropriations procedures have remained unchanged for decades. The budget is still not considered a single piece of legislation; it is still referred to the appropriations committees where it is separated into parts which are sent to different subcommittees. "Taxes and expenditures are (still) decided separately by the separate committees in each house; although the bills on taxes and appropriations are passed by vote of the whole House and whole Senate, there is little evidence that the two groups of bills are related closely to each other when they are considered." [32] Similarly, the benefits and costs of programs authorized in specific appropriations bills are never evaluated in relation to one another. Nor are bills discussed or studied in detail by the full committees, and full House debate is rare. Each House Appropriations subcommittee is still concerned with a different division of the government, and "it is quite natural that a group of men familiar with a particular division of the executive branch will be inclined to take a parochial interest in its welfare." [33] The extreme example is the military budget which has been determined by the Pentagon and the armed services committees with hardly any critical examination by Congress.

That Congress still effectively represents sundry parochial interests, and thus still views the budget as a set of individual and unrelated parts, has been particularly galling to monopoly capital. Various "reforms" that would substitute class-conscious for special-interest budgeting have been suggested by the Committee for Economic Development.[34] Corporate planner and former Budget Director Charles Schultze has denounced the "absurdity of what we are doing now," referring to the plethora of short-run budgets and appropriations bills.

Nevertheless, the executive has succeeded in exercising more and more informal controls over congressional budgetary initiatives and authority (in addition to the formal changes in budgeting already discussed). In the past any bill initiated by a congressman without "legislative clearance" from the Budget Bureau faced enormous obstacles. The Bureau had considerable control over the direction and timing of federal obligations because it reviewed each executive agency's budget requests from Congress and controlled the allocation of Treasury funds to the agencies. This further enhanced the Bureau's and the executive's powers. And there has been more overall executive fiscal planning, with new agencies created to discipline Congress. In 1938, Roosevelt set up a temporary Monetary and Fiscal Advisory Board, made up of the Director of the Budget Bureau, the Chairman of the Federal Reserve System, the Secretary of the Treasury, and the Chairman of the Advisory Committee of the Natural Resources Commission. Later, the Office of Emergency Planning was established to deal with problems cutting across departmental lines. During the Kennedy years, the Budget Bureau, the Treasury, and the CEA were organized into an informal but powerful group responsible for overall fiscal planning (and implicitly, control over Congress). The most recent "reform" at the top was the creation of the Domestic Council to direct program planning for the President and the transformation of the Budget Bureau into the Office of Management and Budget (OMB) by the Nixon Administration. Because of the persistence and strength of special-interest executive agencies and congressmen, "the budget process tends to operate as a constraint on presidential power."[35] The OMB was set up to insulate the President from the budgeting process. Nixon desired more "coordination and evaluation" of federal programs, and OMB is "a sort of elite mini-Government [which] other agencies feel is running roughshod over them." More, Congress "finds [OMB] blind to grass-root realities or complains that it is partly

THE FISCAL CRISIS OF THE STATE

immune to Capitol Hill influence. . . ." [36] Thus, budget policy is increasingly formulated by the executive without any attempt to revolutionize or modernize the congressional appropriations process. The effect of this shift in financial control to the executive has been succinctly described by Schlesinger:

> The Congress, secure in its belief that the basic legislation has established policy, may view its annual consideration of the budget formulated by the experts simply from the standpoint of assuring the most economical attainment of legislative goals. Thus policy formulation, which is so intimately connected with the appropriations levels, may slip into organizational limbo and finally be unconsciously seized by the Bureau of the Budget [today, Domestic Council and OBM]—the one organization that, in theory, should be concerned with economy and efficiency, and should be divorced entirely from policy formulation.[37]

The general result is that budget issues cease to be political issues, and the budget becomes a better planning instrument for the executive. If and when the President's Advisory Council on Executive Reorganization (Ash Council) plans to reorganize the federal executive along functional rather than program lines, administrative power will be centralized even further.[38]

One effect is increasing executive resistance to programs tailored by Congress to local and regional interests—the interests of small-scale capital. In the long run these interests must give way to those of "society as a whole"—a euphemism for the needs of monopoly capital. Thus, for example, there is a long-run tendency for agricultural price supports and water subsidies to decline, and for federal land giveaways to be curbed.[39] And attempts have been made to check guarantees and subsidies to railroads, airlines, waterways, and the merchant marine and to develop a comprehensive federal transportation policy. Another effect is that overall budgetary priorities change very slowly regardless of the wishes of the "current" Administration. Thus, until the peak of the fiscal crisis in 1972–1973 over the past two decades, no major program introduced by previous Administrations has been eliminated. For example, eight years of Republican administration in the 1950s failed to reverse the upward trend in federal spending; in fact outlays on health, education, and welfare were expanded. Now only the executive can interpret and effectively act on the needs of private capital and private interests. With regard to the operation of democratic institutions, one economist has concluded, "The relationship between the legislative and executive branches largely determines the success or failure of democratic government." [40] Is it necessary to add that formal democratic government has declined in proportion to the decline of the budget as an "important instrument of legislative control"?

## POLITICAL POWER AND BUDGETARY CONTROL: STATE AND LOCAL GOVERNMENT

Although the federal government frequently acts in the interests of particular industries and capitalist groups, the executive branch (and increasingly Congress, as well) devotes itself to controlling the social and production relations between capital and labor. In the past, the main domestic problem was the relationship between monopoly capital and organized labor. Today, the executive is more and more preoccupied with the conditions of unorganized labor in the competitive sector, particularly black and other minority workers condemned by racism to the competitive sector and to poorly paid jobs in the monopoly sector. In addition to the relations between labor and capital in the monopoly and competitive sectors, the federal government must regulate those between labor in the competitive sector and the rest of society.

Budgetary control and determination at the state and local levels also is many-sided. The political economies of the fifty states and the economic and social structures of the thousands of local governments, special districts, supramunicipal authorities, and the rest of the 116,000 governmental units vary widely. There is, for example, a near bewildering array of types and amounts of taxes collected at the state and local levels, and there are vast differences in the percentage of funds that originate in federal, state, and local revenue sources. Then there are the variations in taxes per capita, which can be attributed not to variations in wealth and income but to social and political factors such as the strength of organized labor or the prevalence of institutionalized racism. Another factor is the "wide range of responses in the budgets of individual states" to depression, war, and postwar reconversion—and the "similar responses made by states with widely different economic and political characteristics." [41]

Nevertheless, most states share certain political-economic features; some are unique to government at the state level, others are shared by state and local government. These similarities permit us to generalize and describe the essential features of budget making in the great majority of states.

First, although economic and political power are formally separated in capitalist economies, there is an intricate web of informal relations between state and economy, government official and businessman. Such connections exist at the federal level, but the ties between special interests and state and local bureaucracies are far more numerous and intimate. Most state legislatures are instruments of business and commerce, including specific industries and corporations. For "constituents" many state legislators have a cross section of private business—banking, oil and gas, ranching and agriculture, utilities, gambling, wholesale and retail trade, and so on. Businessmen, labor officials, professional groups, lobbyists visit the state capitol not to represent an abstract "social order as a whole," but rather to advance the interests of industry, trade, or corporation. Special-interest politics and budgetary control are central to state and local as well as federal government. But at the state and local levels the special interests prevail.

Who are these "special interests"? Typically there is a one-to-one relationship between local capital in competitive industries and local power elites. At the state level the special interests represent capital not only in the competitive sector but also in the monopolistic and state sectors. Businessmen with statewide or region-wide economic interests constitute the dominant stratum of the capitalist class within state political boundaries and regional economic boundaries. The political-economic perspective of regional capitalists normally reaches beyond the local level and often to the national level, which reinforces special-interest structures within the federal government.

Perhaps the most famous example of the scope and power of regional capital is the symbiotic relationship between the Nevada gambling industry and the state legislature. Other well-known examples are the industries—for example, oil, agriculture and lumbering, mining, shipping—that are dependent on geography and climate. California state universities and colleges work closely with the cattle industry on such programs as cross-breeding, land conservation, animal nutrition, disease prevention, and parasite control, and the Colorado School of Mines serves the mining industry. The Texas Railroad Commission is the instrument of the oil industry, and in Oregon the lumber interests and the legislature work hand in hand. In Illinois

> among the taxpayers' group is a powerful bloc composed of business organizations such as the State Chamber of Commerce, the Illinois Manufacturers' Association, the Chicago Association

of Commerce and Industry, and the Illinois Association of Retail Merchants. . . . In general, all (of these groups) stand for maintaining the status quo and the retention of a "favorable business climate" in tax matters.[42]

The political economy of state government is complex. Under the federal system, "the powers not delegated to the United States by the Constitution, nor prohibited by it to the States, are reserved to the States respectively, or to the people." Local government, thus, is subordinate to—dominated by and dependent on—state government. Accordingly the businessman in the competitive sector (local capital), whose economic interests are confined to a particular city or metropolitan area, normally adopts a statewide political perspective because political power is located in the State House.

Thus, for example, in order to win favorable legislation local capital in retail trade is compelled to organize trade associations on a statewide basis even in the absence of statewide markets or investments.

The second characteristic of state budget making is its limited perspective. Both federal and state governments attempt to regulate the relationships between labor, capital, and government officials, but state governments are not responsible for macroeconomic planning. Further, capitalists and organized labor perceive such issues as collective bargaining, minimum wages, or hours laws in regional terms. For these reasons, the production relations are administered to serve particular industries or sectors of the economy, not the social order. Construction, the most important state and local industry, is organized by regional and local capitalists and is allied with real estate, agriculture, banking, and other industries. Contractors, building suppliers, and construction unions form powerful lobbies in every state capitol and city hall. Each year state legislatures and city councils pass prolabor legislation and budget items. A notable example is the preservation and strengthening of archaic codes that protect markets for building materials and labor power. Such measures underscore the different political economic functions of federal and state (and local) "labor" legislation. The purpose of the former is to maintain social and economic peace throughout the social order. The latter "favors" workers employed by particular industries which themselves are afforded privileged treatment by law and budget. Finally, it should be added that monopoly sector capital and labor, which often are in agreement on national issues, are divided in state and local politics: Taxes required to finance pro-

THE FISCAL CRISIS OF THE STATE

labor programs—property taxes, business income taxes, and so on—cannot be shifted as easily as the federal corporate income tax is shifted.

How is state budget making shaped by local and regional capital and organized labor? First, workers in the competitive sector who are not represented by strong unions (or special-interest groups) have negligible direct or indirect influence. Consequently, little is appropriated for welfare, health, and other services needed by these workers. In this way the federal system deepens divisions between monopoly sector workers and organized, skilled workers in industries such as construction, on the one hand, and unorganized competitive sector workers, on the other. The latter often not only are "passively" excluded from the budget-making process, but also are actively opposed when they attempt to organize and gain political influence. Powerful regional and local businessmen rely on low-paid wage labor, high rents for slum properties, high interest rates on personal loans, high prices in ghetto retail establishments, and so on. Powerful unions are determined to protect hard-won privileges and exclusive spheres of influence. Thus, for example, organized labor normally seeks to keep welfare costs down in order to minimize property and sales taxes, and other local levies paid by workers. Or black organizations that seek public funds for ghetto reconstruction (and oppose urban renewal designed to serve downtown business interests) run athwart the politically powerful alliance between white contractors and white-dominated labor unions.

Second, a high priority is given to "economic development programs"—that is, direct and indirect subsidies granted to particular industries and economic sectors. Summarizing the findings of a comprehensive study of the New York metropolitan area, Robert C. Wood writes that

> the attitudes of the participants [in government], the nature of the political process, and the rules of the political game strengthen the economic trends in being. They leave most of the important decisions for regional development to the private marketplace. They work in ways which by and large encourage firms and households to continue "doing what comes naturally.[43]

Wood continues:

> the system of quasigovernmental agencies, the authorities and public corporations with programs which leap over municipal boundaries buttresses the marketplace . . . as a matter of con-

scious design. . . . Success seems to smile on the transport agencies that favor the auto, the housing project that reclaims a potentially profitable downtown site, the water resources program which responds to a present need rather than anticipating —and helping to shape—the future pattern of development.[44]

The fiscal function of state governments and agencies thus is chiefly to provide social capital and social investment. As will be seen in the next chapter, state and local budgets emphasize education and highway transportation—and the education budget itself is focused on supplying a work force for private capital.

Special interests are even more powerful at the local level. City and local junior colleges train skilled and technical manpower for local industry; downtown business interests (utilities, large retail establishments, banks, etc.) normally determine urban renewal priorities and expenditures; local transit systems and zoning and license laws are designed to serve local business and property owners. Beyond this, local government is also responsive to the needs of regional and national monopoly capital with local plants, offices, and other facilities. Thus, Detroit city government cannot afford to ignore the automobile companies; downtown renewal in St. Louis was shaped by the Busch interests; the Mellons wield great power in Pittsburgh; Wilmington (indeed all of Delaware) in many respects is the private preserve of the DuPonts; the Rockefellers are not without influence in shaping Manhattan's political economy; and so on.

The intimate relationship between big business and local government in American cities is not unique. In Japan, for example, local governments have been described as "clerks" for monopolistic industries which "promote works exclusively for the interests of great enterprise at the expense of local inhabitants." [45] Oliver Williams has termed this the "investor city"—one of four basic types of local government in America. Dominated by local or national capitalists who view it as an instrument of capital accumulation (or as a corporation that should be run in accordance with business principles), the investor city "stands ready to enact zoning variations, reduce tax assessments, provide subsidies, develop industrial parks, install utilities, and do whatever else may be required to keep labor costs low and promote production." [46] In this kind of city the distinction between private and public power is unclear and public investment is a special form of private investment. Several studies of local power in America suggest that the investor city is very common.

Power in the investor city has been consolidated by the

development of city manager and commission government, non-partisanship, and special district government. Corporate liberal businessmen and business-oriented civic reformers introduced commission government and nonpartisanship in the late nineteenth century because of the increasing importance of the city's economic and social functions. Shortages of good streets, electric lighting, public transportation, water and sewage disposal systems, and other facilities were developing. Business wanted forms of local government in which economic and social issues could be resolved in an atmosphere of nonpartisanship—that is, they wanted institutions in which these issues could be settled administratively or bureaucratically. The proliferation of nonschool special districts from the 1940s through the 1960s (special districts make up about two-thirds of U.S. governmental units) has placed more local decision making on an administrative rather than political basis. This development troubles even orthodox political scientists. "One serious argument against [special districts]," John Bollens writes, "is the inability of the public to exert adequate control over them." [47]

Although thousands of municipalities are directly or indirectly controlled by local, regional, or national capitalists, alone or in alliance, the largest cities are controlled by "arbiter governments" (to use Williams' categories). In New York, Chicago, Philadelphia, and other major cities local government perceives its basic task as managing social and economic conflict between and within economic classes. The fundamental characteristic of arbiter cities is the domination of a political machine or charismatic leader. The size of the working class, the influence of local labor organizations, and the heterogeneous character of the business and commercial interests combine to make it difficult or impossible for business to establish clear-cut control. As a consequence, capital has been compelled to establish supramunicipal authorities (e.g., Bay Area Rapid Transit District and Port of New York Authority), economic development corporations, and other agencies that make budgetary decisions outside of the normal political process and hence are relatively insulated from and indifferent to working-class majorities.

Keeping in mind the political framework in state governments and investor or arbiter city governments, budgeting procedures and controls are readily comprehensible. The dominant private interests (particularly the leading industries) predetermine the volume of state spending and the major budgetary priorities. There is little planning at the state and local levels, and the role of financial expertise and integrated decision making (so important at the federal level) is minimal.[48] Although there has been a greater emphasis on "executive leadership" throughout the twentieth century, state agencies still tend to be more or less independent of the governor (and thus more amenable to the influence of special interests). This clearly limits the possibility of an integrated approach to budgeting. In many states earmarking of funds protects the special interests from both the governor and the legislature. In Alabama, to cite the most extreme example, almost 90 percent of all state revenue is earmarked for specific purposes. Over 50 percent of state taxes is earmarked in twenty states; and in another twenty states between 30 and 50 percent is earmarked. One student of state budgeting concludes that "chief executives and legislators have surrendered much of their potential for innovation for a more limited role as reviewers of administrators' requests. State legislators seem to have accepted a more limited supervisory role than the governors." [49] Similar conclusions were drawn by another student of state budgeting after an investigation of the restricted role of the state legislature in the budgetary process in Illinois.

> Despite its formal authority over appropriations, the 1963 General Assembly was virtually powerless in the determination of State expenditures. . . . The legislature had no criteria of its own to apply to [appropriations] bills other than the fact that they were appropriations and therefore worthy of passage. In the absence of such criteria legislative behavior could only produce a stamp of acceptance for decisions made elsewhere. As an institution the legislature was incapable of doing more.[50]

Routine appropriations and incremental budgetary changes are more typical of local than of state government. Normally, current appropriations are kept in line with past spending, and every effort is made to balance the budget, in part because local budget makers are more dependent upon economic conditions within their narrow jurisdiction than their counterparts at the state level.[51] But it is also partly due to the near-total domination of local government by special interests. At the state level the oil industry, the freeway lobby, the railroads, the utilities, the liquor interest, the food chains, and other segments of the economy are forced to haggle for what they want. But at the municipal level mayors, city councils, and city managers tend to be directly responsible to the dominant local industries (which frequently are allied with organized labor). Thus, local budgetary initiatives and planning normally are introduced through the back door in the form of new special districts and/or new federal government aid tied to innovative programs.[52]

Williams identified two other types of local government. "Caretaker government" is found in small towns and rural communities where business interests are marginal and require little or no state-financed infrastructure and where population density is small, education is relatively neglected, and farm or rural families provide many or most of their own services—wells, cesspools, and so on. In other words, caretaker government creates conditions under which residents can take care of themselves; it provides little social investment or social consumption. Caretaker government, which was characteristic of nineteenth-century America, is dying out. The fourth type is rapidly growing in number and size. This is the middle-class and working-class residential suburb which defines its main task as providing life's amenities and specializes in social consumption.


## THE "CHALLENGE TO FEDERALISM"

Because of growing regional and national economic integration, the development of regional economic units with distinct social and economic problems (e.g., transport, education, land-use, health, etc.), and increasing economic concentration and centralization, monopoly capital requires more top-down administration and budgetary planning, especially around regional needs. But because of the persistence of small-business control of state and local governments, the proliferation of special districts and authorities, and the general fragmentation of local political and budgetary power (together with the regressive character of local tax systems) the struggle for centralized political administration and fiscal planning has been a protracted one. At the local level the long-term trend is unmistakable—mayors' terms have been lengthened and their powers of appointment and removal have been broadened. In the larger cities the mayor has been given authority to formulate and execute the municipal budget (New York City has attempted to use PPBS). Similarly, the trend is clear at the state level: Most states have created a more powerful governor and have adopted centralized budgeting systems. And interstate compacts, which are unresponsive to the general public but which are highly responsive to specialized interests, are proliferating.[53]

Far more ominous from the standpoint of small business and other local and parochial interests (not to speak of community-control insurgency movements) is the usurpation of local political and budgetary power by the national state—a trend that is well advanced in developed capitalist societies. In France parliamentary control of the national budget continues to decline.[54] In Japan, during the 1950s and 1960s, "the amalgamation of cities began to be promoted by the Government in connection with regional development plans. . . . [T]he development of capitalism demands . . . a widening of administrative areas."[55] Local government and political federalism in West Germany are under attack by big business and the national state (the official 1966 Report on Financial Reform states that "certain problems of decisive importance cannot be satisfactorily resolved within the limits of the traditional structure of Federalism").[56]

There has been a gradual erosion of the traditional federal system in the United States. Monopoly capitalist groups and the federal executive have been working together to increase federal power in local affairs and, step-by-step, to dismantle local government. The expansion of federal political and fiscal power has ranged from national clean air and water standards and the thousands of federal guidelines that are part of grants-in-aid packages[57] to programs for national coordination of police activity.

Various business-oriented groups and commissions are attempting to "reform" local government and fiscal system. The influential Advisory Commission on Intergovernmental Relations has endorsed broadening local jurisdictions, transferring functions between governments, and sharing fiscal and other responsibilities.[58] And the CED has long sought to create the basis for federal and monopoly capital budgetary planning on the local and regional levels. In a report released in the 1950s, the CED strongly emphasized the importance of local capital budgeting, putting away sums from annual budgets for capital improvements, and increasing debt and developing centralized marketing arrangements to help small municipalities and other local governments raise more money more cheaply.[59] Since the 1950s, the deterioration of local government, mounting regional needs, the worsening fiscal crisis, and the growing power of the people's insurgency movements at the local level have compelled big business to make bolder and more far-reaching recommendations for "reform." In 1966, the CED urged that overlapping layers of local government be curtailed and that only members of policy-making bodies be selected (which would sharply reduce the number of elected local officials). It also recommended that one chief executive (either elected or appointed) be placed in charge of all administrative agencies and that all department chiefs be appointed, and that 54,000 of the country's 80,000 local government units be abolished.[60]

The recommendations outlined above are formulas for federal and big business control of the country's principal regions. Monopoly capital-directed regional planning and government (which ultimately will require that the power to tax be granted regional agencies) and federal spending and tax programs have developed hand in hand. As will be seen in the following chapters, state expenditures increasingly are made with an eye to the development of regional physical capital infrastructure and regional political control, and federal revenue-sharing proposals increasingly are conditional on local support for and participation in regional planning. In our final chapter, we take up the problem of the political significance of this "challenge to federalism" in the context of the economic and fiscal crisis of the system as a whole. But now we must turn to the concrete political-economic analysis of the state budget—first taking up the determinants of the main forms of social capital expenditures (Chapters 4 and 5) and social expenses (Chapter 6), secondly considering the determinants and structure of the revenue-raising system (Chapters 7 and 8).

## NOTES AND REFERENCES

1. The varying strategies and tactics that monopoly capital employs when dealing with different levels and branches of government gave rise to the theory of pluralism, which dominated American political thought during the 1950s and early 1960s.

2. Ira Sharkansky, *The Politics of Taxing and Spending* (Indianapolis-New York: 1969), pp. 34–35.

3. Wlodzimierz Wesolowski, "Ruling Class and Power Elite," *The Polish Sociological Bulletin*, 1 (1965), 31. A brief description of the formal process of changing taxes indicates how complicated the situation is: All tax proposals originate in the House of Representatives Tax bills then go to the Ways and Means Committee which hears testimony from government officials, representatives of business and labor, and other interested persons. It then approves, amends, or rejects the proposal, or writes an entirely new bill After debate in the House, the bill is either approved or rejected (changes in the bill can only be made with the approval of Ways and Means). If the bill is approved, it is next considered by the Senate Finance Committee, which also hears testimony from government, business, and labor officials and other interested persons. If the Finance Committee approves the bill (with or without changes), it is submitted to the Senate for debate,

at which time individual senators may propose amendments. If the bill is passed by the Senate without changes, it goes to the President for his signature or veto. If the bill passed by the Senate is not identical to the one passed by the House, then a conference committee of members from both the Ways and Means and Finance tries to write a "compromise" bill. If accepted by both Houses, the compromise bill goes to the President.

4. Walton Hamilton, *The Politics of Industry* (New York: 1957), p. 9. Other representative works dealing with interest group politics are: Grant McConnell, *Private Power and American Democracy* (New York: 1966); Gabriel Kolko, *Railroads and Regulation, 1877–1916* (Princeton, N.J.: 1965); Robert Engler, *The Politics of Oil* (New York: 1961).

5. *Private Power and American Democracy,* op. cit , p. 279. "Other interest groups" include professional associations such as the professional educators who dominated the Office of Education in pre-Sputnik days.

6. Ibid., p. 244.

7. *The Politics of Industry,* op. cit., p. 9.

8. William Appleman Williams, *The Contours of American History* (New York: 1961); James Weinstein, *The Corporate Ideal in the Liberal State, 1900–1918* (Boston: 1968); Gabriel Kolko, *The Triumph of Conservatism, 1900–1916* (Glencoe, Ill.: 1963); William Domhoff, *Who Rules America?* (Englewood Cliffs, N.J.: 1967); David Eakins, "The Development of Corporate Liberal Policy Research, 1885–1965," (Ph D. dissertation, University of Wisconsin, 1966).

The theoretical issues in the analysis of ruling class and interest groups are discussed in Wlodzimierz Wesolowski, "Class Domination and the Power of Interest Groups," *Polish Sociological Bulletin,* 3–4 (1962).

9. "The New Deal tried to frame institutions to protect capitalism from major business cycles and began in an unclear sort of way to underwrite continuous economic growth and sustained profits" [Paul K. Conkin, *The New Deal* (New York: 1967), p. 75] As Ellis W. Hawley has shown, however, "partial, piecemeal, pressure-group planning" rather than corporate class planning mainly characterized the New Deal [*The New Deal and the Problem of Monopoly* (Princeton, N.J.: 1966), p. 480].

10. There is a final aspect of state power—the state's dependence on banks and other financial institutions to float the state debt. In times of national emergency this dependence has dissolved—for example, during World War II, when the Treasury compelled the Federal Reserve to support federal bond prices, and during the Vietnam War, when the Treasury borrowed from federal trust funds (i.e., from itself) At the state and local government levels the dependence of the state on finance capital for capital funds is great, for reasons taken up in Chapter 7.

11. Jean Marchal, "The State and the Budget," *Public Finance,* 3:1 (1948), 24. One origin of the study of public finance was cameralism. From the sixteenth through the eighteenth centuries, "Cameralism was developed by the advisers and panegyrists of kings and princes . . It embraced all economic, social, and financial facts pertinent to the management of governmental affairs . . . In the thinking of these writers there was no distinction between the private and public sphere of economics" [Gerhard Colm, "Why Public Finance," *National Tax Journal,* 1:3 (September 1948), 195]

12. "The State and the Budget," op. cit., pp. 26–27. Marchal adds that the successful minister of finance was "essentially an accountant, an exact, precise, scrupulously careful man, who has no imagination."

13. "[T]o accommodate these new productive forces at all, the monopoly capitalist state must move out from the wings to the center of the stage,

THE FISCAL CRISIS OF THE STATE

no longer a hidden figure appearing only at moments of crisis, but a permanent actor, its economic actions in the political limelight" [E. J. Hobsbawn, "Capitalist Development: Some Historical Problems," *Marxism Today* (August 1967), p. 37].

14. Lucius Wilmerding, Jr , *The Spending Power, a History of the Efforts of Congress to Control Expenditures* (New Haven, Conn : 1943), p. 193.

15. Ibid., p. 195

16. Basil Chubb, *The Control of Public Expenditures* (London: 1952), p. 1.

17. *The Spending Power*, op. cit , p 194

18. *The Politics of Taxing and Spending*, op. cit.

19. David J and Attiat F. Ott, *Federal Budget Policy* (Washington, D.C : 1965), p 6. European fiscal planning has undergone similar changes. At the end of World War II, one ideologist of monopoly capital argued for the rationalization of the state budget machinery to take into account "national needs " He deplored "countries with a parliamentary government where the executive is not vested with so much authority and where the annual vote for credits offers Parliament an opportunity, which it seldom allows to slip, to question again the principle of the plan itself or to modify its contents " He concluded by favoring the reorganization of public institutions "which still bear the stamp of liberalism" [Robert Jacomet, "The Adaption of Public Finance to the Economic Function of the State," *Public Finance*, 3:1 (1948), p. 210].

20. David Novick, ed., *Program Budgeting-Program Analysis and the Federal Budget* (Cambridge, Mass : 1965), passim.

21. Keith E. Marvin and Andrew M Rouse, "The Status of PPBS in the Federal Agencies: A Comparative Perspective,' in Robert Haveman and Julius Margolis, eds., *Public Expenditures and Policy Analysis* (Chicago: 1970), pp. 451–452.

22. *The Politics of Taxing and Spending*, op. cit., p. 34 "The norms of technical competence and professionalism seem more prevalent than partisan in-fighting in the [Ways and Means] Committee deliberations" (ibid , p. 39).

23. Arthur Smithies, *The Budgetary Process in the United States* (New York: 1955), pp. xiv–xv.

24. *Public Expenditures and Policy Analysis*, op. cit , p. 426

25. Jesse Burkhead, "Review of David Novick, ed., *Program Budgeting-Program Analysis and the Federal Budget*," *American Economic Review*, 56:4 (September 1966), 943.

26. Murray Wiedenbaum, "Institutional Obstacles to Reallocating Government Expenditures," in *Public Expenditures and Policy Analysis*, op. cit., p. 233.

One reflection of these "institutional obstacles" is that little more than one-half of federal expenditures are relatively controllable; the remainder are made out of trust funds or are permanent or indefinite expenditures or fixed charges. Wiedenbaum estimates that only 12 percent of the Labor Department and HEW's budget is controllable; 30 percent of the Agriculture's; 56 percent of HUD's budget. Interestingly enough, the Defense Department's budget contains the largest amount of controllable expenditures—97 percent (ibid., p 239, table I).

27. Aaron Wildavsky, "Rescuing Policy Analysis from PPBS," in *Public Expenditures and Policy Analysis*, op. cit., p. 320.

28. Allen Schick, "The Budget Bureau That Was: Thoughts on the Rise, Decline, and Future of a Presidential Agency," *Law and Contemporary Problems*, 35 (Summer 1970), p. 520.

29. Long-range and overall budgeting in the future is problematic.

Monopoly capital needs political support to get the kind of planning and budgetary priorities it wants. The question of political feasibility is considered in Chapter 9. Suffice it for now to say that the only people agitating for long-run socioeconomic budgeting are left-liberals (social democrats) such as Leon Keyserling who writes that a "five or ten year economic social budget . . would quantify our productive potential in terms of productivity and labor force . set targets for production and for a balance between investment and consumption . . include a quantification of all basic national priorities. . . ." ("The Crisis of Maldistribution and Non-Planning," *Crisis of the American Economy*, Institute of Policy Studies, February 1971). This kind of ambitious socioeconomic planning is unacceptable to monopoly capital, even though in the long run it probably would serve monopoly capital's interests.

30. The Legislative Reorganization Act of 1946 attempted to create a joint committee of members of the House and Senate tax and appropriation committees. Joint committees on the budget also have been suggested at various times during the past twenty years. These and other efforts to improve the allocation of public resources have been challenged and defeated by members in both houses.

31. Aaron Wildavsky, *The Politics of the Budgetary Process* (Boston: 1964), p. 60; Richard F Fenno, Jr., *The Power of the Purse: Appropriations Politics in Congress* (Boston: 1966), p. 316.

32. *Federal Budget Policy*, op. cit., p. 36

33. James R. Schlesinger, *The Political Economy of National Security* (New York: 1960), p. 111. That this situation may be changing is suggested by Sharkansky, who claims that the House Appropriations Committee "leadership generally refrains from putting a member on a subcommittee whose jurisdiction includes an agency with which he identifies closely, and whose programs he would defend with too much fervor" (*The Politics of Taxing and Spending*, op cit., p. 43).

34. See, for example, CED, *Control of Federal Government Expenditures* (New York: 1955), p. 24.

35. "The Budget Bureau That Was" op. cit., p 521. "The capability of the Bureau to function effectively in a presidential role was impaired by the close identification of many examiners with the agencies they were assigned to review" (ibid., p. 533).

36. *Wall Street Journal*, January 29, 1971.

37. *The Political Economy of National Security*, op. cit , p 107.

38. The plan would dismantle seven cabinet-level departments and reassemble them into four superdepartments. The authors hope the plan would "avoid the capture of any one department by any one professional, ethnic, or economic group" [Don Bonafide, "White House Report," *CPR National Journal*, (May 8, 1971), 972].

39. Government-financed tobacco and cotton grading by the Department of Agriculture is a recent case in point. Because of the power of southern congressmen, growers of these crops have been exempted from paying for grading since 1935. In 1969, the cost of grading tobacco leaf was $2.9 million. The Department has requested that Congress eliminate these exemptions, to date with little success. But it is merely a matter of time before the "general interest" will override these special interests. (*San Jose Mercury*, February 26, 1970 )

40. Harold D. Smith, "The Budget as an Instrument of Legislative Control and Executive Management," *Public Administration Review*, 4:3 (Summer 1944), 181.

**41.** *The Politics of Taxing and Spending,* op. cit , pp. 128, 138, and 173.

**42.** Glenn W. Fisher, *Taxes and Politics: A Study of Illinois Public Finance* (Urbana, Ill.: 1969), pp. 178–179. Fisher's is one of the few studies that does more than suggest the symbiotic relationship between particular economic interests and state government power. In most texts on the subject, there is hardly any mention of business or class interests in politics [e g , see Herbert Kaufman, *Politics and Policies in State and Local Governments* (New York: 1963)].

**43.** Robert C. Wood, "The Political Economy of the Future," in Benjamin Chinitz, ed., *City and Suburb* (Englewood Cliffs, N.J.: 1964), p. 151.

**44.** Ibid , p. 152.

**45.** Kiyoharu Nishikawa, "Local Governments and Their Financial Administration in Post-War Japan," *Public Finance,* 18:2 (1963), 116–117.

**46.** Oliver Williams, "A Typology of Comparative Local Government," *Midwest Journal of Political Science* (May 1961), p. 160.

**47.** John C. Bollens, *Special District Governments in the United States* (Berkeley, Calif.: 1957), p. 252.

"Few [special] district officials are elected. Most often only the members of the governing body have elective status, and much more frequently than in other governments the incumbents run without opposition. In many districts no official is chosen by the electorates" (ibid., p. 248)

**48.** *The Politics of Taxing and Spending,* op cit , p. 84 In the eighteenth and early nineteenth centuries when the property tax was the only (or nearly the only) revenue source, there was a close relationship between taxes and expenditures and correspondingly close legislative control of the budget

**49.** Ibid., p. 111.

**50.** Thomas J Anton, *The Politics of State Expenditures in Illinois* (Urbana, Ill : 1966), pp. 246–247. Anton continues that "decisions with regard to large [expenditures] increases, and all other major decisions made in 1963 were determined by the Governor, or persons acting in his name" (ibid)

**51.** *The Politics of Taxing and Spending,* op. cit , p. 126

**52.** Ibid , p. 96.

**53.** Marian E Ridgeway, *Interstate Compacts: A Question of Federalism* (Carbondale, Ill : 1971), p 296.

**54.** Andrew Shonfield, *Modern Capitalism* (Oxford: 1965), pp. 130 and 145.

**55.** "Local Governments and their Financial Administration in Post-War Japan," op. cit., p. 117.

**56.** Elmar Altvater, "West Germany: The Soul Message," *International Socialist Review,* 3:16–17 (November 1966), 394–395.

**57.** See, for example, HEW, *A Guide for Local Government Agencies: Establishing Cost Allocation Plans and Indirect Cost Proposals for Grants and Contracts Within the Federal Government* (Washington, D C , 1970). The issue of revenue sharing and federal power is discussed in more detail in Chapter 8.

**58.** Advisory Commission on Intergovernmental Relations, *Metropolitan America: Challenge to Federalism* (Washington, D.C , 1966).

**59.** Committee for Economic Development, *Defense Against Recession,* March 1954, pp. 45–46.

**60.** CED, *Modernizing Local Government,* July 1966, pp. 8–16. Big business plans for regional government controlled by the giant corporations are perhaps more advanced in the San Francisco Bay Area than elsewhere—no doubt because the Bay Area is the main financial and commercial metropolis for

U.S. imperialism in Asia. More than twenty-five years ago, big business formed the Bay Area Council with the purpose of "furthering the advance of economic and social unity of the area." The Council's policies are formulated by a board of trustees made up of the senior executives of major Bay Area corporations and banks. Of *Fortune*'s 500 top corporations, 27 have headquarters in the Bay Area; 23 are represented on the council [Dan Feshbach, "The Bay Area Council and Regionalization," unpublished manuscript, 1972, p. 3].

# CHAPTER 4
## SOCIAL CAPITAL EXPENDITURES:
## SOCIAL INVESTMENT

### INTRODUCTION

During the last half century or so government expenditures on civilian and military programs have increased absolutely and in relation to GNP in the advanced capitalist countries.[1] Total government spending in the United States increased from less than 8 to over 30 percent of GNP between 1890 and 1960. In Britain and Germany state spending rose from 10 to 40 percent and from 13 to 45 percent, respectively. Over the same period U.S. civilian expenditures rose from 5 to 18 percent of GNP; in England, from 5 to 30 percent; and in Germany, from 10 to 40 percent.[2] In all of the advanced countries government purchases and transfer payments in the general category of civilian expenditures also have increased in absolute and relative terms.

Since World War II total expenditures by all levels of U.S. government rose from 12.8 percent of GNP in 1945–1950 to 22.4 percent in 1966–1970.[3] State and local government spending almost doubled, increasing from 5.9 percent of GNP in 1946–1950 to 11.5 percent in 1966–1970. Federal nonmilitary expenditures also increased during this period (from 1.8 to 2.4 percent of GNP). National defense outlays jumped from 5.1 percent GNP in 1946–1950 to 12.3 percent in 1951–1953, declined to 8.4 percent in 1961–1965, then rose slightly to 8.5 percent in 1966–1970.

Defense, education, health and hospital, and police and corrections outlays at all levels of government increased from 1955–1960 to 1965–1970. Defense spending increased 16 percent between 1955 and 1960 and 53 percent between 1965 and 1970. Education expenditures rose 57 percent between 1955 and 1960 and 80 percent between 1965 and 1970. Increases in health and hospital and police and corrections expenditures during the same period were 60 to 91 percent and 53 to 79 percent, respectively. Increases in highway expenditures declined between 1955–1960 and 1965–1970 (from 42 to 34 percent).

Turning to federal government expenditures, Table 1 reveals that every category rose during the 1960s. Space, educa-

97

## TABLE 1

### TRENDS IN BUDGET OUTLAYS BY MAJOR CATEGORY, FISCAL YEARS 1960–1971
(billions of dollars)

| Category | Outlays | | | | Average Annual Change in Outlays | | |
|---|---|---|---|---|---|---|---|
| | 1960 | 1965 | 1967 | 1969 | 1960–1965 | 1965–1967 | 1967–1969 |
| National defense | 46.0 | 49.9 | 70.6 | 81.4 | 0.8 | 10.3 | 5.4 |
| Space | 0.4 | 5.1 | 5.4 | 4.2 | 0.9 | 0.1 | −0.6 |
| Income maintenance | 24.5 | 34.2 | 43.9 | 56.8 | 1.9 | 4.9 | 6.5 |
| Education, health, manpower | 2.5 | 4.1 | 8.6 | 10.3 | 0.3 | 2.3 | 0.8 |
| Housing and community development | 0.7 | 1.5 | 2.6 | 3.3 | 0.2 | 0.6 | 0.4 |
| Physical resources | 6.4 | 10.2 | 10.3 | 10.8 | 0.8 | 0.0 | 0.2 |
| Interest | 6.9 | 8.6 | 10.3 | 12.7 | 0.3 | 0.8 | 1.2 |
| Other outlays (net) | 4.9 | 5.9 | 7.8 | 6.2 | 0.2 | 1.0 | −0.8 |
| Sale of assets | −0.1 | −1.1 | −1.2 | −1.1 | −0.2 | 0 | 0 |
| Total | 92.2 | 118.4 | 158.3 | 184.6 | 5.2 | 20.0 | 13.2 |
| Total, nondefense adjusted for asset sales | 46.3 | 69.6 | 88.9 | 104.3 | 4.7 | 9.6 | 7.7 |
| Annual % increase | — | — | — | — | 8.5 | 13.0 | 8.3 |

Source: Charles L. Schultze (with Edward K. Hamilton and Allen Schick), *Setting National Priorities: The 1971 Budget* (Washington, D.C.: The Brookings Institute, 1970), pp. 11–12.

tion, health and manpower, and housing and community development increased most rapidly, but the two items that weigh most heavily in the budget—military spending and income maintenance (which is a combination of social consumption and social expense outlays)—also increased sharply. Military spending rose by more than 75 percent and income maintenance outlays by more than 100 percent.

Thus militarism and welfarism emerge as the major federal budgetary priorities. This apparent asymmetry is underscored by the program composition of the federal budget shown in Table 2 (the year 1965 is chosen in order not to confuse the picture with the extraordinary war expenditures since that year). "National security" programs and "public welfare" activities (which include both social consumption and social expenses) absorbed well over 75 percent of federal spending, whereas "economic development" and "government operations" each received only 11 percent.[4] The military and foreign policy establishment dominates federal government payrolls. Of two and one-half million civilian workers in eighty federal departments and agencies, about one million are employed by military and "international relations" agencies. Normally, between three and four million men and women are in the armed forces. The Post Office is the second big federal employer, with more than 600,000 workers. Finally, it was estimated in the early 1960s that over 25 percent of the work force was directly or indirectly supported by state payrolls or state contracts at all levels of government.[5]

Turning to the state and local levels, total government spending increased seventyfold from the turn of the century to the 1960s. Between 1960 and 1969, education outlays rose from $18.7 to $47.2 billion; highways, from $9.4 to $15.4 billion; welfare, from $4.4 to $12.1 billion; health and hospitals, from $3.8 to $8.5 billion; police and fire, from $2.8 to $5.7 billion; and all other categories from $12.7 to $27.8 billion.[6] The number of state government workers increased from 1,057,000 in 1950 to 2,614,000 in 1969. Local government employment rose from 3,228,000 to 7,102,000 during the same period.[7] Education activities absorbed relatively more new employees than other state and local activities. (In 1964, 25 percent of state government workers were in education; by 1966, 40 percent.) Education workers expanded from 45 to 55 percent of total local government employment between 1952 and 1966.[8]

In brief, if the federal government has earned the label "warfare-welfare state," local and state governments deserve the name "productivity state." In addition to its enormous social capital outlays

SOCIAL CAPITAL EXPENDITURES: SOCIAL INVESTMENT         99

## TABLE 2

### PROGRAM COMPOSITION OF THE 1965 FEDERAL BUDGET
(new obligational authority)

| | Amt. ($ millions) | Percent |
|---|---|---|
| National security programs | 59,820 | 44 |
| U.S. military forces | 48,806 | 81.6 |
| Scientific competition (NASA) | 5,304 | 8.8 |
| Foreign nonmilitary aid | 2,826 | 4.7 |
| Foreign military forces | 2,325 | 3.9 |
| U.S. passive defense | 372 | 0.6 |
| Political and psychological competition (USIA) | 176 | 0.3 |
| Arms control and disarmament | 11 | 0.1 |
| Public welfare programs | 45,783 | 34 |
| Life insurance and retirement | 23,402 | 51.1 |
| Public assistance and welfare | 5,976 | 13.0 |
| Aid to farmers and rural areas | 5,398 | 11.8 |
| Unemployment insurance | 4,059 | 8.9 |
| Health | 3,303 | 7.2 |
| Veterans compensation | 2,121 | 4.6 |
| Urban housing and facilities | 1,533 | 3.4 |
| Economic development programs | 14,386 | 11 |
| Transportation facilities [a] | 5,154 | 35.8 |
| Natural resources | 4,278 | 29.7 |
| Education, training, and research | 3,677 | 25.6 |
| Aids and subsidies to business | 1,277 | 8.9 |
| Government operations | 15,616 | 11 |
| Interest payments | 11,102 | 71.1 |
| Housekeeping functions | 3,299 | 21.1 |
| Judicial and law enforcement | 451 | 2.9 |
| Conducting foreign relations | 395 | 2.5 |
| Regulatory programs | 237 | 1.5 |
| Legislative functions | 132 | 0.9 |
| Total | 135,605 | 100 |

[a] Transportation facilities consist of three major programs: land transportation ($3980 million), air transportation ($751 million), and water transportation ($423 million).
Source: Murray L. Weidenbaum, "The Allocation of Government Funds," mimeographed paper based in part on a paper presented to the annual meeting of the Western Economic Association, Eugene, Oregon, August 27, 1964. Data computed from details in *The Budget of the United States Government for the Fiscal Year Ending June 30, 1965* (Washington, D.C.: U.S. Government Printing Office, 1964).

for highway grants and social insurance (social consumption), the federal government monopolizes military expenditures and bears an increasingly large share of welfare expenses (the second form of social expense outlay). And although state and local governments foot a large share of the welfare bill and have developed extensive police and other socially and politically repressive forces (which also are forms of social expenses), most of their budgets are devoted to social capital.

## SOCIAL INVESTMENT: PHYSICAL CAPITAL

Social capital has two general forms—social investment and social consumption. Social investment may be classified as physical capital and human capital. *Physical capital* consists of physical economic infrastructure—for example, roads and highways, airports, railroads, ports, and other transportation facilities; electric, gas, water, sewer, and related industrial development projects; plant and equipment for education and research and development; investments in water and land improvement and related investment in agricultural and mineral exploitation and construction; urban renewal projects such as commercial structures, sports stadiums, parking garages, and so forth. *Human capital* consists of teaching, administrative, and other services at all levels of the education system and scientific and R & D services both inside and outside of the education establishment.

In every advanced capitalist country monopoly capital has socialized part or all of the costs of planning, constructing, and developing and modernizing physical social capital projects. These costs are socialized for two general reasons. First, most physical capital is used to supply goods or services that private capital requires on a permanent basis. Short-term or medium-term profit maximization in electric power production and distribution, water development investments, port modernization, and similar projects is highly important for the corporations and industries immediately affected (e.g., construction firms, private power companies, land development corporations, etc.). But these projects serve a large number of diverse corporations and industries, and from the standpoint of capital as a whole the projects are important mainly because they insure a regular flow of goods or services at stable, minimal prices. Second, projects are socialized because costs often exceed the resources of or are regarded as unacceptable financial risks by the companies immediately concerned.

Physical social capital may be classified as complementary investments and discretionary investments. *Complementary investments* consist of facilities without which private capital projects would be unprofitable; they are determined completely by the rhythm of private capital accumulation (or by the spheres that private capital has chosen to expand and by the technical relations or coefficients between particular private and complementary investments). Thus complementary investments are a special form of private investment, and because private accumulation is increasingly a social process (since the economy is increasingly interdependent) there is no technical limit on state-financed facilities that complement private investments. The purest example of complementary investments are infrastructure projects in underdeveloped capitalist economies that produce one or two primary products for export. Private investment in agriculture or mining (or both) completely determines the purpose, location, scale, and degree of flexibility of railroads, ports, roads, communication and power facilities, and so on. Examples in the United States are rail and road investments in Appalachia, upper Michigan, northern California, and other regions specializing in the production for export of coal, lumber, or other primary products.

*Discretionary investments* are designed to provide incentives for new private accumulation. These projects normally are not judged on the basis of a particular industry's or corporation's profitability, but rather on the basis of a community's or region's overall profitability. Often an investment is both complementary and discretionary. For example, new highway extensions or spurs facilitate the movement of goods and also provide incentives for new investments. However, complementary investments are part of the normal growth of capital, whereas discretionary investments ordinarily are made during times of crisis, when profitable opportunities for capital are lacking throughout the economy, or when particular regions suffer because local industries are declining. Examples of discretionary are the bridge, tunnel, and river projects constructed during the Great Depression in the United States. Both kinds of investments are intended to raise private profit, but discretionary spending may have little or no effect on profits in the short or medium run.

Investments that need not meet the test of the market (directly in the case of private investment, indirectly in the case of complementary social investment) are by definition "inefficient" from the standpoint of capital. Discretionary investments can be wasteful indeed. Until 1902, for example, the French heavily subsidized sailing ships, precisely at the time of the ascendancy of the steamship—

and thereby developed the most technically backward and perhaps least profitable merchant marine of all the advanced capitalist countries. A dramatic contemporary example is the first U.S. government-financed nuclear-powered merchant ship; the $54 million *Savannah*'s yearly operating costs ($3 million) far exceeded revenues.[9]

Because discretionary investments are not likely to pass the test of the market they have little or no quantitative importance in the budget during periods of prosperity and high employment.[10] However, in the context of the federal system and the fiscal crisis at the local level, which compels local governments to compete for new tax-producing industrial and commercial properties by providing low-cost or free facilities for private capital, it is likely that more discretionary investments will be financed at the local level. More important, in the context of the fiscal crisis (i.e., social crisis) of society as a whole, which is forcing monopoly capital to attempt to develop the social-industrial complex, all levels of government will be obliged to subsidize new "solutions" for transportation problems and labor-power development, pollution control, crime control, administration problems in prisons, hospitals, and other institutions, and so on. If and when a fully developed social-industrial complex becomes a reality, billions upon billions of discretionary outlays will be made in the great urban centers, the suburbs, and regions of rural underdevelopment.

In the United States there clearly has been a long-run increase in the volume of complementary and discretionary physical investment, both in absolute terms and in relation to private physical capital outlays.[11] Investments in physical social capital (and human capital) are an increasingly large burden, particularly on state and local budgets. The specific reasons for the growth of the most important forms of physical capital are discussed below. There are three general reasons for this phenomenon.[12] First, and most important, because of the increased complexity and interdependence of production, monopoly capital needs more and better physical capital. More specifically, the growing interpenetration of monopoly capital and the state is related to the increased pace of economic and social change arising from the advance of technology (and thus the more rapid obsolescence of capital equipment) and the increased financial risk attributable to the growth of uncontrollable overhead costs, the sheer size of many investment undertakings, and the lengthening of the lead time before the typical private investment is in full operation and is able to "pay for itself." [13]

Moreover, physical capital outlays generate complex,

long-term, and frequently unexpected economic effects (e.g., the original highways linking suburbs and cities were expected to speed up the flow of commuter and commercial traffic; their actual effect was to produce monumental traffic jams). The growing size, complexity and interdependence of private production and the multifaceted, long-term impact of physical social investments (including the whole process of urbanization) mean that private capital seeks access to or control of not only raw materials, transport facilities, markets and other traditional spheres but also regional land-use patterns, cultural and recreational facilities, and other resources traditionally outside the domain of private capital. In other words, the need for more economic planning and more control of the state budget and state agencies means that all aspects of daily life become potentially important for the growth of private production and profits. This analysis is gaining acceptance among economists of all political persuasions. For example, Richard Musgrave recently wrote that "private goods which demand complementary public investment may come to the fore, and this in turn may raise the share of public investment. . . . The development of urban concentration in conjunction with industrialization calls for municipal programs involving large public investment." [14]

The second reason for the growth of physical social investment is that infrastructure projects are increasingly large in absolute terms, not only because they are more capital-intensive, but also because of their "indivisible" character (i.e., dams, convention centers, sports stadiums, and similar projects must be constructed in large, discrete units). For example, the Boeing 747 jetliner (and, in the future, the SST) has made many air terminals obsolete, requiring the construction of entirely new facilities (including new jetports) rather than the gradual expansion of existing facilities. Another example is the modern supertanker which requires new deep-water terminals on the East Coast and Gulf Coast. Finally, the political clout of small-scale capital and particular monopoly sector industrial interests means that Congress still is compelled to fund a plethora of projects (many of them wasteful) required by special constituencies. In October 1970, President Nixon "grudgingly" signed a public works bill which added 65 new capital projects (and $3.2 billion) to the 37 projects (and $1.3 billion) the Administration had requested.[15] A related trend can be found at the state and local levels, where the competition to attract branch plants of monopoly sector corporations generates an oversupply of government-financed physical infrastructure projects.

## SOCIAL INVESTMENT: TRANSPORTATION

Because of the social character of state capital, nearly every state expenditure is part social investment, part social consumption, and part social expense. Yet there is always a preponderant set of social forces (corporations, industry groups, trade associations, labor unions, political parties, etc.) that determine the kind, size, and location of particular state facilities and activities. Transportation expenditures clearly have a mixed character. However, one set of forces—the "auto complex," or "highway lobby"—largely determines the general nature of the U.S. transportation system. And although suburban roads, city streets, and many commutation facilities are used as social consumption (because the work force requires these facilities),[16] transportation outlays to a large degree are intended to serve private capital. Short-haul and long-haul trucking, delivery and messenger services, rail, air, inland waterway, and a large part of (noncommutation) personal air, car, and other travel are indispensable to the production and distribution of goods by every corporation in every industry. For these reasons, transportation expenditures are discussed under the general heading of social investment.

By the single measure of total volume, transportation outlays (particularly highway spending) are the most important physical capital investments. Federal spending on transportation amounted to $8.8 billion in fiscal year (FY) 1972 (more than double 1960 levels and almost 25 percent greater than in 1970) Aviation and merchant marine and other water transportation received over $1.8 billion and $1.6 billion, respectively. But highway expenditures received the lion's share of the transportation budget—in 1972, about $5 billion of federal money and more than half again as much of state funds. Between 1944 (the date of the Federal Aid to Highways Act) and 1961, the federal government devoted its entire transportation budget to highways.[17] Today, approximately 20 percent of nonmilitary governmental spending is destined for highways. The federal government bears 90 percent of the cost of the interstate freeway system and 50 percent of the cost of other primary roads (up from 20 percent between 1921 and 1962). In area redevelopment schemes highways receive the greatest part of state subsidies. For example, more than 80 percent of federal funds allocated to Appalachia for economic development have been spent on road and highway construction because planners needed the cooperation of state governors who joined with electric power, steel, and other private interests to block alternative "solutions" to the area's problems.[18]

Until recently, the politics of highway construction fore-closed competing modes of transportation, especially urban mass transit and rapid interurban railroad service, primarily because highway projects serve the interests of many specific industries and segments of the economy as well as monopoly capital in general. It now is widely recognized that economic growth in recent decades has been spearheaded by automobile and related production, decentralization of industrial and commercial activities, suburban residential construction, and a vast expansion of recreational facilities—all of which require a huge complex of interstate freeways, state highways, access roads, bridges and tunnels, and ancillary facilities. Rejecting public transportation and toll highways (although not user taxation in the form of the gas tax), the state has "socialized intercity highway systems paid for by the taxpayer—not without great encouragement from the rubber, petroleum, and auto industries." [19] Two examples of the auto complex will suffice. In 1962, the combined forces of the trucking companies, port groups, and barge companies blocked legislation that would have given the railroads more freedom to cut rates. And in 1965, an attempt by the Johnson Administration to compel truckers to pay higher user charges failed.

Initiated and supported by the auto complex, road transportation projects also receive powerful support from many other sectors of monopoly capital and the general public. For large-scale industry the availability of truck transportation is the key factor in location decisions.[20] For the car-owning commuter the transportation budget constitutes a giant subsidy (and thus is a form of the socialization of the costs of variable capital). Although the politics of highway construction are controlled by the auto complex, highways offer car owners free access and unused capacity.[21] Highways also provide "a low marginal price per mile by auto once [the auto owner] commits himself to ownership"; this is especially advantageous because he must meet fixed payments. Thus car owners' use of public transportation is minimal.[22] Finally, mass transit capital construction and operating costs are very high; such facilities require a large volume of traffic to make them pay.[23] In the past the combination of these factors has loaded the dice against mass transportation systems.

Auto transport is extraordinarily costly: hence the large fiscal burden on the state. In the United States, about 20 percent of GNP is spent on transportation (in the Soviet Union, roughly 7 percent) because of high capital requirements ($5 million per freeway mile) and vast unused physical capacity (partial underutilization of autos in transit and of highways during nonpeak hours and full underutilization of vehicles during working hours).[24]

Transportation costs and hence the fiscal burden on the state are not only high but also continuously rising. It has become a standard complaint that the expansion of road transport facilities intensifies traffic congestion. The basic reason is that motor vehicle use is subsidized and thus the growth of the freeway and highway systems leads to an increase in the demand for their use. Furthermore, the state has not been able to extricate itself fiscally by constructing more elaborate systems, precisely because freeways and highways have spawned more and more suburban developments—where road expenditures per capita are much higher than in the cities—at greater and greater distances from the urban centers. One study found that gains in transportation efficiency resulting from the development of urban garage facilities and improved routes were almost immediately absorbed by the further dispersal of residential and commercial construction.[25] As will be seen in Chapter 5, freeway construction also intensifies the cities' fiscal crisis by removing land from the tax roles. And commuting population places an extra burden on city expenditures in the form of traffic control, parking facilities, and similar outlays. A final factor in the fiscal crisis is waste and corruption in the construction of the interstate freeway system.[26] Much if not most of the waste is attributable to the fact that local officials use the interstate system to meet strictly local transportation needs. This practice is, in effect, encouraged by the federal government: state governments receive larger federal subsidies for interstate system construction than for other primary road projects.[27]

For all of these reasons the cost of transportation and the costs that fall on monopoly capital itself (e.g., delays in deliveries) both steadily increase. Thus large banks, construction companies, construction materials concerns, large-scale local business, and a host of other interests have allied with agencies at all levels of government (and have created new agencies) to overcome the auto lobby's resistance to mass transit. Under a 1966 amendment to the Urban Mass Transportation Act, HUD subsidized a series of pilot projects. The Nixon Administration's 1970 budget included $200 million for mass transit development, and the head of the Urban Mass Transportation Administration announced that $1 billion in additional funds was required by the cities in 1971.[28] By 1972, mass transit spending had reached $1 billion yearly. Plans for large-scale mass transit systems have already been implemented, one in Washington, D.C., the other in the San Francisco Bay Area. (The Bay Area Rapid Transit [BART] is the first new public transit system to be built in the United States in 50 years.) Studies by radical groups in the Bay Area and radical economists in Washington have disclosed that both systems were planned by leading monopoly sector corporations not to meet the needs of the people but to serve large downtown corporations, banks, and insurance companies, which need centralized office facilities and a transit system that can move suburban white-collar office workers to and from the commercial and financial districts.[29] And monopoly capital in the Pittsburgh area, increasingly worried about foreign competition in steel and the relative decline in orders from Detroit, has responded to the transport crisis with a plan for "transit-expressways"—elevated trains mounted on steel and concrete structures. The project, sponsored by the Port Authority of Allegheny County, is dominated by the Mellon interests, big steel, and Westinghouse Electric Corporation. Backed financially by the state of Pennsylvania, the project also has received aid from the Housing and Home Finance Agency in the Department of Commerce. Even the automobile companies are trying to get into the act by developing mass transit bus systems that move along electronically controlled guideways. All in all, more than twenty cities are building or expanding and modernizing mass transit rail facilities, and the Urban Mass Transit Administration is spending tens of millions on research and development.[30]

Far from solving the problem, these and similar efforts probably will intensify the overall irrationality of the country's transportation system—and deepen the fiscal crisis as well. More than thirty federal agencies regulate or promote particular modes of transport. Many of these agencies compete with one another. The federal executive will not be able to rationalize and streamline transportation until it controls the federal agencies that still serve the conflicting and often contradictory interests of particular industries. And according to a subcommittee of the Joint Economic Committee,

> the way in which Congress handles transportation legislation—with urban mass transit considered by the Banking and Currency Committees, highways by the Public Works Committees, other forms of transportation by the Commerce Committees, and trust fund legislation by the Ways and Means and Finance Committees—places further obstacles in the way of coordinated approach to transportation policy.[31]

Powerful interests opposed to unified transportation planning have spokesmen in the key committees. For example, Don Clausen (D-Cal.) of the Roads Subcommittee of the House Public Works Committee strives mightily to maintain the monopoly of the auto lobby over the Highway Trust Fund.[32] Even the executive branch is cool to overall transportation planning—suggesting that transportation priorities are still largely determined by the monopoly corporations' immediate economic interests. For example, in August 1969, Nixon rejected his own Secretary of Transportation's plans for a unified urban transportation policy based on the trust fund approach (not annual appropriations, the course favored by Nixon). Even the Department of Transportation itself is more concerned with carrying out the will of Congress (which is preoccupied with the needs of the transportation industry) than developing overall transportation systems.[33] Finally, although BART and a handful of other projects indicate that under favorable conditions monopoly capital can develop regional transportation planning, there have been many failures (e.g., local competitive sector interests defeated monopoly capital's attempt through the Bay Area Council to develop and implement overall port modernization and development).

The enormous duplication, overlapping, and waste in transport spending is attributable to the influence and power of specific industrial, regional, and other interests at the various levels of government. An ever-increasing burden is placed on the state budget by the proliferation of specific and unrelated programs. For example, the domination of the aviation industry by eastern banks insures that the industry receives privileged treatment by the Department of Transportation. As a consequence of their dependence on financial institutions, local governments pay huge sums to the banks when subway, bus, and other facilities are "municipalized."[34] Harbor and port bills remain classic examples of pork-barrel legislation. Finally, the railroads represent a potentially bottomless pit for federal spending. Dozens of modest programs such as HUD subsidies for modernization and extension of electrified track on the Long Island Railroad ($30 million in 1967) are under way. But juicier subsidies for the industry (and for the banks that hold railroad bonds and stocks) are in the offing. In 1970, the Nixon Administration wanted to authorize the Transportation Department to loan $750 million to the Penn Central and the Department of Defense to guarantee a bank loan of another $200 million. All in all, it has been estimated that the costs of nationalizing the railroads (which in the long run is inevitable) could run from between $20 and $50 billions.[35]

There is another reason to expect transportation needs (and budgets) to expand. The development of rapid transport and the modernization of the railroads, together with the extension of the freeway systems, will push the suburbs out even further from the urban centers, putting still more distance between places of work, residence, and recreation. Far from contributing to an environment that will free suburbanites from congestion and pollution, rapid transit will, no doubt, extend the traffic jams and air pollution to the present perimeters of the suburbs, thus requiring still more freeway construction, which will boost automobile sales. There are almost 90 million on the road today, and the number of cars is growing more rapidly than the number of people. Further compounding future road transport needs will be new corporate liberal programs seeking to disperse people from the major population centers.[36] What is in prospect is larger amounts of spending on both auto and mass transit during the next decade ($40 billion will be needed by mass transit alone, according to the Urban Mass Transportation Administration).

In conclusion, the record to date suggests that full-scale regional planning (and, ultimately, interregional planning) will be needed to economize on the transportation budget (and to that degree alleviate the fiscal crisis), to expand social investment, and to maintain the growth of production and accumulation in the monopoly sector. In turn, this will require the continued expansion and development of regional planning agencies, and, ultimately, regional government.[37]

In the past major changes in political organization have been necessary for the growth of monopoly capital and the development of monopoly capital budgetary priorities. Centralization of power at the federal, state, and local levels has provided a favorable milieu for private accumulation. There is no reason to believe that the relationship between political organization and capital accumulation will change. Monopoly capital in combination with the federal executive and elements in Congress have taken steps in the direction of regional government and regional planning, but these have been tentative steps because of the opposition of the majority of Congress, clientele agencies in the federal executive, local business, branches of organized labor, white-collar and middle-class suburban governments, and minority and radical community organizations and groups. As *Business Week* writes, "the mayors and city transit officials crying out for Apollo-size federal money grants will have to learn that they must accept federal NASA-type management—unless there is more regional cohesiveness and planning." [38] Overcoming this opposition is a top priority of monopoly capital. The hold of competitive capital, white-collar suburbanites, and special interests of all types over local government is a formidable barrier to the development of the social-industrial complex. When and if the complex becomes a national political force, it may be possible to open up new spheres for private investment and simultaneously reduce the transportation budget's contribution to the fiscal crisis. Until then, overall transport planning will remain the pipe dream of a few corporate liberal politicians.[39]

THE FISCAL CRISIS OF THE STATE

## SOCIAL INVESTMENT: HUMAN CAPITAL

Capital accumulation and economic growth in the monopoly sector depend on the introduction of new production processes, new materials, new products, and on the integration of science and technology. Always important for economic growth (and frequently the spur for capital accumulation),[40] scientific and technological R&D services and well-educated scientific, technical, and administrative laborpower today are indispensable. Technical change and capital accumulation also are all becoming closely integrated and R&D and education are now the costliest form of social investment.[41]

Capital accumulation and economic growth depend on the growth of the productive forces, which include land, raw materials, fuels, and other forms of constant capital, methods of work organization, laborpower and labor skills, and technology. Technology is part of but not totally identified with the social productive forces. Although it appears that technology determines the growth of production, in the last analysis the advance of technology, its uses, and its distribution between the various branches of the economy are all determined by the relations of production.[42] The rate of and distribution of material gains from technical progress are, in fact, determined in the collective bargaining process. In the nineteenth century the transformation from a labor-using to a labor-saving technology ultimately was caused by the disappearance of opportunities for industrial capitalists to recruit labor "extensively" from the artisan and peasant classes at the prevailing wage rate. During the latter half of the century the established industrial proletariat faced less competition, labor organizations were strengthened, and workers were able to win wage advances. Thus, at root it was labor-capital struggle (together with competition in product markets) that compelled industrialists to introduce labor-saving innovations.[43]

Throughout the twentieth century elementary and secondary education increasingly has stressed practicality. Thorstein Veblen was one of the first to note this when he wrote that business "feels the need of a free supply of trained subordinates at reasonable wages," parents "are anxious to see their sons equipped for material success," and youth "are eager to seek gainful careers." [44] Forty years ago the National Education Association (NEA) advocated increased federal aid to education because of the "development of the machine age and power age." [45] But despite the rapid advance of technology during the first half of the century, industrial and financial corporations trained the greatest part of their work force until World War II. In the context of the further technological possibilities latent in the scientific discoveries of the late nineteenth and twentieth centuries, this was a profoundly irrational mode of social organization. Technical-administrative knowledge and skills, unlike other forms of capital over which private capitalists claim ownership, cannot be monopolized by any one or a few industrial-finance interests. The discoveries of science and technology spill over the boundaries of particular corporations and industries, especially in the epoch of mass communications, electronic information processing, and international labor mobility. Capital in the form of knowledge resides in the specialized skills and abilities of the working class itself. In the context of a free market for laborpower—that is, in the absence of a feudal-like industrial state which prohibits labor mobility, an impossibility in a fully developed capitalist society [46]—no one corporation or industry or industrial-finance interest group can afford to train its own labor force or channel profits into the requisite amount of R&D. Patents afford some protection, but there is no guarantee that a particular corporation's key employees will not seek positions with other corporations or industries.[47] The cost of losing trained laborpower is especially high in companies that employ technical workers whose skills are specific to particular industrial process—skills paid for by the company in question. Thus, on-the-job training (OJT) is little used not because it is technically inefficient (it apparently is very efficient technically) but because it does not pay.

Nor can any one corporation or industrial-finance interest afford to develop its own R&D or train the administrative personnel increasingly needed to plan, coordinate, and control the production and distribution process. In the last analysis, the state is required to coordinate R&D because of the high costs and uncertainty of getting utilizable results. Central funding of R&D is thus needed in spheres that private capital considers poor investment risks. Further, technological change has

> tended to reduce the difference in input structure distinguishing the major groups of industries. . . . [T]he proliferation of new materials and new methods tends to increase the variety of inputs to each sector [and] breaks down the primary identity of major industrial blocks. . . . Thus as a principal consequence of technological change the diverse major industries in the U.S. economy tend to become interlocked in increasing interdependence. In the job market there is . . . increasing demand for people who can contribute to the coordinative and integrative functions required by the larger and more complex system.[48]

World War II provided the opportunity to rationalize the entire organization of science and technology in the United States. As Maurice Dobbs argues,

> modern war is of such a kind as to require all-out mobilization of economic resources, rapidly executed decisions about transfer of labor and productive equipment, and the growth of war industry, which ordinary market-mechanisms would be powerless to achieve. Consequently, it occasions a considerable growth of state capitalism. . . .[49]

The intervention of the state through government grants to finance research programs, develop new technical processes, and construct new facilities, and the forced mobilization of resources converted production to a more social process. The division of labor and specialization of work functions intensified, industrial plants were diversified, and the technical requirements of employment became more complex and frequently more advanced. The end result was a startling acceleration of engineering technologies and the chemical, physical, medical, and other sciences.

At the war's end monopoly capital once again had to finance its own R&D and train its own technical work force. The continued rationalization of the work process required new forms of social integration which would enable social production to advance still further. The first step was the introduction of the GI Bill which socialized the costs of training (including many if not all of the living expenses of labor trainees) and eventually helped create a labor force that could exploit the stockpile of technology created during the war.

But the GI Bill did little directly to expand the supply of higher education and R&D facilities. Beginning in the mid-1950s, monopoly capital increasingly became preoccupied with maintaining and accelerating economic growth. More specifically, the large corporations began to recognize the crucial role of "human capital" in the development of modern capitalism. A series of CED studies emphasized the role of technical change, in the development of new products, new production methods, new materials, and new needs.[50] The CED recognized that marketing techniques and facilities had to be modernized so that demand could be stabilized and plant and equipment investment could be made with the "long view." It also stressed the importance of mathematical, scientific, and technical training for technical change and capital accumulation and the importance of the state in supplying social capital, particularly human capital.[51] In 1961, the influential Commission on Money and Credit (organized by the CED) wrote that "high priority should be given to budgetary provision for basic research and the training of research talent. Such aid should be placed on a sustained basis, and it should play a key role in the government's contribution to higher education." [52]

. In the late 1950s and 1960s, this emphasis on technical progress and the expansion of educated laborpower (together with the above-average rise in the school-age population, the result of the World War II baby boom) stimulated a rapid expansion of lower-level technical education and the establishment of a vast system of higher education by local and state governments. In addition, this emphasis stimulated a transformation of private universities into federal universities through research grants and other subsidies and the creation of a well-organized, comprehensive, and economical program to exploit technology, which included not only the education system itself, but also foundations, private research organizations, countless federal agencies, and last but not least the Pentagon. This new system required enormous capital outlays, a large expansion of teaching and administrative personnel, an upgrading of teachers at all levels, more extensive education and related services, specialized teacher-training programs, more scholarships, libraries— in short, enormous new burdens on the state budget. Local government expenditures per pupil increased from $380 to $534 (first quartile) and from $787 to $1154 (highest quartile) between 1964–1965 and 1968–1969.[53] In 1968–1969, $19 billion was spent on higher education; almost $13 billion (or almost 70 percent) was provided by the state.[54] During the past few decades education outlays and the share paid by various levels of government have increased significantly.[55]

The decision to expand the education system and extend education services into entirely new areas had far-reaching effects on production relations. Perhaps the most significant was the state's replacing the family (and factory and office) as the main socializing agency of the youthful apprentice work force. And the reorganization of the labor process and the free availability of masses of technical-scientific workers permitted the rapid acceleration of technology, which has been crucial to the growth of and harmonization of production relations within the monopoly sector.

Technical-administrative knowledge became a significant form of labor power (and increasingly of capital) with the new,

THE FISCAL CRISIS OF THE STATE

rationalized social organization of the labor process and technology in the form of new State and Junior College systems, private R&D companies, "think tanks," and federal contracts. The relative importance of living laborpower declined, and the importance of capital equipment (or dead labor) increased. Statistical studies indicate that the growth of aggregate U.S. production is caused increasingly less by an expansion of labor inputs and the stock of physical capital, and more by upgrading labor skills, improving the quality of physical capital, and bettering the organization and control of work. In brief, socialization of the costs of training laborpower has spurred the substitution of men by machines; this, in turn, expands total production and accelerates the growth of the relative surplus population—and increases the need for social expense programs, including education programs which are needed not only to attempt to turn the surplus population into capital, but also to legitimate the system in an epoch when education increasingly is required to get and keep well-paying jobs.[56] One indication of this process is that between 1962 and 1968, 95 percent of employment growth was in the "upper half" of the labor market (workers with a high-school diploma or better). Another indication is that between 1958 and 1967, the number of full-time and part-time scientists and engineers employed by universities and colleges grew at an annual rate of 6.9 percent.[57] Still another is that between 1964 and 1968, state government R&D expenditures grew at an average annual rate of 20 percent.[58]

The continued substitution of "mind work" for manual work, the increasing emphasis on new product development, and the growth of the high-technology industries will increase demands on education and R&D budgets at all levels of government. To the degree that the social-industrial complex makes more rapid headway in the sphere of education, we can expect more burdens on the budget. Although the federal government now does not envision large-scale spending programs on new technology (but rather a preliminary series of small steps to promote closer government-business cooperation in developing and exploiting technology),[59] federal appropriations are bound to expand in the future. There are hundreds of potential targets for the social-industrial complex. "For six months," Sterling Green wrote in early 1972, "some 300 people in a dozen executive agencies have been generating ideas for 'targeted R&D.' There are projects which have immediate usefulness and, preferably, can be adopted by private industry to generate sales, jobs, profits, and new investment and exports." [60] Perhaps even more pressure on the budget will stem from the increased demand for higher education and training by women, oppressed minorities, older workers whose skills are redundant, and others now confined to competitive sector employment and low-level, low-pay jobs in the monopoly and state sectors. With regard to private education *Business Week* writes,

> the financial crisis in higher education shows no signs of abating. Now that the nation's colleges and universities have cut costs to the bone—with few signs of substantial improvement—they are turning to new sources of income as a way out. . . . When schools look for new sources of income, the most obvious alternative is the government.[61]

Only at the elementary school level is there expected to be a slowdown in growth—thanks to the (unexpected) recent decline in the birth rate.

In the last analysis, the only way to ameleriorate the fiscal crisis in the schools and colleges is to place the production and distribution of education on a more "efficient" basis. This includes abandoning traditional liberal arts programs (except in upper-class schools) and substituting "career education." At the secondary level this "reform" is well under way in Hawaii and other states. The essence of the "reform" is to reorder and modernize school curricula to insure that every youth has a "marketable skill" no matter when he or she leaves school. A related trend is the move toward OJT—paid for by the state. Beginning in the mid-1960s, the Department of Labor began to shift the emphasis from institutional training to OJT (which rose from 5 percent of Manpower Development Training Act (MDTA) programs in 1964 to 41 percent in 1968).[62] Other changes (which probably will accelerate) are higher tuitions and fees (together with long-term, low-interest loans), more coordination among private and state schools to eliminate duplication of facilities and overlapping services,[63] and increased centralization of administrative and budgetary control (including federal control). For example, North Carolina, a growing industrial state with relatively few traditional industrial interests to resist "modernization," has established a statewide system of 20 industrial education centers which at present enroll more than 50,000 students. Last but not least, programs to tighten up the whole system of rewards and discplines in the schools (i.e., to restore repression to education) are likely to multiply.[64]

Although in the early 1970s there was an oversupply of educated labor power in many (although by no means all) fields, in the long run the education system will continue to expand—albeit with a different set of priorities which state and education bureaucracies expect will produce more "efficiency."

# NOTES AND REFERENCES

**1.** An increase in government expenditures follows from the general theoretical scheme developed here. The general scheme ignores the many specific factors governing the relation between the growth of private and state spending. Specific factors include: the relative importance of economies of scale in the state and monopoly sectors; the rapidity with which wage and cost increases are transmitted from the monopoly to the state sector; the volume of labor reserves in comparison with the stage of development of the economy (which affects the size of the surplus population and hence the volume of social expenses); the position of a particular country in the world capitalist system (which affects the size and type of military budget); climate, population density, and many other factors (which affect the volume and composition of social capital expenditures); and so on.

**2.** Richard A. Musgrave, *Fiscal Systems* (New Haven, Conn.: 1969), pp. 96 and 98, tables 4–1, 4–2, and 4–3. See also, Solomon Fabricant, *The Trend of Government Activity in the U S. since 1900* (New York: National Bureau of Economic Research, 1952); M Slade Kendrick, *A Century and a Half of Federal Expenditures* (New York: National Bureau of Economic Research, 1955)

**3.** Calculated by Richard England, "Capitalism and the Military-Industrial Complex: A Comment," *Review of Radical Political Economies*, 4:1 (Winter 1972). England bases his calculations on U S Department of Commerce, *National Income and Product Accounts of the United States, 1929–1965*, Table 3.10, and U.S. Department of Labor, *Manpower Report of the President, 1971*, Table G–12.

**4.** These priorities are relatively new. In the pre-World War II peacetime periods the federal government spent little on either the military or welfare. In relation to GNP (and excepting World War I), total federal outlays were more or less stable until the 1930s, reaching a low point of about 2 percent in 1912–1913. War-connected expenditures (including current military spending, veterans' programs, interest on the national debt incurred during the war, etc.) have increased from 2 to 13 percent of GNP since 1929, thanks to World War II, U.S. leadership in the world capitalist system, the cold war, the Korean War, and the war in Vietnam. Non-war-connected spending has risen from about 1 percent of GNP to 8 percent [David J and Attiat F. Ott, *Federal Budget Policy* (Washington, D.C.: 1965), p. 6].

**5.** John R. Bunting, *The Hidden Face of Free Enterprise* (New York: 1964), pp. 145–146, citing a Brookings Institution study by Victor K. Heyman.

**6.** U.S. Department of Commerce, *Pocket Data Book, USA, 1971* (Washington, D.C.: May 1971), p. 91, table 79.

SOCIAL CAPITAL EXPENDITURES: SOCIAL INVESTMENT

7. Ibid., p. 95, table 84.

8. Daniel H. Kruger, "Trends in Public Employment, 1946–1966," in Daniel H. and Charles T. Schmidt, Jr., eds., *Collective Bargaining in the Public Services* (New York: 1969), pp. 6 and 8.

9. *San Francisco Chronicle,* January 26, 1967.

10. Thus, e g., there is a trend in Australia to rationalize the country's transportation system in the direction of fewer expenditures and modernized services. This was necessary because of the gross inefficiencies of the railroads and transport in general, which arose from state ownership and investment policies formulated independently of market criteria [B. U. Ratchford, *Public Expenditures in Australia* (London: 1959)].

11. In the 19th century federal outlays were relatively insignificant. Transportation and communications facilities were provided mainly by private capital; education, medical and health, natural resource, and related expenditures were insignificant; and research and development programs were nonexistent The federal government served private capital primarily in nonfiscal ways. Land theft and land grants, immigration policies, monetary controls, tariff and patent laws, and similar activities made labor power and land available to private capital cheaply and "represented and strengthened the particular legal framework within which private business was organized" [Henry W. Broude, "The Role of the State in American Economic Development, 1820–1890," in Harry N. Scheiber, ed , *United States Economic History: Selected Readings* (New York: 1964)] without requiring significant outlays of state capital. For example, between 1862 and 1866, 100 million acres of public land were given to the railroad companies at little or no cost to the federal budget. State and local governments responsive to the needs of mercantile capital (as contrasted with industrial capital) underwrote the majority of state subsidies to private merchants and other businessmen [Louis Hartz, *Economic Policy and Democratic Thought: Pennsylvania, 1776–1860* (Cambridge, Mass.: 1948), pp. 290–291]. Between 1827 and 1866, 6.3 million acres of land were given to aid canal and river development. Again, actual state expenditures were small. Waterway development absorbed only $114 million in state funds between 1790 and 1890 (but $1.4 billion between 1890 and 1931).

12. If the state failed to own or control physical capital infrastructure, one capitalist group could monopolize this infrastructure and destroy competing capitalist groups.

13. A good discussion of these tendencies can be found in John Kenneth Galbraith's *The New Industrial State* (Boston: 1967), passim.

14. *Fiscal Systems,* op cit., p. 77

15. *Business Week,* October 17, 1970, p. 101.

16. The whole problem of urbanization and urban decay and renewal is taken up in the next chapter.

17. The first federal road aid to the states came in 1912. The purpose was to help to finance post roads. In 1916 and 1921, Congress again appropriated funds for state highway systems. By way of contrast, during the first decade of this century, there was a great boom in electric interurban railroads. The state neither financed developments nor underwrote investments nor shared losses. The interurbans were financed by syndicates and groups of local businessmen.

18. *Wall Street Journal,* June 28, 1965

19. Payntz Taylor, *Outlook for the Railroads* (New York: 1960), p 91. An excellent historical analysis of the decisive importance of the automobile in twentieth-century U.S. economic development is Paul A. Baran and Paul M. Sweezy, *Monopoly Capital* (New York: 1966), chap. 8.

**20.** According to a *Business Week* survey, the availability of truck transport was cited by 75 percent of the businessmen questioned, and was the most frequently mentioned requirement ("Plant Site Survey, A Study Among *Business Week* Subscribers," *Business Week* Research Reprint, 1964). The State of Michigan, controlled by the auto industry, boasts the country's largest continuous stretch of interstate freeway Serving the auto industry directly, Michigan's highways are also used to advertise that state's transportation advantages for private capital in general (e g, see Consumers Power Commission advertisement in the *Wall Street Journal,* February 24, 1966)

**21.** A provocative thesis is that the argument that roads "benefit" everyone in a capitalist society is analagous to the argument that slave quarters "benefit" everyone in a slave society Because of their physical features both roads and slave quarters can be used for recreation The political consensus that developed in the 1950s—the grand era of road building and suburbanization—thus is attributable partly to the technical features of roads, not to any consciously designed plan for promoting the general well-being

**22.** Roger Sherman, "A Private Ownership Bias in Transit Choice," *American Economic Review,* 57:5 (December 1967), passim.

**23.** Larry Sawers, "Metropolitan Transportation Planning: A Review of *The Urban Transportation Problem,*" *Review of Radical Political Economics,* 2 (Spring 1970), 69.

**24.** For a good analysis of the contradiction between the social nature of transportation and private ownership of vehicles, see George Shaw Wheeler, "The Crisis in Transport," *Czechoslovak Economic Papers* (1965).

**25.** A Rand Corporation study cited by John W Dyckman, "Transportation in Cities," *Scientific American* (New York: 1965)

**26.** Stanley Meisler, "Super Graft on Super Highways," *Nation,* April 1, 1961.

**27.** *Federal Transportation Expenditures,* Report of the Subcommittee on Economy in Government of the Joint Economic Committee, August 17, 1970 (Washington, D.C., 1970), p. 11.

**28.** *Wall Street Journal,* December 24, 1971. In California (as of 1972) revenue from a 5 percent sales tax on gasoline is earmarked for mass transit.

**29.** Dan Feshbach, "The Bay Area and Regionalization" (unpublished manuscript). Feshbach shows that blue-collar communities and the most heavily industrial areas are not served by BART Needless to say, BART was sold to the people by the big corporations as "total transportation"—as a "cure for the Bay Area traffic congestion problem" [Pacific Studies Center, "BART, Regionalization, and Pacific Rim Strategy" (unpublished manuscript)] This same study shows that the big banks own land around and near BART stations, which will serve as their office headquarters and other office facilities Further, "Hunters Point (one of San Francisco's two black ghettos) and the industrialized parts of Contra Costa County are nearly missed, while tiny Orinda and Lafayette have stations of their own" (ibid.).

See also, Ralph Ives, Gary W Lloyd, and Larry Sawers, "Mass Transit and the Power Elite," *Review of Radical Political Economics,* 4:2 (Summer 1972).

**30.** "Attacking the Mass Transit Mess," *Business Week,* June 3, 1972.

**31.** *Federal Transportation Expenditures,* op. cit., p 3.

**32.** American Trucking Institute, *The Geography of Survival,* May 1971.

**33.** The same conclusion can be drawn about other kinds of physical social investment, which remain the subject of pork-barrel legislation. For example, in 1972, the Nixon Administration was pushing for modernized bus lines (clearly in the interests of the auto complex and small-scale capital and smaller and medium-sized municipal governments), whereas the big-city mayors were pushing for rapid mass transit ("Attacking the Mass Transit Mess," op. cit., p. 63).

**34.** The purchase of the N.Y. subways by the city government in 1939 netted the banks $500 million.

**35.** *Wall Street Journal*, January 6, 1972. In June 1972, Jack Anderson wrote that Senator Vance Hartke (D-Ind.) and other friends of the railroads and big truckers

> are trying to sneak through a bill that could cost the taxpayers more than $5 billion. Called the Surface Transportation Act of 1972 . . . the bill would set up a $5 billion fund under the Secretary of Treasury. The money could then be loaned for 15 years at token interest. A single carrier . . . could borrow as much as $750 million. One of the many loopholes is in the definition of "loan." The "loans" could conceivably be written off as gifts. In any case, they would not have to be paid back until 15 years after completion of a project. . . .

(*San Francisco Chronicle*, June 4, 1972).

In mid-1972, *Business Week* wrote that "the Transportation Department estimates that the nation's railroads will require $15 billion worth of new cars and locomotives by 1980. No way is in sight to raise that $15 billion without federal assistance . . ." (*Business Week*, June 24, 1972, p. 98).

**36.** Mass transit will also increase population density within the urban centers. BART can be considered the prototype.

> Planned highrise around the stations in addition to high density residential and commercial land uses between the stations will permit the crowding of even more people into Berkeley. The existing zoning in Berkeley will allow a 120 percent increase in population. Already, $850 million of construction planned or under way will be located around BART stations. The tremendous increase in office space near BART stations (78 percent increase in San Francisco) will bring a daily invasion of commuters, with their traffic, parking and smog problems. With BART being built, the anticipated population explosion will be a self-fulfilling prophecy. BART will cause far more congestion than it can relieve.

("BART, Regionalization, and Pacific Rim Strategy," op. cit., p. 8.)

**37.** In the San Francisco Bay Area regional planning and regional government promise to profit big business by providing the framework for what monopoly capital calls "orderly growth." "Size, type, and location of new markets and investment opportunities are created by careful design of infrastructure . . ." which in turn requires metropolitan government in one form or another [Les Shipnuck, "Corporate Regionalism and Community Control" (unpublished manuscript)]. Again, according to a Bay Area Council vice-president, "from a business point of view, it makes the greatest common sense to organize the Bay Area on a political basis that corresponds to economic reality" ("BART, Regionalization, and Pacific Rim Strategy," op. cit., p. 12).

**38.** "Attacking the Mass Transit Mess," op. cit., p. 61.

**39.** For example, see the interview with then Transportation Secretary John A. Volpe, *San Francisco Examiner and Chronicle*, September 21, 1969.

**40.** William Leiss, "The Social Function of Knowledge," *Social Theory and Practice*, 1:2 (Fall 1970), 5–7.

**41.** Like physical infrastructure projects, education outlays also have a mixed character. Education spending is in part a form of social consumption for middle-class and upper-class children in the sense that privileged schooling reproduces inequalities within society. Education once was regarded as the bulwark of democracy, but in fact schooling became "the instrument for creating those very inequalities [it] was designed to prevent" [John K. Norton and Eugene S. Lawler, *Unfinished Business in American Education* (Washington, D.C.: NEA (1946), p. 29].

Further, one central purpose of elementary education is so to structure personalities and behavior patterns that the social order is maintained. In the past, e.g., U.S. public schools had the special function of Americanizing immigrant populations. In this sense a large share of the education budget is in the nature of social expense outlays (not social costs).

**42.** Rather than vice versa. Technology by itself determines nothing. Ideas such as Galbraith's "industrial state" thesis, based on the "imperatives of technology," seem to be objective, but in fact are fetishistic. They place technology above man and make man a slave to technology. Various theories of the "convergence" between the United States and the Soviet Union make the same fundamental methodological error.

**43.** The change in technology then "works back upon" or modifies the relations of production, but not mechanically or because of any "imperative." The immediate decision to accelerate labor-saving technology belongs to capitalists; the ultimate decision rests with the production relations. The acceleration of the use of labor-saving techniques had the long-term effect of stratifying the working class into many unskilled, semiskilled, and skilled layers. Broad-based working-class organizations, class consciousness, and class unity were subsequently more difficult to achieve.

**44.** Thorstein Veblen, *The Higher Learning in America* (New York: 1957), p. 144.

**45.** *Report of the National Conference of the Financing of Education*, July 31–August 31, 1933 (Washington, D.C., 1934).

**46.** We add "fully developed" because in Japan labor mobility is comparatively negligible; many techniques are available (blacklisting, company housing, etc.) to retain workers trained by particular employers. But even in Japan the relations of production are becoming "modernized" and there is more and more voluntary labor mobility.

**47.** Gar Alperovitz relates the following story in a letter to the author:

> I recently ran into a high-priced corporate lawyer who explained the process corporations use to "lock-in" (that's the term) their highly trained specialists: they make them party to special stock option plans which, over time, make them eligible for more and more stock *if they stay*. If they leave, they lose a lot. Also, if they take their boodle *all at once*, the tax load is enormous . . . so they drag on. Finally, if they take the stock *and hold it*, its value expands; so there is an impulse for them to hold. However, once they get any stock, they are subject to high taxes—which they can usually only meet by selling some stock (thus making it impossible to realize greater gains). A further technique comes in here: the company offers a loan (*if* the guy will stay) so he can pay his tax bill and hold onto the stock. All of this is enough to "lock-in" anybody, according to the lawyer— with a real hammerlock.

Such are the machinations required by large-scale capital in an epoch in which the disparity between the social nature of production and private ownership of the means of production is truly stupendous!

48. Anne P. Carter, "The Economics of Technological Change," *Scientific American*, 214:4 (April 1966), 9.

49. Maurice Dobb, *Capitalism Yesterday and Today* (New York: 1962), p. 75.

50. For example, CED, *Economic Growth in the United States: Its Past and Future* (Washington, D C., February 1958), p. 51.

51. CED, *Paying For Better Public Schools* (December 1959); *The Budget and Economic Growth* (April 1951). In a pamphlet called *Growth and Taxes: Steps for 1961* (February 1961), the CED recommended large increases in federal spending for education.

52. Commission on Money and Credit, *Money and Credit: Their Influence on Jobs, Prices, and Growth* (Englewood Cliffs, N.J.: 1961).

Organized labor also has supported expanded education budgets [see, e.g., Committee for Economic Progress, *Taxes and the Public Interest* (Washington, D.C.: June 1963), p. 12] for a number of reasons—as an avenue for upward economic and social mobility and a way to create more jobs directly, and also to expand productivity in the monopoly sector. Because the costs of state education are borne by the working class and small business class, whereas the benefits are monopolized by monopoly sector labor and capital, organized labor has everything to gain and little to lose (excluding the jobs of the surplus population) if education budgets are expanded.

53. Office of Education, National Center for Educational Statistics, *Current Expenditures by Local Education Agencies for Free Elementary and Secondary Education* (Washington, D.C., September 1970).

54. Office of Education, National Center for Educational Statistics, *Financial Statistics of Institutions of Higher Education: Current Funds, Revenues, and Expenditures, 1968–69* (Washington, D.C., 1970), p. 5, Table I.

55. Office of Education, National Center for Educational Statistics *Higher Education Finances: Selected Trends and Summary Data* (Washington, D.C., 1968), p. 3, Table I.

56. Thanks to Marianne Rodenstein for this formulation.

57. National Science Foundation, *Resources for Scientific Activities at Universities and Colleges, 1969*, Surveys of Science and Resources Series, NSF–70–16 (Washington, D.C., May 1970), p. xi.

58. National Science Foundation, *Research and Development in State Government Agencies, Fiscal Year 1967 and 1968*, Surveys of Science and Resources Series, NSF–70–22 (Washington, D.C., May 1970), p. vii. Because much R&D financed by the national state is "nongrowth" oriented (i.e., military R&D with little or no spillover benefits for the civilian economy) there does not seem to be any direct connection between federal R&D outlays and growth [Amitai Etzioni, "Federal Science, an Economic Drag, Not Propellent," in Seymour Melman, ed., *The War Economy of the United States* (New York: 1971), p. 133, citing work of Robert Solo]. But it is undeniable that the direct, long-run impact of military R&D has been very large.

59. In 1972, the Nixon Administration outlined a program that would promote the licensing of government-owned patents; permit the National Science Foundation to support applied research in industry; encourage the development of small, high-technology concerns by enabling small-business investment companies to make more risk capital available, and establish prizes for outstanding technical achievements (*Wall Street Journal*, March 17, 1972).

**60.** "Drive for Technological Gains Will Reshape Economy," *Ann Arbor News*, March 12, 1972, p. 7.

**61.** "College Push for More Public Money," *Business Week*, January 29, 1972, p. 38.

**62.** Howard Wachtel, "Looking at Poverty from a Radical Perspective," *The Review of Radical Political Economics*, 3:3 (Summer 1971), 13.

**63.** "Colleges Push for More Public Money," op. cit.

**64.** According to studies by Herb Gintis, the practical element in education today is precisely the repressive element—i.e., "personality structuring" in accordance with the need to produce "human capital" ["The New Working Class and Revolutionary Youth," *Socialist Revolution*, 1:3 (May/June 1970)]. The repressive element in education is well documented in such books as Jules Henry's *Culture Against Man*, Raymond Callahan, *Education and the Cult of Efficiency*, and Charles Silberman, *Crisis in the Classroom*.

# CHAPTER 5
# SOCIAL CAPITAL EXPENDITURES:
## SOCIAL CONSUMPTION

## INTRODUCTION

Social consumption outlays can be classified into two subgroups: goods and services consumed collectively by the working class and social insurance against economic insecurity. The first group includes (1) suburban development projects (e.g., roads, elementary and secondary schools, and recreation facilities, together with home mortgage subsidies and guarantees); (2) urban renewal projects (e.g., high rises for white-collar, technical, and professional workers, mass transit, parking garage, and other commuter facilities); and (3) related projects such as some child care and hospital and medical facilities. The second group includes workmen's compensation, old age and survivors insurance, unemployment insurance, and (in the near future) medical and health insurance.[1] In general the greater the socialization of the costs of variable capital, the lower will be the level of money wages, and (*ceteris paribus*), the higher the rate of profit in the monopoly sector. For this reason, monopoly capital often actively supports the expansion of social consumption expenditures.

Modern capitalist societies are compelled to allocate an increasing share of the social product to social consumption spending, particularly for workers in the monopoly sector. The general reason is that nineteenth-century rural and farm families typically provided their own water supply, waste disposal systems, transportation and communications, housing, and recreational and cultural facilities. And the cities extended family systems, ethnic organizations and groupings, and private philanthropy constituted a kind of social insurance against sickness and old age, unemployment, and other catastrophic events. By contrast, modern capitalism requires mounting social consumption outlays because of growing interdependencies in industrial, commercial, transportation, housing, and recreational patterns. With the increased proletarianization of the general population, intensified specialization of functions and division of labor, and rampant suburbanization, it has become more and more difficult for the typical working-class family to supply its own amenities. And because of private ownership of the means of production and the absence of overall social planning there is considerable duplication and overlapping of facilities and economic waste; hence social consumption outlays are especially burdensome.

## SUBURBAN EXPLOITATION OF THE CITY

Two related questions are at issue in an analysis of social consumption: first, the determinants of the total volume of social consumption, and second, the distribution of outlays on social consumption within the working class. In this and the following sections we will discuss the growth of social consumption in the cities and suburbs, which requires analysis of the political-economic relations within the modern metropolitan area. As will be seen, the political relations between city and suburb reflect the social relations between working class and capitalist class, as well as social relations between monopoly sector and competitive sector workers.[2]

Until the late nineteenth century "native" Protestant industrialists and businessmen ran most American cities,[3] which ensured that the forces of capitalist production would develop relatively unchecked and unhampered. Land itself began to be seen mainly as a marketable asset, and not (as in Europe) as a place or home. Indeed, the rectangular gridiron characteristic of nearly all North American cities was established to widen the market and facilitate speculation in urban land.

By the last half of the century immigration and industrialization had decreed the central political fact in the growing urban centers: the elementary division of classes under capitalism —capitalists and workers. But men of property were relatively few in number and divided among themselves. Scandalized by rampant corruption and unable to control their environment, the upper classes sought refuge in the villages on the periphery of the city, where market forces were pushing out the farmers. Public transportation systems and the automobile, which vastly increased the accessibility of the peripheral area, were drafted into the service of the fleeing upper and middle classes. Class relations soon manifested themselves in a new form: city-suburb relationships. At the same time businessmen shifted the focus of their political activities and attempted to run the city from the State House.

For the great majority in the middle classes—commercial property owners and businessmen, independent professionals, and the new corporate retinue—the city became a wasteland which they could not control and therefore could not enjoy. Hence they became suburbanites—to control their environment (in particular to get more space), acquire political autonomy, and escape from big-city politics.[4] Only the near-rich and very rich could afford non-residential land-use and thus create livable enclaves within the core city. Some remained.

Class conflict, which in an earlier period sharply divided the city, finally was placed on a metropolitan basis. The result was the 1400 governments of the New York metropolitan area, the 457 tax-levying bodies in Illinois' Cooks County, and the proliferation elsewhere of state organs—municipalities, trusteeships, school, sewer and other special districts. The fundamental class issues of state finance—the relative burden of taxes and the division of state expenditures between the different social classes—reemerged, but in a new form. The new suburban political units were compelled to defend themselves against city programs—tax redistribution, central-city income taxes, consolidation or merger of the entire metropolitan area.

These struggles have become more complicated and diffuse with the exodus of the more prosperous sections of the working class, particularly monopoly sector workers. The automobile and freeway and federal mortgage insurance programs opened up hundreds of thousands of subdivisions in the new suburbs. Federally subsidized suburban development began in earnest in 1932, when the Federal Home Loan Bank Act put the credit of the state behind financial institutions chartered by state and federal governments. And the creation of the Federal Savings and Loan Insurance Corporation in the same year protected small savers and thus helped savings and loan associations mobilize capital for suburban housing mortgages and development. Partly as a result, savings and loan capital rose twentyfold (to $120 billion) between 1945 and 1967. Mortgage debt on nonfarm residential properties increased from about $25 billion during World War II to roughly $250 billion in 1968, when there was an outstanding $50 billion in FHA-insured mortgages and another $34 billion in VA-guaranteed mortgages. In recent years 80 percent of all new private homes have been built in the suburbs. *Business Week* has written,

> on the record the government's program to promote the construction of middle-class housing has been enormously successful. Mortgage insurance . . . has made it possible for middle-income

earners [i.e., monopoly and state sector workers] to become home owners, and in doing so it has created and maintained a huge market for modern, well-equipped, medium-priced houses, especially in the suburbs.[5]

While the proportion of the suburban work force employed in business and professional occupations continues to increase, the number of semiskilled and skilled workers living in the suburbs also rises.[6] Traditional class divisions are being reproduced outside the city limits, generating political struggles between, and within the suburbs as well as between suburb and city.

The suburb and the city have evolved a relationship very similar to the one that developed between the imperial powers and their colonies which produced and exported primary commodities.[7] Just as the export economy offers a natural resource, the city provides at no cost its central location and hence enormous advantages to economic activities in communications, trade, and exchange. (If communications, trade, and exchange are the city's raison d'être, centrality is its most valuable resource.) Central-city services (banks and other financial houses, law offices, research, advertising and public relations services, and central office administration for the giant corporations), which are essential to monopoly capital, expand rapidly. Meanwhile, with the development of modern one-story plants (which cannot be located in the city because land values are too high) and the rise of trucking and air freight (which have made locations along the freeways and near airports more desirable), manufacturing and warehouse and other facilities—and the better-paid monopoly sector working-class jobs—move to the periphery. What is left is small-scale manufacturing, retail trade, and food and other competitive sector services where productivity and wages are relatively low. In effect, except for downtown bank and corporate activity, the city becomes the competitive sector—a reservoir of cheap labor.

One difference between the export economy and the city is that a natural resource sooner or later is exhausted, whereas a central location increases in value with more intensive use. This simple fact accounts in large part for the simultaneous dynamism and decay of the central city. The export sector in the colonies was partly or wholly owned by foreign capital, and sometimes even the working force was of foreign extraction. Key downtown economic activities are owned mainly by suburbanites. The wage share generated by these sectors is small and the share going to salaries (and therefore suburbanites) is correspondingly large. "The central cities [i.e., downtown areas] are becoming more and more specialized in functions which require chiefly professional, technical and clerical workers," one economist has written, "but the skilled and literate groups are precisely those segments of the population which are increasingly choosing to live outside the urban center." [8] When the export economy expanded the largest part of the rise in income was channeled abroad as repatriated profits. When the city's economy expands profits and salaries are "repatriated" to the suburbs. To be sure, suburbanites patronize central-city stores, thus contributing to sales-tax revenues, and bear some of the burden of property taxes on suburbanite-owned real assets. Moreover, income taxes siphon off some of the flow, and grants-in-aid from state and federal governments return it to the city. Nevertheless, the only study available indicates that the income-employment multiplier is lower in the central city than in outlaying districts. Incomes earned in the central city thus tend to be "exported" to the suburbs.[9] From the standpoint of both the imperial power and the suburb, the system is partly self-financing: Resources are transferred from the colony and the city and paid for with the increased income (repatriated earnings and profits) generated by the expansion of demand for central-city services. This one-way transfer of resources tends to pauperize colony and city alike.

Extending the analogy further, commodities and services not available locally to the colonists were imported. For the "new colonists" suburban living itself takes the place of luxury and other goods not available locally. Foreigners utilized the colonial social and community services at little or no cost. Suburbanites similarly exploit transport, hospital, police, fire, and other services.[10] Thus the suburbanite appropriates two sets of social consumption facilities and services. Meanwhile, the central city must widen its highways to accommodate peak rush-hour traffic, invest in more parking and police services and traffic control systems, and bear the burden of generally increased costs of congestion, including air pollution. The flight of industry erodes the value of the existing tax base, and, at the same time, the removal of land from the tax base reduces the tax base itself.[11] In Roy Bahl's words,

> The flight of higher income families and some industries to the suburbs has eroded the fiscal capacity of the central city. At the same time, the suburban residents, through an interaction with the core city, draw heavily on public services and multiply such

city problems as traffic congestion and air pollution. This charge of fiscal mercantilism—the exporting of the tax base from the central city and the importing of service costs—finds much support in empirical research.[12]

The argument that central-city voters will rebel against meeting the needs of the suburbanites (and thus that city expenditures may be less than "optimum") ignores the fact that the city bureaucracy has little choice in the matter, and that the voters have little or nothing to say about either the volume or composition of the city budget. A study of fifty-five city governments in the San Francisco-Oakland area revealed that the property tax rate and level of per capita expenditures were higher in the central city than in the dormitory, industrial, or balanced suburbs. The dormitory suburb enjoyed the lowest tax rate and its per capita expenditures were only 58 percent of those in the central city.[13] Suburban parasitism is suggested by another analysis which showed that the expanding suburban population was correlated with all categories of city expenditure except outlays for recreation facilities, whereas the central-city population did not appear to influence the level of per capita expenditures.[14] And a third study demonstrated that the ratio of central-city public payrolls to payrolls in the entire metropolitan area increases with the proportion of the population living in the suburbs.[15]

The exploitation of the predominantly working-class city by monopoly sector workers and middle-class and capitalist-class suburbanites probably has intensified since World War II. There has been a historic shift in the terms of trade between suburb and city—to the advantage of the former. Salaries tend to advance more rapidly than wage payments and wages tend to expand more rapidly in the monopoly sector than in the competitive sector. The shift is reflected also in the increasing number of residential and mixed suburbs (compared with industrial suburbs). And although the typical metropolitan area has become more economically self-sufficient, or autarkic, the central city increasingly specializes in "export" services. Thus the city experiences a certain amount of economic growth but little economic development. Finally, it should be stressed that to the degree that the evolution of city-suburb relationships is attributable to the ability of monopoly sector workers and capital to escape the city, suburban exploitation of the city is rooted in the nature of monopoly sector production relations. In other words, the city-suburb relation is one (of many) specific mechanisms that have created the impoverishment of one-third of the working class —the competitive sector work force.

## SOCIAL CONSUMPTION IN THE SUBURB

The proximate determinants of the volume and composition of social consumption are the tax base and tax rate structure and the interrelations between private commodities and public goods. The tax base and rate depend on private wealth or income and the taxable surplus (the state's ability to appropriate private income, which is conditioned by various socioeconomic forces), respectively. The interrelations between the demand for private and public goods are both technically determined and socially conditioned. There is, for example, an objective need for more road mileage per capita in the suburbs than in the densely populated city; highway expenditures are inversely correlated with population density. Putting aside the investment aspects of road building, suburban families "consume" relatively more roads, and the distribution of road expenditures is biased in their favor. The demand for social services is also socially conditioned. Education outlays, for example, ordinarily receive a higher priority in middle-class suburbs than in working-class districts. For this reason alone, it is likely that professional, technical, white-collar worker communities will allocate a larger part of available resources to education than blue-collar working-class communities with a comparable tax base and number of school-age children.

A community with a relatively high level of private income and wealth can afford quality social services. More significant, the class character of suburban communities is relatively uniform and suburban governments are more responsive to the needs and demands of their constituencies. The suburbs use zoning ordinances to preserve their exclusive character and to bar housing that fails to pay its own way in property tax revenue. "Government is a 'Chinese Wall,'" Scott Greer has written, "protecting the character of the people in the neighborhoods, the character of school and school children their children will know, and the investment in property." [16] Sealed off into autonomous political units, the suburbanites monopolize local political power and thus are able to mobilize resources for the requisite volume of social consumption. In Greer's words,

> the layout and maintenance of streets, parks, schools, the shape
> of commercial and residential developments, are not only sources
> of interdependence for those committed to the place—their control is so managed that effective action by the interdependent
> population is possible. Beyond this, taxation, the police power,

the right to license and control, are assigned to the municipality as they cannot be to a local area in the absence of specific formal government. In this sense the municipality creates further bases for interdependence and a more powerful local community.[17]

It is true that only a fraction of the suburban population participates in public affairs, and voting is no heavier in the suburb than in the city.[18] But community leaders are drawn from a relatively homogeneous stratum, politics are generally nonpartisan, and "schism in community occurs rarely if at all; there is little to split and fight about." [19]

The voluntary exchange theory of public finance, first advanced in the nineteenth century by De Viti de Marco and Wicksell,[20] sheds a good deal of light on the nature of collective decisions. The theory was never meant to be a "historical account of how States arose . . . (but) a logical explanation, from the economic angle, of why States continue to exist." [21] This approach is based on the assumption that the state acts in the economic interests of the people and contends that state revenues and expenditures are determined by the same principles that govern the private marketplace. "Taxes . . . appear as voluntary payments," Musgrave has written, "rendered by the individual in exchange for services supplied by the public economy, and in accordance with his evaluation of those services." [22]

In this extreme form, and applied uncritically to society as a whole the notion of voluntary exchange is devoid of real content. But with one important modification, and if carefully restricted to suburban communities, the theory makes sense. The modification is necessary because the reality of state authority and compulsion is clearly incompatible with the basic principle of voluntary action. Benham has suggested a solution to this difficulty: "Each [citizen] would voluntarily agree to be compelled to pay [taxes], provided the others also agreed. The outward semblance of force and sanctions in imposing taxation would clothe a reality of voluntary judgment and preference." [23] William Baumol has shifted the perspective from revenues to expenditures and "base[s] an economic theory of the state on an extension of the external economy improvement." [24] The more up-to-date version asserts that it pays the individual to enter into a coercive and collective arrangement because only then are his economic desires and needs realizable. Precisely the same thing can be said about class needs—the perpetuation of privilege and status. State economic activities in the area of social services are thus explicable only within the frame of reference of welfare economics and its key concepts—externalities, spillovers, public goods, on the one hand, and the class character of capitalism, on the other. To put the case formally, the costs of entering into a coercive agreement fall below the benefits that accrue from suburban government's ability to "capture" externalities, create public goods, and protect class privileges and status. This is the basic organizing principle of suburban government from the standpoint of state expenditures.

As well-to-do suburban families gravitate to communities that provide more quality social consumption, those communities gain a more solid financial base for the expansion of social services. And families can choose communities that offer certain types of services (and scrimp on others).[25] An affluent retired couple may select a community with lavish recreational facilities, whereas a family with many children will carefully scrutinize the local school system. "There is only one business in this community," according to the principal of the Scarsdale (New York) High School, "and it's education." [26] With a median income of $25,000 annually, Scarsdale is a beacon light for foundation executives and other professionals and education-minded parents. Although there is no market for social services comparable to the private marketplace, there is a ready-made substitute for the private market, a means by which preferences can be expressed—family mobility.

This does not mean that the allocation of resources among the suburbs is "optimum" in any absolute sense. Families in one suburb may shop in another and use the recreational facilities in a third. Sewer, water, and school districts almost invariably cut across municipal lines. One group of suburban families may therefore be paying more than their "fair share" for the amenities which all use and enjoy. And social consumption may be undersupplied because a majority of voters in one community reject the burden of certain expenditures (e.g., roads) which they are confident other communities or government units will accept. From the perspective of the suburban areas as a whole, however, the allocation of economic resources between private and social consumption, together with the specific "basket" of social services, would seem to be satisfactory. Certainly, it is unrealistic to refer to a generalized shortage of public goods and social services in the suburbs. There exists a market for social consumption—a market with its own concrete institutional forms and legal foundations. The characteristic institutions constitute formal middle-class democracy. The legal foundations date to the epoch when the subdivisions and schoolyards were agricultural land and the village was incorporated by a society of farmers. The legal instrumentalities, which predate industrialization, are thus appropriated by the modern suburbanites. Most important, the market is constantly expanding the need for social consumption to complement private spending (roads, marinas, park services, beaches, traffic control, etc.) and grows with the demand for private consumption.[27] Needless to say, this imposes more fiscal burdens on local government.

## SOCIAL CONSUMPTION IN THE CITY

The political economy of the city is very different from that of the suburb. Because competitive sector workers are concentrated in the core cities incomes and residential values are lower and the tax base correspondingly meager. Hence social consumption outlays designed to meet the needs of city dwellers (in contrast to city expenditures serving suburban commuters) are comparatively low. Several statistical studies demonstrate that geographic and demographic factors do not figure importantly in the determination of municipal expenditures, but rather that per capita local government spending is closely correlated with income and wealth.[28]

If wealth and income differences between city and suburb were the only differences, we would have to conclude that comparable opportunities to choose the requisite amount and types of social consumption are open to low-income city workers. But there is another set of differences. In the suburbs power has a relatively clear-cut class basis, and elected government serves suburban residents more or less directly. By contrast, most cities have at-large electoral systems (or combination of ward and at-large systems). Elected officials represent the city as a whole—and tend to serve the wealthy, downtown businessmen, and other dominant private interests. Working-class community and neighborhood interests are underrepresented or unrepresented, in part because of the at-large electoral systems, in part because of the typical city's vast size. These factors, together with increased mobility and the wide range of choices in the modern metropolitan area, further reduce working-class political activity. Until the community-control movement (led by black workers and others from the army of the unemployed) emerged in the 1960s, physical withdrawal or the search for new diversions "absorbed" working-class discontent.

The political economies of the suburb and city (and the availability of social consumption) depart in another respect. Absentee landlords of residential structures and owners of larger commercial property have no direct stake in the volume and quality of urban social services, except for police and fire services, which almost always are superior quality in the central cities (whereas educational services are almost always superior in the suburbs). Further, "citizen's committees" consisting of bankers and businessmen often decide which issues will (and will not) be placed before the public in referendums. If the situation gets out of hand, private capital can and does threaten to move to more "attractive" areas, where taxes are low and social services are pinched.

Finally, monopoly capital seeks to take class issues out of the political sphere by strengthening the city bureaucracy and the supramunicipal authorities. The great majority of urban-center school systems, for example, are partly or wholly isolated from municipal politics and are operated bureaucratically. In Pittsburgh, to cite an extreme instance, the school board has absolutely no budgetary ties with City Hall, and board members are selected by judges of the local Court of Common Pleas. When vacancies occur "the judges rely heavily on the city's civic leaders, mostly businessmen and their wives, but with a sprinkling of labor leaders and prominent Negroes." [29] In Greer's words, "the powers and resources necessary to the urban centers of large-scale society are thus organized *outside* of the *framework* of municipal government, leaving the framework archaic and passive." [30]

These lines of thinking lead inescapably to the conclusion that within the framework of the urban political economy there are few real opportunities for the working class, particularly the tenant population and the lower-income strata, to express their preferences through "establishment" political institutions. Urban families are able to "choose" a neighborhood that provides an appropriate life style (children orientated, skid row, the "Village," etc.), but highly different neighborhoods are incorporated into a single political unit. Thus the structure of choices and political decision making in the city is altogether different from that in the suburb.

In conclusion, it is worth noting that the great disparities between the volume and quality of social services ordinarily do not lead to a mass exodus to the suburbs. There are obvious barriers to working-class mobility, particularly black mobility. Racist policies and practices, including the inability to acquire mortgages to finance suburban residential dwellings (especially where minimum financial requirements are imposed on prospective home builders) are two formidable obstacles. Another factor that reduces mobility is the lack of adequate public transportation for workers who cannot afford to commute by auto. But the structural explanation of the proliferation of social consumption facilities in the suburbs, the ex-

THE FISCAL CRISIS OF THE STATE

pansion of social consumption outlays in the cities designed to serve the commuting population, and the disparities between social consumption in the suburbs and cities is rooted in capitalism itself, particularly the dominance of monopoly capital, the social oppression of blacks and other minorities, and the bifurcation of the work force into the competitive and monopoly (and state) sectors.

## FROM URBAN RENEWAL TO REGIONAL PLANNING

The specific consequence of suburban "imperialism" is a decline in overall profitability within the city, especially in commerce and trade. Another consequence is the increasing difficulty of getting office workers to and from their jobs.

> The local elites have an urgent need to get educated, disciplined middle class technocrats and managers [and white-collar workers] to the bureaus and offices from which the nation's businesses and governments are run. This is becoming increasingly difficult as central city living conditions continue to deteriorate, as the suburban frontier steadily recedes, and as commuting becomes ever more time-consuming.[31]

Still another consequence is the growing shortage of city housing for technocrats and managers and white-collar workers, despite the fact that most new urban housing in the 1950s and early 1960s was designed for middle-income and upper-income families.[32]

The confluence of a decline in profitability, inadequate commutation systems, and the shortage of middle-income housing has forced business and the state to map out urban renewal plans and investments in every city. Urban renewal expenditures have a highly mixed character, and until the creation of HUD at least thirteen different federal agencies with more than forty programs were involved in urban reconstruction. The development of mass transit systems designed specifically for the commuting population and the subsidization of middle-income housing in the core cities are forms of social consumption. The redevelopment of shopping districts, the construction of new shopping malls, and the building of new sports stadiums and convention centers are forms of social investment. And the underwriting of land purchases and transfers to real estate interests and speculators for new office building construction is a source of speculative profits pure and simple. One writer has described this aspect of urban renewal "as a way of taking

SOCIAL CAPITAL EXPENDITURES: SOCIAL CONSUMPTION    135

land from old users and selling it in large quantities to new ones, at a much lower price than would otherwise prevail." [33] Another has estimated that New York City alone has been compelled to spend $160 million per square mile of cleared land in subsidizing the difference between the present market value of land and land value in its new uses.[34]

Urban renewal programs cannot be considered steps toward rational, overall social planning, but rather specific responses to particular needs of monopoly capital and downtown business. Regional development agencies, supramunicipal authorities, and city halls that control urban renewal in fact reinforce the "decisions" of the marketplace. The state urban renewal budget thus has contributed not only to the dynamism of the downtown districts but also to the decay of the remainder of the city. Precisely because they aggravate the irrationalities of capitalist development, urban renewal expenditures are bound to expand in the future and exacerbate the overall fiscal crisis. To the degree that the core city is "renewed" with the aim of harmonizing with suburban development, the development of the suburbs and the underdevelopment of the cities will be intensified. However, to the degree that the core city is reconstructed as a competitor to the suburbs, the underdevelopment of cities will be deaccelerated, but facilities of all kinds will be further duplicated and multiplied. In either event urban renewal outlays will continue to heap new and expanding burdens on the state budget.

In recent years corporate liberal organizations such as the CED, the federal government, and regional associations of large corporations have concluded that social consumption facilities must be planned on a regional basis (just as they have recognized the importance of regionally planned social investments). The problem is made particularly acute by the increasing irrationality of economic development in the metropolitan region. Large monopoly sector corporations are moving office headquarters as well as manufacturing and related facilities to the suburbs. Since 1965, for example, twenty-two large companies (among them American Can, Shell Oil, and Johns Manville) have relocated headquarters near New York city. And the flight of manufacturing and other facilities from the central city is accelerating. In the New York suburbs "it is estimated that 150,000 of the 750,000 new jobs created during the last decade were blue-collar jobs. But the number of blue-collar workers who found homes in the New York metropolitan area suburbs during the same period increased by only 50,000." [35] Clearly, federal housing programs must concentrate more on building and subsidizing suburban homes for low-income workers to insure that the movement of people keeps pace with the movement of jobs. This will also require regional planning agencies and (ultimately) regional government. According to HUD Undersecretary Richard Van Dusen,

> The best long-term solution is gradually to create metropolis-wide housing agencies, composed of representatives from all the communities, that would choose the sites for future subsidized, low-cost units by majority vote. The suburb thus selected would then receive Federal grants to help pay for the extra services required by their new, low-income residents.[86]

Finally, as the great metropolitan areas become more economically integrated and as the suburbs grow in size and number, transportation, water supply, sewerage, and air pollution, as well as land-use and housing issues more and more are transformed into regional issues that require overall regional planning. In short, the development of capitalism requires the constant widening of administrative units. Neither the autonomous suburbs nor the central-city bureaucracies are able to ensure the profitable accumulation of social capital. And, eventually, integrated regional economies will develop integrated expenditures and taxing policies and powers.

## ECONOMIC INSECURITY AND SOCIAL INSURANCE

The second major group of social consumption expenditures are transfer payments to workers and their families in the form of social insurance against work-related accidents and illness, old age, retirement, death, unemployment, and disease and sickness not related to work. All of the major social security programs (except workmen's compensation) were introduced in the 1930s and 1940s—the railroad retirement system, old age and survivors' insurance (OASI), unemployment insurance (UI), veterans' life insurance and various retirement plans for state government workers. In the near future some kind of national health insurance program will be instituted.

Since their inception, social security payments have expanded rapidly. UI benefits have risen both in absolute terms and in relation to average wages, and eligibility periods have been lengthened. OASI payments have increased even more, partly because more workers are retiring, but mainly because Congress periodically has boosted benefit levels. Between 1964 and 1972, OASI payments rose from $19.2 to $43.6 billion and UI benefits increased from $3.7 billion to $5.1 billion.[37] It is estimated that the most comprehensive proposals for national health insurance, the Kennedy-Griffith plan, will cost the federal government $70 billion by 1974. Currently, the social security system (chiefly OASI and UI) consumes about one-fifth of the federal budget. At the state and local levels, however, social security payments (primarily pensions for state workers) are relatively small—but spending on health care and hospital and related services is much higher.[38]

The basic purpose of social security is widely misunderstood. Only workers who are economically redundant are eligible for workmen's compensation, old age insurance, and unemployment benefits. In other words, the expansion of social security is the direct effect of technological, cyclical, and other forms of unemployment that accompany capitalist economic development. Thus it appears that social security benefits should be classified as social expenses not as social consumption expenditures.

Although social security contributes to social and political stability by conservatizing unemployed and retired workers, the primary purpose of the system is to create a sense of economic security within the ranks of employed workers (especially workers in the monopoly sector) and thereby raise morale and reenforce discipline. This contributes to harmonious management-labor relations which are indispensable to capital accumulation and the growth of production. Thus the fundamental intent and effect of social security is to expand productivity, production, and profits. *Seen in this way, social insurance is not primarily insurance for workers, but a kind of insurance for capitalists and corporations.*

Monopoly capital has long recognized the importance of economic security for production and profits. In the words of a CED pamphlet on economic growth, private "pensions give a clear incentive to better labor, they reduce labor turnover, by lessening financial worry. . . ."[39] And corporate leaders have long agitated for programs that spread the risks and/or socialize the costs of economic insecurity. The first major step was workmen's compensation (insurance against work-related accidents and sickness). In his influential study of corporate liberalism in the United States, James Weinstein has shown that workmen's compensation was initiated by industrial leaders well before such insurance became mandatory under the law.[40] A president of International Harvester stated that the aim of workmen's compensation was "to strengthen and develop the esprit de corps"—that is, to keep up worker morale and discipline.

Other social security programs were supported by corporate leaders. Beginning in the 1880s, the American Association for Labor Legislation, which was organized by vanguard corporate liberals, agitated for broader social insurance, including national health insurance (a model health insurance bill drafted by the Association in 1914 was submitted to a number of state legislatures). But it was not until the New Deal, when the working class won the right to organize and bargain collectively that monopoly capital and the state created a modern social security system.[41] Perhaps the most influential group in drawing up the Social Security Act of 1935 was the Business Advisory Council. This benchmark in the history of social insurance legislation was very much the product of corporate liberal planning.

What are the specific features of the retirement system embodied in the Social Security Act? As Milton Friedman has written,

> social security is in no meaningful sense an insurance program in which individual payments purchase equivalent actuarial benefits. It is a combination of a particular tax—a flat-rate tax on wages up to a minimum—and a particular program of transfer payments. . . . [H]ardly anyone approves of either part separately. Yet the two combined have become a sacred cow . . . a triumph of imaginative packaging and Madison Avenue advertising.[42]

The flat-rate tax up to a minimum income insures that low-income, competitive sector workers pay the same amount (or relatively more) as high-income, monopoly sector workers. The "particular program of transfer payments" based on income received in the past insures that high-income workers receive relatively more benefits than low-income workers. The system thus tends to redistribute income from competitive sector to monopoly sector workers and reproduce and deepen the divisions within the work force.

This fact explains an apparent contradiction: Although "hardly anyone" approves of "either part [of the system] separately," OASI is seldom debated or challenged in Congress. Organized labor is more or less satisfied because the system redistributes income in its favor. Monopoly capital is also relatively happy because the system insures comparative harmony with labor. If monopoly sector workers were compelled to contribute as much as they receive upon retirement, current money wages would have to be slashed sharply. But if retired workers received what they actually paid in, retirement benefits would be impossibly low. In either event, monopoly sector labor-management relations would be seriously impaired. Workers would bitterly resist technological and other changes that threatened their jobs, the ability of the unions to maintain discipline would be undermined, and in most industries management would be faced with more uncertainty.

Technological unemployment and automation are burning issues in labor-management relations. Leaders of big unions, prodded by the rank and file, fight for programs that will protect the unemployed, members forced into early retirement, workers laboring in unsafe conditions, and others whose normal work life is subject to the convulsions arising from new technologies, capital accumulation, changes in the composition of market demand, and so forth. Monopoly sector unions have compelled monopoly capital to supplement OASI with an elaborate system of private pensions. More and more union members receive increasingly liberalized fringe benefit packages. Pensions, pay for time not worked, supplemental unemployment benefits (SUB), severance pay, medical and health benefits—all have been rising steadily. According to one study, fringe benefits jumped from 16.1 percent of payroll costs in 1947 to 29.9 percent in 1967. And monopoly sector workers have received the lion's share of increased benefits.[43]

The growth of pensions has been especially rapid. According to Bureau of Labor Statistics (BLS) studies, normal retirement benefits after thirty years of service increased 5 percent between 1957 and 1961, 25 percent between 1961 and 1964, and 40 percent between 1964 and 1968. Dorothy R. Kittner reported that the percentage of unionized workers covered by retirement plans jumped from 11 percent in 1948 to 38 percent in 1954 to 76 percent in 1966.[44] Predictably, rank-and-file workers have agitated for more of a good thing, and fringe benefits (especially pensions) have become an increasing drain on corporate profits. The labor brokers who head the big unions have been caught in the cross fire between the rank and file and the monopoly corporations. On the one hand, they cannot ignore their members' demand for increased and more comprehensive benefits. On the other hand, they normally are eager to avoid militant struggle with the corporations.

The brokers have tried to solve this dilemma by urging the federal government to expand social security programs (particularly OASI) more rapidly. When pensions were a small portion of labor costs, when high unemployment rates disciplined the work force, and when wage rates normally were not administered through collective bargaining, monopoly capital's support for OASI was comparatively lukewarm (partly because state pension systems potentially compete with private insurance companies). But as pensions add more and more to the wages bill, corporate leaders become increasingly enthusiastic about raising social security benefits and making coverage more comprehensive. The breakthrough came in 1949, when UAW president Walter Reuther perceived that the "easiest" way to win further increases in OASI was to wrest expensive pension plans from the Big Three auto companies—which then would pressure the federal government into raising OASI benefits in order to reduce their own costs.[45]

The effect of the "Reuther system" is that corporations socialize the costs of variable capital and thus defend their profits, union leaders conserve their hegemony over the rank and file, and and labor discipline and morale are maintained. As long as the monopoly sector expands on the basis of labor-saving technology and as long as there is labor-capital consensus, OASI benefits will increase at more or less regular intervals.

Social security was further liberalized in 1972. Widow's benefits and minimum monthly benefits were increased and retirement tests were eased. Automatic cost-of-living adjustments will certainly be added in the future. And proposals to unhinge social security payments from payroll taxes and allow the Social Security Administration to draw funds from the general treasury have gained new support, particularly in the Senate.

The Social Security Act was designed to insure smoothly functioning labor-management relations in the monopoly sector. Its purpose was to underwrite the living standards of monopoly sector workers, not working-class consumption. Initially, workers in small-scale firms, agriculture, and other branches of the competitive sector (not to speak of workers in domestic employment and petty commodity production) were totally excluded from coverage. Even today, UI benefits in low-income states (especially in the South), where the monopoly sector is relatively undeveloped, are low compared with benefits and eligibility periods in high-income states, where monopolistic industries are comparatively well-developed. Most competitive sector workers were excluded from the system because of the indifference of monopolistic corporations and the opposition of small-scale, competitive capital which requires a ready supply of cheap labor and resists any program that would put a floor under wages.[46]

Of course, the political system does not permit monopoly capital to translate its economic requirements directly into effective legislation and budgeting. Capitalists must contend for power with other classes and strata. In the last analysis the content of the social security system is determined politically—and although the system has not been fundamentally reformed coverage gradually has been extended, even to competitive sector workers, thanks to the effort of organized labor and progressive political forces.

> In 1940, just under 58 percent of all persons in paid employment were eligible for coverage, but by 1967 the figure had increased to about 93 percent. Legislation during the 1940's extended coverage to railroad workers for the survivor benefits in effect under Social Security. . . . The 1950 Act was one of the most sweeping in terms of expanding coverage. On a compulsory basis, it brought regularly employed farm and domestic workers, nonfarm self-employed persons (except professional groups), and Federal civilian employees not under the Federal employee retirement system into the program. State and local government employees not under retirement systems and employees of nonprofit institutions were added on an elective basis. In 1954, coverage was extended to certain additional regularly employed farm and domestic workers, farm self-employed. and certain professional self-employed people. . . . The 1956 Act extended coverage still further. . . .[47]

Finally, the 1969 legislation extended benefits to 4.5 million more workers in the competitive and state sectors (small business, agricultural processing concerns, and state hospitals and institutions of higher education). Thus, the system continues to expand not only owing to the economic requirements of monopoly capital but also because of the political forces at work in the society as a whole, and the state's need to win mass loyalty.

The contradiction between the state's accumulation and legitimization functions has reached a head in the debate over the kind and scope of national health insurance that will become available to the working class. In fact, the anatomy of America's political economy is being laid bare by the disputants.

This complex situation involves several key elements. First, union health and medical care plans constitute a growing drain on corporate profits. W. W. Kolodrubetz reported that contributions to health insurance plans in 1966 exceeded $8 billion, or about 40 percent of total fringe benefit costs.[48] And Kittner discovered that the number of union workers covered by health and medical insurance plans increased from 18 to 91 percent between 1948 and 1966.[49] Second, organized labor and progressive political movements demand a national health insurance program because of the skyrocketing costs of health and medical care. Third, private health insurance companies (both profit and nonprofit)—and nonprofit hospitals—also are in financial trouble. As Renée Blakkan writes, "faced with rising hospital and drug costs on the one hand and already-gouged consumers who will not stand further payment increases on the other, the companies have only one way out—the government must assume payments." [50]

The debate focuses on two questions: Who will receive how many and what kind of benefits? Who will foot the bill? During the late 1960s and early 1970s, two major (and several minor) bills were proposed. The plan put forward by the Nixon Administration in February 1971 would require all employers to purchase a minimum standard health insurance policy for employees and their dependents. Costs would be "shared" by the companies and workers in the form of a payroll tax, but of course the payroll tax (as the OASI and UI payroll tax) would be shifted back to workers or forward to consumers. The Nixon plan is in the mainstream of traditional social security programs. It would exclude some competitive sector workers (part-time and seasonal workers and domestics) and low-income individuals who are not supporting unemployed children (i.e., a portion of the absolute surplus population).[51] The Nixon plan makes one other distinction between better-paid and poorer-paid workers. Families of four or more people earning over $5000 annually would "share" the costs of health and medical insurance with employers. Under a separate Family Health Insurance Plan the government would pay all of the costs for families earning less than $3000 and share costs with families earning between $3000 and $5000. Thus, in unionized industries the amount of benefits and coverage would be determined through collective bargaining, but in nonunionized industries (and for the unemployed) benefits and coverage would be established unilaterally by employers, within government-defined limits. Finally, Nixon's scheme would place a relatively heavy burden on workers and employers (assuming that the payroll tax could not be shifted) in low-wage competitive industries because these industries now provide little or no health and medical coverage and because payroll taxes would constitute a relatively high proportion of total payrolls.

The Nixon plan makes a partial distinction between monopoly sector workers, competitive sector workers, and the unemployed. The second major national health care proposal, the Kennedy-Griffith bill, makes no such distinction: The poor are not set apart from the nonpoor. This plan seeks to socialize not only the costs of disease and non-work-related accidents and sickness afflicting monopoly workers, but also the social expenses of production. It contains fewer deductibles than the Nixon plan and offers more comprehensive health care coverage; it would be financed half from payroll and income taxes and half from general federal revenues. The plan is actively supported not only by organized labor but also, and especially, by welfare rights groups and other representatives of the poor. The latter have put their weight behind the bill because it would, in effect, redistribute income from the owning classes and monopoly sector workers to competitive sector workers—to the poor and unemployed. Hospitals, medical organizations, and others oppose Kennedy-Griffith because it would create a health security board (appointed by the President), which would supervise the entire health care industry. Further, and most important, it would effectively eliminate the private health insurance companies—and thus is being resisted by large-scale capital on both ideological and practical grounds. As Senator Kennedy noted,

> only the health insurance industry stands to lose if [the Health Security Bill] is passed—and I believe that we have already witnessed the failure of that industry to serve the people. . . . [U]nder the Health Security Act . . . the major part of the funds will flow through the Federal government. The cost to the nation, however, remains the same. The higher federal payment is offset by a reduction of equal amount in spending for private insurance and out-of-pocket payments.[52]

These are strong words coming from an establishment politician, and it is likely that a plan more closely approximating Nixon's will finally be approved by Congress. It also is likely that the incomes of the private insurance companies, profit-making hospitals and nursing homes, drug companies, hospital equipment manufacturers, and medical professionals will continue to rise and the burden on the taxpayers will continue to expand. Between 1946 and 1967, hospital costs rose almost 450 percent (or six times the rate of advance of the consumer price index. And a BLS study estimated that hospital fees would rise more than 200 percent between 1968 and 1975.[53] Demand for medical care, far from being choked off by higher prices, rises still further because of increased state subsidies and payments. And although the Nixon and Kennedy-Griffith plans envision a system of cost controls,[54] it is probable that a judgment made in 1970 will stand the test of time:

> The great boom of the 1960's in the health industries was largely the product of government subsidization of the market. For years the government has directly or indirectly fed dollars into the gaping pockets of the dealers in human disease. In addition

THE FISCAL CRISIS OF THE STATE

to direct payments for health care, for educating health manpower, and for hospital construction, it has granted tax reductions to individuals for their medical expenses. . . . It has expanded purchasing power of the so-called nonprofit hospitals by granting them tax exemptions, and, until recently, by exempting them from minimum wage and labor relations laws. It has directly supported basic biological and chemical research to the tune of billions of dollars and has sponsored dramatic advances in electronics. . . . And in 1966, the biggest government subsidy of all—Medicare and Medicaid—got going. By 1969, federal, state, and local governments picked up more than a third of the tab for the nation's health needs, and all signals were go for a steadily increasing government-guaranteed market.[55]

The limit will be reached when the state is paying the full cost of all medical and health care. And because neither the Nixon nor the Kennedy-Griffith plan seeks to establish government delivery of health and medical services, drugs, and equipment, the production and distribution of medical care will remain in the hands of private capital and self-employed physicians and others. This contradiction between social production and private ownership almost guarantees that state health and medical care expenditures, far from leveling off, will continue their unrelenting rise.

## NOTES AND REFERENCES

1. It should be stressed that our discussion is confined to the ways that the state underwrites consumption directly. Given the totality of input-output relations in the economy, the state underwrites consumption indirectly in many ways. For example, by subsidizing investment in R&D in agriculture, the state helps to keep food prices low, and thus the subsistence wage relatively low. Obversely, by subsidizing social consumption in health, the demand for drugs, medical equipment, etc., is kept high, thus indirectly underwriting investment in the drug and medical supply industries.

2. These are by no means the only social relationships in the metropolitan centers. Thus generalizations based on analysis of class cannot be applied uncritically to any city, suburb, or city-suburb. But we are less interested in differences between metropolitan areas than in their similarities. The history of American cities is complicated and rich in unique detail. Our purpose is not to do justice to this history, but rather to isolate the essential and universal elements that bear on the question of the volume and distribution of social consumption.

**3.** Edward C. Banfield and ·James Q. Wilson, *City Politics* (New York: 1966), p. 38.

**4.** William M. Dobriner, *Class in Suburbia* (New York: 1963), pp. 64–77.

**5.** *Business Week,* May 27, 1972, p. 80. *Business Week* also reports an AFL–CIO study which concluded that union members are more likely to live in the suburbs than in working-class neighborhoods near their factories ("Trouble Plagues the House of Labor," *Business Week,* October 28, 1972, p. 70).

**6.** Bernard Lazerwitz, "Metropolitan Residential Belts," *American Sociological Review,* 25 (April 1960), 249

**7.** Eric Schiff, "Direct Investment, Terms of Trade, and the Balance of Payments," *Quarterly Journal of Economics,* 56 (February 1942); Paul Baran, *The Political Economy of Growth* (New York: 1957).

**8.** Benjamin Chinitz, "City and Suburb," in Chinitz, ed., *City and Suburb* (Englewood Cliffs, N.J.: 1964), p. 28.

**9.** Frederick W. Bell, *The Economics of the New England Fishing Industry: The Role of Technological Change and Government Aid,* Federal Reserve Bank of Boston, Research Report No. 31, February 1966, p. 23. According to Roy W. Bahl [*Metropolitan City Expenditures* (Lexington, Ky.: 1969)], there are no definitive studies on how much suburbanites pay for city services they use.

**10.** Harvey Shapiro, "Economies of Scale and Local Government Finance," *Land Economics,* 39 (May 1963), 178.

**11.** Mordecai S. Feinberg, "The Implications of the Core-City Decline for the Fiscal Structure of the Core-City," *National Tax Journal,* 17 (September 1964), 216.

**12.** *Metropolitan City Expenditures,* op. cit., p. 19.

**13.** Julius Margolis, "Municipal Fiscal Structure of a Metropolitan Region," *Journal of Political Economy,* 65 (June 1957), 232.

**14.** Harvey E. Brazer, "The Role of Major Metropolitan Centers in State and Local Finance," *American Economic Review, Papers and Proceedings,* 47 (May 1958). This study is confirmed by more recent data: Woo Sik Kee, "Central City Expenditures and Metropolitan Areas," *National Tax Journal,* 18 (December 1965).

**15.** Julius Margolis, "Metropolitan Finance Problems," in James Buchanan, ed., *Public Finances: Needs, Sources, and Utilization* (Princeton, N.J.: 1961).

**16.** Scott Greer, *The Emerging City* (New York: 1962), p. 147.

**17.** Ibid., p. 116.

**18.** Ibid., p. 147.

**19.** Ibid.

**20.** James M. Buchanan, *Fiscal Theory and Political Economy* (Durham, N.C.: 1960), p. 35.

**21.** F. C. Benham, "Notes on the Pure Theory of Public Finance," *Economica,* 1 (November 1935), 451.

**22.** Richard Musgrave, "The Voluntary Exchange Theory of Public Finance," *The Quarterly Journal of Economics,* 53 (February 1939), 214. To put it another way, "the tax tends to take away from each and all that quantity of wealth which they would have voluntarily yielded to the state for the satisfaction of their purely collective wants" [Gerhard Colm, "Why Public Finance," *National Tax Journal,* 1 (September 1948), 196, quoting Graziani].

**23.** "Notes on the Pure Theory of Public Finance," op. cit., p. 157.

**24.** William Baumol, *Welfare Economics and the Theory of the State* (Cambridge, Mass.: 1952), p. 12.

**25.** George J. Stigler, "The Tenable Range of Functions of Local Government," in Edmund S. Phelps, ed., *Private Wants and Public Needs*, rev. ed. (New York: 1965), p. 171; Charles M. Tiebout, "A Pure Theory of Local Expenditures," *Journal of Political Economy*, 64 (October 1956), passim.

**26.** Quoted by Eric Pace, "Poor Little Rich Village," *New York Times*, May 26, 1965.

**27.** Richard Musgrave, *Fiscal Systems* (New Haven, Conn.: 1969), p. 79.

**28.** See, e g., the following studies: Stanley Scott and E. L. Feder, *Factors Associated with Variations in Municipal Expenditure Levels* (Berkeley, Cal.: 1957); Harvey E. Brazer, *City Expenditures in the United States* (New York: National Bureau of Economic Research, 1959); John C. Bollens, ed., *Exploring Metropolitan Community* (Berkeley: 1961); Seymour Sacks and W. H. Hellmuth, *Financing Government in a Metropolitan Area* (Glencoe, Ill.: 1961); Robert C. Wood, *1400 Governments* (Cambridge, Mass.: 1961).

**29.** Robert Bartley in the *Wall Street Journal*, June 17, 1966.

**30.** *The Emerging City*, op. cit., p. 191.

**31.** Ralph Ives, Gary W. Lloyd, and Larry Sawers, "Mass Transit and the Power Elite," *Review of Radical Political Economics*, 4:2 (Summer 1972), 70.

**32.** According to Martin Anderson's *The Federal Bulldozer* (Cambridge, Mass.: 1964), 90 percent of all new housing units built under urban renewal in the 1950s were middle and upper income.

**33.** Matt Edel, paper presented at the December 1969 meeting of the Union for Radical Political Economics.

**34.** Raymond Vernon, "The Myth and Reality of Our Urban Problems," in *City and Suburb*, op. cit., The practical experience and literature on the subject of urban renewal is vast and the general conclusions widely accepted. Urban renewal means people removal, especially black removal: Families are transferred from the downtown periphery to deteriorating districts elsewhere in the city, the neighborhoods are blighted by freeway construction, and public housing is linked to slum clearance (and thus the failure to create and use more open spaces). As Charles Abrams wrote in his *The City as the Frontier* (New York: 1966, p. 220), "since the welfare of the building industry had won equal place with the people's welfare in the 1949 Housing Act, it seemed inevitable that sooner or later the interests of lower-income families would be forgotten." Martin Anderson's *The Federal Bulldozer* (op. cit.) analyzes the coalition of banks, newspapers, department stores, downtown real estate owners, academic intellectuals, city planners, and city politicians that has made urban renewal what it is. Originally introduced at the expense of both the urban working class and small business, urban renewal began to protect the latter in 1964 when Congress passed a housing bill that provides concessions and compensation for small business.

**35.** "The Battle of the Suburbs," *Newsweek*, November 15, 1971, p. 62.

**36.** Ibid., p. 70.

**37.** Charles L. Schultze et al., *Setting National Priorities: The 1972 Budget* (Washington, D.C.: The Brookings Institution, 1972), p. 21, table 1–6.

**38.** Between 1950 and 1968, expenditures at all levels of government for health and medical care rose from $1.3 to $13 billion (or over one-third of total national health costs). This spending includes state outlays for medical facilities and services and Medicare and Medicaid.

**39.** CED, *Economic Growth in the U.S.: Its Past and Future* (February 1958), p. 49.

SOCIAL CAPITAL EXPENDITURES: SOCIAL CONSUMPTION     147

**40.** James Weinstein, *The ·Corporate Ideal in the Liberal State, 1900–1918* (Boston: 1968).

**41.** With the introduction of collective bargaining in the monopoly sector, wages increasingly were regulated by labor and management. At the same time the monopolization of product markets insured that declines in product demand in particular industries or throughout the monopoly sector resulted in decreases in production not in prices. Thus economic contraction in the monopoly industries more and more had a negative impact on employment rather than on wages. For this reason social security as a system for regulating production relations has become increasingly important over the years.

**42.** Milton Friedman, "The Poor Man's Welfare Payment to the Middle Class," *The Washington Monthly,* May 1972, p. 16. The standard work on social security is Joseph A. Pechman, Henry J. Aaron, and Michael K. Taussig, *Social Security: Perspectives for Reform* (Washington, D.C.: The Brookings Institution, 1968).

**43.** The payroll costs of 79 large corporations were reviewed [cited by E. Robert Livernash, "Wages and Benefits," *A Review of Industrial Relations Research,* vol. I (Madison, Wisc.: Industrial Relations Research Association, 1970), p. 120]. Another study cited by Livernash estimated that between 1929 and 1967 employee benefits increased by 9.6 percent per year, in contrast to the average yearly increases in wages and salaries of only 3.9 percent. Still another study showed that between 1959 and 1966 benefits were liberalized each year for 80 to 90 percent of workers covered by major union contracts, that benefits were introduced or liberalized for 40 percent of all union workers, but that only 20 to 25 percent of nonunion workers received benefits for the first time or were favored by liberalized benefits (ibid., p. 121). More evidence that benefits are concentrated in the monopolistic sector is provided by a study showing that 70 percent of all workers covered by SUB plans are employed in four key monopolistic industries (autos, steel, rubber, and cement) (ibid., p. 124).

**44.** Ibid., p. 127.

**45.** The technique was to negotiate a pension plan with the Big Three that guaranteed retired workers a maximum of $100 monthly. The companies were compelled to pay the difference between OASI benefits and the $100. This scheme created strong incentives for the corporations to throw their full support behind increases in OASI benefits—which Congress soon passed.

**46.** Even at present all of the needs of older people (including many retired monopoly sector workers) are not met. According to the federal government's own definition, about one-third of all individuals sixty-five or older live below the poverty line. In 1968, almost one-quarter of all poor people were sixty-five or older [Howard Wachtel, "Looking at Poverty from a Radical Perspective," *Review of Radical Political Economics,* 3:3 (Summer 1971)]. Thus, what monopoly capital is willing to accept in social security programs is limited to the amount of benefits required to enable the monopoly sector work force to reproduce itself and to keep labor-management relations peaceful.

**47.** James R. Ukockis, "Social Security: Development and Financing," *Monthly Review,* Federal Reserve Bank of Kansas City, April 1968, p. 10.

**48.** "Wages and Benefits," op. cit., p. 132.

**49.** Ibid., p. 133.

**50.** Renée Blakkan, "Health Plans Guarantee Profits," *Guardian,* March 27, 1971, p. 6.

**51.** This is a perfect example of how workers who produce neither surplus value nor children who are potential surplus value producers are treated in capitalist society.

**52.** Quoted in the *Missouri Teamsters,* February 18, 1972.

**53.** Cited by the *Missouri Teamsters,* April 5, 1968.

**54.** Both the Nixon and Kennedy-Griffith plans would attempt to build in cost controls by a system of prepayments: A hospital or doctor group would receive a certain amount per patient per year. Needless to say, this scheme gives doctor groups and hospitals every incentive to pad costs in order to make claims for more funds more credible and turn away patients (the less treatment and hospitalization the patient gets, the more the hospital makes). The Kennedy-Griffith plan presumably would minimize cost padding by imposing a formula under which payments could grow no faster than the rate of growth of new tax receipts or the growth of an index averaging cost of living, population growth, and services covered, whichever is less.

**55.** *The American Health Empire: Power, Profits, and Politics,* A Health-PAC Book prepared by Barbara and John Ehrenreich (New York: 1970), p. 96.

# CHAPTER 6
# SOCIAL EXPENSES OF PRODUCTION:
# THE WARFARE—WELFARE STATE

## INTRODUCTION

In this chapter we consider the problem of the effects of monopoly sector capital accumulation on the state budget in general and the military and welfare budgets in particular. Our thesis is that there is a tendency for social expenses of production to rise over time and that the state increasingly is compelled to socialize these expenses.[1] Our argument is based on the general model of capitalist production and distribution set forth in Chapter 1.

Monopoly sector productivity and productive capacity tend to expand more rapidly than the demand for labor and employment. Further, this tendency is exacerbated by the expansion and the socialization of the costs of social capital. This is of crucial importance in the analysis of the growth of the modern welfare system and foreign economic expansion and imperialism. Welfare and military spending are determined by the needs of monopoly capital and the relations of production in the monopoly sector. Surplus productive capacity (or surplus capital) creates political pressures for aggressive foreign economic expansion. And surplus laborpower (or the surplus population) also builds up political pressures for the growth of the welfare system. Thus the structural determinants of both military spending and welfare outlays are broadly the same and the two kinds of spending can be interpreted as different aspects of the same general phenomenon.

The welfare state tends to expand because of the growth of the surplus population which has relatively little purchasing power of its own, and the warfare state tends to grow because of the expansion of surplus capital which cannot be disposed of at home (in part because of the growth of the surplus population). For these reasons, the problem of maintaining an adequate level of aggregate demand is fundamentally a problem of expanding markets and investments abroad and subsidizing competitive sector (and unemployed) workers at home. In sum, both welfare spending and warfare spending have a twofold nature: The function of the welfare system is not only to control the surplus population politically but also to expand demand

and domestic markets. And the warfare system not only keeps foreign rivals at bay and inhibits the development of world revolution (thus keeping laborpower, raw materials, and markets in the capitalist orbit) but also helps stave off domestic economic stagnation. Thus we describe the national government as the *warfare–welfare state*.[2]

It should be stressed that some surplus goods are taken off the market by the surplus population with purchasing power provided by the welfare system. Similarly, part of the surplus population is employed by the state in the military and to staff the welfare agencies established to control the remainder of the surplus population. Thus, monopoly capitalism is in part a self-correcting system. However, as productivity continues to expand, the welfare system tends to grow too slowly to generate enough purchasing power to acquire surplus goods, on the one hand, and to generate enough employment for the surplus population in the state sector, on the other. This means that welfare and military expenditures tend to increase simultaneously.[3]

In sum, to control the surplus population foreign markets must be expanded and controlled, and to expand and control foreign markets the surplus population must be controlled. If foreign markets are not expanded and controlled, decelerating economic growth forces cutbacks in outlays on the surplus population. And if the surplus population is not controlled, social and political disorder forces the state to turn inward and slow down foreign expansion. During the 1960s, these dialectical tendencies appeared to be quite strong in the United States.

## SURPLUS CAPITAL AND THE WARFARE STATE

Militarism and imperialism (and antiimperialism) are inherent features of capitalist economic development [4]—notwithstanding the differences in origin, form, and ultimate effects of such adventures as the English-Dutch trade wars, wars of imperial conquest in Asia and Africa, wars fought for national independence in Latin America, civil wars in Europe and America, wars between developed imperialist powers (World War I and World War II), and wars of national liberation today. This is the general context in which we will examine the U.S. military budget. The specific context is the post-World War II period in which U.S. monopoly capital has expanded overseas in the milieu of the developing socialist world (which to a large degree has closed off access to laborpower, raw materials, and markets on favorable terms), third world national liberation struggles, the decline of the old European colonial powers, and the military defeat of the Japanese empire.

Analyzed from the vantage of this context, the roots of American militarism can be traced directly to the tendency for the monopoly sector to generate surplus capital. Monopolistic producers need and seek foreign markets and investment outlets in order to keep aggregate demand in step with productive capacity. Every dollar of sales above the break-even point goes directly into profits— that is, marginal sales revenue over the level of capacity utilization that allows corporations to cover costs is all gravy. Thus since World War II nearly every monopoly sector corporation has reorganized its production, financing, and marketing facilities in order to expand foreign sales, either directly or through overseas branch plants and subsidiaries. And since the early 1950s, corporation after corporation has been transformed into a "multinational" (or "international") company.[5]

Employment in the monopoly sector also depends on foreign economic expansion. For more than fifty years organized labor has supported corporate and federal programs that promote commodity exports and the control of foreign sources of raw materials and markets by U.S. capital. Unions have opposed investments that "export" jobs to countries that offer laborpower. (Until the early 1970s, most investments did not fall into this category.) Overseas branch plants provide a market for the parent corporation despite nationalist economic policies (e.g., high tariffs and import quotas in Europe and the Third World).[6] Investments designed to exploit agricultural and mineral raw materials required by U.S. industry also have been supported by organized labor. Finally, until recently U.S. capital sought to take over established European concerns, not to create fresh competition for U.S. industries, but rather to prevent European capital from competing with U.S. capital. Thus, although the short-term effect of many foreign investments may be to reduce the demand for labor at home and expand it abroad, the long-term effect has been to expand and control U.S. foreign markets and hence to support the home economy.

An additional consideration is that the growth of productivity normally is limited by the size of the market. Monopoly capital does not introduce economies of large-scale production, finance, and marketing in order to lower unit labor costs unless the costs of new R&D, equipment, techniques, sales facilities, and the like can be recovered from expanded sales. Moreover, harmonious labor-management relations are indispensable for increased productivity which is essential if the United States is to be competitive economically. In turn, a competitive economic position and foreign economic expansion are required to ensure harmonious labor-management relations.[7] These considerations strongly support the conclusion that organized labor and capital in the monopoly sector have had an important common interest—namely, foreign economic expansion and control of overseas markets. And the absolute and relative surplus populations also have an economic interest in overseas expansion: Periods of war and rapid foreign economic growth open up job opportunities for workers who normally are confined to the competitive sector or are unemployed.

American overseas expansionism began in earnest with the closing of the frontier and the Open Door notes of the 1890s. The roots of the modern American economic empire are many and varied (and also somewhat tangled). But one decisive factor was the alliance between conservative labor leaders and corporate chieftains. Both sides agreed to throw their political support to the economic expansionists in order to expand and control foreign markets and thus increase the absolute size of the national income pie. They expected (correctly) that the effect would be to soften or mute labor-capital struggles over the distribution of income.[8] At the same time, other interests joined or helped forge the expansionist consensus: importers and exporters, shipping and insurance companies, raw material processors, bankers, and farmers.[9] Throughout the 1920s and 1930s (with the exception of a few years in the early New Deal period), the basic goals of U.S. foreign policy and diplomacy were to expand exports and maintain American hegemony.[10] During World War II, union leaders participated with monopoly capital in every phase of the administration of the war program. And the corporate liberal-imperialist consensus flourished in the 1950s and 1960s under the banner of "bipartisan foreign policy."

The growth of the modern military-industrial complex and the Pentagon establishment cannot be attributed only to economic factors. The Pentagon has spent hundreds of billions of dollars since World War II not to protect specific markets or investments or gain new markets, but to expand U.S. economic, political, and cultural hegemony. In other words, the military-industrial complex and U.S. militarism are inconceivable outside of the context of world capitalist development, with its emphasis on national competition and its great fear of socialism and the world revolutionary movement. A full analysis of the growth of U.S. militarism and the military budget over the past three decades is beyond the scope of this book. But we are able to identify those factors in the arms race, the structure of the military-industrial complex, and the wars against national liberation struggles that are likely to force the federal government to continue to expand the military budget into the foreseeable future.

First, the continuous expansion of world capitalist production, the extension of capitalism into the Third World, and the proletarianization of the world population enlarges the arena both for capital accumulation and for class and national conflict. The increasing instability of the world capitalist social order, the transformation of compromise-minded bourgeoisie nationalist movements into national liberation struggles (especially in Vietnam), and the birth of new socialist societies, have "dictated" increased military spending by the "mother country." Today, overseas expansion meets more and more resistance and the defense of empire is more and more costly. The U.S. government has been compelled to develop a series of military blocs, a far-flung network of military bases, and an enormous domestic military establishment. Further, the cold war requires the constant upgrading of military technology in order to maintain parity in the balance of terror, and the opposition at home to the Vietnam War requires the development of hypermodern technological substitutes for the fire power traditionally supplied by foot soldiers. Last, but not least, there

> is clearly in process . . . a competition among the industrial nations to sell arms to the developing [sic] nations of the world. In the Indian subcontinent and the Middle East these sales have contributed to an intense arms race; while in North Africa, sub-Saharan Africa and most of Latin America the situation is still . . . that of an "arms walk." [11]

Equally clear is the encouragement that the U.S. government and businessmen have given to Japanese rearmament since the 1960s, in part to build up a satellite-developed capitalist power, in part to get more arms orders for U.S. contractors.

Second, the major so-called private military producers have established what seems to be a permanent tap on the federal budget and thus have a long-run stake in the arms race itself. Industrial procurement amounts to about 50 percent of the Pentagon's budget, and the proportion of all military orders received by the largest fifty defense contractors increased from 58 percent during World War II to 66 percent in 1963–1964.[12] In military production "the initiative, risk-bearing and similar manifestations of enterprise appear to have become characteristics of the buyer rather than the seller." [13] Thus, the big military contractors participate readily with defense programs regardless of the rationality of these programs in terms of overall national capital interests. So do the subcontractors and other suppliers, who have been described as but the visible part of a huge iceberg.[14]

The proof that a handful of large corporations has a permanent hold on the military budget lies in the fact that the same firms continue to receive the largest share of military contracts despite the rapidly changing nature of defense spending. The volatility in the ranks of the major weapons suppliers during the late 1950s and early 1960s was more apparent than real, and it was not attributable to the changing military budget but rather to mergers and short-term joint ventures by contract construction companies.[15] The resources of most of these corporations are so specialized, the emphasis on quality and technology rather than volume and low price is so great, and the absence of mass distribution is so pronounced that they are unable to shift a significant amount of resources to nonmilitary production for the private sector. Hence these companies must be subsidized indefinitely. Recent attempts to help some of these corporations to enter the private market by and large have failed.

> In view of the consistently poor results that these diversification efforts have yielded in the past and the extreme reluctance of the company managements to invest substantial amounts of their own funds in these ventures [government subsidies to do commercial work] would seem to offer little encouragement.[16]

What are the consequences of the inability and unwillingness of the major arms producers to diversify into civilian markets and the political power exercised by these contractors and the banks that have helped finance them? On the one hand, the profit rate in this branch of the state sector generally has been higher than the "normal" rate throughout the economy. And on the other, when military contracts are withdrawn or reduced and the arms manufacturers suffer temporary losses, the government typically moves in with new subsidies or loan-underwriting programs. The most dramatic case is the $250 million government-guaranteed loan extended to Lockheed by a consortium of banks.

Needless to say, the arms contractors and the Pentagon are so interrelated as to constitute in many respects an entity—

the military-industrial complex. This interrelationship works to strengthen both sides of the complex. But the Pentagon itself has become relatively autonomous. Vernon Dibble writes,

> Like all large corporations, it seeks to expand, and to reach out for monopoly control over its environment. It sets up or takes over subsidiary corporations like nonprofit think tanks. It diversifies its products [which] now include not only weapons, strategic theories, and military skills. They also include ideological indoctrination, social research, . . . social work, and . . . "advanced educational and medical techniques.[17]

Summarizing the extent and scope of the complex, Dibble defines the *garrison state* as

> (1) a large and powerful military that penetrates deeply into civilian life; of (2) the great importance of civilians in military affairs, the increasing resemblance between military officers and civilian executives in politics and business, and the greater contact and cooperation between officers and civilians in politics, in science, and in business; such that (3) the traditional boundaries between civilian and military society break down; and (4) the military are blended into an alliance with government and with large corporations. . . .[18]

Thus huge cost overruns and waste are not uncommon. Over $10 billion was spent in the 1950s and 1960s for weapons and hardware that never reached the production stage (over $3.5 billion went for military aircraft).[19]

The third factor that can be expected to maintain current levels of spending is that technological advance in monopoly sector civilian production is dependent on a large and growing military scientific and technological establishment. Historically, the military often has been the medium for the modernization of civilian production. The classic examples are Prussia and imperial Japan. At the end of the eighteenth century, Prussia devoted over 70 percent of the national budget to the military, in part because private industry lagged in adopting and developing new techniques.[20] Even today some Japanese industrialists believe that rearmament is needed to advance technology in the private sector.[21]

In the United States the military is politically the most acceptable sphere for the development of technology beyond private capital's technical and/or financial capabilities. As economic growth becomes increasingly dependent on new products and production process, the military's role in supplying technology for nonmilitary uses is expanded.[22] Some of the major growth industries are in the state sector in whole or part (e.g., electronics, computers, scientific instruments) and directly or indirectly owe their expansion to militarism and war. To this degree, military R&D must be considered forms of social investment, not social expenses (although in terms of supplying capital to industry, total military spending must be considered primarily an effect, not a cause, of accumulation in the monopoly sector). In turn, the civilian development of military technology under the auspices of monopoly corporations and the universities and private R&D firms augments military requirements still further and activates new military R&D and production. For example, originally developed to power the first battleships, the dynamo later found a market in urban lighting, was improved by civilian engineers, and finally was reintroduced into military production at a higher level of efficiency. The story of the development of aircraft, atomic power, plastics, electronics, and other innovations is very similar.

For all of these reasons Congress has little real power to determine the level and composition of military spending and the capitalist class has little desire to do so (although it does have the power). As the CED wrote early in the 1960s, "we have . . . urged the expenditure of *whatever funds are determined to be needed* for defense purposes by competent and responsible authorities."[23] As for Congress, Administration military appropriations bills are routinely passed (and congressmen do not even have the right to vote for or against particular military spending programs). Thus, military spending probably will increase—even if at the same (or somewhat slower) rate as the GNP. Military R&D spending (including space and atomic energy R&D), which increased from less than $1 billion in 1950 to about $7 billion by the mid-1960s, also is likely to expand.[24] Although both military and civilian employment in the armed forces have declined, appropriations will probably rise because of the shift to a full-volunteer army and the need to offer pay scales that attract and keep technically competent military personnel. Present and future wars of national liberation will compel the United States to continue to augment "conventional" and counterinsurgency forces. And finally, failure to achieve a real détente with the Soviet Union (and thus check Soviet influence and power in the northern tier of Africa, the Mideast, and India) will compel the militarists and capitalist class to keep up spending on nuclear strike and counterstrike capabilities. The arms treaty negotiated by the

Nixon Administration with the Soviet Union in 1972 provides a ceiling on the number of nuclear missiles and warheads, not on military spending. Thus, the Pentagon and Nixon himself on his return from Russia in 1972 were quick to point out that the treaty cannot be expected to liberate funds from the defense budget for civilian programs (i.e., the social-industrial complex). The government will spend billions to replace and modernize existing missiles, warheads, submarines, and so on. In fact, after signing the treaty, Nixon requested that Congress raise the military budget for fiscal 1973 by $6.3 billion. In I. F. Stone's words

> superiority is still the basic doctrine of the U.S. arms program. As Nixon told Congress on his return from Moscow, "no power on earth" will be allowed to become "stronger than the United States of America in the future. This is the only national defense posture which can ever be acceptable to the United States." The doctrine was stated more explicitly in Laird's latest defense posture statement: "An assessment of the future defense needs of the United States must include a program to assure our continued technological superiority." That spells perpetual arms race, since the other side—irrespective of any new cooperation in trade or other matters—cannot lag too far behind for fear we may be developing a first strike capacity.[25]

## SURPLUS POPULATION AND THE WELFARE STATE

Poverty and government relief programs also are inherent features of capitalist development. Capitalism is in part the history of peasants and farmers, home-workers, petty craftsmen and tradesmen, and others forced into poverty by the advance of capitalist agriculture, factory production, mass retailing, and so on; in part the history of industries and entire regions becoming economically impoverished as a result of changes in technology and market forces; in part the history of poverty generated by recessions and depressions and by particular industrial and occupational structures that confine some people to low-income, unstable employment.

Capitalism is also in part the history of state welfare policies and programs. Government relief dates back at least to the early sixteenth century, and in general outline it has not changed. In their influential study of the modern welfare system Piven and Cloward write,

THE FISCAL CRISIS OF THE STATE

The key to an understanding of relief-giving is in the functions it serves for the larger economic and political order, for relief is a secondary and supportive institution. Historical evidence suggests that relief arrangements are initiated or expanded during the occasional outbreaks of civil disorder produced by mass unemployment, and are then abolished or contracted when political stability is restored. . . . [E]xpansive relief policies are designed to mute civil disorder, and restrictive ones to reinforce work norms. In other words, relief policies are cyclical—liberal or restrictive depending on the problems of regulation in the larger society with which government must contend.[26]

Unrestrained capital accumulation and technological change create three general and related economic and social imbalances. First, capitalist development imposes great stresses and strains on local and regional economies; second, capitalist growth generates imbalances between various industries and sectors of the economy (particularly, the monopoly and competitive sectors); third, accumulation and technical change reproduce inequalities in the distribution of wealth and income. These imbalances (once described by Eric Hobsbawn as "the rhythm of social disruption") not only are integral to capitalist development, but also are considered by the business classes to be a sign of "healthy growth and change." Furthermore, the forces of the marketplace, far from ameliorating the imbalances, normally magnify them because of the multiplier effects of changes in demand on production.

These imbalances were also present in earlier phases of capitalism. Modern capitalism, like nineteenth-century capitalism, is unplanned. But the modern version differs in two fundamental respects, which explains why permanent subsidies to the poor are budgetary phenomena attributable to the growth of monopoly capitalism. First, an economy dominated by giant corporations operating in monopolistic industries tends to generate more inequalities than a more competitive economy. The source of inequality is monopolistic price fixing. Shortages and surpluses of individual commodities now manifest themselves in the form of social imbalances. For example, a decline in the auto industry is not followed by lower prices and wages, but by increased unemployment. In addition, the national (and, increasingly, the international) character of monopoly sector markets means that economic and social imbalances are no longer confined to a particular region, industry, or occupation, but rather tend to spread throughout the economy. Finally, federal policies for economic stability and growth soften the effects of economic recessions and lead to the survival of inefficient businesses—and hence in the long run to the need for more subsidies.

The second difference between competitive and monopoly capitalism concerns the way in which economic and social imbalances are perceived and acted upon. Competitive capitalists exercise relatively little control over prices, production, and distribution. Unemployment, regional underdevelopment, and industrial bankruptcy appear to be "natural" concomitants of "free markets." Moreover, the level and structure of wages are determined competitively; individual capitalists are not able to develop and implement a wage policy, and thus the impact of wage changes on the volume and composition of production, the deployment of technology, and unemployment appears to be the consequence of impersonal forces beyond human control. Because imbalances of all kinds are accepted by capital and the state as natural and even desirable, and because the ideology of capital is the ruling ideology, the inevitability and permanence of imbalances and transitory crises tend to be accepted by society.

With the evolution of monopoly capitalism and the growth of the proletariat, this fatalistic attitude undergoes profound changes. Business enterprise gradually develops economic and political techniques of production and market control. Oligopolistic corporations gradually adopt what Baran and Sweezy have termed a "live-and-let-live attitude" toward each other.[27] In this setting the imbalances generated by capitalist development begin to be attributed to the conscious policies of large corporations, big unions, and government agencies rather than to impersonal market forces. Corporate capital, small-scale capital, and the working class alike begin to fix responsibility for the specific policies on particular human agents.

The central premise of the consensus between monopoly capital and organized labor is that a rapidly growing GNP is the best insurance against labor unrest and militancy, which disrupt the production process. The bigger the national income pie, the less bitter the conflicts arising over its distribution. Similarly, it has been taken for granted that overseas expansion and the deepening of the domestic market are the best insurance against social and political disorder.

In practice, this idea has not worked out as the power elite and corporate policy planners once hoped. The general reason is that the gains from technical progress and economic growth have not been distributed equitably, but rather have been concentrated in the hands of the large corporations dominating the monopoly sector, together with the professional, technical, white-collar, and blue-collar strata in the monopoly and state sectors. More specifically, there is no automatic mechanism by which competitive sector workers share in the gains from technical progress in proportion to their numbers and needs. On the contrary, precisely because technological change generates a relative surplus population, capital accumulation in the monopoly sector tends to create even more poverty. Similarly, there is no mechanism insuring that small businessmen and farmers in the competitive sector get their "fair share" of the increments to national income attributable to technical progress and capital accumulation.

Furthermore, the benefits of social investment and social consumption tend to flow primarily to monopoly capital and organized labor, but the costs devolve to competitive sector capital and labor. In other words, not only does the traditional functioning of the monopoly sector impoverish the competitive sector but also the growth of social investment and social consumption tends to intensify the contradictions between the two sectors. Specifically, from the standpoint of the monopoly industries it is more rational to combine technical laborpower with capital-intensive technology than to combine unskilled or semiskilled laborpower with capital-saving technology because the costs of training technical laborpower are met by taxes paid by competitive sector capital and labor. Thus, the size of the surplus population in relation to the monopoly sector work force does not play an important role in regulating monopoly sector wage rates (in particular, in the technical/white-collar strata, because unskilled laborpower does not compete with technical laborpower). The effect is that in the long run (although not during short-run periods of abnormally high demand for labor) the surplus population grows in size because of the expansion of the monopoly sector. "The lower classes," in Joseph Pechman's blunt words, "have not been able to hold their own in the private economy." [28]

Unable to gain employment in the monopoly industries by offering their laborpower at lower than going wage rates (and victimized by sexism and racism), and unemployed, underemployed, or employed at low wages in competitive industries, the surplus population increasingly becomes dependent on the state. Welfare programs of one kind or another are financed by appropriating tax funds from the better-paid monopoly and state sector workers and channeling these funds directly or indirectly into the hands of the surplus population, together with the state agencies, bureaucrats, professionals, and others who administer welfare programs. In other words, the real income of monopoly sector workers is increased by the socialization of the costs of social investment and social consumption, and then reduced by the taxation and/or inflation required to finance the social expenses of production made necessary by this very same monopoly sector growth. In this sense, the state budget can be seen as a complex mechanism that redistributes income backward and forward within the working class—all to maintain industrial and social-political harmony, expand productivity, and accelerate accumulation and profits in the monopoly sector.[29]

## POLITICAL STRUGGLE
## AND THE MODERN WELFARE SYSTEM

Like workers in the monopoly industries, the surplus labor force requires more and more state-financed social services and benefits. Unlike organized labor, they are forced to struggle for an increased share of the budget largely alone. Monopoly capital has no direct economic interest in their welfare (their consumption levels are not a form of capital), and while organized labor favors any plan to put a floor under wages (e.g., minimum wage laws, etc.), it is less eager to foot the welfare bill. As long as the structures of racist and sexist institutions are intact, the surplus population will not be able to compete for the better monopoly sector jobs. And because small-scale capital wants wages kept low it will continue to oppose social programs that increase competitive sector wages.

As a consequence of the legitimization crisis of the state and the deterioration of competitive sector workers' standard of living during the past two decades or so (a period of general economic expansion), increasing numbers of surplus workers have become militant in their opposition to budgetary priorities that favor the monopoly sector. National movements and organizations of black and other minorities, women, welfare rights groups, and local insurgency movements and community groups struggling against local welfare, health, and other bureaucracies have compelled the federal, state, and local governments to broaden welfare standards, develop new welfare-related programs, increase intergovernmental grants, and so on. For example, it was only after the black rebellions in the cities in the mid-1960s that the Federal Housing Administration promised to underwrite urban housing loans and to guarantee a minimum of 90 percent of urban housing investments made by insurance companies.[30] Of much greater importance in the long run is the emergence of a new sense of "people's rights"—especially, the right to material survival. In Richard Cloward's words, there is a "vast pool of people in the cities eligible for relief but not getting it." [31]

The awakening of the surplus population has led to a proliferation of state programs designed both to repress insurgency movements and groups that refuse to be coopted and to "cool" these movements and organizations.[32] The welfare system has vastly expanded with the development of HEW, HUD, OEO, and other federal agencies and thousands of new local, state, and quasi-state agencies. And subsidies, particularly for education, retraining, child care, housing, transportation, and health (mainly Medicare and Medicaid) have increased. Public assistance payments, which until the 1960s were less than 2 percent of the federal budget, have mounted sharply in recent years because eligibility provisions have been liberalized, more people have taken advantage of their rights,[33] and benefits have been raised.

At state and local levels, however, bitter political opposition to expand welfare and social programs for minorities and the poor persists. One reason is that politically influential small businessmen and farmers in the competitive sector need a sizable labor reserve to keep wages low and profits up. Another reason is that monopoly capital has few programs at the state or local level that reflect its class priorities. Still another is the general opposition among professionals, white-collar and monopoly sector workers, and other taxpayers to welfare. Finally, local and state governments have resisted increases in welfare and actually slashed welfare budgets in the past two or three years because of the fiscal crisis. Although the federal government underwrites well over one-half of welfare payments, state and local governments still control the welfare programs and strive to keep a lid on benefits. Even during the late 1950s and early 1960s, when the fiscal crisis (and social crisis) was much less severe, state and local governments generally tried to keep welfare programs to a minimum. For example, a study of Illinois state finances showed that up to 1965 every state agency receiving federal grants had expanded—with one notable exception, the Public Aid Department.[34]

The resistance of state and local governments to welfare spending precisely when welfare needs have increased by leaps and bounds has forced the national government to attempt to redefine the entire issue and to forge new programs that will meet minimum needs and satisfy insurgency movements. Until recently, corporate leaders viewed the wages system as the central (if not only) mode of social discipline and were convinced that the growth of a permanent welfare system and bureaucracy would undermine the wage system and social discipline. It was feared, for example, that control of public funds would gradually slip into the hands of "sentimental" welfare workers and even the poor themselves. No better expression of the traditional position of business and the national government can be found than President Roosevelt's message to Congress in 1935:

> The lessons of history confirmed by the evidence immediately before me show conclusively that continued dependence upon upon relief induces a spiritual and moral disintegration fundamentally destructive to the national fiber [meaning "capitalist social order"]. To dole out relief . . . is to administer a narcotic, a subtle destroyer of the human spirit. It is inimical to the dictates of sound policy. It is in violation of the traditions of America.[35]

Guided by this tradition, local, state, and federal government officials concentrated during most of the 1960s on devising more stringent controls and getting people off the welfare rolls and into "legitimate" employment. The first shot was fired by the city manager of Newburgh, New York, who tried to clamp down on "welfare chiselers" in 1961. Almost without exception the national press endorsed Newburgh's welfare "reforms" (later, Newburgh's eighteenth-century approach to the issue was declared illegal by the courts).[36] But research suggested that fraud was a peripheral problem. For example, a 1963 HEW study found that less than 5 percent of welfare recipients were ineligible and that many of these were on the rolls because of administrative errors.[37] In fact, as welfare and related social programs grew during the 1960s and early 1970s, it became increasingly clear that it was not the welfare client who was defrauding the government, but rather many of the businessmen and professionals who indirectly or directly received state contracts and grants. Under the Medicaid program, for example, an estimated $1 billion went down the drain in New York City alone as a result of

> medical groups sending patients from one practitioner to another for additional services which weren't needed. Private nursing homes [that] billed the city for patients who had been dead. . . . Physical therapists [who] were paid for treating nursing home patients on days when the therapists weren't even at the home in question. . . . Foot doctors [who] moved from the suburbs

into New York City slums "to take advantage of the lucrative Medicaid practices." . . . Druggists [who] sent in bills for double the prescription they filled, or for more expensive drugs than they actually provided. . . . Dentists [who] charged the city for bridgework never constructed and pulled teeth unnecessarily to make room for expensive false teeth.[38]

And as a result of the FHA's program to insure mortgages on inner-city homes,

> Slumlords take over decaying buildings and make slight surface repairs; corrupt or misguided FHA officials overassess the property value; then an unsuspecting black family purchases the home. After a short time the houses prove so decrepit they are abandoned and condemned, leaving the landlord with a fat profit, the family without a home, and the Federal government holding a lease on the property.[39]

There also have been numerous instances of "unethical" business practices and outright fraud in laborpower training and development and education programs.

Partly because the welfare-fraud thesis had been discredited, the federal government began to propagate the idea that the welfare problem was attributable to the absence of employment opportunities and day care centers for mothers who were heads of families and the lack of the "right attitudes and values" toward society in general and wage work in particular. In 1962, HEW Secretary Ribicoff attempted to develop reforms that would "rehabilitate and restore" the poor to "productive roles in society"—mainly by finding ways to push welfare mothers into the labor force.[40] Because over 70 percent of children receiving welfare under the Aid For Dependent Children (AFDC) program were (and are) under twelve, "human resource development" programs and child-care facilities, it was hoped, would significantly reduce the ranks of what one corporate liberal group called "high cost citizens" and limit the growth of urban districts with an "increasing absence of self-supporting taxpayers." [41] In other words, for the first time the federal bureaucracy recognized that GNP and total employment and poverty and the welfare rolls could grow simultaneously. Later in the decade came an implicit recognition that poverty is an integral feature of the capitalist system and that welfare expenditures and income maintenance should be seen not as temporary expedients needed during times of recession and depression but as permanent features of the political economy.[42]

SOCIAL EXPENSES OF PRODUCTION

Thus, the national state began to experiment with various laborpower-development and job-creation schemes. Job creation in the state sector was not a new idea (tens of thousands of unemployed workers were hired by the Works Progress Administration and the Public Works Administration during the 1930s. But laborpower training for the poor, a relatively modern conception, has received the most emphasis (in fact, the 1972 budget by the Nixon Administration did not include funds for public employment). The 1964 Manpower Development and Training Act serves two purposes. First, it subsidizes OJT programs (OJT spending in relation to total MDTA outlays has risen from less than 10 percent in 1964 to over 50 percent currently) in both the competitive and monopoly sectors, but chiefly the former. Second, MDTA itself trains workers (directly or via state contractors) for the competitive sector and low-paid state sector jobs. "The largest government training operation as implemented under the Manpower Development and Training Act," writes Jerome Joffe, "has primarily provided training for low-skill high-turnover jobs in both the rising sectors in the central city, e.g., nurse's aide, and the traditional low-wage industry occupations, e.g., sewing machine operator." [43] In effect the federal government has been attempting to transform social expense outlays (welfare) into social capital for the competitive sector.

The limits of current MDTA programs are clear. It does socialize some of the costs of laborpower training for small-scale capital (and thus has won support from small business), but it fails even to begin to solve the problem of poverty. Precisely because newly trained workers are sent to the low-income competitive sector (and to low-wage state sector jobs), the problem is not job availability, but a living income for poor families. Further, HEW itself estimated in 1968 that less than 2.5 percent of all welfare recipients could work if there were sufficient day care facilities. [44]

Because traditional housing, welfare, and MDTA-type programs cannot significantly relieve poverty the federal government has underwritten health and food outlays directly and is making plans to underwrite poor people's housing (via a system of housing allowances which would give a poor family an average of $900 yearly to be applied to housing, allowing the family to shop in the market for its own shelter). [45] Of far greater importance in the long run is the system of income allowances (negative income tax proposals) which would grant permanent concessions to the poor. One plan put forth by the Nixon Administration would guarantee a minimum income of $2400 yearly for welfare families and graduated subsidies for the working poor. A close approximation to the Nixon plan is a bill passed by the House in 1971 (HR 1) which would abolish welfare entirely, except for the aged, disabled, and families with preschool children. For welfare recipients HR 1 would guarantee a parent employment paying almost $2500 annually in the private sector or in an expanded federal government job corps. HR 1 would double the number of people eligible for welfare and would cost over $15 billion the first year. But in the long run the sponsors of HR 1 hope that tens of thousands of people would become wholly or partly self-supporting because of new training programs and the growth of public service (i.e., social-industrial complex) jobs in education, health, environmental protection, public safety, and related areas. Experimental programs to achieve total social control are already in operation in a number of states; they seek to

> "modify" the "behavior" of the poor. Through a "point system" farcically called "Incentives for Independence" recipients can win a point, worth $12.50, every two weeks if their children work in so-called community projects; if they attend school regularly, "cooperating with the teacher"; if they join a group such as the Boy or Girl Scouts. Parents and adults can also win points. A mother with children whose father has gone can get $12.50 every two weeks if she tells the state agency where he is so the agency can force him to support the children. Two points a month are also won for "Improvement in housing standards by self clean-up or self-repair of dwelling.[46]

Whether systems of social control such as "Incentives for Independence" and welfare reforms that tie grants to work (including programs designed to subsidize capital in the competitive sector by footing a portion of the wage bill directly) will succeed and develop further without undermining social discipline and the ideology of hard work (i.e., the fear of economic insecurity) remains to be seen. As Piven and Cloward showed, relief payments expand during periods of social and political disorder—and are contracted when disorder is reduced (e.g., since the black rebellions of the mid-1960s). But social and political order normally is restored only when poverty is reduced by an economic upswing. As we have seen, however, one of the sources of poverty is precisely the expansion of the monopoly sector. In the last analysis, therefore, the social expenses of production are likely to continue to grow. It would appear that one basic condition for the political containment of the surplus population as well as the leveling out (or reduction) of welfare spending is the full development of the social-industrial complex—including urban and rural social and economic redevelopment. And whether the social-industrial complex can become a reality is a political question, which will be considered in Chapter 9.

## SURPLUS CAPITALISTS
## AND SOCIALISM FOR THE RICH

The final expense of stabilizing the capitalist social order consists of the funds needed to keep local and regional capital securely within the corporate liberal political consensus at home and to maintain the client ruling classes abroad. The latter take the form of foreign aid, particularly balance-of-payments assistance through the International Monetary Fund; World Bank and Agency for International Development (AID) loans which strengthen Third World export industries and buttress the rule of local bourgeoisies whose economic interests are based on export production, processing, and trade; and outright military and nonmilitary grants-in-aid.

More corporate capital must forge alliances with traditional agricultural interests (especially those of the southern oligarchy) and small-scale capital. The votes of southern and midwestern farm congressmen and other representatives bound to local and regional economic interests (e.g., shipping, soft coal mining, fishing) are indispensable for the legislative victories of corporate liberal policies. It is no less important that state legislators, municipal governments, and local newspapers, TV stations, and other opinion makers support urban renewal, education, health, housing, and transportation.

The political support of small businessmen, farmers, and other local and regional interests is extremely costly. Billions of dollars of direct and indirect subsidies are required by the farmers, especially the large growers who dominate the farm associations and many local and state governments. The first New Deal farm plan—the so-called domestic allotment plan—was introduced to quell a midwestern farm revolt.[47] Since the 1930s, price support, acreage restriction, credit, soil conservation, and rural redevelopment and rehabilitation programs—all designed to conservatize the farmers—have proliferated.

> It was soon discovered that these programs were, on the whole, more helpful to the "top third" of the farmers than they were to the "lower two-thirds." . . . The small landowners, tenants, sharecroppers, wage hands, and migrant workers who composed the majority of the farm population received only indirect

THE FISCAL CRISIS OF THE STATE

benefits and, in some cases, were actually harmed by these programs.[48]

Today, large commercial farmers make up less than 15 percent of the farm population, but receive an estimated 63 percent of farm subsidies.[49]

 Subsidies in various forms—particularly allowances to finance the relocation of small business—are also required to placate small-scale capital adversely affected by corporate-oriented urban renewal programs. The Small Business Administration has an extensive financial-aid program, including a policy of underwriting small banks. The fishing industry receives capital grants for new boat construction. And the federal government pays the difference between the cost of constructing ships in the United States and the estimated costs in foreign shipyards, which amounts to roughly 50 percent of total construction costs. Further, the state expends about $125 million annually to help pay for merchant shipping operating costs.[50] Finally, stockpiling of "strategic materials," offering the textile industry favorable buying prices, and the licensing of various occupations also fall wholly or partly into the category of political subsidies.

 In all urban centers of the underdeveloped U.S. economic colonies and semicolonies there is a vast and growing impoverished population which cannot find employment in the capital-intensive branch plants and subsidiaries of the international corporations. Because of this increasingly restless, potentially revolutionary population corporate and government leaders charged with administering the empire call for more "foreign aid," loans, grants, and technical assistance. The general aim of foreign aid programs is to maintain the world capitalist social order and to create the conditions for its further expansion. The need for welfare programs, wars on poverty, foreign aid, and other ameliorative programs knows no limit, or, more accurately, is limited only by the boundaries on the application of modern technology and the spread of capitalism itself.

# NOTES AND REFERENCES

1. In the nineteenth century, private capital paid for a relatively large portion of social expenses. On the one hand, private police and other repressive forces (including private armies in the underdeveloped capitalist countries) were not uncommon. On the other hand, the welfare system was effectively a system of private charity. In the second decade of the twentieth century, monopoly capital attempted to pay for its own social expenses through a system known as *welfare capitalism.* Welfare capitalism failed because no one corporation or industry could either plan effectively or finance a system designed to maintain harmony in the social and political orders. In fact, monopoly capital cannot afford programs necessary to maintain harmony in the relations of production.

2. Admittedly this is an awkward and contradictory term. Yet the national state is not exclusively a warfare state, nor certainly completely a welfare state It is both. On the one side, militarists and imperialists dominate the Pentagon, the military-industrial complex, etc. On the other, corporate liberals and reformers are influential in the welfare agencies (e.g., HUD and HEW). Because of its contradictory character no single word can describe the state adequately.

3. Military spending (including space and foreign affairs) in 1955, 1965, and 1972 was $42.3, $59.3, and $85 6 billion, respectively. "Income maintenance" spending in the same years was $15.1, $34.6, and $84.6 billion, respectively (however, a large portion of these outlays was in the nature of social consumption, not social expenses). Between 1964 and 1972, social expenses in the form of public assistance and Medicare and Medicaid rose from $3.3 to $9.8 billion and from $0.2 to $12 4 billion, respectively. It should be added that the Johnson and Nixon Administrations financed the increased military spending mainly through inflation (i.e., by the state's borrowing from itself) in order not to jeopardize congressional funding for domestic programs.

4. This is not to say that militarism and imperialism are unique to capitalism. If imperialism is understood to mean "the extension of political power by one state over another, [then] all through the sixty centuries of more or less recorded history" imperialism has been a principal feature in human relations [Margery Perham, *The Colonial Reckoning* (London: 1963), p. 1]. But militarism and imperialism have a systematic character in capitalist development. The present author has summarized the differences between precapitalist and capitalist expansionism as follows:

> [P]recapitalist and capitalist societies differ in five general ways: first, in precapitalist societies, economic expansion was irregular, unsystematic, not integral to normal economic activity. In capitalist societies, foreign trade and investment rightly are considered to be the "engines of economic growth." Expansion is necessary to maintain the rhythm of economic activity in the home or metropolitan economy and has an orderly, methodical, permanent character. Second, in precapitalist societies, the economic gains from expansion were windfall goals, frequently taking the form of merely sporadic plunder. In capitalist societies, profits from overseas trade and investment are an integral part of national income, and considered in a matter-of-fact manner. Third, in precapitalist societies, plunder acquired in the course of expansion often was consumed in the field by the conquering armies, leaving the home economy unaffected. In capitalist societies, exploited territories are fragmented and integrated into the structure of the metropolitan economy. Fourth, in precapitalist societies debate within the

THE FISCAL CRISIS OF THE STATE

ruling classes ordinarily revolved around the question whether or not to expand. In capitalist societies, ruling class debates normally turn on the issue, what is the best way to expand. Last, in relation to colonialism, pre-capitalist and capitalist societies also differ in a fundamental way. In the former, colonialism (land seizure, colonist settlement, etc.) was the only mode of control which the metropolitan power effectively could exercise over the satellite region . . . [C]apitalist societies have developed alternative, indirect, and more complex forms of control.

(James O'Connor, *The Meaning of Economic Imperialism*, The Radical Education Project, Ann Arbor, undated, pp. 1-2.) We also tried to show that industrial capitalist expansion is more aggressive and universal than mercantilist capitalist expansion (ibid., pp. 2-3).

5. The internationalization of capital is documented in Harry Magdoff, *The Age of Imperialism* (New York: 1969). A summary of theories of foreign expansion based on analysis of the monopolistic structure of large-scale corporations can be found in *The Meaning of Economic Imperialism*, op. cit., pp. 11-12. The economic theory of why twentieth-century U.S. imperialism is more aggressive and universal than nineteenth-century British imperialism also can be found in this article (ibid., pp. 16-17).

6. James O'Connor, "International Corporations and Economic Underdevelopment," *Science and Society*, 34:1 (Spring 1970), 47-48.

7. Stephan J. Scheinberg, "The Development of Corporate Labor Policy, 1900-1940" (Ph.D. diss., University of Wisconsin, 1966).

8. The seminal work on the history of U.S corporate capitalism during this period is William A. Williams, "The Age of Corporate Capitalism," *The Contours of American History* (Cleveland, Ohio: 1961); also see his *The Tragedy of American Diplomacy* (New York: 1962). A recent work by Ronald Radosh documents the role of labor leaders in foreign policy [*American Labor and United States Foreign Policy* (New York: 1969)].

9. The role of the farmers is taken up in William A. Williams, *The Roots of the Modern American Empire* (New York: 1969).

10. Robert Freeman Smith, "American Foreign Relations, 1920-1942," in Barton J. Bernstein, ed., *Towards a New Past: Dissenting Essays in American History* (New York: 1969); Lloyd C. Gardner, *Economic Aspects of New Deal Diplomacy* (Madison, Wisc.: 1964). For a summary and comparative study of conservative, liberal, and radical interpretations of the U.S. foreign policy, see Walter Cohen, "U.S. Foreign Policy: A Radical Study Guide," *Pacific Research and World Empire Telegram*, 3:3 (March/April/May 1972).

11. U.S. Senate Committee on Foreign Relations, "Arms Sales and Foreign Policy," in Seymour Melman, ed., *The War Economy of the United States* (New York: 1971), p. 34.

12. William Baldwin, *The Structure of the Defense Market, 1955-1964* (Durham, N.C.: 1967), p. 9.

13. Murray Wiedenbaum, "The Defense-Space Complex: Impact on Whom?" *Challenge*, 13-14. (April 1965), 46.

14. Michael Reich and David Finkelhor, "Capitalism and the Military-Industrial Complex: The Obstacles to Conversion," *Review of Radical Political Economics*, 2:4 (1970).

15. *The Structure of the Defense Market*, op. cit., p. 17.

16. Murray Wiedenbaum, review of *The Modern Public Sector: New Ways of Doing the Government's Business, American Economic Review*, 58 (June 1968), 626.

# SOCIAL EXPENSES OF PRODUCTION

**17.** Vernon K. Dibble, "The Garrison Society," in *The War Economy of the United States,* op. cit., p. 181.

**18.** Ibid.

**19.** *Economic Analysis and the Efficiency of Government,* Hearings before the Subcommittee on Economy in Government of the Joint Economic Committee, 91st Congress, Part V, Supersonic Transportation Development, May 7, 11, 12, 1970, p. 951. I. F. Stone provides an interesting sidelight on the power of the Pentagon:

> When Kennedy and Khrushchev finally got the nuclear test ban treaty in 1963, Kennedy had to sign a virtual treaty with the Pentagon assuring it that testing would go on at a greater pace than ever underground. . . . The Pentagon is looking for similar assurances this time. At the same House Appropriations Committee hearing on June 5 [1972], Admiral Moorer, chairman of the Joint Chiefs of Staff, "suggested," according to the *New York Times* report the next day, "that the Defense Department's acceptance of the arms control agreement [signed by Nixon in Moscow] might depend on the Administration's approval of modernization of the offensive strategic forces." This is how our own military barons bargain in the neo-feudal system of Washington. [*New York Review of Books,* June 29, 1972.]

**20.** Tsunesaburo Tokoyama, "Bread or Gun," *Public Finance,* 9:4 (1954), 383.

**21.** According to Japanese industrialist Yuichi Yuasa, "many phases of the defense industry require a high degree of technology and can be expected to pull up the technological level of Japanese industries in general" (John C. Roberts, "Remilitarization of Japan," *Nation,* December 19, 1959, p. 469).

**22.** Paul Rosen (Baran), "Militarism and American Technological and Scientific Progress," *Monthly Review* 9 (March 1957); Phillip Morrison, "The Innovation Industry," *Monthly Review* 11 (July/August 1959).

**23.** CED, *Growth and Taxes: Steps for 1961* (New York, February 1961), p. 6 (italics added).

**24.** Seymour Melman, *Our Depleted Society* (New York: 1965), p. 77. In a series of works including *Pentagon Capitalism* (New York: 1970) and *The War Economy of the United States* (op. cit.), Melman has argued that modern America has seen the development of a new ruling group defined more by its relations to the means of destruction than by its relation to the means of production. This is not the place to analyze his thesis, but it should be pointed out that from a Marxist point of view the state budget is merely the way that surplus value (and thus wealth and power) is appropriated Surplus value still has to be produced, and thus those who own the means of production are in a decisive position to control the production of wealth and power (as opposed to its distribution). Furthermore, the same people ultimately exercise control over the major corporations in the monopoly sector, the big banks and financial intermediaries, and the military contracting firms. In short, militarism in America is based on forces that run much broader and deeper than the development of a "new class."

**25.** *New York Review of Books,* op. cit., p. 12. The biggest single offsetting factors are the attempt by the U.S. to get Germany and Japan to direct more of their resources into military production and by the Sino-Soviet split, which the Nixon Administration brilliantly exploited, and which effectively keeps down the U.S. arms budget. We must make clear, however, that the popularly expected "Vietnam dividend" (the moneys saved when and if the Vietnam War ends) is a complete myth [e.g., see Dorothy Brockhoff, "Mr. Wiedenbaum Goes to Washington," *Washington University Magazine,* 40:2 (Winter 1970), 5]. In 1969,

Charles Schultz estimated that taking into account weapons systems already approved and the expected costs of improving them, a $100 billion Vietnam "dividend" (added to the anticipated increases in taxes due to economic growth) would be reduced to $30 billion by 1974 [*The Progressive*, 37:6 (June 1969), 41–42)]. By 1972, establishment economists conceded that the "dividend" would be zero.

26. Francis Fox Piven and Richard A. Cloward, *Regulating the Poor: The Functions of Public Welfare* (New York: 1971), p. xiii.

27. Paul A. Baran and Paul M. Sweezy, *Monopoly Capital* (New York: 1966), p. 48.

28. Joseph A. Pechman, "The Rich, the Poor, and the Taxes They Pay," *The Public Interest*, 17 (Fall 1969), 25.

29. Schultz et al. write that "as social insurance grew, the need for welfare assistance was expected to diminish." [Charles L. Schultz et al., *Setting National Priorities: The 1972 Budget* (Washington, D.C.: The Brookings Institution, 1972), p. 73.] Musgrave also writes that "there is every reason to expect that . . . the ratio of transfers (including expenditures for low-income-oriented merit goods) will tend to decline with rising income." Many liberal economists and commentators have expected the growth of the education budget to reduce the welfare rolls—and poverty in general. These predictions, expectations, and hopes were unrealistic because liberal theory lacks a scientific methodology for studying and comprehending modern capitalist development. [Richard Musgrave, "The Voluntary Exchange Theory of Public Finance," *The Quarterly Journal of Economics*, 53 (February 1939), 82.]

30. *Business Week,* July 20, 1968.

31. *Wall Street Journal*, April 24, 1969.

32. One standard orthodox argument is that the growth of social welfare programs is attributable to economic growth and the progressive income tax. For example, according to H. Wold, increases in tax revenues in relation to national income have made it possible to finance social insurance plans that could not have been introduced otherwise because of taxpayer resistance ["Economic and Financial Aspects of Social Insurance Schemes," *Public Finance*, 5:3 (1950), 240] This kind of argument ignores two factors: first, monopoly capital's need to expand social consumption as a form of capital; second, the reality of political threats to harmonious corporate rule. Wold tells us only that the state has the resources to finance social consumption and social expenses, not how the state got the resources nor why the state uses the resources to expand expenditures for these particular purposes.

33. Schultz, et al. (op. cit., p 138) have estimated that the proportion of poor people on welfare increased from 18 to almost 50 percent from 1966 to 1971 and that "between 1966 and 1970, total money payments for AFDC (federal, state, and local) rose from $1.8 billion to $4 8 billion, or by 27 percent a year" (ibid., p. 174). Schultz's explanation of this increase is a typical example of bankruptcy of liberal thought.

> Most of the increases occurred in the large industrial states. A variety of factors contributed to the increase—rising numbers of broken families, more liberal standards of eligibility, increases in the proportion of eligible persons applying for benefits, migration from the South to the North and from rural to urban areas. Rising unemployment contributed to further rapid increases in 1970. [Ibid.]

Needless to say, these are all proximate causes, not underlying reasons for the expansion of welfare. The underlying reasons are the growth of capitalist production and the struggles of the surplus population.

SOCIAL EXPENSES OF PRODUCTION                                173

**34.** Thomas J. Anton, *The Politics of State Expenditures in Illinois* (Urbana, Ill.: 1966), p. 259.

**35.** Quoted in Paul Jacobs, "America's Schizophrenic View of the Poor" (unpublished manuscript).

**36.** William B. Rollins and Bernard Lefkowitz, "Welfare a la Newburgh," *The Nation,* October 16, 1961.

**37.** *Wall Street Journal,* August 16, 1965.

**38.** *San Francisco Chronicle,* January 6, 1972.

**39.** Marc Allan Weiss, "A House Is Not a Home" (unpublished manuscript, 1972). Weiss continues: "The by-product of this process is that HUD is now the *largest* landowner in many central cities—over 240,000 units worth $2.4 billion. Through this ownership it will be much easier to assemble land for urban renewal. Once again racism is an ally of the regional planners."

**40.** *Wall Street Journal,* August 16, 1965

**41.** Advisory Commission on Intergovernmental Relations, *Fiscal Balance in the American Federal System,* Vol. I (Washington, D.C., October 1967), p. 4.

**42.** Throughout the 1960s, the number of welfare recipients rose by almost 10 percent yearly (*Wall Street Journal,* April 24, 1969). It should be added that the notion that unemployment and poverty are beyond any individual's control is a ruling-class idea that dates back to the early twentieth century. However, the revival of the idea in the 1960s was based not on the reality that unemployment and poverty are beyond any individual's control but on the reality of left and insurgency political forces.

**43.** Jerome Joffe, "The Limits of Urban Policy," *Review of Radical Political Economics,* 4:2 (Summer 1972), 101.

**44.** HEW, *Estimated Employability of Recipients of Public Assistance Money Payments* (Washington, D.C , July, 1968). In 1968, only 1 percent of welfare recipients were able-bodied men. Twenty-four percent were old age recipients; 8 percent were permanently and totally disabled; 50.3 percent were children; 2.9 percent were incapacitated parents in the home; 1 percent were blind. Only 13 percent were mothers (one-fifth were already in training).

**45.** Medicare and Medicaid (which increased state payments for health in relation to total health outlays from 25 percent to over one-third after 1966) and food stamps directly underwrite consumption.

**46.** Renée Blakkan, "New Welfare 'Incentives' Virtually Enslave the Poor," *Guardian,* October 27, 1971, p. 4.

**47.** This revolt was led by the Farm Holiday Association over the issues of foreclosures and low farm prices. See John L. Shover, *Cornbelt Rebellion: The Farmer's Holiday Association* (Urbana, Ill.: 1955).

**48.** Willard Range, "The Land and the Landless: Georgia Agriculture, 1920–1940," in Harry N. Scheiber, ed., *United States Economic History: Selected Readings* (New York: 1964), pp. 466–467

**49.** James O'Keefe, "The Effects of Price Support Programs on Low Income Farmers" (unpublished manuscript). Another estimate is that the "top 10 percent of farmowners received from 36 percent (tobacco) to 72 percent (sugarcane) of all price support payments" [Howard Wachtel, "Looking at Poverty from a Radical Perspective," *Review of Radical Political Economics,* 3:3 (Summer 1971), 12].

**50.** C. Lowell Harriss, "Subsidies in the United States," *Public Finance,* 16:3–4 (1961), 276.

:

# APPENDIX: THE SOCIAL EXPENSES
## OF ENVIRONMENTAL POLLUTION

The uncontrolled expansion of monopoly capital production creates another fiscal burden on the state: social expenses of private production—that is, outlays required to repair or prevent damage to the physical environment Automobile transportation is a major source of social expense: Oxygen is consumed; crop-and-animal-destroying smog is produced; rivers and oceans are polluted by lead additive gasolines; the land is fouled by the construction of freeways. The expenses of ameliorating environmental damage do not enter into the accounts of the auto industry, which seeks to minimize its own costs and maximize sales and profits. Other branches of the monopoly sector also pollute the air and water and poison animal and plant life. Many industries are unwilling voluntarily to treat toxic chemical waste or to develop sources of energy which will not, as fossil-fuels, pollute the air. Nor do the social expenses of consuming limited water resources figure into the accounts of monopoly capital. Of the approximately 25 trillion gallons of water used in the United States every day, over 13 trillion are used by industry and about 7 trillion by agriculture. All in all, industry is responsible for over 70 percent of all waste water and over two-thirds of suspended solids in the air. Between 40 and 60 percent of the waste loads treated by municipal sewage plants come from the roughly 300,000 industrial plants that dump their waste into municipal sewers.

Agribusiness generates still more pollution. To minimize crop losses (and thus costs) it uses chemicals harmful to crops, animals, water purity, and human life itself. Further, nonbiodegradable synthetic (e.g., plastic) consumer and capital goods create still more pollution.[1] For example, plastic containers reduce production costs, but the taxpayer gets the bill for burning or burying used containers. Last but not least, monopoly sector growth is largely based on new products and thus a rapid rate of product obsolescence and more waste and pollution.[2]

By and large, private capital refuses to bear the expenses of reducing or eliminating air and water pollution, conserving the soils, preserving forests, wilderness areas, and wildlife sanctuaries, and generally working to maintain ecological balances. In the past these expenses were almost completely ignored—at the cost of near-ruination of the environment. Few antipollution laws were on the books and those, more often than not, were ignored. Further, special interests frequently were able to "bend" the law. One classic case was the exemption of the Merrimack River from pollution control until 1946 because of the power of local textile, leather, and paper industries, all heavy polluters. Today, because of the increasingly social character of production and unplanned monopoly sector growth, pollution is threatening not only the ecological balance (and thus has generated a nationwide environmental movement), but also profitable capital accumulation itself, particularly in real estate, recreation, agriculture, and

SOCIAL EXPENSES OF PRODUCTION

other branches of the economy in which land, water, and air are essential resources to capital.[3]

Although some industries (e.g., the National Coal Association) continue to put out anti-anti-pollution propaganda and some labor unions have joined the battle against environmentalists and their allies,[4] the trend is toward stiffer antipollution legislation and environmental controls. More important from the standpoint of the fiscal crisis, the portion of the state budget devoted to reducing pollution has begun to increase at all levels of government. The state has begun to make antipollution subsidies available to private capital, as loans, guarantees, grants, tax-exempt bonds. The auto industry probably will receive subsidies to help finance the transition to the electric or fuel-cell car. And subsidies for public utilities to finance the transition to solar, nuclear, or sea energy will no doubt expand. Corporate farmers will insist on being "compensated" for crop losses arising from bans on DDT and other harmful chemicals. More federal funds will be spent to help regulate outdoor advertising, alleviate conditions in recreational areas, finance the costs of land purchase or condemnation, landscaping, and roadside redevelopment, and otherwise meet the expenses of "esthetic pollution." In short, there is developing a new "pollution-industrial complex." As Martin Gellen notes,

> Like the defense suppliers and the educational-manpower conglomerates, the pollution control industry now enjoys the good fortune of being legislated into success. Lavish profits will come from ready-made markets bolstered by special laws controlling pollution levels of factories, special tax write-offs for the industrial buyers of abatement equipment, and plenty of R&D money for the pollution controllers themselves.[5]

Potential profits in the pollution-control industry are in fact truly "lavish." A McGraw-Hill survey estimated that industry as a whole was expected to spend almost $5 billion in 1972 to clean up pollution,[6] an increase of more than 50 percent from 1971. Former Secretary of the Interior Udall has stated that "waste treatment is a proper business cost." And the Water Quality Act of 1965 requires state governments to establish and enforce water purity levels for interstate waterways within their boundaries.

However, legislation and moral suasion are only two elements in the solution to the pollution problem. The other essential ingredient is government money. A move toward total environmental planning will be needed if the job is to be done without inflicting unreasonable financial pressure on specific corporations and industries. No one corporate farmer can afford to pay the expenses of conserving soils, water, and plant, animal, and human life. No single manufacturer can absorb the expense of producing nonpolluting vehicles.[7] No municipality can afford to build adequate sewer-treatment plants. No airline can meet the expenses of noise pollution or modernize air traffic facilities and control. And industries such as paper, chemicals, primary metals, and other large-scale polluters cannot afford to treat and dispose of their waste properly without financial help in one form or another.[8] These facts are understood by corporations and industries, Congress, and the Administration. As Senator Muskie (chairman of a Senate Public Works subcommittee at the time) said in 1966,

> just ordering a city or an industry to stop polluting isn't the answer. The costs of treatment are simply overwhelming. If we mean it when we say that our national policy is to enhance the quality of our water resources, then we've got to be willing to put up the money to get the job done; and the present spending level doesn't begin to reflect the magnitude of the problem.[9]

It is difficult or impossible to tell how much money the state will pour into pollution control in the years to come. According to one report, the federal share of local waste-handling costs is now about 18 percent. The report continues,

> On January 1, 1970, the nation's municipal waste-handling systems presented the need for the investment of $4.4 billion, and were generating additional needs at the rate of over $800 million a year. With expected growth of the system, and inflation occurring at an average rate of 3.5 percent a year, total investment requirements will conservatively amount to $10 billion over the five years 1970–1974 if all existing deficiencies are remedied and no new deficiencies are allowed to occur.[10]

Nevertheless, although the Nixon Administration asked Congress to appropriate $4 billion in federal grants to local communities over an eight-year period to help local communities build more sewage plants (municipal authorities were expected to raise another $8 billion through bond issues), when Congress appropriated $800 million in 1971 for such plants, Nixon vetoed all but $214 million (because of general inflation and the fiscal crisis). In 1972, Congress overrode a presidential veto and appropriated $18 billion for municipal sewage plants and related facilities.

Air pollution control also is expected to be very expensive. Federal expenditures in this area (excluding programs dealing with auto pollution) were projected by HEW to expand from $132 million in 1970 to $490.4 million in 1975.[11] All in all, the President's Council on Environmental Quality estimated in 1971 that the total cost of cleaning up air, water, and solid waste pollution would amount to over $105 billion—of which industry was expected to pay little more than 40 percent.[12]

# NOTES AND REFERENCES

1. Barry Commoner, *The Closing Circle* (New York: 1971).

2. All waste is not pollution; waste becomes pollution only when waste is so concentrated that natural recycling is impossible. The fact that industrial and related plant is so concentrated in urban areas means that waste is highly concentrated, and in turn that the portion of total waste that is pollution is very high [Gayle Southworth, "Some Notes on the Political Economy of Pollution" (unpublished manuscript, 1972), p. 5].

3. For example, California's foothill subdivisions used up more than 500,000 acres of land between 1960 and 1970 According to a study by California's Division of Soil Conservation [*Environmental Impact of Urbanization on the Foothill and Mountainous Lands of California* (Sacramento, 1971)], subdivision development has created "significant environmental problems such as water pollution, loss of fish and wildlife habitat, damage to water courses, lakes and reservoirs, impairment of recreational opportunities, and sediment and flood damage to property." The report concludes that "the impact of people's activities is creating conditions that are destroying the values that people are seeking." When air, water, and other forces of production are impaired to the point of threatening profitable accumulation, antipollution outlays cease to be social expenses of production and become social capital, specifically, social investments.

4. *Wall Street Journal,* November 19, 1971

5. Martin Gellen, "The Making of a Pollution-Control Complex," *Ramparts,* May 1970, p. 24.

6. "Spending Races to Catch up to the Need," *Business Week,* May 13, 1972. The same survey estimated that business antipollution outlays in relation to total capital spending are expected to rise from 4 percent in 1971 to 5 3 percent in 1975.

7. New car buyers in 1972 were already paying $300 more on the average for pollution-control devices. Estimates of the cost of a pollution-free vehicle run from $1,000 to $10,000 greater than today's auto and truck prices. Passing these expenses on to the consumer would greatly restrict the market for new cars and spell financial ruin for the industry

8. There have been exceptions to this rule. In Pittsburgh, for example, the Mellon interests reduced air pollution produced by their steel mills in order to preserve the values of their downtown real estate. Again, in Europe, Ruhr Valley industries have established cooperative associations in which municipalities and the industries themselves coordinate and control water waste treatment.

9. *Wall Street Journal,* June 23, 1966.

10. U S. Department of the Interior, Federal Water Pollution Control Administration, "The Economics of Clean Air," March 1970, p. 6.

11. *The Costs of Clean Air,* Second Report of the Secretary of Health, Education, and Welfare (Washington, D.C., 1970), p. 3.

12. *Newsweek,* August 16, 1971.

# CHAPTER 7
# FINANCING THE BUDGET:
# STATE ENTERPRISE AND STATE DEBT

## INTRODUCTION

The state can finance increased budgetary outlays in three general ways: first, by creating state enterprises that produce surpluses which in turn may be used to underwrite social capital and social expense expenditures; second, by issuing debt and borrowing against future tax revenues; third, by raising tax rates and introducing new taxes. The first two will be discussed in this chapter. Tax exploitation and the growth of the tax state will be considered in Chapter 8. We will attempt to show that neither the development of state enterprise nor the growth of the state debt has resulted in the fiscal liberation of the state. Indeed the purpose and effect of state enterprise is to underwrite private profit. Some enterprises are organized to break even and fail to yield any surplus at all. Others produce a surplus which typically is used to underwrite and expand private capital. Still others generate a surplus, part of which is plowed back into the enterprise itself, but management is prohibited in various ways from expanding and encroaching on the private sector. In all three cases, state enterprise is typically established by a partnership between the state and monopoly capital and is managed in the interests of accelerating capital accumulation in the monopoly sector. Thus nationalization of industry and the development of state enterprise typically have not resulted in surpluses and lower taxes or prices, but rather in new state debt and increased state fiscal dependence.

State debt incurred at both local and national levels effectively expands private profits and extends the sway of monopoly capital. The growth of state debt normally does not exacerbate the fiscal crisis, but neither does state borrowing alleviate the crisis. State and local government debt has been partly "self-liquidating" in the sense that social capital formation is indirectly productive and contributes to private capital accumulation and the expansion of production, employment, and income, and hence the tax base. Federal government debt also has partly "paid for itself" during periods when actual output is less than potential output by expanding credit and increasing the level of aggregate demand, production, employment, income, and the tax base.

## STATE ENTERPRISE: GENERAL CONSIDERATIONS

From a technical standpoint there are few if any important barriers to the accumulation of state capital in the directly productive spheres of the economy. Within the state sector there is no shortage of scientific, technical, skilled, or unskilled labor, nor is there a lack of organizational and administrative know-how. Within the ranks of local and national government agencies there is an abundance of knowledge and experience in the areas of labor relations, financing, marketing, and other aspects of modern business management. Further, lands presently owned by various levels of government could yield sufficient raw materials, fuels, and other necessary physical resources.[1] To be sure, unless the state financed its production activities by simply issuing debt to itself, state capital would be compelled to purchase money capital at the same interest rate that private capital is forced to pay. Thus, if state capital confined itself to the competitive sector, it would fail to generate more than minimal "normal" rates of return. In this event, any real possibilities for the state's fiscal liberation would obviously be closed off. But if the state were to establish enterprises in the monopoly sector, where the rate of profit is relatively high and stable, the resulting surpluses could help finance general budgetary expenditures.

But these technical possibilities are completely unrealistic from a political standpoint. In American capitalist society state investments are normally confined to indirectly productive projects. Obviously it is in the interest and within the reach of monopoly capital to seize all profit-making opportunities for itself and to resist the encroachment of state capital on its own "natural territory." Indirectly productive investments (i.e., social capital) increase private profits and expand monopoly capital's natural territory. Monopoly capital also wants the state to remain dependent on tax revenues and thus fiscally weak—to reduce the possibility that a popular government would reorder the allocation of material resources.[2] Finally, it is ideologically important for private capital to monopolize profit-making activities in order to perpetuate the myth that the state is too incompetent to manage directly productive capital.

Monopoly capital employs many and varied methods and techniques to prevent the state from acquiring and managing directly productive capital. Economic domination gives the owning class ideological domination as well—that is, the entire legal system is based on the interests of monopoly capital. This means that equity financing of state enterprise often is ruled out, which denies an enterprise a financial cushion and exposes it to real risks when interest charges on loan capital exceed earnings.[3] The pinch can be especially painful if state enterprise is managed on the principle of balanced-budget pricing (i.e., if it is forced to set prices at levels that will just cover costs, no more, no less). For example, unable to raise equity capital and forbidden to generate internal surpluses, British nationalized enterprises increased their debt five times over through 1961. At that time the government modified its financial policies, but one legacy of British nationalization is still a swollen debt structure. Further, in the event that interest charges are large relative to the state's tax resources, there is the danger that temporary unprofitable operations will require cutbacks in normal activities and services. For example, at the municipal level, especially in the smaller cities, state enterprise (except for utilities, which private capital itself seeks to monopolize) is especially risky. In addition, simple bankruptcy proceedings normally are not available to state enterprise.[4]

In Europe many state enterprises are allowed to issue marketable equity stock. But the legal framework within which these enterprises operate mitigates against their self-actualization. In Austria, France, and Germany nationalized industries have an indeterminant status in law—and in some cases there are no statutes governing their operation. The most diversified Italian state enterprise, the Industrial Reconstruction Institute (IRI) consists of more than 120 companies which employ over 250,000 workers. IRI has acquired about one-third of its equity capital from the state and legally is permitted to pay out dividends and interest to the state equal to the average prevailing throughout the economy. Nevertheless, the state does not expect, nor does it receive, regular dividend payments. In effect, the state's role is to support the rate of profit throughout the economy, which has earned it the appelation "rentier who never squeals." [5]

The development of state enterprise is inhibited also by private capital's unrelenting opposition on ideological grounds. "Remember that government, however necessary," warns Robert C. Tyson, chairman of the U.S. Steel finance committee, "has nothing to give except that which is first taken away." [6] What Tyson means is that the state cannot create wealth directly because it is confined by men like Tyson to management of unproductive and indirectly productive assets; the Tysons propagate the notion that it is part of the natural order of things for the state not to be direcly productive. Local governments could free themselves fiscally by taking over hundreds of utilities (franchises granted fifty to seventy-five years ago will expire shortly). For example Gainesville, Florida, derived over 23 percent of its general revenues from surpluses generated by its electric utility operations in 1965. But powerful forces seek to keep the utilities in private hands or to prevent them from generating surpluses should they fall to the state. The Municipal Finance Officers Association argues that utilities should not generate surpluses but rather are created to furnish services at cost (a striking illustration of the anomaly of public officials attempting to keep the state dependent on private capital).[7]

In the United States no significant political force has advocated state enterprise (except when private businesses such as urban transit companies cease to be profitable). As early as the third quarter of the nineteenth century the business-dominated courts introduced new criteria making it unconstitutional to use tax moneys for other than "public purposes," which did not include state enterprise.[8] Farm groups agitated for state control to prevent monopoly abuses, but their campaigns for state ownership were sectional and limited to a handful of activities (and in the last analysis they sought to control and regulate private capital, not abolish it).[9] And although it is true that American unions once agitated for state industry, they were motivated solely by a desire to win material advantages for limited groups of workers in the face of employer hostility to collective bargaining and trade unionism.[10]

During crisis periods (e.g., World War II), monopoly capital has used the state to directly develop and manage directly productive activities in the interests of economic expansion and technical development. However, with the return to "normalcy" the state is rapidly stripped of its capital assets. From 1946 to 1949, for example, the cumulative percentage decline of state-owned producer durable assets exceeded 40 percent. As late as 1955, the Hoover Commission estimated that there were over 2500 commercial and industrial facilities within the Department of Defense. In the wake of the Commission's investigations and the Budget Bureau director's follow-up recommendations, the federal government abandoned most of these activities to private capital.[11] Even in the climate of corporate-dominated federal policy and working-class quiescence of the early Johnson Administration, the government was compelled to promise to sell off the few remaining enterprises competing with private business (e.g., nuclear fuel production) in order to win a business consensus for its (probusiness) policies.[12] The culmination of private capital's war against state enterprise may well be the full development of the social-industrial complex—the movement of private capital that seeks to take over state functions and facilities (e.g., education, land development, public housing, etc.). A politically unopposed social-industrial complex would bind the state even more tightly to the needs and interests of monopoly capital.

## STATE ENTERPRISE IN EUROPE

State enterprise in Europe is extensive and well developed.[13] Furthermore, it appears that state capital has grown at the expense of private capital. Consequently, the European experience must be considered on its own terms. In the European economies where state capital coexists with private capital, possibilities for the fiscal liberation of the state are very limited because productive capital has been nationalized but not socialized. State enterprise exists to still political unrest and underwrite losses of private capital, not to develop productive facilities in order to free the state from tax finance.[14] It exists primarily to serve, not compete with, private capital. Profits from state enterprise are either limited by statute, diverted to private consumption, or used to encourage the private sector at the expense of the state sector.[15]

European feudalism was characterized by widespread baronial ownership of the means of production. In the era of mercantilism the state also acquired productive assets, which it retains in some forms (e.g., state forests) to this day. Moreover, the European market was always relatively small, and the scale of operations of the typical private enterprise was comparatively modest. To ensure that technological development would not stagnate, the state was compelled to extend the range of state enterprise to industrial activities private capital would not undertake. State capitalism thus helped to keep the European economies competitive with each other and later with the United States.

European governments normally have responded to general or specific economic and political crises by setting up mixed enterprises or decreeing nationalization, not by providing indirect subsidies, underwriting investment, and so on. In France (except for the nationalized railroads), the first major group of enterprises coming under public ownership were victims of the financial crisis of the 1930s. Called upon to support a number of bankrupt firms, "the state, in return for its financial assistance, received a portion of the capital stock, thus transforming the firms into mixed companies." [16] But the most extensive nationalization occurred directly after World War II.

> In March, 1944 the National Resistance Council, which grouped together the principal elements of the resistance movement, called for "the return to the nation of the great means of monopolized production, fruits of common labor, of the sources of energy, the wealth underground, the insurance companies, and the large banks." A doctrine of public ownership was incorporated into the preamble of the Constitution of 1946 by the statement that "every good, every enterprise, whose use has or acquires the characteristics of a national public service or of a de facto monopoly must become the property of the community.[17]

In Italy the business and financial classes saw the nationalization of particular industries—for example, railroads and telephone and telegraph communications—as merely extensions of the state's public works policy.[18] During the Great Depression there was little resistance to the nationalization of directly productive industries; in Italy (as in most European countries) the state supported the banks and evolved "mixed companies" to protect the value of private bank shares.[19] In the context of European capitalist development it was natural for the state to give massive support, including outright purchase, to private capital—not to remove capital from the private sphere, but to keep productive activities in operation.

It was not until immediately after World War II that the British government nationalized industries that had been particularly hard hit by the Great Depression. Nationalization rescued most of the industries (particularly rail transport and coal) from bankruptcy.[20] In Austria nationalization purged the economy of private German capital and reduced the danger that private property would be appropriated by the Allies under the Potsdam agreement (enterprises taken over by the Russians during the occupation were transferred to the state).[21] And in Greece, to hasten development of the national economy, the state established directly productive enterprises which were to be turned over to private capital after "the formation of the proper economic environment which will permit their successful management by private enterprise." [22]

During the interwar period European nationalization was spearheaded by national power elites and ruling classes; during and after World War II—especially in England, France, and Austria—labor and left-wing parties played a crucial role. In both periods nationalization occurred in the context of mass agitation against private capital. However, nationalization typically has been introduced and implemented by conservative forces seeking to stabilize the social and economic order. A comparative study of eight European countries (and Japan) failed to disclose any positive relationship between the relative size and development of social democratic parties and the size of the state sector. European social democracy, with the single exception of the British Labour Party, has not favored state enterprise on political grounds (nor have social democratic parties resisted state policies underwriting private capital).[23]

Because of its largely conservative character, European state enterprise has not promoted the fiscal liberation of the state, but rather has strengthened private capital. Many state enterprises—especially the nationalized sector in Britain, the Italian state railways, and some French state corporations (e.g., coal production)—are not run on commercial principles and are forbidden by law to generate profits or are otherwise financially hamstrung.[24] British state enterprise originally was compelled to balance its budget "over a period of good and bad years"; since 1961, however, public corporations have enjoyed greater flexibility in pricing decisions. Further, the nationalized sector is expected to follow wage, price, investment, and other policies aimed at stabilizing the British economy, not freeing the state fiscally. Thus, for example, public corporations are expected to "buy British"—that is, purchase materials from British private monopolies rather than from lower-cost overseas suppliers. Throughout western Europe, when state enterprise competes directly with private capital, the law frequently limits the scope of the state corporation's actions in other ways.[25]

Even when state industries generate surpluses, the surpluses typically are not available to the state treasury because the enterprises normally are not managed by government representatives, but rather by autonomous administrations. In France, for example, managers of enterprises in which the state holds less than 30 percent of total assets are not accountable to Parliament. Sealed off from prevailing political pressures, most European state enterprises operate on private capitalist principles and hence reinforce rather than threaten the rule of the market. Ironically, two important features of French state enterprise

> have been a high degree of expansionary drive, involving continuous pressure for investment and introduction of new tech-

niques, and a surprisingly intense concern with the development of economically rational methods of determining prices and budgets. The nationalized firms have known how to develop their productivity, enlarge their fields of action, and watch their costs. . . . In an economy where the spirit of conservatism has too often taken the place of the spirit of enterprise in the psychology of the private enterpreneur, the nationalized sector sometimes appears to be the last refuge of those traditionally "capitalist" virtues: audacity, the taste for large-scale operations, dynamism.[26]

Summing up, Sheahan writes,

the [French] government firms have largely escaped direction by other agencies of the government and have acted very much as private enterprise might have done in the same markets. [And, in terms of day-to-day control, although] "the state firms are more open to supervision than private companies are . . . at the same time the channels are open for the firm itself to shape the governmental choices that control its own environment.[27]

State enterprise sometimes even cooperates with private monopolies and is a party to monopolistic agreements. For example, Baum suggests that the state-owned French coal industry has helped keep oil prices high and that the state railroad industry has engaged in semicollusive economic practices with the private truck industry.[28]

Edmond Langer's conclusions on the Austrian experience can be applied to European state enterprise in general:

In most cases, the nationalized sector produces the commodities and services which private industry does not produce. Moreover, it supplies its goods and services to the private sector on very favorable terms. It is doubtful whether under a private-economy system the industries which are nationalized would be able to offer the same terms. This means that private industry is the prime beneficiary of the nationalized sector which supplies it with its basic product and service requirements. Economically speaking, no antagonism therefore seems to exist, except in infrequent individual cases.[29]

In extreme cases state enterprises are compelled to support private capital at the expense of the state enterprises themselves (such as BOAC, which has had to support the British aircraft industry by buying equipment at home rather than shopping for it abroad).

In Italy, a similar situation has developed. IRI has been one of "the principal factors in reconstruction and industrial development since World War II." According to Apicella,

> the functions of public enterprise in the economic policies of Italy's government since the war are substantially similar to those of public enterprise before the war, namely, the provision of the most favorable conditions for (economic) development at the greatest possible rate without any concurrent aims of nationalization or complete control of the productive sectors concerned.[30]

Until the development of the National Hydrocarbons Corporation (ENI) in the postwar period "acquisition of share holdings by the state (did) not by itself put the latter in a position to implement an industrial policy going beyond the preservation and development of the undertaking concerned." [31] But one of the principal aims of even ENI has been to encourage the participation of private capital in every phase of the industry except in those areas where hydrocarbon resources were originally discovered. The general political economic function of state industry in Italy is summarized by Posner and Woolf thus:

> The account we have given of IRA and ENI could, in large part, have been told of any two large holding companies in Italy—Fiat, Montecatina, Edison, and so on. The method of raising investment finance, the effort for growth in the Mezzogiorno, the independence of ENI from the international oil companies, are distinguishing features of the public sector: but has there been much more than this? In the future, unless there are changes in the character of the direction from above, Alfa Romeo or Alitalia or even Italsider will operate in a manner similar to firms whose shareholders are individuals and institutions in the private sector.[32]

Indemnity policies also have strengthened private capital. In Britain, France, and Italy very generous payments to former stockholders often have limited the enterprise's investment capacity—while permitting private capital to expand into other sectors of the economy. Another factor confining the state fiscally is that a great part of productive state capital consists of backward industries that under the best of circumstances cannot generate a large surplus year in and year out. As for the dynamic industries monopolized or participated in by state capital, legislation and administrative rulings limit the state's ability to develop an overall industrial policy that might finance the general state budget. For example, British laws have been amended to prohibit nationalized firms from producing equipment for their own use.

## THE STATE DEBT: HISTORICAL ASPECTS

Athough state enterprise unquestionably gives national planning agencies more leverage in the field of fiscal and monetary policy and investment planning, government-owned business does not liberate the state fiscally. In fact, the main purpose of state enterprise is to strengthen the private sector of the economy. The intent and effect of state borrowing is similar to the intent and effect of state enterprise. On the one hand, the growth of state debt gives the treasury more power in monetary and fiscal planning. On the other, the institution of the debt normally tightens capital's grip on the state. The general reason is that whereas private capital borrows in order to expand profits and thus has the capacity to repay outstanding loans directly, the state borrows in order to expand social capital (and thus private profits) or social expense expenditures. The expansion of social capital influences the state's capacity to repay its debt indirectly (to the degree that the growth of social capital accelerates private accumulation, employment, wages, profits, and the tax base). Similarly, the growth of social expenses also influences the state's capacity to meet its debt obligations indirectly (to the degree that increases in social expense outlays maintain aggregate demand, income, employment, and the tax base). But neither social capital nor social expense outlays enlarge the state's capacity to repay the debt directly. In effect, the security of state loans is the power to tax and the ability to expand the tax base by enlarging GNP.

Ironically, between the seventeenth and nineteenth centuries, private capital stripped the state of its directly productive capital (i.e., profitable business) in order to strengthen the private economy. The early breakup of the state monopolies and the formation of the state debt were merely different aspects of the same general process. "The formation of the public debt," writes the author of a classic article on the subject, "served as a springboard for the mobilization of a structure of private corporate power over crucial areas of the political economy (banking, commerce, empire, fiscal affairs)." [33] Far from replacing private debt, the growth of the state debt in the nineteenth century provided the basis for its expansion. [34]

THE FISCAL CRISIS OF THE STATE

In turn, the expansion of both state and private borrowing provided the foundation for the expansion and strengthening of a rentier class. Ultimately, the state became financially dependent on and therefore politically indebted to this class of bankers, investment houses, and other money brokers (e.g., debt service in France at the turn of the century amounted to one-third of the state budget).

In nineteenth-century Europe the state debt "predominantly arose out of the exigencies of war." [35] Because the tax system was comparatively rigid and unproductive, capital and state combined to minimize or conceal the immediate costs of war by issuing debt or acted to "delay the open accounting of those costs until the nation was fully committed to the undertaking." [36] The effect of debt-financed wars and imperial expansion was inflation, the reduction of real income going to the working classes, and "the concentration in the hands of active businessmen of the large resources upon which the state at war may draw in the shape of either taxes or loans." [37] It was thus war and imperial expansion (together with the simultaneous growth of public and private debt) that created the rentier class which Marx described in a deservedly famous passage as the "aristocracy of finance":

> By the "aristocracy of finance" must be understood not merely the large bond negotiators and speculators in government securities, of whom it may be readily understood that their interests and the interests of the government coincide. The whole modern money trade, the whole banking industry, is most intimately interwoven with the public credit. Part of their business capital must be invested in interest-bearing government securities that are promptly convertible into money. Their deposits, i.e., the capital placed at their disposal and distributed, by them, among merchants and industrialists, flow partly out of the dividends on government securities. The whole money market, together with the priests of this market, is part and parcel of this "aristocracy of finance," and in every epoch the stability of the government is synonymous to them with Moses and the prophets.[38]

## FEDERAL GOVERNMENT DEBT
## IN THE UNITED STATES

As in Europe, the U.S. national debt has played an important role in the accumulation of capital and the creation and growth of an "aristocracy of finance." Between 1790 and 1860, the state debt diverted about $80 million from consumption to the capital market, and from 1866 to 1900 this form of "forced savings" amounted to $600 million.[39] The precondition for this "forced savings" and redistribution of income and wealth was the original role of the state debt in bringing about control of the state by the bankers and monied classes. According to Ferguson, "funding the debt was the economic counterpart of the Constitution." [40] In effect control of the national treasury was placed in the hands of the commercial and banking interests which owned the debt. These interests were so powerful that the debt was attacked by Jeffersonians and Jacksonians as a "political institution" and as a source of corruption.

The "aristocracy of finance" still exists and is still very powerful. Banks and corporations still invest in "interest-bearing government securities that are promptly convertible into money." It remains true that the "capital distributed among merchants and industrialists flow[s] partly out of dividends on government securities." More, the dozen or so investment banks that monopolize the flotation of government securities profit enormously from the state debt. All in all, government debt—federal, state, and local—plays an important role in propping up the financial system, and thanks to the new agencies established by Congress during the 1960s to put federal borrowing power behind housing and other congressional programs, federal and federally assisted borrowers (including the Treasury) took almost 40 percent of available market credit in 1972.[41]

However, because of the expansion of private business credit and home mortgage and consumer credit over the past three decades (due in large part to government underwriting and guarantees), the state debt today constitutes a relatively small part of total debt (and profits from the state debt make up a relatively small part of the financial institutions' total profits. In 1946 (because of borrowing during the war), government debt was about 62 percent of total debt; in 1965, less than 30 percent (although state and local debt rose from 4 to 9 percent of total debt during this period, federal debt declined from 58 to 22 percent). In absolute terms the federal debt grew from $40 billion in 1940 to $450 billion in 1972.

Although federal borrowing agencies increased their share of the market dramatically in 1970–1971, the financial institutions no longer hold much power over the federal budget. During and after World War II, when federal debt skyrocketed, the dependence of the state on finance capital completely evaporated when the Treasury compelled the Federal Reserve System to support the price of new federal debt issues. Price supports lasted until the Treasury Accord of 1951 restored the Federal Reserve's independence.[42] However, since then the Federal Reserve from time to time has supported government bond prices (e.g., in 1958, when the market for long-term government bonds was extremely weak).

The fundamental reason that the Federal Reserve System has lost much of its independence and that the "aristocracy of finance" no longer exercises the power over the national state it once did is not the declining importance of the state debt in relation to the private debt. Rather, it is the growing interpenetration between the monopoly sector (which itself is closely linked to the big financial institutions) and the state bureaucracy, together with the development of class-serving domestic and foreign policies and budgetary priorities (as contrasted with interest-group policies and priorities). In particular, federal tax policy is used to regulate the economy as a whole, and the federal debt is incurred mainly as a result of planned budgetary deficits designed to expand general economic activity. Because of the state's relative autonomy, government bonds increasingly have taken the form of "special issues"—securities intended for distribution only among government bodies and government pension and other funds. In effect, the national state increasingly has been financing its annual deficits by borrowing from itself. Whereas marketable securities increased by only 30 percent between 1946 and 1970 (December), special issues grew by 250 percent.[43]

Nevertheless, the increase in the *absolute volume* of marketable and special securities has been about the same. In absolute terms special issues rose from $22.3 billion in 1946 to $78.1 billion in 1970, whereas marketable bonds increased from $189.6 to $247.7 billion over the same period.

Why was the "aristocracy of finance" willing to increase its holdings of national debt by about $58 billion during a period of inflation and rapidly rising stock prices? They weren't. On the one hand, finance capital increasingly refused to buy long-term federal bonds, thus forcing the Treasury to issue relatively more short-term bills and notes and shorten the length of the debt. In 1950, the average length of the federal debt was in excess of eight years. It dropped to about five to six years between 1951 and 1963. And after 1964, when inflationary pressures started to build up, the debt had to be shortened still more.[44] The percentage of the national debt in bonds declined sharply between 1965 and 1970 (from c. 50 percent to little more than 20 percent). As the debt has become shorter and shorter, it has become more liquid (more like money), and thus more inflationary, in turn forcing the government to put out more special issues, which have fueled the inflation and fiscal crisis.

On the other hand, finance capital increasingly has

refused to buy even short-term federal debt, preferring state and local bonds, mortgages, private bonds, and stocks. Since the end of World War II, insurance companies and mutual savings banks have liquidated more than 50 percent of their federal debt holdings. Commercial-bank federal debt holdings have also declined, although not nearly by as much (because short-term notes and bills give the banks needed liquidity), and corporate and individual holdings have remained about the same. Who then has taken up the slack? State and local governments, whose holdings of federal debt instruments have increased threefold.[45] In sum, it is clear that the "aristocracy of finance" is extremely reluctant to support its own government by buying up federal debt, even when interest rates rise and the debt is shortened. The upshot has been that the same people who have tried to force the government into noninflationary paths of budget finance have in effect compelled the state to turn its debt into near-money and increasingly engage in the most inflationary type of finance—borrowing from itself. One effect of inflationary finance is to push up interest rates and hence increase federal debt service. Even in the comparatively noninflationary period of 1954–1964, when federal debt rose by 14 percent, interest payments increased by 68 percent, and interest income by 147 percent.[46] In 1972, debt service rose to an all-time high of $21 billion. In this way, inflationary finance places a fiscal burden on the state directly. In the future, even in the highly unlikely event that the federal government begins to run budgetary surpluses, debt service can be expected to expand because the "political forces seem to be that the possibly offsetting surpluses . . . will not be allowed to reduce the outstanding debt. These forces will tend to push through tax reductions or expenditure increases in such periods in lieu of debt retirement. As a result, we can expect that the national debt will move upward over time in a stair-like fashion." [47] Another effect of inflationary finance is to generate higher prices in the monopoly sector and higher wages in the competitive, monopoly, and state sectors (wage increases in the competitive sector depend on the rate of inflation; in the monopoly sector and to a lesser degree the state sector, wage rises depend on productivity and cost of living) and hence worsen the fiscal crisis indirectly. Inflationary finance also means higher interest rates (so that the "aristocracy of finance" can protect their profit margins), which also indirectly fuels the fire of inflation and intensifies the fiscal crisis. Finally, when the Federal Reserve System expands commercial-bank reserves to help the Treasury finance new issues that would otherwise be sold at unacceptably low prices, more credit is created and more inflation ignited.

# STATE AND LOCAL GOVERNMENT DEBT

Federal borrowing and the federal debt and state and local government borrowing and debt are governed by very different political economic principles.[48] Federal debt is incurred as a result of budget deficits and is not directly related to the acquisition or construction of social capital or social expense physical facilities. And the national debt is serviced from general Treasury funds not from income generated from specific assets. Most state and local government debt is incurred to finance social capital and expense outlays and physical capital facilities (together with physical facilities such as prisons to meet social expenses). State and local governments frequently borrow to cover deficits, but debt incurred in this way is always short term and very limited in amount.

The most significant difference between federal and state and local borrowing concerns the relationship between finance capital and the federal and state and local treasuries. The only important power that financial institutions exercise over the federal government is their ability to compel the Treasury to pay high interest rates (and even this power has been greatly diluted by the shortening of the debt and the growth of special issues). At the state and local levels banks and other financial institutions keep their profits high and growing not only by demanding (and getting) high interest rates but also by influencing or controlling how borrowed funds are expended.[49] In general, state and local governments can borrow funds from local financial institutions (and if bond issues are big enough, from national financial institutions) only under certain restrictive conditions.

Rule number one is that finance capital does not make funds available for any economic activity that competes with private capital. Beyond the obvious ideological issues, there are two reasons for this rule. First, banks and other major leaders typically are owned or controlled by the same people who have investments in private commerce, manufacturing, and other nonfinancial profit-making spheres. Second, a significant portion of the income of the banks and money brokers springs from state and municipal securities; hence the "aristocracy of finance" normally wants to keep state and local governments dependent on the banks and other financial institutions.

Rule number two is that private bankers normally do not underwrite local and state bond issues unless they are reasonably certain that the borrowed funds will be used to finance social capital projects that expand the tax base by encouraging private investment and economic activity. General obligation bonds must "pay for themselves" in the indirect sense of increasing potential tax revenues. Thus, in effect, local governments mortgage their taxing powers to the banks. Revenue bonds (e.g., self-liquidating airport modernization bonds) are expected to pay for themselves directly. The same can be said of the new industrial revenue bonds which are tax-exempt securities issued by a government entity to finance the construction of industrial plants to be leased to private capital.[50] Public industrial financing programs "originally were designed to overcome problems created by an inadequate supply of credit in rural areas." During the early 1960s, however, "States began to use the promise of industrial aid financing as an inducement for firms to locate in a particular State. Most recently, many States have been forced to adopt laws authorizing industrial aid financing of some type to remain competitive with neighboring States in the competition for new industry." [51]

The mechanisms of financial control over local and state governments vary from locality to locality. In some areas "conservative investors are known to avoid bond issues whose purposes they believe are beyond the proper scope of local government." [52] In others (perhaps a majority) any tendency toward "irresponsible" local spending means that local government units suffer a setback in their credit ratings. In some cities so-called citizens' committees made up of bankers, brokers, and businessmen screen capital projects before bond referendums are sent to the voters.[53] At times voters have defeated bond referendums supported by local financiers and businessmen, and state and local governments have turned to lease-purchasing arrangements and industrial revenue issues. Perhaps most important, bond market underwriters have considerable monopoly power (or, more precisely, monopsony power) because there are tens of thousands of governmental units that attempt to sell bonds and only a handful of big buyers.[54] For example, in 1965, New York City hit on a plan to balance its budget by a borrow-now, pay-later program which would enable the city to sell municipal securities at favorable prices. But the financial syndicate that planned to purchase $63.9 million of bonds changed its mind because a taxpayer group threatened litigation. New York lost its only customer and was compelled to borrow at higher rates of interest.[55]

State and local government social capital outlays have risen dramatically during the past two decades—particularly in the last eight or ten years. State and local borrowing and debt service have expanded concomitantly. Both general obligation bonds (secured by either future tax revenues or the "full faith and credit" of local government) and revenue bonds have expanded, but in recent years the latter have increased more rapidly. Between 1950 and 1964, total state and local government debt increased by 339 and 236 percent, respectively. Between 1960 and 1969, state and local government debt outstanding increased in absolute terms from $19 to $40 billion and from $23 to $40 billion, respectively. Township, special authority, and other local debt outstanding rose from $28 to $64 billion during the same period. In terms of the volume of annual issues, state and local borrowing jumped from $2 billion yearly in 1945 to $16 billion in 1968, subsequently skyrocketing to $23.1 billion in 1971.[56] Future prospects are that state and local borrowing and debt will continue their expansion (in 1967, Representative Wright Patman estimated that through 1975 "public facility" needs would rise to almost $500 billion, of which $328 billion would be required by state and local agencies. In turn, about one-half of these outlays were expected to be financed by tax-exempt municipal securities).[57]

Although high interest rates force local and state governments to cut back borrowing temporarily, one study showed that in 1966 the high cost of borrowing did not stop, but merely postponed the construction of new social capital projects. Although

> the empirical literature on how State and local governments in fact have responded to credit market conditions is sparse [this literature] does indicate that these governments cut back on their borrowing when interest rates were above their upward postwar trend and that they borrowed more when rates were below that trend [but] there has been no measured response to the upward trend itself.

A more recent Federal Reserve study bears out the findings of the earlier study and suggests that local governments went ahead with capital projects even though costs continued to mount throughout the late 1960s. Thus, 1971 borrowing was at an all-time high of $23.1 billion not only because of the "natural growth in demand for debt-financed projects, but also [because governments wanted] to reinstate debt plans abandoned in fiscal 1970." [59] This study showed that interest-rate movements did not cause state and local units to postpone or cancel long-term borrowing. It also showed that legal interest ceilings were either raised or removed altogether in order to clear the path for higher levels of debt finance.

To be sure, it has become increasingly difficult for local and state governments to sell bonds, and increased spending at the local level means that more tax funds are needed, narrowing the basis for debt service and inhibiting the capacity of local units to borrow more.[60] Nevertheless, debt finance and debt service probably will continue to mount because more social physical capital outlays are needed and because in the long run spending seems to be insensitive to higher interest rates and borrowing costs. Moreover, current state and local spending (financed from current tax revenues) is increasing more rapidly than total expenditures. For example, between 1955 and 1966, state and local government monthly payrolls increased by 168 percent, whereas total spending rose by only 60.8 percent.[61] Today, state and local payrolls constitute more than 50 percent of total expenditures (although at the federal level, direct payrolls make up only 15 percent of the budget, giving the national state more flexibility).

In sum, although the development of new municipal bond funds will direct more small savings to the money market for state and local bonds, it can be concluded with some confidence that more federal revenue sharing will be needed not only to finance current outlays but also to refinance local and state long-term debt. The reasons are the wage inflation in the state sector (including the wage costs of capital construction projects, which make up over 90 percent of state and local bond-financed outlays, excluding expenditures for existing structures and land purchases), high interest rates and debt service, reduced tax bases, and mounting demands on state and local budgets. According to available evidence, even industrial revenue bonds are not paying their own way in terms of increasing the tax base.[62]

The need for federal funds to refinance state and local debt and meet rising current expenditures will be even greater when and if more state and local borrowing takes the form of "social-industrial" capital—that is, social capital in the form of physical facilities for day care, laborpower retraining, low-income housing and recreation, and other projects which (unlike traditional social capital facilities) have little or no payoff in terms of raising the tax base in the short and middle run. Of course, the Federal Reserve could lessen the fiscal burden by engaging in an expansionary monetary policy, but its real political-economic function is to help the Treasury to float new issues at relatively high prices, meantime using selective policies to keep up stock prices—not to relieve the burden on local taxpayers and local governments. Finally, needless to say, the price of federal refinancing of local and state debt will be more federal control over local projects and more top-down regional planning.

THE FISCAL CRISIS OF THE STATE

# NOTES AND REFERENCES

**1.** In nineteenth-century America the state sold public lands at declining prices which were too low to add any revenue to the Treasury (or gave land away) [Lewis H. Kimmel, *Federal Budget and Fiscal Policy, 1789–1958* (Washington, D.C.: The Brookings Institution, 1959), p. 18].

**2.** Rudolf Goldscheid, "A Sociological Approach to the Problem of Public Finance," in Richard A. Musgrave and Alan T. Peacock, eds., *Classics in the Theory of Public Finance* (New York: 1958).

**3.** During the first years of nationalization in Britain the financial structure of state-owned industry was extremely rigid. Interest payments were considered prior charges to be paid whether or not the enterprise generated any surplus.

**4.** For a good discussion of the whole issue of municipal enterprise, see John Due, "The City of Prineville Railway—A Case Study in Government Enterprise," *The Quarterly Review of Economics and Business*, 5:4 (Winter 1965).

**5.** Andrew Shonfield, *Modern Capitalism* (New York: 1965), p. 188.

**6.** Robert C. Tyson, "The Private Impact of Public Spending," address to the Public Expenditures Survey of Wisconsin, Milwaukee, September 29, 1964.

**7.** Alan Rabinowitz, *Municipal Bond Finance and Administration* (New York: 1969), p. 46.

**8.** *Modern Capitalism*, op. cit., p. 306.

**9.** Thanks to Horace Davis for educating me on the subject of state enterprise and the farm movement in the United States. Professor Davis writes:

> The National Nonpartisan League mounted an on-going campaign for state ownership of nearly everything except the land, in 1916 in North Dakota. In a couple of years they had captured the Republican Party through participation in the primaries and enacted their whole program, including a state-owned bank, a state-owned grain elevator, state hail insurance, and state financing of home purchase; they campaigned for federal ownership and operation of the railroads. . . . In Nebraska, also a farm state, the state government under the leadership of Charles Bryan, brother of William J., went into the business of marketing coal to break a local ring, and held out the threat of further state entry into business unless the local monopolists behaved themselves. This was in the early 1920's." (Letter to the author, February 14, 1971.)

**10.** Peter Henle, "A Chronicle of Trade Union Positions on Government Ownership," *Monthly Labor Review* 88 (July 1965).

**11.** A 1963 Budget Bureau directive warns civil servants proposing to use public enterprises for the "provision of a product or service" that

> the existence of the government-owned capital assets is not in itself an adequate justification for the government to provide its own goods and services. The need for continued government ownership and operation must be fully substantiated. . . . Even the operation of a government-owned facility by a private organization through contractual arrangement does not automatically assure that the government is not competing with private enterprise. . . . This type of arrangement could act as a barrier to the development and growth of competitive commercial sources. (*Modern Capitalism*, op. cit., pp. 298–299).

**12.** M. J. Rossant, *New York Times*, June 7, 1965. In late 1969, the Atomic Energy Commission was ordered to prepare to sell its three uranium enrichment plants to private capital. Thus, "what started as total government ownership and control of the 'industry of the future' has become an industry dominated by and organized for private profit with the public paying most of the costs" (Lee Webb, "U.S. to Sell Vast Uranium Complex," *Guardian*, December 1969).

The growth of state capitalism is evidenced by the fact that state capital makes up a growing share of total U.S. capital stock. From 1902 to 1946, the government's share of the value of total national capital assets (excluding military assets) rose from 6 6 to 20.6 percent [Solomon Fabricant, *The Trend of Government Activity in the United States Since 1900* (Princeton, N.J.: 1950), p. 19, Table 3, p. 20, Table 4]. The greatest part of government assets, however, consists of noncommercial assets. Goldsmith has estimated that in 1955 the government's share of "total reproducible tangible assets" was about 13 percent and that only 2 percent of all assets was operated directly by government enterprise [Raymond W. Goldsmith, *The National Wealth of the United States in the Postwar Period* (Princeton, N.J.: 1962), p. 98, Table 24, p 99]. The state's share of the total stock of producer durable goods was only 3 percent, or $5.9 billion of $199 9 billion; its share of total structures was about 20 percent (ibid., pp. 117–118, Table A–5). The proportion of total land operated or managed by the state was 13 percent, but private interests monopolized the ownership of livestock, and the greatest part of state-owned land consisted of parks, reserves, and other non-income-producing properties. It is interesting to note that prior to the federal property inventory report of June 30, 1956, issued by the Committee on Government Operations, public domain lands were listed as having "no value."

13. In Europe between 20 and 30 percent of total directly productive investment consists of state investment [A. A. Arzumanian, "State Monopoly Capitalism and the Working Class," *Problems of Economics* 8:6 (October 1965), 51–52]. In the United Kingdom, although only 14 percent of GNP originated in nationalized firms in 1958–1959, "public authority" investments comprised about 40 percent of total investments [W. A. Robson, *Nationalized Industry and Public Ownership* (London: 1960), p. 76]. The weakness of state enterprise in England is indicated by the fact that the share of GNP originating in the public corporations fell to 11 percent in 1969 [Michael Barratt Brown, "Against the Conservative Attack on Public Enterprise," *Bulletin of the Institute of Workers Control*, 9 (1971), 7].

In France the state directly operates more than 20 percent of total assets, including nearly the entire coal and gas industry, one-half of the automotive industry, and about one-third of chemical fertilizers (*The National Wealth of the United States in the Postwar Period*, op. cit., pp. 98–99). Of the major European countries, only Germany has a relatively small state sector; a large part of state capital was transferred to private interests after World War II. In Finland state investment amounts to about 20 percent of total investment [William J. Fredrickson, "Economic Recovery of Finland Since World War II," *Journal of Political Economy*, 68 (February 1960), 30]. In Belgium and Holland, however, the share of total assets operated by the state is only about 6 percent.

14. According to Marx and Engels economic crisis proved that the bourgeoisie lacked the capacity "to manage modern productive forces," and thus forced the growth of state enterprise [Tom Wengraf, "Notes on Marx and Engels' Theories of the Development of the Capitalist State" (unpublished manuscript, September 1970)].

15. "The beneficent character of state intervention in favor of monopoly profit results from the fact that the state does not seek profit for itself

but for the capitalist . . ." [Paul Boccara, "Introduction to the Question of State Monopoly Capitalism," *Economic Bulletin*, New Series, no. 13 (January 1968), 12].

**16.** Warren C Baum, *The French Economy and the State* (Princeton, N.J.: 1958), pp. 32–39.

**17.** Ibid., p. 175. At first the nationalization movement included demands for worker participation in management and worker control. But attempts at tripartite management (workers-consumers-government) failed, and "powers over the management of the public enterprises have been progressively transferred to the general manager and his staff, on the one hand, and to the various ministries, on the other" (ibid., p. 184). See also, Adolf Sturmthal, "The Structure of Nationalized Enterprises in France," *Political Science Quarterly*, 67:3 (September 1952), and "Nationalization and Workers' Control in Britain and France," *Journal of Political Economy*, 61:1 (February 1953).

**18.** Vincenzo Apicella, "The Development of the Public Sector," *Annals of Public and Co-Operative Economy*, 35:1 (January/March 1964), 6.

**19.** The fascist government encouraged the banks to supply credit to businesses that were no longer solvent. Then the banks were forced to support their own shares under pressure from panics in the stock market. "Ultimately, the only escape from bankruptcy for the vast interlocked complex of industrial and financial interests was a take-over of the assets, as well as the liabilities, by the state" (*Modern Capitalism*, op. cit., pp. 178–179).

**20.** R. Kelf-Cohen, *Twenty Years of Nationalization: The British Experience* (New York: 1969).

**21.** Edmond Langer, "Nationalizations in Austria," *Annals of Public and Co-Operative Economy*, 35:2–3 (April/September 1964), 116–117.

**22.** Pella Lenouda, "Public Enterprise in Greece," *Public Finance*, 18:3–4 (1963), 290–291.

**23.** V. P. Duggal, "Socialist Labour Parties and the Size of the Public Sector in Some Countries," *Annals of Public and Co-Operative Economy*, 35:4 (October/December 1964).

**24.** *Modern Capitalism*, op. cit., p. 191.

**25.** A good example is the Renault works in France, which finances its investments via bank loans and the issuance of debentures and thus faces heavy interest and sinking fund charges Moreover, untypically, Renault must distribute 50 percent of its profits to its employed personnel, the remainder going to the state treasury. Renault receives no special tax privileges and actually receives fewer state contracts than its private competitors [Jean Marchal, "Investment Decisions in French Public Undertaking," *Annals of Public and Co-Operative Economy*, 35:4 (October/December 1964), 264–265].

**26.** John Sheahan, *Promotion and Control of Industry in Postwar France* (Cambridge, Mass.: 1963), p. 193.

**27.** Ibid., pp. 190 and 33.

**28.** *The French Economy and the State*, op. cit., p. 213.

**29.** "Nationalizations in Austria," op. cit., p. 156.

**30.** "The Development of the Public Sector," op. cit., p. 22.

**31.** Ibid.

**32.** M. V. Posner and S. J. Woolf, *Italian Public Enterprise* (Cambridge, Mass.: 1967), p. 128.

**33.** Manuel Gottlieb, "Political Economy of the Public Debt," *Public Finance*, 11:3 (1956), 269.

**34.** The public debt expanded at the expense of consumption, not savings, first, because savings were interest-elastic (mainly because corporate or internal business savings were relatively small), whereas investment was interest-inelastic, and second, because the debt was financed by indirect taxation falling mainly on the working classes and small business and professional groups. Thus, in Marx's words, the debt was "one of the most powerful levers of primitive accumulation" [*Capital*, Vol. I, Modern Library Edition (New York: 1906), 827–829]. The debt also played an important role in the accumulation of capital in the early nineteenth century in that debt interest provided a stable source of income for the capitalist class, thus releasing other funds for more risky and speculative ventures.

35. "Political Economy of the Public Debt," op. cit., p. 266. For example, between 1820 and World War I, a period of relative peace, the British national debt actually declined. In the United States there was a similar decline in the federal debt from the end of the Civil War to World War I.

36. B. J. F. Steinmetz, "Is the Growth of Public Debt a War Phenomenon or a Capitalistic Phenomenon?" *Public Finance*, 4:4 (1949), 363–364.

37. "Political Economy of the Public Debt," op. cit., p. 266.

38. Karl Marx, *Eighteenth Brumaire of Louis Bonaparte*, quoted in "Political Economy of the Public Debt," op. cit., p. 268, n. 8.

39. Paul B. Trescott, "Some Historical Aspects of Federal Fiscal Policy, 1790–1956," in *Federal Expenditure Policy for Economic Growth and Stability*, Joint Economic Committee, U.S. Congress (Washington, D.C., 1957), p. 79. Budget surpluses in the nineteenth century (particularly during the first half) generated by tariff revenues and the sale of public lands were used to retire the debt, which fell from $81 million in 1825 to $7 million in 1832. Small farmers, small businessmen, and workers were exploited, first, because high tariffs reduced real incomes, and second, because tariff revenues were used to pay interest on and retire the debt, thus redistributing income to debt holders.

40. E. James Ferguson, *The Power of the Purse: A History of American Public Finance, 1776–1796* (Durham, N.C.: 1961), p. 341.

41. Compared with 12 percent in 1969. Today, 40 federal agencies have the right to borrow in the market, including the Export-Import Bank, the Maritime Administration, and TVA. These also include five "sponsored agencies" (the most important of which are the Federal Home Loan Banks and the Federal National Mortgage Association) which are privately owned but backed by government credit. These sponsored agencies use the federal government as insurer, guarantor, and market intermediary. The newest federal borrowing agencies are a rural telephone bank, the Environmental Financing Agency, and "Sally Mae," a secondary "Marketmaker" for college student loans ("An Administration Lid on Agency Borrowing," *Business Week*, January 22, 1972). Budgetary planners are concerned about the proliferation of these agencies because they allocate credit outside of the framework of normal budget planning. In 1972, the Nixon Administration wanted to rationalize the whole system by creating a federal bank that would borrow for most of these agencies and also by limiting the volume of loan guarantees that federal agencies offer private borrowers.

42. According to Lynn Turgeon, "large corporations have been willing to put up with the restrictive monetary policy [that followed the Accord] because they are financially independent of the banking system as a result of ample reserves resulting from legislated subsidization [rapid depreciation and investment tax credits]" (communication to the author). Taken as a whole, it is clear that restrictive monetary policy together with "legislated subsidies" have the effect of allocating credit resources to the big companies in the monopoly sector, another example of their enormous power.

THE FISCAL CRISIS OF THE STATE

**43.** Nonmarketable securities ("savings bonds") have hardly grown at all, increasing from $56.2 billion in 1946 to $59.1 billion in 1970.

The *motive* for expanding special issues was primarily to avoid paying the high interest rates that followed from the Treasury Accord of 1951 and the Fed's subsequent restrictive monetary policy (thus, between 1950 and 1957, special issues jumped from 14.8 to 20.7 percent of total national debt).

**44.** It should be added that between 1957 and 1963–1964, the rate of inflation was relatively low and the government was able to lengthen the debt temporarily and rely less on special issues. Since the mid-1960s, the Treasury has had to shorten the debt and put out more special issues to finance growing deficits.

**45.** "[State and local governments] find U.S. government securities a safe outlet for their excess working cash balances, pension funds, and money held in the future anticipation of expenditures such as the proceeds from bonds. Investors such as savings and loan associations and corporate pension funds also like to keep a portion of their assets in a liquid, low risk form such as government securities . . ." [Ansel M. Sharp and Bernard F. Sliger, *Public Finance* (Homewood, Ill.: 1964), p. 167].

**46.** Victor Perlo, "The U.S. Government and the Economic Cycle," *World Marxist Review*, 18:9 (September 1965), 35–37. It could be argued that a growing debt (and thus a growing debt service) in modern capitalism is not only a concomitant, but perhaps a necessary condition for economic growth.

**47.** James Buchanan, *The Public Finances* (Homewood, Ill : 1960), p. 361.

**48.** It should be noted that to the degree that state and local governments hold federal debt, some state and local debt is in reality national debt. Because of the tax-exempt features of local bonds (see Chapter 8) national debt is magically transformed into tax-free securities. The cost of floating these securities is reduced (local governments save perhaps as much as $700 million yearly because they can sell their securities at higher prices), but this merely shifts the cost to the federal government because the wealthy individuals who hold these bonds escape taxation under the individual income tax.

**49.** Banks, small business, and taxpayer and other groups have placed all kinds of legal restrictions on state and local borrowing, including constitutional prohibitions against some kinds of indebtedness, bans on "full faith and credit" debt in some states, requirements for prior legislative approval and/or referendums or both, etc.

**50.** The trend toward the provision of public credit for direct private use has accelerated in recent years. Confined to a handful of states in the South prior to 1958, industrial revenue bond sales never exceeded $12 million yearly. Despite the opposition of many bankers and corporate law firms, the Treasury, and the SEC, more and more states have issued increasing amounts of these securities. By 1967, over forty states had passed enabling acts permitting the use of lease-rental financing, and the total volume of industrial revenue bonds outstanding came to almost 10 percent of all tax-exempt issues, or $1 3 billion [Alan Rabinowitz, *Municipal Bond Finance and Administration* (New York: 1965), passim].

**51.** U.S. Department of Agriculture, Economic Research Service, *Financing Industrial Development Through State and Local Governments* (Washington, D.C.: December 1967), p. iv.

**52.** *Municipal Bond Finance and Administration*, op. cit., p. 43.

**53.** For example, in 1966, the Finance Committee (consisting entirely of bankers and brokers) of St. Louis' Bond Issue Screening Committee reduced health and hospital bond requests by more than 50 percent and park, recreation, and cultural project requests by two-thirds (*St. Louis Post-Dispatch*, July 10, 1966).

**54.** *Municipal Bond Finance and Administration*, op. cit.

**55.** *New York Times*, November 19, 1965.

**56.** "Planned and Actual Long-Term Borrowing by State and Local Governments," *Federal Reserve Bulletin*, December 1971, p. 977.

**57.** Statement of Wright Patman, Subcommittee on Economic Progress, Joint Economic Committee, *Financing Municipal Facilities* (Washington, D.C.: December 5, 1967).

**58.** Paul F. McGouldrick and John E. Petersen, "Monetary Restraints and Borrowing and Capital Spending by Large State and Local Governments in 1966," *Federal Reserve Bulletin*, July 1968, p. 554. Although in 1966 large state and local units reduced long-term borrowing by 20 percent of planned levels, "the deferral of long-term borrowings did not result in equivalent reductions in capital outlays within that period" (ibid., p. 552) Most governments borrowed short term or fell back on liquid assets. High interest rates had a negligible effect on contract awards (ibid , p. 563). Further, local interest ceilings and other legal restrictions on borrowing cause local government to postpone, not abandon capital projects (ibid., p. 561).

**59.** "Planned and Actual Long-Term Borrowing by State and Local Governments," op. cit., p. 979.

**60.** *Municipal Bond Finance and Administration*, op. cit., p. vii. Rabinowitz writes that "it would be too much of an overstatement to suggest that state and local governments, in their bond financing, are becoming orphans in the marketplace. But it would be an understatement bordering on delusion to suggest that all is well or that all can continue as in the past" (ibid.).

**61.** U.S. Department of Commerce, *Chart Book on Governmental Finance and Employment, 1966* (Washington, D.C.: 1966), pp. 2 and 15.

**62.** U.S. Department of Agriculture, Economic Research Service, *The Impact of New Industry on Local Government Finances in Five Small Towns in Kentucky*, Agricultural Economic Report No. 191 (Washington, D.C.: September 1970), p. iv. Precisely because the new plants were established to take advantage of pools of unemployed workers, their negative impact on local finances was minimized (because the towns did not have to develop new services for new residents).

# CHAPTER 8
# FINANCING THE BUDGET:
# THE TAX STATE

## INTRODUCTION

Tax finance is (and always has been) a form of economic exploitation and thus a problem for class analysis. It is no less true today than in the past that "external protection and power, and the enrichment of some classes at the expense of others (are) the purpose of contributory systems" [1] and that "tax struggle is the oldest form of class struggle"—as Marx wrote over a century ago. Therefore the state must attempt to establish equitable forms of taxation in order to conceal the inequitable content of the tax structure and the exploitive nature of the class structure. History has shown that when the state is no longer able to conceal tax exploitation or justify it ideologically, there is the risk of a tax revolt (and thus a class revolt) and an intensification of the state's fiscal problems (and thus political problems).

## IDEOLOGIES OF TAX EXPLOITATION

Every important change in the balance of class and political forces is registered in the tax structure. Put another way, tax systems are simply particular forms of class systems. When capitalism was developing within European feudal society, the bourgeoisie used the tax system to compel the nobility to adapt the state to the requirements of private capital accumulation. In preindustrial U.S. capitalist society tariffs increased steadily until the late 1820s, but the class interests of farmers and southern planters, which conflicted sharply with those of the rising, protectionist-minded industrial bourgeoisie, prevailed for the moment and tariffs were cut back dramatically during the early 1830s. Later, when the Civil War destroyed the southern planter class and thus weakened the western farmers politically, a strengthened industrial bourgeoisie was able to increase tariffs. In a still later stage of capitalist development the tax structure mirrored the imperatives of imperialist expansion. The classic example is the imposition of a poll tax on tribal and peasant labor in order to recruit wage labor for the foreign-owned plantations and mines. Throughout history tax systems have reflected international rivalries and have been registered in the booty (once a respectable and important, albeit unstable, source of revenue) seized from or the reparations forced on the vanquished.

Ruling classes normally attempt either to conceal or to justify or rationalize tax exploitation ideologically. New taxes are served up with slogans—for example, "tax fairness or equity" or "improving incentives." And the state must "explain" increased tax rates and broadened tax bases in such terms or invite increased tax evasion, a flight from newly taxed economic activities, organized political opposition, and other forms of tax revolt.

This was true even in the feudal era, when the domination of one class by another was transparent and accepted as a permanent feature of society. When they first appeared in the budgets of the feudal nobility taxes contained "equity" criteria based on the principle that different classes had different rights and duties. For example, "the nobility of eighteenth-century France," Louis Eisenstein writes, "were serenely certain that they contributed special benefits to society that called for a special immunity from taxes. They . . . had incentives that had to be preserved for the welfare of others." [2] By contrast, the dominant classes in nineteenth-century America attempted (with moderate success at times) to conceal tax exploitation. The working class was small and undeveloped and thus personal income taxes were not feasible, the only wealth tax was the property tax, and the tariff became the most important source of revenue—one that was relatively "invisible" because it took the form of higher commodity prices. Even today, import and export taxes are held up as models of taxation in underdeveloped countries precisely because they are easy to conceal. One economist has written of the "political advantage" of export taxes because they hide the burden that falls on peasant farmers engaged in export production.[3]

Tax exploitation also is concealed from the taxpayer in advanced capitalist societies. And indirect taxes (e.g., sales and excise taxes) remain important sources of state and local revenue. The Tax Foundation has estimated that roughly 150 taxes are "hidden" in the price of a loaf of bread, and about 600 taxes in the price of a house.[4] However, far more important, tax exploitation normally is accepted because the ideology of the dominant monopoly capitalist class is accepted.[5] The justification for exploitation is based on three general concepts: the old idea of *incentive* and the new ideas of *ability to pay* and *equal treatment for equals*. Put briefly, the incentive rationale asserts that if profits are taxed too heavily, the accumu-

THE FISCAL CRISIS OF THE STATE

lation of capital and thus the growth of production and employment will diminish, and that if the incentives of wealthy families and investors and their financial institutions (which monopolize the supply of money capital) are impaired, the supply of investable funds will dry up. In other words, the official ideology of taxation asserts that taxes must not reduce incentives both to supply and to invest money capital. These propositions are, of course, true within the framework of capitalist production: Those who advance them can sabotage production if they do not receive what they consider to be acceptable profit margins and personal incomes.

The ability-to-pay doctrine holds that every member of society—capitalist and worker alike—should pay taxes commensurate with personal income. Needless to say, this principle is suspended when it conflicts with the incentives doctrine. For example, dozens of loopholes ensure that income from capital ownership is substantially tax-free. Further the use of income, not wealth, as the measure of ability to pay clearly discriminates against workers and in favor of capital. Nowhere in the capitalist world are unrealized capital gains taxed, even though they clearly increase an individual's ability to pay taxes.

Another ideological element in the theory of taxation is based on ability to pay. The hidden premise of the principle is that the benefits of state expenditures accrue more or less equally to every taxpayer. This argument is invalid: Local, state, and federal budgetary priorities are determined by the need to expand social capital (social consumption and social investment) and social expenses of production (welfare and warfare spending).[6] Thus the ability-to-pay doctrine is ideological, not because it is illogical, but because its premise is false.

The final justification of tax exploitation is the idea that "equals should be treated equally." Unassailable in principle, this doctrine is prejudicial to the working class in practice. Capitalist society is not a society of equals. There are owners and nonowners, monopoly capitalists and competitive capitalists, organized workers and unorganized workers, oppressive social groupings and oppressed minorities, rich and poor, and so forth. Thus, a tax system that treats "equals equally" merely reinforces existing inequalities.

## TAXATION OF THE CAPITALIST CLASS

The federal government uses tax rates and the tax structure as instruments of fiscal policy for economic stabilization and growth. In the 1960s and again in the early 1970s, rates and structure were changed in an effort to stimulate investment spending and capital accumulation. Like expenditure policy aimed at socializing the costs of constant and variable capital, tax policy is largely designed to expand private profits and private economic activity, which means that the state must not impair capital's incentives to save and invest. Thus, theoretically, taxation of the income or wealth of the capitalist class is at best impractical.

Superficially it seems that the monopoly capital class is taxed in a number of ways. In the United States (and most advanced capitalist societies) there are corporation income taxes, gift and inheritance taxes, taxes on commercial property, payroll taxes on business, and the individual income tax. In fact, most taxation on corporate income is absorbed by consumers (workers and small businessmen), not by the corporate owners. Gift and inheritance taxation is minimal and relatively easy to avoid or evade. Commercial property taxes are also shifted mainly to tenants or consumers (or back to workers). Payroll taxes are shifted to workers altogether. And the individual income tax structure provides many opportunities to escape high marginal rates of taxation. Only in times of national crisis has there been a serious attempt to tax income accruing to capital. All income in excess of 8 percent of invested capital was appropriated during World War I; Congress legislated an undistributed profits tax late in the depression (1936–1939); a 95 percent excess profits tax was imposed during World War II, with the stipulation that revenue from it and the corporate income tax should not exceed 80 percent of a corporation's net income (the true rate of taxation was obscured by a complicated system of credits and allowances); and, finally, during the Korean War, a temporary 30 percent excess profits tax was imposed.[7]

Historically, there is a close connection between the development of the corporate income tax and the individual income tax. The first individual income tax (1913) exempted the vast majority of workers and was applied only to wealthy individuals. Capitalists responded to the threat of America's first (and short-lived and last) class tax by agitating for a corporate income tax as a substitute for the individual income tax. Nelson Aldrich led this movement in the Senate, and in 1909 Congress enacted the first corporate tax. From the outset, business leaders have favored taxing their corporate rather than personal income because monopoly sector corporations control prices and thus can shift the corporate income tax to consumers. Consider the evidence. In 1920, when the tax rate was 12.5 percent, after-tax earnings were 12 percent of net book value of large

THE FISCAL CRISIS OF THE STATE

manufacturing corporation. In 1955, with the tax rate at 52 percent, the after-tax earnings figure was 13 percent.[8] Although the problem is highly complex and hotly debated, it is generally agreed that "when measured from changes in the rate of return (profit), shifting is close to 100 percent."[9] In both the monopoly and the competitive sectors (which cannot absorb the tax because profits are so meager) the corporate income tax is similar to a general sales tax levied at a rate in proportion to the corporation's profit margin.[10]

Although there are no general business taxes in the United States, capitalists are nominally subject to various wealth taxes. The most important of these is the property tax, which, in fact, falls mainly on the working and small-business classes. Within the core cities residential property assumes the larger (and commercial property, the smaller) burden of property taxation.[11] Central-city property values show a relative decline because of the "suburbanization of industry" and the proliferation of freeways, public parking, and other facilities, which removes land from the tax rolls. And the flight of relatively well-to-do workers, professionals, and small businessmen to the suburbs has further reduced revenues from residential property taxes.[12]

Available studies indicate that owners of residential buildings usually shift the property tax to their tenants—the vast majority of whom are workers. And it has been estimated that about 75 percent of property taxes on local industry and retail establishments are shifted to consumers.[13] Finally, a recent federal study showed that over three million households, the vast majority of them low-income families, pay more than 10 percent of their income in property taxes.[14] In short, it is not surprising that economists generally agree that the property tax is harshly regressive.[15]

The only other U.S. wealth taxes are estate and gift taxes. Modest levies were imposed early in the century, but not until the New Deal did populist elements in Congress (at first with Roosevelt's support, which was later withdrawn) attempt to raise estate and gift taxation significantly. The taxes were raised, but as Bernstein notes, "when combined with such regressive levies as social security and local taxes . . . the Wealth Tax of 1935 did not drain wealth from higher-income groups, and the top 1 percent even increased their shares during the New Deal years."[16] Since 1942, estate and gift taxes have remained basically unchanged. Although nominal federal estate-tax rates range from 3 percent on $5,000 to $10,000 to 77 percent on $10,000,000 or more, the actual average rate is little more than 10 percent. The difference is attributable to exemptions for life estates and for gifts made more than three years before death.[17] In his study of federal taxation Joseph Pechman writes that "about 3 percent of the estates of adult decedents and less than one-fourth of the wealth owned by the decedents in any one year are subject to estate and gift taxes." [18] Thus even though U.S. monopoly capitalists have accumulated enormous wealth since World War II, revenue from estate and gift taxes run below $4 billion annually—roughly 2 percent of total federal revenues (or less than half their percentage contribution in the early 1940s).[19]

Monopoly capitalists pay no general business tax and their unrealized capital gains go tax free. To be sure, wealthy indi-viduals who receive dividends and interest income are taxed at high marginal rates under the individual income tax, but the corporate owners and their top managers receive the greatest part of their in-come in the form of tax-free interest from municipal bonds and realized capital gains, which are taxed at relatively low rates. For example, less than 2 percent of the richest families own about 87 percent of municipal school bonds.[20] Favorable treatment of capital gains, together with the enormous benefits from income-splitting at high income levels, reduce taxes on the rich by about one-half, and personal deductions reduce taxation still further to about one-third of potential levels under the nominal rate structure. All in all, the average tax rate at the upper end of the income scale is probably as low as 20 percent.[21] Because the monopoly capitalist class (but not the working class) has been able to establish loopholes in the tax system "the individual income tax has hardly made a dent in the buildup of this massive concentration of wealth despite the facade of progressive rates." [22]


## TAX EXPLOITATION OF THE WORKING CLASS

Changes in tax rates and the tax structure, the main forms of modern fiscal policy, have increasingly favored corporate profits and growth. And with the tax shelters and loopholes available to monopoly capitalists, the whole system is based, in effect, on the exploitation of the working and small-business classes, particularly monopoly sector workers whose taxable incomes are relatively high.

In addition to shifted property and corporate income taxes, the social security and sales and excise taxes and the individual income tax are exploitative. The social security payroll tax used to finance old age insurance and unemployment insurance (outlays for social consumption) is regressive, falling most heavily on the low-income worker, because a flat rate is applied to taxable earnings without regard to income levels.[23] It is especially regressive for workers who do not stay in the labor force long enough to accumulate sufficient credited employment to qualify for primary benefits.[24] Although worker and employer nominally contribute equally to the payroll tax, "most economists agree that the entire payroll tax really falls on wages—that wages would be higher by approximately the amount of the employer's contribution if no such contribution were on the books." [25]

Excise taxes are levied by both state and federal governments, and most state and many local governments impose general sales taxes. In part or whole regressive, these taxes also are particularly burdensome to low-income workers.[26] State sales taxes were introduced in the 1930s to reduce the burden on residential, commercial, and industrial property owners. By 1967, state governments were raising nearly two-thirds of their tax revenues from sales and gross receipts taxes, whereas individual income taxes contributed only 16 percent.[27]

With the growth of new social classes and class formations, the forms of tax exploitation change. During the nineteenth century an indirect tax—tariffs—was the major source of federal revenue. Today the individual income tax raises roughly one-third of revenues at all levels of government. Experimented with briefly during the Civil War, the first real income tax was passed by Congress in 1894, after more than a decade of farmer, small-business, and working-class agitation against big business. The tax rate was a flat 2 percent, which, as noted earlier, would have been paid only by a handful of wealthy individuals. In 1894, the tax was declared unconstitutional by the U.S. Supreme Court.

In the nineteenth century (particularly the first half), the farmer, business and commercial, and planter classes received the vast majority of national income, and of course they were not willing to tax themselves. Only with the creation and growth of a massive and propertyless working class was an income tax politically feasible—a tax with ample loopholes, so wealthy families could escape its high marginal rates.

With the growth of a modern proletariat, the individual income tax was also ideally suited to the needs of monopoly capital. For one thing, the income tax cannot be shifted to profits. For another, the tax is progressive in form, although regressive or proportional in content. Thus the myth of "tax equity" could be preserved. Loopholes, generally perceived as aberrations in an otherwise equitable system (liberal politicians are forever seeking to "close the loopholes"), are, in fact, a normal and necessary part of the income tax structure.

Not surprisingly, the income tax has encroached more and more on wage income since it was first introduced. The national state systematically reduced personal exemptions and credits for dependents from $4000 (for a family of four) in 1913–1916 to $2400 in 1970. In 1913–1916, a single person was granted an exemption of $3000; in 1970, only $600. And, until 1943, labor income was taxed at a rate 10 percent lower than profit income because of the absence of comparable treatment of personal expenditures for "business purposes" such as personal depreciation allowances, education expenditures, and so forth. Further, in terms of actual purchasing power, real exemptions have fallen by even greater amounts. Finally, popular consciousness of the tax burden has been reduced by tax withholding —the most subtle form of tax exploitation (before withholding was introduced in 1940, there was widespread tax evasion among lower-income families). Currently, about 85 percent of income taxes are collected at the basic 20 percent rate, which applies to two-thirds of all returns.[28]

The average effective rate of taxation on the highest incomes is no more than 25 percent (it is less than 5 percent for very low-income families), chiefly because of the special treatment granted capital gains income, income exclusions (interest from local bonds), deductions (important chiefly to higher-bracket families) and income splitting and exemptions (which benefit high-income relatively more than low-income families).[29] In all probability, no one other than independent professionals, professional and technical workers, and small and middle businessmen pays more than 15 to 20 percent because of the ease of funneling income into nontaxable forms (e.g., expense accounts) and widespread tax evasion among farmers and those who receive interest income and annuities. In recent years the state has failed even to pretend that the flat war tax surcharge of 10 percent is progressive. And the 1965 tax cuts benefit the rich far more than the poor—for the former the decrease in tax rates is permanent, but for the latter (whose money income is rising and thus subject in the future to higher marginal rates) the decrease is only temporary.[30]

To summarize, the tax system performs two major functions. First, it permits monopoly capital to expand its income and wealth, and thus plays an important role in reinforcing it as the dominant class. Even when these outlays nominally are covered by taxes on profits, increased state outlays increase profits and fall on

THE FISCAL CRISIS OF THE STATE

real wages because corporate taxes are shifted to consumers in the form of higher prices. Second, to meet the costs of social capital and social expenses, the system appropriates capital from small business and the working class. Thus by limiting their ability to accumulate liquid savings, the tax system forces workers to remain workers—and in the long run it compels the working class to be more and more dependent on capital and ultimately on the state. This is one interesting contradiction of the tax system: on the one hand, the tax burden falls most heavily on the working class; on the other, the working class requires more and more expenditures (social consumption and social expenses) precisely because of its working-class status. It may be true that the greater the level of tax exploitation, the higher the level of government expenditures, and hence the need for even greater tax exploitation.

## REVENUE SHARING
## AND THE CRISIS OF FEDERALISM

The federal government appropriates the lion's share of tax revenues generated by capital accumulation and economic growth. As employment and incomes increase, the progressive individual income tax "catches" a larger portion of the increment to income than do regressive state and local property and sales taxes.[31]

Nevertheless, state and local governments are compelled to spend increasing amounts on social capital projects and social expense programs. In addition to forcing local governments to raise taxes on workers and small business, monopoly capital has won concessions in the form of industrial property tax relief, free industrial plants and facilities, and so on. A contradiction thus exists between the expanded fiscal burdens heaped on the states and localities and their ability to meet this burden. The contradiction reflects conflicts within the existing power structure—monopoly capital is relatively powerful at the federal level whereas competitive capital is comparatively strong at the state and local levels. In effect, monopoly capital forces small business and labor to underwrite the expansion of the monopoly sector but does not increase their ability to finance social capital and social expense outlays.

Consequently, state and local governments must raise taxes and introduce new taxes (between 1957 and 1970, state and local taxes increased by over 100 percent in the vast majority of the states). At present, 45 states have sales taxes and 37 have income taxes. And Congress has tried to use tax-credit devices to force other

FINANCING THE BUDGET: THE TAX STATE                    211

states to introduce income taxes. Moreover, since the 1950s, the federal government has had to channel more and more tax revenues to the states, and state governments in turn have had to allocate more funds to local governments.[32] Between 1955 and 1968, federal aid to state and local governments increased from about $3 to over $17 billion annually, and the number of major grant programs rose from 44 to 95 (in 1968, there were more than 400 programs and specific grant authorizations; 128 were in the field of education).[33] Even as early as 1960, about 40 percent of city revenues came from federal and state government grants. By 1966, 15.8 percent of all state and local revenues originated at the federal level. All in all, federal aid to state and local governments expanded from less than $10 billion in 1962 to over $27 billion in 1970.[34]

Despite these grants, state and local governments have had to scurry about seeking new sources of taxes and revenues. By the late 1960s, the local fiscal crisis was almost completely out of hand. Local politicians, school boards, and special districts pleaded with their state governments for more help and the states turned to Washington. The so-called mayors' lobby—the Legislative Action Committee of the U.S. Conference of Mayors—has been making strong direct appeals to the federal government for aid to the big cities (and in 1971 actually forced the release of $700 million in model cities funds authorized by the Congress but held up by the President).

For local politicians and businessmen the problem is that funds are not available in sufficient quantities when and where they are needed by local government and local capital. Until recently, federal grant programs actually redistributed revenues from the industrial to the nonindustrial states and from the larger states where the fiscal crisis was most severe to the smaller states.[35] However, for the monopoly capitalist and the federal executive, the problem is that too many projects established under the auspices of too many governments and special districts receive too many funds. Concerned less with the fiscal crisis in particular states and cities, and more with the fiscal crisis as whole, corporate planners and the federal government are preoccupied with the many "major administrative difficulties" created by the "rapid, uncoordinated, piecemeal expansion of the Federal grant system." [36] In short, national planners are worried chiefly about efficiency—meaning, ultimately, corporate profitability and accumulation. As the CED puts it, "home rule for those who can handle it." What this means is that "big business is uniting behind plans to set up regional administrative governments that usurp present local government powers (taxation, zoning, policing, eminent domain) in order to make domestic economic expansion more efficient and centrally planned." [37] Other capitalist agencies such as the National Industrial Conference Board have developed ideas for regional fiscal planning,[38] which, in turn, will ultimately require regional government—new political structures through which Federal funds will be channeled. In brief, revenue-sharing programs developed by big business boil down to new policies to reduce or eliminate the power of local government and substitute regional planning and regional government organized by monopoly capital.

One big step in the direction of regional planning and government came in 1966, when Congress passed the Comprehensive Health Care Planning and Services Act. This legislation eliminated a number of categorical public health grants and

> substituted a single grant for comprehensive health care services. . . . An added dimension of this particular "experiment" with the consolidated grant approach was the condition that each state create or designate an agency with responsibility for developing comprehensive plans of health services. These plans are expected to provide for careful distribution of state and federal funds among the various health services and to constitute the basis for *federal review* of state health programming. Two other aspects of this legislation are worth noting. First, there is a *declared administrative intent to designate significant decision-making activities to the regional offices.* . . . As the Federal official responsible for the administration of this program stated recently, *"The Regional Office will be where the action is."* Second, accompanying the new single grant program was a project grant program supportive of *areawide health planning.*[39]

Similarly, the federal government requires that highway funds and funds for local transit lines be applied to projects that are integrated into regional transportation plans. That the new system of consolidated grants is designed to eliminate duplication and waste at the local level (translation: "eliminate the power of small-scale capital and local governments") is evidenced by President Nixon's own special revenue-sharing proposal. Under the Nixon plan, 130 of 500 specific programs would be consolidated into six major grant areas— urban community development, rural community development, education, manpower training, transportation, and law enforcement (all major areas of social capital and social expense outlays). The special revenue-sharing plan is described by the Administration itself as providing "full State and local discretion over *implementation* of broad *national* objectives mandated by Congress." [40] In other words, the federal government defines policies and plans and local governments put them into practice. The first revenue-sharing bill, passed in September 1972 (which will distribute $20 billion to local government and $10 billion to the states over five years) permits local authorities to use their funds only for public transport, public safety, and environmental protection.

Closely related to plans for regionalization are programs designed to force state and local governments to stretch their tax capabilities to the limit. Revenue sharing is intended to provide the financial and political clout for regional planning and regional government, not relieve local fiscal crises directly. Evidence from both the U.S. and Canada suggests a tendency for local (provincial in Canada) "tax effort" to be reduced as federal aid increases.[41] Those who would "modernize" revenue sharing seek to avoid this danger. In the words of the Nixon Administration's general revenue-sharing proposal, federal funds granted to a particular state

> will be adjusted according to how well it has attempted to meet its people's needs through its own revenue-raising powers. A State that does an above average job on this score will have its share adjusted upward. This provision is designed to provide an incentive for States and localities *to maintain and even expand their own tax effort* when that is appropriate.[42]

Not surprisingly, the 1972 revenue-sharing bill distributes relatively more funds to states that make relatively strenuous "tax efforts."

To summarize, the purpose of the Nixon Administration's (and any conceivable national government's) revenue-sharing program is, first, to save money by consolidating specific federally funded projects into general program areas; second, to create regional authorities (and ultimately regional governments), which will permit monopoly capital and the social-industrial complex to make an "end run around" local government; third, to force state and local governments to squeeze the taxpayer even more. But this strategy rests, uncomfortably, on two assumptions: first, that federal monies will be available in sufficient quantities to finance the regionally based social-industrial complex, and, second, that big business and the federal government will be able to reduce or eliminate the power of small-scale capital (and the competitive sector) in local and state government, and, further, that community-control movements, labor groups, radical and revolutionary organizations, and other social forces with everything to lose and nothing to gain will not be able to stop top-down regional planning and government.

The first assumption is somewhat tenuous. Although

THE FISCAL CRISIS OF THE STATE

the U.S. Treasury does appropriate the largest share of tax revenues generated by capital accumulation and economic growth and has committed itself to $30 billion of revenue sharing, the federal government's enormous and growing fiscal obligations are becoming more difficult to meet. In May 1972, the Brookings Institution announced that the Treasury would need all incremental tax revenues for the following two years to pay for current obligations and programs already authorized, and that higher spending would require higher taxes (the Nixon Administration immediately responded that the budget would be pruned here and pared there and that funds would be available for new programs). Moreover, after "subtracting" the Department of Defense budget (which is almost sacrosanct), payments into various trust funds, interest obligations on the public debt, and other fixed and semifixed expenditures, less than one-third of federal revenues is available for revenue sharing (no more than 5 percent of GNP).[43]

But the second assumption is much more dubious. Whether competitive sector capital, professional classes, community and insurgency groups, state employee organizations, welfare rights organizations, and sections of organized labor that are influential in local politics will allow supergovernment to be imposed from above by a federally subsidized social-industrial complex is unpredictable. But this question will not yield to economic analysis alone. The scope and limits of capitalist reform require political analysis and judgment. It is to such analysis and judgment that we turn in the concluding chapter.

## NOTES AND REFERENCES

1. Rudolf Goldscheid, "A Sociological Approach to the Problem of Public Finance," in Richard A. Musgrave and Alan T. Peacock, eds., *Classics in the Theory of Public Finance* (New York: 1958), p. 203.

2. Louis Eisenstein, *The Ideologies of Taxation* (New York: 1961), pp. 222–223.

3. Frank A. Jackson, "Political Aspects of Export Taxation," *Public Finance*, 12:4 (1957), 291.

4. Cited by Sylvia Porter, *San Francisco Chronicle*, November 29, 1966.

5. The situation in the underdeveloped countries is very differ-

ent because the bourgeoisie is small, weak, and generally ineffective as a ruling class. Forced levies in the form of inflation substitute for voluntary taxes as tax exploitation.

6. The most amazing aspect of this situation is that bourgeois economists actually claim that the distribution of the benefits of state expenditures favor the working class (especially the poor) at the expense of the owning classes! One economist writes that "a redistributive system is, of course, the type which is characteristic of the modern state" [James Buchanan, *Fiscal Theory and Political Economy* (Chapel Hill, N.C.: 1960), pp. 18–19]. A survey in the late 1950s indicated that more than 40 percent of all taxpayers at the lower end of the income scale believed that the government took away more in taxes than it returned in services. [Morris Janowitz et al., *Public Administration and the Public* (Ann Arbor, Mich.: 1958)]. Almost 70 percent of those sampled by the Opinion Research Corporation in the summer of 1972 said that they thought they paid too much for what they got in the way of federal services (*Business Week,* June 17, 1972, p. 102). The overall effects of state expenditures on the distribution of income and wealth between economic classes have not been analyzed, but some researchers have reported on the effect of state spending on personal-income distribution. A study of 1961 and 1965 spending concludes that "the general pattern of distribution of all major expenditure benefits is significantly 'pro poor'—on any reasonable assumption concerning the incidence of benefits" [Tax Foundation, *Tax Burden and Benefits of Government Expenditure, By Income Class, 1961 and 1965* (New York: 1967), p. 28]. This study (and subsequent studies by the Council of Economic Advisors and the Bureau of the Census) assumes that all benefits from state spending flow directly to individual families and that business organizations per se do not receive any benefits, and hence that the owning class does not benefit indirectly from state spending which underwrites their corporations in various ways. In other words, the Tax Foundation study assumes that America is not a class society—hardly a "reasonable assumption."

7. Progressives, reformers, liberals, and conservatives alike have agreed that excess profit taxation should be confined to wartime crises. The reason is that excess profits taxation would contribute to basic changes in the distribution of wealth and income and, ultimately, class structure. This is why, to take the first example in twentieth-century American history, "occasional progressives such as Woodrow Wilson and William G. McAdoo presented a united front with those opposing excess profits taxes (after World War I)" [H. Larry Ingle, "The Dangers of Reaction: Repeal of the Revenue Act of 1918," *The North Carolina Historical Review,* 49:1 (January 1967), 72].

8. Jerome R. Hellerstein, *Taxes, Loopholes, and Morals* (New York: 1963), pp. 67–68.

9. Marian Krzyzaniak, ed., *Effects of Corporation Income Tax; Papers Presented at the Symposium on Business Taxation* (Detroit: 1966), p. 13. Depending on the particular economic assumptions, a case can be made that the corporations shift the income tax not only to consumers, but also back to workers in the form of lower wages, as well as to investors in the nontaxed sectors. In the latter case the burden is passed within the capitalist class (ibid., p. 85).

10. There are also a number of loopholes in the corporate income tax. The most glaring is the oil depletion allowance. In 1964, the top twenty-two oil refiners paid only 4 percent of their more than $5 billion gross profits in income taxes. In 1965 and 1966, the percentage rose to 6.9 and 8.5 percent, respectively. When the depletion allowance came under increasing attack politically in the late 1960s, the oil industry announced that any cut in their allowances

THE FISCAL CRISIS OF THE STATE

:

would result in higher prices and thus effectively be passed on to consumers (*Wall Street Journal*, July 23, 1969; September 5, 1969).

We should add that state governments have corporate and bank taxes of various kinds. In California, for example, about one-third of state revenue comes from such taxes. The degree to which these taxes are shifted forward to consumers, backward to workers, or sideways to other businesses is unknown because most large corporations sell out of state.

**11.** One reason is that commercial and industrial property (unlike residential property) is not bought and sold with great frequency and its "fair market value" is almost impossible to estimate accurately. Capitalists thus can undervalue their holdings whereas homeowners cannot. Another reason is that in some cities (e.g., Houston) major industries themselves fix the value of their properties for tax purposes.

**12.** Mordecai S. Feinberg, "The Implications of the Core-City Decline for the Fiscal Structure of the Core-City," *National Tax Journal*, 17 (September 1964), 217. Revenues from property taxes actually rose in the ten largest U.S. cities between 1950 and 1960 But if assessed rates and prices had not changed, revenues would have fallen in four of the ten.

**13.** Richard Musgrave's study of Michigan property taxes, cited in California Assembly, Interim Committee on Revenue and Taxation, *Taxation of Property in California*, December 1964, p. 30. Little or no shifting occurs if there are rent controls, long-term leases, or real competition between landlords for tenants.

**14.** *Wall Street Journal*, January 15, 1971.

**15.** Dick Netzer, *Economics of the Property Tax* (Washington: 1966), pp. 40–62. One economist has written, "The unevenness of its base, the wide variations in rates, and the imperfections in its administration probably make (the property tax's) impact such as to move the tax system as a whole away from, not toward, ability to pay" [Jesse Burkhead, *Public School Finance* (Syracuse: 1964), p. 185]. See also Gerhard Rostvold's review of James Maxwell, *Financing State and Local Governments* (Washington, D.C. 1965), *American Economic Review*, 56 (September 1966), 947.

**16.** Barton J. Bernstein, *Towards A New Past: Dissenting Essays in American History* (New York: 1968), p. 175.

**17.** *State Inheritance Tax Rates and Exemptions* (New York: 1966), p. 165.

**18.** Joseph Pechman, *Federal Tax Policy* (Washington, D.C.: 1966), p. 182.

**19.** Lillian Doris, *The American Way of Taxation: Internal Revenue, 1862–1963* (Englewood Cliffs, N.J.: 1963), pp. 181–182. Only in Europe, directly after World War I, were capital levies remotely possible; there was considerable popular discontent with war profiteering and the conscription of manpower. The classic article on the political economy of wealth taxation in this period is Manuel Gottlieb, "The Capital Levy After World War I," *Public Finance*, 7:4 (1952).

**20.** Phillip M. Stren, *The Great Treasury Raid* (New York: 1964), p. 191.

**21.** John G. Gurley, "Federal Tax Policy," *National Tax Journal*, 20:3 (September 1967), 320. This article is a brilliant review of Joseph Pechman's *Federal Tax Policy*, op. cit.

**22.** Ibid., p. 321. This estimate may be contrasted with the standard estimate that the progressive individual income tax makes the total tax system slightly progressive within the $10,000–$15,000 income range, and even more progressive above the $15,000 level. (See, e g., the estimates made by one of monopoly capital's own institutions, Tax Foundation, Inc., *Tax Burdens and Benefits* . . . , op. cit., p. 13, Chart 1.)

See Joseph Pechman and Benjamin Okner, *Individual Income Tax Erosion by Income Classes* (Washington, D.C.: The Brookings Institution, 1972), for the most up-to-date study of the extent to which loopholes erode the income tax. Pechman writes that "the structure of the [income] tax has remained remarkably stable . . . despite all the talk about closing loopholes" [Joseph A. Pechman, "The Rich, the Poor, and the Taxes They Pay," *The Public Interest*, 17 (Fall, 1969), 26].

**23.** "Those who earn less than the taxable ceiling pay 10 4 percent, not 5.2 percent, of their earnings in payroll taxes, and these rates are scheduled to rise. A family of four with income under about $8,700 pays a larger payroll tax than income tax" (*Setting National Priorities*, op. cit )

**24.** Ernest C. Harvey, "Social Security Taxes—Regressive or Progressive?" *National Tax Journal* 18 (December 1965), 408.

**25.** Charles L. Schultze et al , *Setting National Priorities: The 1972 Budget* (Washington, D C.: The Brookings Institution, 1971), p. 212. The authors continue, "A study by John A Brittain of the Brookings Institution that has not yet been published supports this contention and produces a great deal of theoretical and empirical evidence to support it." However, an earlier study indicated that two-thirds of all U S. corporations add payroll taxes to prices (i e., shift the taxes to consumers) [Lewis H. Kimmel, *Taxes and Economic Incentives* (New York: 1950), p. 182]. In either event, the effect is generally the same—the working class pays.

**26.** Tax Foundation, Inc., *Retail Sales and Individual Income Taxes in State Tax Structures* (New York, 1962), pp. 29–30. The federal tax law of 1965 clearly reflected the regressive nature of these taxes; it was expected to reduce excise tax revenues by almost $5 billion over a four-year period. Excise taxes on tobacco, gasoline, alcohol, and other wage goods were retained, but taxes on a wide range of luxury and semiluxury products were cut. [T. W. Calmus, "Burden of Federal Excise Taxes by Income Classes," *Quarterly Review of Economics and Business*, 10:1 (Spring 1970).

**27.** Bureau of the Census, *State Government Finances in 1967* (Washington, D.C.: 1968), p. 7, Table I.

**28.** In 1916, only 400,000 returns were actually taxable; taxable returns jumped to 2.5 million in 1925, 4 million in 1939, over 32 million in 1950, and more than 55 million today. In 1913, the rate was 1 percent on the first $20,000 taxable income (after deducting personal exemptions). Today the figure is 20 percent on the first $20,000. In 1913, individual and corporation income taxes together yielded a little more than $35 million; today the individual income tax alone yields about $85 billion. Most advanced capitalist counties have experienced the same trends. In Japan, for example, the number of income taxpayers rose from 1 million to 19 million between 1935 and 1945, and the contribution of the income tax to national income jumped from less than 1 percent to 10 2 percent [Sei Fujita, "Political Ceiling on Income Taxation," *Public Finance*, 16:2 (1961)].

**29.** Available studies also indicate that taxation as a whole is at best proportional and at worst regressive with respect to income, although some studies indicate a degree of progressivity in the higher-income brackets. See, for example, Mabel Newcomer, "Estimates of the Tax Burden on Different Income Classes," in *Studies in Current Tax Problems* (New York: Twentieth Century Fund,

THE FISCAL CRISIS OF THE STATE

1937): Gerhard Colm and Helen Tarasov, *Who Pays the Taxes?* Temporary National Economic Commission, Monograph No. 3 (Washington, D.C.: 1941); Richard Musgrave et al., "Distribution of Tax Payments by Income Groups: A Case Study for 1948," *National Tax Journal* (March 1951); Richard Musgrave, "Incidence of the Tax Structure and Its Effects on Consumption," *Federal Tax Policy for Economic Growth and Stability*, papers submitted by panelists before the Joint Committee on the Economic Report, U.S. Congress, 1955; Richard Goode, *The Individual Income Tax* (Washington, D C.: 1964), p 263; "Who Really Gets Hurt By Taxes," *U.S. News and World Report*, December 9, 1968. Ross Abinati of San Jose State College has estimated that the average effective tax rate on the incomes of all strata of the working class and managers, officials, proprietors, and farmers is roughly 30 to 32 5 percent. A few years ago Herman P. Miller, head of the Census Bureau's population division, estimated that the average tax rate for all levies (at all levels of government) is: $2000–$4000, 34.6 percent; $4000–$6000, 31 percent; $6000–$8000, 30.1 percent; $8000–$10,000, 29.2 percent; $15,000–$25,000, 30 percent; and $25,000–$50,000, 32.8 percent.

30. S. D. Hermamsen, "An Analysis of the Recent Tax Cut," *National Tax Journal* (December 1965), 425.

31. State and local taxable surpluses are low not only because the federal government appropriates the largest part of taxable surplus (a subject considered in Chapter 9), but also because the effect of a rise in state and local spending on local output (and the tax base) through an increase in demand is relatively small owing to spending "leakages" to other states and cities. Another factor restricting local taxable capacity is that if taxes are too high, individuals are free to live or work in other localities and businesses are free to move to "tax havens."

32. However, between 1950 and 1962, the portion of local government spending paid for by federal grants remained unchanged at about 1.5 percent. The concept of federal grants to the states actually has a long history. The idea was first suggested by Thomas Jefferson in 1805. A series of proposals made in the course of the nineteenth century were either defeated in Congress or vetoed by the President, and it was not until 1887 that the first real grants were made to agricultural experimental stations connected with land-grant colleges. The first highway grants were made in 1916.

33. Harry L. Johnson, ed., *State and Local Tax Problems* (Knoxville, Tenn.: 1969), pp. 103–104.

34. *Business Week*, October 17, 1970, p. 101. Hand in hand with the expansion of federal grants has gone federal control. "All too often, federal officials in an agency with large grants to distribute deal directly with their bureaucratic counterparts in state or local governments, undercutting the authority of mayors and governors and weakening their control over their own budgets" (*Setting National Priorities*, op. cit., p. 159.)

35. This conclusion is based on the relation between tax payments and federal revenues received [Tax Foundation, Inc, *Allocating the Federal Tax Burden by State*, Research Aid No. 3 (New York: 1964), p. 31, Table 7].

36. *State and Local Tax Problems*, op. cit, pp. 103–104. In 1970, there were 1019 programs that involved some sort of federal aid (*Business Week*, October 17, 1970, op cit.).

37. Fred Cohen and Marc Weiss, "Big Business and Urban Stagnation," *Pacific Research and World Empire Telegram*, 1:2 (September 1969), 7. Cohen and Weiss are the source of the CED quote.

38. For example, see, Michael E. Levy and Juan de Torres, *Fed-*

eral *Revenue Sharing with the States: Problems and Promises* (New York: National Industrial Conference Board, 1970), p. 114.

**39.** *State and Local Tax Problems,* op. cit., pp. 64–65 (italics added).

**40.** The Domestic Council, Executive Office of the President, *Highlights of Revenue Sharing: Reform and Renewal for the 1970s* (Washington, D.C.: 1971), p. 13.

**41.** N. A Michas, "Variations in the Level of Provincial-Municipal Expenditures in Canada: An Econometric Analysis," *Public Finance,* 24:4 (1969). Some U.S. cities that receive relatively large amounts of federal grants spend relatively more per capita than cities that receive comparatively little in federal grants. But few economists are willing to conclude that this means that grants-in-aid have actually encouraged the increased spending (*State and Local Tax Problems,* op. cit.) In states that impose fund-matching requirements, state grants-in-aid to communities have no doubt added to total spending.

**42.** *Highlights of Revenue Sharing . . . ,* op. cit., p. 13. More specifically, Nixon's formula is not based on how wealthy a community is, but on how hard the community is trying to meet its needs through its own tax resources. The program allocates money to the states on a per capita basis with a "tax effort" adjustment. Monies then are distributed to localities based on shares of revenue raised locally. States and localities unable to raise tax funds thus are penalized [The Domestic Council, Office of the President, *Revenue-Sharing Chart Book* (Washington, D.C., 1971)]. Nixon proposed $5 billion in general revenue-sharing and $11.4 billion in special revenue-sharing funds. That Nixon meant business became very clear when the Administration made public its education bill in 1970. The measure did not provide any new funds for the states; it was described by *The New York Times* as a money-saving, not a revenue-sharing bill (it sought to save money by consolidating various federal education programs).

**43.** "[B]udgetary outlays over which Congress has no year-to-year control rose by 51 percent between 1967 and 1971. These so-called uncontrollables now account for more than two-thirds of all federal spending . . ." (*Fortune,* March 1972, p. 2).

# CHAPTER 9
# THE SCOPE AND LIMITS
# OF CAPITALIST REFORM

## INTRODUCTION

The fiscal crisis of the capitalist state is the inevitable consequence of the structural gap between state expenditures and revenues. It is our contention that the only lasting solution to the crisis is socialism. However, the state might be able to ameliorate the fiscal crisis by accelerating the growth of the social-industrial complex. Politically, the complex consists of the slowly evolving alliance between sections of monopoly capital and the surplus population, together with low-paid monopoly sector labor. Economically, the complex consists of the transformation of social expenses into social capital by mounting socioeconomic programs both to provide new subsidized investment opportunities for monopoly capital and to ameliorate the material impoverishment of the surplus population. Sociologically, the complex consists of the creation of a new stratum of indirectly productive workers—the small army of technologists, administrators, paraprofessionals, factory and office workers, and others who plan, implement, and control the new programs in education, health, housing, science, and other spheres penetrated by social-industrial capital.

The hoped-for long-term effect of the more rapid development of the social-industrial complex is an increase in productivity throughout the economy. Such growth might help alleviate the fiscal crisis because each dollar of government expenditure might be more "efficient" in the sense of adding to the economy's long-run productive capacity, thus expanding total income and the tax base and easing the burden of financing the budget. In other words, the fundamental purpose of the complex is to gear the state sector more closely to the monopoly sector—the dynamic sector in terms of growth of production.

Competitive sector capital has little to gain from the social-industrial complex. Production in this sector expands on the basis of increased employment, not investment in large-scale, capital-intensive or sophisticated technologies. Further, the demand for administrative laborpower is relatively small. Small businessmen thus are normally indifferent to expenditures for higher education, R&D, and similar outlays. Many small-scale capitalists are hostile to the education establishment because the extension of higher education reduces the supply of low-paid, unskilled and semiskilled laborers. Furthermore, small business is forced to pay taxes that find their way into the pockets of monopoly capital, organized labor, or the surplus population (e.g., the welfare budget). Finally, competitive sector capitalists reject welfare and social programs beyond the bare minimum because they cannot comprehend the problem of the surplus population in class terms.

Organized labor also is opposed or indifferent to the more rapid development of the social-industrial complex. Unions in the competitive sector (primarily the construction trades) stand to lose everything and gain nothing. Monopoly sector unionized workers are at best indifferent and at worst opposed to the complex because their taxes will finance social-industrial investments and programs and because unorganized surplus-population workers will receive the bulk of new jobs. Certainly, the "free" collective bargaining developed since World War II in the monopoly sector will have to be changed substantially (perhaps dismantled entirely) to make the complex work.

A third factor in the political-economic equation is the military-industrial complex, which seems to be ambivalent to the further development of the social-industrial complex. On the one hand, some military contractors have received social-industrial capital subsidies, contracts, credits, and the like. These contractors have grown accustomed to the state's providing capital and markets and care little whether the markets are for military or civilian hardware, systems, or services—as long as the markets are subsidized or guaranteed. On the other hand, during the past three decades large-scale military spending has been the only kind of state outlays consistent with both economic stabilization and growth and the political realities of American society. Overseas commitments at times have compelled the federal government to adjust other parts of the budget to the exigencies of the cold war, small-scale hot wars, and the war in Southeast Asia. The corporate ruling class has little discretion in the determination of either the volume or type of military expenditures.

The military-industrial complex also involves organized labor employed by the military suppliers, as well as many small businessmen whose material survival depends on military subcontracts, trade and service activity around military bases, and the like. The

THE FISCAL CRISIS OF THE STATE

penetration of the military-industrial complex into nearly every corner of the U.S. economy and its central role in maintaining American hegemony in the world system pose enormous obstacles to diverting a significant amount of military production to civilian production even if the state makes it profitable to do so. And last but not least, many state contractors themselves must be weaned from one kind of state contract, production method, and way of thinking to another.

Obviously, the full development of the social-industrial complex requires enormous changes throughout American society, particularly in the contours of the political-economic system. A number of forces are at work producing these changes. First, monopoly capital, including branches of the military-industrial complex itself, must attempt to solve the fiscal crisis and the problem of inflation, on the one hand, and the problem of insurgency and radical movements among the surplus population on the other. Second, and related to the first point, movements among the poor, minority groups, women, youth, and other sections of the population are demanding basic changes in society, especially institutional changes that will alter the distribution of income and economic opportunities in their favor. Third, Europe and Japan not only are on their feet economically but also in many fields are outcompeting the United States, and increasingly are interested more in world markets (including markets in the socialist countries) than in expanding American "protection" against possible "aggression" from the socialist world. In the United States as well, more and more capital is being internationalized, or invested in international corporations which trade and invest with anyone for a profit—including the socialist countries in eastern Europe and the USSR. And a general sense that the American empire has become intolerably expensive in both lives and money is reflected in the growth of neoisolationist sentiment. The state bureaucracy itself signals its willingness to replace some military-complex activity with social-industrial investments and programs. In fact, this combination of factors blocked additional funds for the SST and almost scuttled the Lockheed loan.

Government and business are attempting on a broad front to enlist "allies" in the struggle with those opposed to the social-industrial complex. Urban coalitions that work with black militants have been established. Students and youth are promised that America can reform itself and offered new careers and economic opportunities that will "serve the people." And the regional economic and political infrastructures that are being set up will, it is hoped, take root and provide the framework for the accumulation of social-industrial capital. Other practical and ideological steps include dozens of experimental programs and investments in education, health, transportation, pollution control, and other fields.

Nevertheless, the Congress still is controlled by interests indifferent or opposed to the social-industrial complex. Large-scale monopoly sector capital, the smaller technological companies in the state sector, and the surplus population have relatively little influence or power in the House or Senate. As a result, the forces that are attempting to forge the social-industrial complex must compete in elections at all levels of government, but especially at the federal level where the "prize" is the Treasury. The coalition needs a political instrument—a political party.

Without a political party it is not likely that the social-industrial complex will move beyond the experimental stage. Neither the Democratic nor the Republican party is a suitable instrument for the complex, at least as these parties were constituted through 1971. To be sure, both are organized and managed by groups drawn from a wide variety of classes and strata. Both are responsive to the banks and financial institutions, interlocked with the military-industrial complex and monopoly capital, and depend in varying degrees on the votes of organized labor, professionals, managerial and white-collar workers, small businessmen, farmers, ethnic minorities, the poor, and so on. However, the class alignments embodied in both parties tend to be antagonistic to any change in the status quo, particularly to those implicit in the social-industrial complex.

The class interests represented by the Democratic party are, in order of their political importance, first, the corporate liberal wing of the monopoly capitalist class (especially in the "growth industries") and ethnic capital in the monopoly sector and some branches of the competitive sector (e.g., ethnic banking and construction); second, organized labor, including organized labor in the construction trades; third, the surplus population, including unorganized competitive sector workers, minorities, and the poor. Many interests in the first group and millions of workers and unemployed in the third stand to gain by allying and building a social-industrial complex. Organized labor (particularly the construction unions) has "good reason" to fight the complex. Organized labor's opposition is especially threatening today because another factor breaking up the traditional harmony between monopoly capital and labor is the former's flight overseas in search of cheap laborpower for its labor-intensive branch-plant operations. Monopoly capital thus is forced to be especially wary of any new program that might seriously undermine labor morale and discipline. In fact, the corporate liberal wing of the Democratic party with its new constituency of blacks and other minorities and the poor is presently at loggerheads with organized labor, and the split within the party (reflecting the differences between the old and new corporate liberal politics) may not be healed easily. To transform the Democratic party into an instrument of capitalist reform it probably will be necessary to neutralize the influence of organized labor (by ignoring its programs and local political representatives) and put an end to the AFL-CIO's veto power over Democratic presidential nominations.[1] Of course, there is a problem: To use Richard Scammon's metaphor, the Democratic party without organized labor is like a car without an engine—the body and upholstery may be beautiful (thanks to wealthy liberal campaign donors), but the car won't run.

The class forces and alignments within the Republican party differ in significant ways. The core of the Republican party is middle-scale and large-scale capital in the traditional industries, small business, competitive sector and professional and managerial strata. The Republicans also are the party of the hard-core military contractors. Both small businessmen and military contractors who cannot shift to nonmilitary production are attempting to stunt the growth of the social-industrial complex. They are also trying to define the complex in acceptable ways. For example, in 1971, the Nixon Administration subsidized the retraining of hundreds of out-of-work aerospace technicians for top positions in local government—suggesting that the needs of ex-employees of military contractors have a high priority in Republican party planning. Where the social-industrial complex is a living reality, the tendency in the Republican party is to argue that private capital should play a more active role—if not control the complex outright.

To summarize, dominated as it is by traditional industrialists and bankers and local and regional capitalists, the GOP is an extremely ineffective candidate to nurture the social-industrial complex to maturity. The complex will require much more economic and social planning in transportation, urban redevelopment, education, and other spheres—precisely the kind of planning that monopoly capital (especially in technology-intensive growth industries) is capable of and that small-scale business abhors. In 1972, the Nixon Administration's political economic instincts were to deal with the fiscal crisis by planning to cut back expenditures, not pushing for more rapid development of the social-industrial complex.

It seems that the only hope for reform-minded big businessmen and reformist state officials is to get organized labor out of the Democratic party (or to neutralize its influence within the party).

THE SCOPE AND LIMITS OF CAPITALIST REFORM

But the unions could not conceivably use the Republican party to advance their own ends because of the influence in the party of labor's arch antagonist—small business. And without organized labor's support (votes and money), it would be extremely difficult, perhaps impossible, for the Democratic party to win a national election. Politically, the situation seems to be a standoff. If social-industrial programs continue to grow in number, variety, and comprehensiveness, it probably will be on a more or less experimental basis, without significant enabling legislation or massive infusions of money.[2]

## TAXABLE CAPACITY AND THE TAX REVOLT

In the last analysis, our comprehension of the fiscal crisis and the social-industrial complex is no more or less keen than our understanding of the social, political, and economic struggles of society's principal economic classes and strata. Budgetary needs may remain unsatisfied and human wants may go unfulfilled, but if those who are dependent on the state do not engage in political struggle to protect or advance their well-being, the fiscal crisis will remain relatively dormant. For example, in the State of Illinois, "in most municipalities . . . the present revenue structure will support moderate increases in expenditures in the coming years. [But] at the same time municipal officials are aware that strong and conflicting pressures for better service prevail side by side with demands for lower taxes."[3] An important exception is the Illinois city of East St. Louis, where the fiscal crisis is severe precisely because social conflict in that divided city is tumultuous. Again, in New York City, where the social crisis is extremely intense, municipal expenditures have been rising by about 15 percent annually, revenues by only 5 or 6 percent. Although there is a tendency for the ratio of state spending to GNP to increase, there is little or no correlation between level of per capita income and the ratio of state spending and taxation to GNP.[4] Apparently, different levels of political consciousness and social-political struggle exist in countries (and, by extension, regions) that have similar levels of per capita income, and thus the fiscal crisis is less latent (or more volatile) in some countries (and regions) than in others.

The ultimate scope and limits of capitalist reform depend on the ongoing political struggles and movements that shape the social-industrial complex. Monopoly capital strives to define and control the complex in terms of its own perceived interests. David Rockefeller writes,

THE FISCAL CRISIS OF THE STATE

In view of the emerging demands for revision of the social contract, a passive response on the part of the business community could be dangerous. Any adaption of our system to the changing environment is far more likely to be workable if those who understand the system's problems share in designing the solutions. So it is up to businessmen to make common cause with other reformers . . . to prevent the unwise adoption of extreme and emotional remedies, but on the contrary to initiate necessary reforms that will make it possible for business to continue to function in a new climate. . . .[5]

Summing up the corporate liberal view, Rockefeller continues,

now with the social contract again up for revision, new social and environmental problems are generating increasing pressure for further modification and regulation of business. By acting promptly, business can assure itself a voice in deciding the form and content of the new social contract.[6]

Corporate liberals seek a "new social contract," one that involves governmental decentralization and regionalization and the meshing of private corporate management "inventiveness" with the sovereign power of the state.[7] To achieve "responsible decentralization," they would establish "local control fronts" [8]—nonprofit community corporations linked to regional-planning agencies through which federal funds would be channeled from the state treasury to private corporations engaged in social-industrial investment. More and more, the issue of the growth of the social-industrial complex and regional planning are inseparable. And because regional planning requires corporate-dominated regional government, whether the fiscal crisis will be ameliorated by the complex depends on whether large-scale capital and the federal executive can persuade local government to cooperate or force it to submit.

In sharp contrast are the efforts of minority, community control, women's liberation, and other movements to socialize decision making from below. These popular movements seek what the corporate planners might term "irresponsible decentralization." They are engaged in struggles not only over the amount of state funds allocated to social investment and social consumption facilities and programs, but also over control of transportation, health, education, day care, and other activities and projects. What is increasingly at stake is both the distribution of the social product between and within the main economic classes and the uses to which the social product is put. Thus, the social-industrial complex and the move toward decentralization embrace contradictory and potentially explosive goals. If the social crisis that underlies the fiscal crisis is not exacerbated by the emergence of a strong left-wing revolutionary movement (or a right-wing, fascistic movement), a fully developed social-industrial complex is a real possibility. But if American politics takes a sharp leftward or rightward turn, it is clear that the social, economic, and political meaning of the complex will be drastically altered.

We must turn now to the question of the current tax revolt. It should be stressed from the start that "tax revolt" has different meanings for different people at different times. Historians would agree that people always have disliked and resisted paying taxes. The "resistance" may take the form of mild grumbling and petty cheating on tax returns or violent overthrow of government—or any action in between. Historians would also agree that resistance has been associated with many factors—for example, rule by foreign power, the distribution of the tax burden, the uses of tax revenues, the ability of people to shift economic activity to nontaxed fields, the ease with which the taxed population can sell their products and thus acquire cash for the tax man, the general level of poverty, and so on. In the present period, with the vast majority of the people proletarianized and without direct access to the means of production, resistance to taxation flares up when those upon whom the burden falls feel that the tax structure is inequitable and/or when the purposes of state expenditures are rejected. Complaints that "taxes are too high" may mean that "my taxes are too high and someone else's are too low," "government spending is too high," or that "the government is spending too much for someone else and not enough for me"— or all three.

Tax resistance can have extremely serious political consequences for the established order in advanced capitalist societies. The basic reason is that the average worker cannot escape or avoid individual income taxes, sales and excise taxes, and other levies that fall directly on income or consumption. In earlier phases of capitalism, when the majority of taxpayers still had ties with the family farm, trade, or business, people often could abandon taxed economic activities and return to untaxed subsistence production. This no longer is possible because the vast majority of taxpayers are workers with specialized skills or functions that are useless in subsistence production. Thus, although, in Marx's words, "tax struggle is the oldest form of class struggle," political struggle against tax exploitation is the only meaningful form of tax revolt today. Voting "big spenders" out of office, organizing political movements, refusing to pay taxes as an act of political conscience—these are a few of the many forms of political noncompliance. Some argue that there is an exception to the "rule" of political struggle—that workers can fight for higher money wages to make up for the burden of higher taxes and thus force the state to finance budgetary expansion through inflation (or indirect taxation), not increased direct taxation. However, because the income tax is progressive it neutralizes in part or in whole the "relief" obtained through wage struggles. In the last analysis, tax resistance is likely to fail if it is not overtly political.

At present, taxpayer resistance is expressed in economic and political terms. Wage struggles are conducted partly to recover wages lost to higher direct taxation and inflation. To the degree that they succeed, wage struggles aggravate inflation, and thus both reflect and intensify the fiscal crisis. Similarly, political tax resistance reflects and intensifies the gap between state expenditures and revenues. Thus, the tax revolt, which is sparked by the volume and composition of state expenditures and the distribution of the tax burden, makes it more difficult to finance rising budgets in the future.

Although taxpayers include small businessmen, professionals, and the working class, resistance is not organized along class lines. Tax issues are rarely seen as class issues, partly because of the general absence of working-class unity in the United States, and partly because the fiscal system itself obscures the class character of the budget.

Tax issues normally are seen as interest-group or community issues and thus have served to divide, not unite the working class. The growth of thousands of autonomous tax-paying units and the proliferation of special districts and supramunicipal authorities tends to set community against community, tax district against tax district, suburb against city. The basic class issue of state finance— the distribution of taxation and the division of expenditures among different social classes—thus emerges in a new form. The core cities attempt to force the suburbs to pay their "fair share" of city expenditures; the relatively well-off suburban population resist core-city programs—tax redistribution, central-city income taxes, commuter taxes, consolidation or merger of tax districts, and so on. Some suburbs are taking the offensive by offering inducements to private capital in order to establish more autonomous industrial and commercial bases.

In sum, the monopoly sector work force, the small-business and professional classes, and the owning class are fighting to keep and extend privileges won partly at the expense of the surplus population, particularly the surplus population employed in the competitive sector.

The property tax also meets increasing resistance. Decades ago its function was to finance public improvements that benefited property owners. Today, there is little or no such connection between the tax and expenditures (except schools). Rather, there is a trend to use the revenues to finance expenditures many property owners oppose. Home owners in many cities are mounting tax referendum campaigns aimed at downtown business interests whose properties are undervalued for tax purposes. And there is widespread sentiment in the suburbs that the property tax should be replaced in whole or part by other sources of revenue—sentiment that right-wing state and local politicians exploit in behalf of small-scale capital. Partly as a consequence of its unpopularity, property taxation accounts for a relatively small part of state and local revenue (5 percent at the state level, 50 percent at the local level). Furthermore, taxes on personal property have been almost completely abolished. And in 1971–1972, a series of state court decisions declared property-tax financed public education unconstitutional because children in low-yield tax districts are thus denied equal protection under the law.

Potentially of far greater long-run significance than local and state resistance is a federal tax reform movement, which is gaining momentum (we say "potentially" because the movement to lower federal taxes on the poor is motivated in part by the desire to stifle opposition to lowering taxes on business still more). According to a recent Opinion Research Corporation poll, more and more people believe that a larger share of future tax increases should be paid by corporations and wealthy individuals.[9] In 1970, the Nixon Administration reversed its earlier position and requested Congress to pass reforms that would take less from the poor and more from corporations and wealthy families. The proposed reforms included guarantees that at least 50 percent of a rich individual's income would be taxed and that poverty-level families would be freed from any federal income tax and a series of loophole-closing measures. That year Congress raised personal exemption levels for the first time in recent history. In 1972, House Ways and Means Chairman Wilbur Mills and Senator Mike Mansfield persuaded Congress to agree to review all 54 tax loopholes over the next few years.[10] Finally, the McGovern-Kennedy social-industrial forces pledged a minimum tax on the rich and the abolition of income taxes on the poor, and several movements are agitating against state and local loopholes (e.g., the Cali-

THE FISCAL CRISIS OF THE STATE

fornia Peace and Freedom party is attempting to end California's special tax treatment of capital gains income).

Suburban resistance to increased taxation, agitation against the property tax, the urban-suburban cold war, and local and national tendencies toward tax reform (not to speak of tax avoidance and evasion) can be attributed to two factors: first, the rising level of taxation and increasing consciousness of inequities in the tax structure; second, criticism of prevailing expenditure priorities. Let us consider these in turn.

The rising level of taxation is attributable to the introduction of new taxes and the upward drift of tax rates on property, consumption, and (at the state level) personal income. State and local taxes in relation to per capita income have increased in every state since 1942. Property taxes alone rose from $22.6 billion to roughly $37 billion between 1964–1965 and 1970–1971. And federal payroll taxes take an increasingly large share of personal income. In 1973, social insurance taxes will rise to about $63.7 billion (up from $54 billion in 1972), or two-thirds of the amount collected under the individual income tax.[11] According to a recent Gallup poll, nearly 70 percent of the population believes that taxes are "too high," an increase from 52 percent in 1965.[12] The question is whether this sentiment ultimately will circumscribe the state's fiscal planning functions. Put differently, does the working class have a certain taxable capacity? If so, under what conditions will mounting state expenditures press against these limits and bring the fiscal crisis to a head?

There are no hard and fast answers to these questions. Perhaps a useful way to approach them is to compare the economy's taxable capacity when the competitive sector was preeminent with today's monopoly capitalist economy. Three lines of analysis are open. First, the epoch of competitive capitalism ended in the late nineteenth century and thus predated both world wars and the continuing struggle between the capitalist and socialist worlds. The role of the federal bureaucracy was relatively limited and the role of Congress, which was (and is) the handmaiden of special-interest groups, was comparatively large. Thus, the scope for independent action by the state was narrowly circumscribed.

Second, in competitive capitalism the long-run tendency for the economy to generate excess capacity of capital and unemployment (or surplus capital and surplus population) was relatively weak. In a more or less fully employed economy, the private sector necessarily is deprived of any economic resources utilized by the state (or there is little potential taxable surplus in a fully employed economy). Consequently, planned increases in state outlays have to be financed by a corresponding rise in tax rates or by inflation, which will be resisted more or less vigorously by the population. Furthermore, actual taxable surplus in the epoch of competition was relatively small. Costs of reproducing the work force in relation to GNP were high because an advanced productive base could not be developed in an economy of small-scale, competitive enterprise. For this reason there undoubtedly was a definite limit on the proportion of total product that the state could appropriate without seriously impairing incentives to work, save, and invest, and thus threatening to undermine the tax base itself.[13] In sum, the liberal state's financial independence was limited because taxable capacity was relatively small and the executive branch relatively undeveloped.

In the era of monopoly capitalism the character of the fiscal system (as that of the entire society) undergoes a profound change. The powers of the special interests in the legislative branch dwindle and the authority of the class-conscious political directorate in the executive branch grows, widening the scope of independent state action. The normal tendency of monopoly capitalism is toward the creation of surplus capital and surplus labor. To the degree that capacity remains idle and the surplus population remains unemployed, state expenditures tend to raise not only the level of aggregate demand but also real output, incomes, and the tax base. In this sense, state expenditures tend to be partly self-financing and virtually costless in terms of the industrial capacity and laborpower utilized. However, the price of the corporate liberal consensus between monopoly capital and organized labor is a policy of high employment. High or full employment clearly mitigates against the process of self-financing of state expenditures and deepens the fiscal crisis because an expansion of state expenditures tends to be inflationary.

Third, because of the tremendous productive capacity of monopoly capitalism, it would appear that larger and larger portions of wage income can be taxed without affecting economic incentives or risking political tax resistance. However, much of this surplus is not available to taxation because part of it takes the form of selling expenses included in commodity prices (e.g., packaging, model and style changes, advertising, etc.), and because the state encourages private consumption by underwriting social consumption and social expense outlays.[14]

We can safely conclude that at one budgetary level full employment of economic resources will be reached. And at another, higher level, the state will have appropriated the entire surplus available in taxable form. At this point, further increases in state spend-

THE FISCAL CRISIS OF THE STATE

ing will require the enlargement of the tax base. This will necessitate a reallocation of state expenditures even more in favor of private accumulation and the social-industrial complex in order to accelerate capital accumulation and the growth of real income.[15]

In sum, private accumulation and the expansion of income have increased the tax base, opening the way for the state to finance the programs and activities essential to further profitable accumulation in the monopoly sector. However, state expenditures have become increasingly integral to the process of monopoly capitalist accumulation. In the long run the state must encourage private accumulation more and more in order to generate the economic growth required to raise tax revenues that are needed to strengthen an economic system whose first and overriding purpose is profit making and accumulation. As the "growth dividend" becomes increasingly elusive, state and private economic activity must be ever more closely meshed. The passive servant of private property in an older era, today the federal government must come actively to its defense.[16]

State and local government remains even more dependent fiscally. First, the effect of a rise in state and local expenditures on the local tax base through an increase in demand and income is relatively small because of spending leakages to other states and localities. Second, the local taxable surplus is comparatively small because personal income tax appropriates the greatest part. Third, state and local taxes catch a relatively small part of the growth dividend. Finally, if state and local taxes are too high, individuals are free to live or work in other localities and businesses are free to move to tax havens. For these reasons, expenditures are tied closely to revenues, and increases in state and local spending depend more and more on federal grants. Of course, some states are more willing than others to use the fiscal capacity available to them—for example, states engaged in an all-out competition for new industry no doubt fail to exploit their actual tax capacity. But from a practical standpoint, the main political issue at the state and local levels is frequently "economy in government."

Another consideration is that the growth of tax revenues depends on the growth of the economy's taxable sectors—particularly the absolute size of the working class, together with the level of wage income. There is a strong tendency in the U.S. economy for competitive sector employment to increase because of the growth of the surplus population. To the degree that the low-wage competitive sector absorbs unemployed workers and new workers into the work force (and also to the degree that the system generates total or partial unemployment), it is clear that wage income will grow relatively slowly

**THE SCOPE AND LIMITS OF CAPITALIST REFORM** 233

(or remain stagnant) and thus that the tax base will increase slowly (or stagnate). However, in the absence of quantitative studies of the expansion of competitive sector employment in relation to the growth of monopoly sector output, it is difficult to know how much weight to give to this process.

In any case, the main limits on taxation are not the size of the work force or the level of wage income or any other "economic" factor but rather are political in nature. "Taxation will reach a practical limit when the political and social resistance by taxpayers becomes so serious that the government is prevented from imposing an additional tax burden," writes Sei Fujita.[17] In other words, a society's taxable capacity depends on its political capacity to adjust to change, especially to new social and class needs. Thus, tax structures and patterns of expenditures that once were considered equitable may be rejected today. And tax ratios that once were believed to be high may now be considered relatively low. For example, twenty-five years ago Colin Clark suggested that the maximum (noninflationary) tax GNP ratio was 25 percent—a limit that Clark considered to be political in character. Although there is no way to prove or disprove the point (precisely because the budget is inflationary), a figure of 30 percent might be more accurate today. Certainly, during World War II, taxes in America rose to unprecedented heights without engendering any significant resistance. And in Europe aggregate tax rates are relatively high (between 30 and 40 percent in comparison with about 28 percent in the United States). However, political movements organized around the tax issue have had little success, partly because tax evasion is widespread, partly because the European working class is accustomed to high taxes (and higher levels of social consumption), and partly because the comparatively small size of military budgets and earmarked funds gives European governments relatively more flexibility in spending tax revenues.

The political limits of taxation (or political ceiling on tax rates) obviously depend on the nature of the state (and the expectations that the population has toward the state power) and the budgetary priorities and composition of expenditures. Although most U.S. politicians apparently believe that "who will pay" is a more important question than "for what," taxpayers are becoming increasingly sensitive to present-day budgetary priorities. One study conducted in the early 1960s concluded that popular sentiment was running against space spending and subsidized agriculture and in favor of domestic welfare and education programs. But a majority of the population sampled did not approve expanding any government program through higher taxation.[18] A 1969 Harris Poll concluded that two-thirds of all taxpayers resented the way that the government was spending their money, stating that "the central motive for paying taxes has begun to disintegrate." Those polled opposed foreign aid, Vietnam war spending, space and defense increases, and federal welfare outlays. According to the Opinion Research poll cited earlier, 50 percent of Americans believe today that "they pay too much for what they get from the government." [19] Finally, in the current debate on federal revenue-sharing no one in the establishment has suggested that the national government cut taxes and then let the people decide whether to bail out local and state governments by increasing or decreasing local and state tax payments voluntarily. No doubt the reason is that the people would reject present-day spending priorities.

What is the long-run significance of popular attitudes on taxation and spending for social and political change? This is a difficult question because the tax issue cannot be separated from the question of state expenditures and spending priorities. It will become even more complex as the weakness of the growth dividend forces the federal government to raise taxes, and as popular disapproval of spending priorities compels the national state to conceal these new taxes. Thus, the new tax that we may be burdened with will be an indirect tax falling disproportionately on the monopoly sector— in all likelihood a value-added tax (VAT), which is used in some European countries where the working class is much more conscious of the class character of the budget and society.[20]

In the past the issue has been so complex and confused that the right wing has enjoyed a near monopoly on the question of taxation. For its part, the left has not exploited the tax issue because it has been wedded to the modern liberal tradition that has sought an enlarged government role in the economy and has paid little or no attention to the structure and burden of taxation. However, there are signs that progressive and left forces are breaking their self-imposed silence on taxation and are beginning to link up the issues of tax exploitation and expenditure priorities. Some unions, particularly state employees unions such as the Transport Workers Union in New York and sections of the American Federation of Teachers, are incorporating demands that the tax burden be shifted to the rich and to business into their programs for higher wages and better working conditions. This enlarged perspective on state finances represents an advance in understanding of the fiscal system, but it is clear that even a total critique of the relationship between expenditures and taxation is insufficient in and of itself. Of greater importance is a demonstration of the relation between state expenditure priorities and the pattern and pace of private capital accumulation, especially accumulation in the monopoly sector. For example, tax referendum campaigns organized around the issue of the burden of property taxation on residential versus commercial property have a limited impact on people's understanding and the actual burden of the fiscal system if they fail to include a critique of the class character of education, urban renewal, and other expenditures. Past struggles by populist, progressive, liberal, and left movements have shown dramatically that under conditions of monopoly industry and administered prices it is extraordinarily difficult at best and normally impossible to influence significantly the distribution of the tax burden (and thus the distribution of wealth and power) without a simultaneous challenge to both state and private spending priorities.

Moreover, a movement that seeks to transcend special-interest politics would have to demonstrate the symbiotic relationship between foreign and domestic spending. Even on the left it is sometimes not appreciated fully that overseas economic expansion and imperialism are required to maintain corporate liberalism at home by expanding national wealth and income, thus muting domestic struggles over the distribution of income and wealth. At the same time, the growth of domestic social and welfare spending—particularly the growth of the social-industrial complex—is the precondition for the maintenance of class harmony and popular acquiescence to militarism and imperialism. The welfare-warfare state is one single phenomenon, and military and civilian expenditures cannot be reduced significantly at the expense of one another. Thus, an understanding of the relation between taxes and expenditures, between state and private capital accumulation, and between overseas and domestic economic expansion requires comprehension of the totality of world capitalism—a difficult but not impossible undertaking precisely because there is a large constituency ready to support a massive expansion of the social-industrial complex at the expense of military, space, and foreign aid spending.[21] However, it will be difficult for corporate liberal capitalists to develop a political instrument to get the social-industrial complex off the ground and into self-sustained growth. This combination of factors holds out a potential opportunity for the American left. While the social-industrial complex is designed to alleviate the fiscal and legitimization crises simultaneously, in the last analysis it will probably intensify both.

## MOVEMENTS OF STATE WORKERS

At once a cause and effect of the tax revolt is the opposition to state budgetary priorities by state employees and state clients and dependents. Progressively tighter budgets, stagnant or declining real wages and salaries, and falling social services spending have unleashed a torrent of criticism against state government by state workers and dependents. Public employee unions have been growing by leaps and bounds. The American Federation of State, County, and Municipal Employees (AFSCME) expanded from 150,000 members in 1950 to 400,000 members in 1972; over 60 percent of the membership hold blue-collar jobs. The other two labor unions that have grown most rapidly since the late 1950s also are state worker organizations—the American Federation of Government Employees and the American Federation of Teachers (AFT). In California, where membership in both the liberal AFT and the more conservative California State Employees Association has increased significantly, at least 45 new groups have organized more than 22,000 state workers along occupational lines.[22] In New York the state worker movement encompasses nearly every public employee—even unskilled and semiskilled hospital workers, traditionally neglected by labor organizations. Thus, in the early 1960s, New York's Local 1199, Drug and Hospital Workers, and the AFSCME began the state's first large-scale drive to organize the mass of hospital workers. In the country's biggest city 25 percent of all union members are public employees. Less than one-third of U.S. cities with 10,000 or more people had one or more municipal employee organizations in 1938; in 1950, two-thirds of all cities were partly unionized; it was estimated that 80 percent of the cities were unionized in 1969.[23] At the state level government employee associations have grown significantly (they have made little progress at the local level, no doubt because in the past they were a kind of company union). And at the federal level membership in the two major postal unions affiliated with the AFL-CIO (National Association of Letter Carriers and United Federation of Postal Clerks) as well as the major independent union (National Postal Union) grew rapidly during the 1960s. More than one million civilians employed by the federal, state, and local governments belong to a labor organization. Between the mid-1950s and 1970, unionized state workers rose from 5 to about 11 percent of total union membership.

Not only are there more unions and union members, but also state worker organizations are becoming better organized. Union leaders foresee the day when there will be a single postal union, and an affiliation between the new American Postal Workers Union and the Communication Workers of America (which have 330,000 and 550,000 members, respectively) is likely in the future. There have been mergers between National Education Association and AFT locals and lengthy national discussions seeking to merge the two or-

THE SCOPE AND LIMITS OF CAPITALIST REFORM          237

ganizations completely. There also has been a series of mergers between organizations representing professors and other university employees.

State unions also have become more militant in their demands for better pay, shorter hours, and better working conditions. Thirty years ago not one state employee organization had a strike policy; even unions affiliated with the AFL or the CIO had no-strike provisions in their constitutions. Today the situation is very different. Government unions have called more strikes, which have lasted for longer periods and have involved more workers. In 1953, there were only thirty strikes against state and local governments; in 1966 and 1967, there were 152 and 181 strikes, respectively. During the quarter century prior to 1966, only 129 teachers' strikes were recorded; in 1966, there were 33.[24] In 1967–1968, the AFT alone conducted 32 major walkouts and ministrikes involving nearly 100,000 workers. In March 1970, 200,000 postal workers went on strike, and during that year and the next dozens of cities and towns were hit by major and minor strikes of municipal workers—including policemen and firemen. In June 1971, New York's District Council 37 (AFSCME) and the Teamsters opened up a new phase in the struggle between state workers and the state administration. Responding to the state legislature's refusal to ratify a Council 37 retirement plan which had been approved by New York's mayor and city council, unionists sabotaged drawbridges, stalled trucks at strategic points, let water pressure sink to dangerously low levels and raw garbage flow into Manhattan's rivers, and generally displayed an unheard-of militancy. In fact, many state workers' strikes have been called by independent unions or ad hoc committees without any formal union affiliation.[25] Even professional employee organizations are changing their character—for example, the American Nurses Association renounced its no-strike policy in 1968. And in urban transit the prewar voluntary arbitration system has broken down almost completely (as state ownership has replaced private ownership) and strikes have increased steadily since 1940.[26] It is widely expected that more and more unions will become more and more militant.[27]

The growth of unionism and rank-and-file militancy is attributable to a number of factors. Routinization of advancement, overall bureaucratization of white-collar work, and the remoteness of the average worker from his or her supervisor all provide fertile ground, but the main reasons spring from the fiscal crisis itself. State employees (and dependents and clients) increasingly are aware that they are subject to a gradual erosion of material standards because of budgetary priorities that favor social investment, the tax revolt, inflation, and state policies designed to restrain inflation. Most strikes

THE FISCAL CRISIS OF THE STATE

are called over wage demands (which cannot be linked to rising profits).[28] The fiscal crisis also subjects state workers (and clients) to profound qualitative changes in their relations with state administrators and politicians. Workers and administrators thus are engaged in both quantitative and qualitative struggles which interpenetrate at nearly every point in the state sector. For example, the struggle for black studies programs in higher education and (recently) at the secondary level is at once an attempt to win control over state expenditures and to produce basic changes in the school curriculum and in social relations between students and teachers. And teachers' unionism weaves the issues of control of the schools, curriculum development, programming classroom time, and racism into the traditional themes of wages, hours, and conditions. In brief, the social meaning of the fiscal crisis goes well beyond immediate budgetary issues.

Most state employee organizations have embraced traditional modes of unionization and struggle, particularly the emphasis on "economism," perhaps because in the climate of corporate liberalism state workers (however militant) have access to no compelling alternative tradition. Many observers believe that traditional economism will fail state employees, not only as the labor movement has failed monopoly sector workers by binding them to the corporate-defined and corporate-dominated political consensus, but also, and more immediately, because state unionism will be unable to "deliver the goods."

Monopoly sector and state workers occupy different places in the political economy. Large corporations protect profits directly by passing on wage increases to consumers in the form of higher prices. State administrators do not have any equivalent "taxing" mechanism; wage increases normally are absorbed by higher taxes. The monopoly corporations' long-term response to militant economism has been to protect profits by accelerating labor-saving technological change in order to increase productivity and lower unit labor costs. Thus they contribute greatly both to inflation and to an increased absolute volume of available goods. It is difficult for state administrators to absorb higher wages by raising productivity. Indeed, some are under pressure to retard the application of technology, and, in any case, they do not have operative profitability criteria to guide decision making. In short, wage struggles in the state sector cannot "pay for themselves" as they do in the long run in the monopoly sector. Further, in the event that efficiency can be improved, the resulting savings are not passed on to the workers involved but rather to the general treasury.

A crucial function of monopoly sector unions is to

maintain labor discipline in the face of mechanization and technological unemployment. State sector unions do not share this function because the basis for the expansion of state sector production is the expansion of taxation, not productivity and profits. Thus, state sector unions are actually dysfunctional from the standpoint of regulating production relations—their wage demands are inflationary and they play little or no role in maintaining labor discipline.

The state normally resists state unionism and wage demands more adamantly than monopoly corporations, which can pass on wage increases and must maintain discipline. Furthermore, labor struggles in the state sector often are opposed by the tax-paying working class (and small businessmen, farmers, etc.). As a result, pursuing these struggles in traditional trade unionist ways might worsen the condition of state workers because the struggles worsen the fiscal crisis itself. A good example of the contradictory position of "economistic" state unions is provided by the United Professors of California (UPC). On the one hand, UPC wants higher salaries for its members, even at the risk of a major confrontation with the state government. On the other hand, it seeks increases in income and sales taxes to pay for higher salaries, and thus risks losing allies among the tax-paying working class.

A final point is that state unions ordinarily must stay on the defensive insofar as economic demands are concerned. In the private sector traditional unions demand and normally get their "fair share" of increases in corporate profits. Because the state's income is dependent on the tax base and tax rate, state unions are normally unable to go on the offensive, except insofar as state workers struggle to keep up with monopoly sector workers. Thus, to the extent that state workers confine their activity to traditional economism, the dynamics of their struggles are very different from those in the monopoly sector. In sum, there is no general understanding of the function of the state in capitalist society, and especially of the fact that state employees are not employed by the "people" but rather by the representatives of private capital as a whole. Put another way, there is no general understanding that the growing antagonism between state employees and state administrators conceals an objective antagonism between wage labor and capital.

What are the qualitative aspects of labor struggles within the state sector, particularly struggles engaged in by service workers—teachers, social and welfare workers, probation officers, public health employees, doctors, nurses, hospital personnel, city planners, employees in recreation, and so forth? On the one hand, the education of service workers consists largely of technical-scientific training. They are taught the rudiments of the scientific method, the history of their "profession," their obligations as public servants, and so on. In the course of their education and work experience service workers learn that society consists of a system of social relations that can be modified or totally transformed. On the other hand, the fusion of economic base and political superstructure and the fiscal crisis have led to the "rationalization" of state jobs, the introduction of efficiency criteria, the waning of professional standards, and in general the transplantation of capitalist norms from direct production in the private economy to the state administration. Thus, for example, teachers who view themselves as educators are required to patrol school halls and cafeterias and generally perform social control functions that many find incompatible with their self-image.[29] College professors accustomed to campus autonomy are subjected more and more to the authority of the trustee, regent, and legislator. Probation officers must cope with more red tape and control from the top; social work is everywhere being streamlined; nurses are compelled to work at many tasks that traditionally have been accomplished by aides and volunteers. In short, state technical and service workers are being proletarianized in the context of a fiscal squeeze that often does not permit compensatory wage and salary increases. Furthermore, the expansion of state sector careers and jobs reduces the dependency of workers on private capital and thus tends to reinforce any feelings of hostility toward the business and commercial world.

State workers—particularly service workers—are attempting to resolve these conflicts. They are nominally in the service of "society," "the public welfare," "quality education," "public health," and so forth—the words and phrases normally used to describe the functions of the state administration. However, because they have been trained to think in terms of social relationships, many service workers quickly learn that indirectly they serve private capital and that their jobs really consist of establishing the preconditions for profitable business, training "human capital" rather than educating human beings, and exercising control over subject populations—especially in activities in which the incipient social-industrial complex has already begun to rationalize state programs. In other words, a contradiction arises between the formal and informal requirements of their employment. Of course, a majority of state workers are keenly aware that they "live off" their clients in the sense that they would not have their jobs without them. But many have chosen to undermine their own positions—that is, their formal positions in the state hierarchy. One response has been a redefinition of their jobs—the development of a new kind of job consciousness, an attempt truly to serve the people. Younger workers tend to reject the state administration's real goals and practices (most older workers tend to remain loyal to "city hall" or the traditional political bosses). They are able to relate easily as "oppositionists" independent of specific positions within the state bureaucracy. For example, social workers tend to define the main beneficiaries of social services as their clients, whereas supervisors and administrators view the "public" as the main beneficiary.[30]

Service workers share another bond: They all require state funds for their real and nominal functions. In fact, when attempting to perform their nominal function they are immediately faced with a gross shortage of resources—classroom space, buildings, land, hospital beds, welfare funds, training resources, and so on. Their nominal function requires far more resources than their real function—social control and social investment. Thus, service workers can develop a kind of "class" consciousness and relate easily to one another over questions of staffing, facilities, and funding. Needless to say, a similar conclusion may be drawn with regard to their dependence on the state budget to meet their own material needs.

Another response has been a step-up of activity against the state administration and its values and goals in general and the social-industrial complex in particular. For example, at the national level the AFT and the AFL-CIO opposed Nixon's appointment of Sidney Marland as U.S. Commissioner of Education; Marland is at once an opponent of collective bargaining for teachers and a proponent of the social-industrial complex. The AFT also is struggling against "performance contracting" in the schools—a favorite port of entry into education for private capital. At the local level AFT teachers are fighting new plans to pay teachers according to "productivity" rather than level of attained education and seniority.

Nevertheless, there still is no general consciousness of the broader relations into which state workers and service workers enter. Only a handful of state workers have made the leap and begun to identify politically with their clients. Welfare workers in New York City, for example, are developing political alliances with welfare rights organizations. And there are signs that other state workers—bus drivers, health workers, and others—are developing this new kind of awareness. The AFT, for example, is consciously developing social unionism. This evolution is necessary because traditional trade unionism cannot speak to the needs of state workers as public employees and because it is difficult for state unions to take the offensive economically as monopoly sector organized labor is able to do. Thus,

THE FISCAL CRISIS OF THE STATE

fresh militancy tends to center around qualitative issues of job control, the nature of public service, and so on.

## MOVEMENTS OF STATE CLIENTS

The new militancy of state clients and dependents—welfare recipients, students (especially minority students), patients dependent on public hospitals and health programs, prisoners and parolees, patients in mental institutions, and others—also both reflects and deepens the fiscal crisis. By substituting "dead laborpower" for "living laborpower," the monopoly sector creates a relative surplus population which is forced to seek jobs in the competitive sector. And the breakup of the family system and traditional precapitalist production such as subsistence farming generates an absolute surplus population. The mass of state clients is drawn from both strata. Partly because of the expansion of the monopoly sector and partly because of the proletarianization of hundreds of thousands of ex-farmers, women, and others drawn into capitalist production, there is a tendency for wage increases in the competitive sector to be slow and modest. Workers tend to be impoverished and increasingly need the state to satisfy material needs. But because of the tax revolt, the cost of social investment and social consumption, and higher wages won by state workers (together with institutionalized racism and sexism within the state sector), it is increasingly difficult for the state to meet its clients' needs. This is especially true in the context of inflation and relative economic stagnation and for the unorganized rural poor, most of whom remain excluded from social legislation such as unemployment insurance and Fair Labor Standards Acts. "The more vocal and better organized urban poor," states the President's National Advisory Commission on Rural Poverty, "gain most of the benefits of current antipoverty programs." [31]

There is a growing awareness that advanced capitalism works to the disadvantage of competitive sector workers (and the rest of the surplus population) and low-paid monopoly sector workers and that economic exploitation and racial and sexual oppression are interdependent. As a result, unions such as California's United Farmworkers Organizing Committee, community coalitions such as New York's Black Coalition, national coalitions such as the National Tenants Organization (founded in 1969 by 250 local tenants groups) and the National Welfare Rights Organization (with 125,000 members in 800 chapters established expressly to help the eligible poor get relief), and other movements and organizations of the surplus population and state dependents that have sprung up in recent years have been extremely militant and more radical than state sector workers.

Militancy is necessary because these organizations represent groups that do not have access to the traditional modes of labor struggle. Collective bargaining is impracticable for state dependents if only because it is impossible to define appropriate bargaining units and to locate the ultimate state authority with whom to bargain. Further, although black people allied with other minorities have elected public officials in a number of cities, political power at the national and regional level has been elusive because of the weakness of most competitive sector workers and the rest of the surplus population in the major political parties. State clients and the poor are forced to conduct their struggles in highly unorthodox ways. Their leaders argue that the people are engaged in a permanent struggle against the establishment—a struggle that includes demonstrations, marches, fasts, nonviolent and violent resistance, political pressure, electoral politics, and every other technique in the armory of political activism.

These organizations and movements are also more radical in the profound sense that they are not wedded to the parochial political perspective that characterizes monopoly sector unions and to a lesser degree state employee unions. Perhaps the chief reason is the interrelationship between economic impoverishment and social oppression, which makes the black movement (together with other minority movements) the most likely candidate to unify state dependents and state workers. Consumer and women's liberation groups work with student or professional organizations (e.g., the Student Health Organization, which is made up of medical and nursing students, and the Medical Committee for Human Rights) in health and medical care. In New York there is relatively close collaboration between state welfare clients and workers. Black transit workers in Chicago and black-led caucuses in other cities are being forced to tie their demands for better pay and working conditions to minority and community demands for fare reductions or freezes and the maintenance of routes and services. In nearly every major American city, blacks and oppressed minorities and women constitute a majority of the municipal work force, and issues of race and sexual politics serve to unite workers and clients.

Student and teachers groups increasingly are aware of the link between state expenditures and taxation. For example, in May 1971, a CFT-organized March for Education in Sacramento was supported not only by every public employee union in the state but also by numerous student and community groups. One reason certainly was that the CFT demanded not only adequate financing of public schools at all levels of education but also "fair and reasonable tax reforms to support these expenses based on ability to pay" and more rapid school integration and stepped-up minority hiring. This is a good example of how popular movements within the state sector can and do combine demands for more resources for state workers and dependents with demands for more progressive taxation and higher taxes on business. Perhaps of greater long-run significance, political leaders such as Bella Abzug (D-N.Y.) and Ronald Dellums (D-Cal.) are encouraging the NWRO to organize coalitions of the working and nonworking poor, including rank-and-file unionists in low-paying industries, minority group caucuses, women's domestic worker unions, the unemployed, and so on. Moreover, there are moves afoot to unite black and white workers in the surplus population—for example, in early 1972, the first National Housing Conference in Chicago brought together poor people from black, brown, Italian, Slav, Irish, and Puerto Rican communities. And, finally, there is the alliance between surplus population organizations and the antiwar movement, which joined with organizations of state and private workers in a NWRO-sponsored mass demonstration in Washington to demand an end to the war, minimum income guarantees, and the defeat of Nixon's repressive Family Assistance Plan.

An alliance of a majority of the surplus population, especially if it were supported and to a degree defined by radical state worker organizations would have great impact on American economic and political development. Perhaps the only way for the state to contain such a movement is to accelerate the growth of the social-industrial complex, which combines the voting power of the surplus population with the money and power of significant groups of monopoly capitalists and state contractors. This is becoming particularly true given the alliance between surplus population organizations and the antiwar movement; with cutbacks in military spending the only jobs available would be in the social-industrial complex. However, it will be very difficult politically to generate the massive legislation needed to finance social-industrial programs and investments. Furthermore, the new social-industrial jobs presently are not much better than those offered by the traditional competitive industries and the lower rungs of the monopoly sector. The Nixon Administration's Work Experience and Training Program, for example, has not led to more demanding jobs or to significantly higher pay scales.[32] If in the final analysis the complex frustrates the expectations it creates for better jobs and better pay, it will breed more problems for the establishment than it solves. In sum, whether or not the social-industrial complex becomes a reality, there seems to be a good chance that the state will be able neither to coopt the present "movement of the poor" nor channel its activities into politically harmless avenues.

## COUNTERATTACK BY THE STATE

The economic and political struggles around the issues of the distribution of the tax burden, the volume of state expenditures, and budgetary priorities have pitted interest group against interest group, white-collar suburbanite against city dweller, white worker against black worker, taxpayer against state worker, state worker against labor in the monopoly sector, and so on. Struggles within and against the state have not been fought along class lines and hence do not necessarily pose any serious political threat to the established social order. In fact, many of these struggles have polarized the working class.

Nevertheless, the state has not succeeded in normalizing the relations of production in the state sector. On the one hand, the federal government has been "tightening up" hiring policies to screen out radicals and militants [33] and has centralized nearly all labor relations under the Department of Labor. (However, many of the conflicts that flare up at the state and local levels are still settled on an irregular or ad hoc basis.) On the other hand, state agencies have tried to develop administrative solutions to these struggles and conflicts or to contain them within new institutional arrangements. In fact, corporate liberals are no less concerned with the ideological and political aspects of insurgency movements than with their strictly economic aspects. "Every strike by public employees creates at least as great a crisis of public opinion as it does a crisis of transportation or education or whatever else may be involved," writes W. Willard Wirtz.[33] Thus, as Aronowitz has said, "the problem of finding a mechanism for dealing with public employee unions and locking them firmly into the system as an ally instead of a disruptive force has occupied sophisticated liberals for the past several years." [34]

It is rather that the "problem" is basically unresolvable because the "mechanism" is nonexistent. The government normally mediates between labor and capital, establishes the "rules of the game," and generally attempts to keep conflicts from spreading into other industries or otherwise getting out of hand. But there is no organ to mediate between the government and state employees because the government itself is one of the parties to labor-management disputes. Perhaps because of this, for example, over 100,000 disputes in the Post Office, are unresolved and bargaining over grievance procedures is close to collapse.[35] Many suggestions have been made to keep disputes manageable: fact finding with recommendations, strikework agreements, a labor peace agency, joint labor-management committees, permanent mediation panels, special panels such as the Atomic Energy Panel, labor courts, prohibitions on national affiliations to curb strike potential, and so on.[36] None is especially popular with either administrators or unionists. The best that state officials propose is "maximum practicable participation [by state employees] in developing and in administering their employment relationship." [37] Many urge compulsory arbitration, but most courts hold to the idea that the "people" are a sovereign entity and thus only elected officials have the right to dispose of public funds. So it is likely that in the foreseeable future compulsory arbitration will be confined to grievances under existing collective bargaining contracts and will not be used to resolve conflicts over new or renewed contracts.[38]

The second reason that it is difficult to establish arrangements that will keep workers and unions "firmly locked into the system" is that there exists a near-universal ban on strikes against the state. A federal statute makes it a criminal offense to strike against the government, and every federal employee union is obliged to renounce the right to strike. Nearly everywhere at the state and local levels strikes are condemned in law or press release by administrators as "illegal" and "immoral" actions against the public welfare.[39] Many states are strengthening their antistrike laws. In March 1969, for example, New York hardened several provisions of its antilabor Taylor law. And the 1971 Supreme Court decision banning most strikes in the state sector (excluding strikes against state contractors) appears to be the last judicial word on the subject—at least for the time being.

Although some establishment liberals support the right of state employees to strike, official commissions and study groups are not able to answer the most crucial issue involved: Can collective bargaining be effective without the right to strike? The state administration's answer is an unqualified yes. The unions' answer is an unqualified no. Several years ago the Advisory Commission on Public Employee Relations report to Governor George Romney (one of the three or four most influential studies of the issue), stated, "our view is that we have not yet reached the point where this 'ultimate issue' has to be or can realistically be decided." [40] One labor mediator put his finger on the crux of the matter when he said that "if freedom from public employee strikes is earnestly sought . . . the public employee organizations must be given a *quid pro quo* for its non-strike pledge." [41] However, nowhere does 'the mediator or anyone else involved suggest just what the quid pro quo might be.

The third and final reason why it is unlikely that state sector relations of production will become institutionalized in the near future is that local and state governments increasingly cannot afford to "lock" state workers into the "system." During the 1950s and most of the 1960s, many state agencies were willing to adopt the principle of parity between wage and salary workers in the state and unionized private sectors. However, because of inflation and the fiscal crisis, the national state is trying both to slow down the growth rate of monopoly sector money wages (and organized competitive sector industries) and to abandon the principle of parity. In this regard, Nixon's New Economic Policy was a great turning point. Meanwhile, local and state governments are trying to ameliorate the fiscal problem by imposing their own wage freezes or at least to harden their response to wage demands. Thus, the New York legislature refused to grant needed pension increases to New York City municipal workers, California froze college professors' salaries in 1970, and so on. Even compulsory arbitration of local wage disputes (adopted over the protests of some government officials) has failed to keep wage demands in line with the cities' fiscal capabilities. Pittsburgh, for example, "is in serious financial difficulty" because of wage hikes awarded policemen and firemen by arbitration. [42] Other local governments are "kicking the problem upstairs" by using employees' salary demands to pressure state governments (and the federal government) to redistribute tax monies through grants-in-aid. [43]

Despite the difficulties of negotiating with the state and the illegality of strikes, the refusal of many federal agencies to bargain in good faith, and the fines and jail sentences heaped on union militants, state workers and their organizations have struck or slowed down or otherwise hampered state operations when necessary. [44] For example, New York's Condon-Wadlin law banning strikes in the state sector is completely ineffective. And despite the fact that administrators are unhappy when unions challenge civil service-type approaches to personnel questions, unilateral determination of pay scales by state bureaucrats, and "managerial prerogatives" within the state agencies, there are more and more collective contracts of increasingly broader scope. Juridically, the benchmark came in the late 1950s and early 1960s with certain changes in the attitudes of key state bodies toward state employee unionism. New legislation and executive orders guaranteed public workers the right to organize and to participate through their representatives in determining the terms and conditions of employment. [45] In the past decade or so twenty-seven states have introduced some form of collective bargaining law for state employees, although there is wide divergency among states with regard to the categories of work affected and whether the state is required to bargain.[46] It is difficult to estimate how many local agencies have actually signed collective contracts with unions. One study suggests that collective agreements are widespread in Pennsylvania. In the late 1960s, workers in at least 575 local government units (of 3440) had collective contracts.[47] Finally, the first important collective bargaining settlement involving federal employees was signed in 1970 between postal unions and the U.S. Postal Service.

Union militancy in the state sector clearly has the potential for radicalizing both state employees and their organizations. For example, unlike monopoly sector unions, state labor organizations normally cannot justify wage demands on the basis of rising profits. They argue in terms of the need for "better public services," "quality education," "good health care delivery," and so on (and rising cost of living). But union militancy has fostered reactionary responses to such issues as racism, popular control of state institutions, and "professionalism." The experience of New York City teachers in their battles with administrators and parent and community groups over control of the schools offers abundant evidence of this danger. And even in the state sector, trade unions as such are poor instruments of radical social change because they are compelled to emphasize disciplined rank-and-file activity, tight organizational structures, and the union shop—not political education and mass activity at the base, two important factors in the politicization of workers.

## BEYOND REFORM

During the past few years tens of thousands of state workers and more state dependents have become politicized and radicalized to one degree or another. Some of the new radicals are ex-student New Leftists who are attracted to service occupations such as teaching and social work. Others are professional and semiprofessional workers. Still others are blue-collar workers squeezed by inflation and the fiscal crisis, and black workers in such fields as sanitation and public transportation who are carrying the struggle against institutionalized racism into the state agencies. There also has been a process of politicization and reaction in traditionally conservative branches of the state, particularly the police forces. Furthermore, the Nixon Administration and local police forces have conducted a series of counterrevolutionary actions against the black liberation and antiwar movements. Less dramatically, the Community Action Programs established in the mid-1960s, which provided a measure of community participation in a number of federal programs, have increasingly come under the influence and control of local governments.

Putting aside the radical roots of particular state sector occupations, it is important to emphasize that a majority of state employees labor in a socioeconomic milieu that breeds politicization and radicalization. One factor is the general nature of the work process in state industries. In the past, there was a more or less rigorous separation between the private and state economic spheres. However, with the interpenetration of economic base and political superstructure this division has become less and less pronounced. It has become increasingly apparent to many state employees that they are not "public servants" but indirect employees of private capital. At the same time, the work process is still guided by political norms. Thus state workers and clients can attack on "managerial prerogatives" without seeming to interfere directly with private property and the profit system. For example, the San Francisco Social Services Employees Union has forced the welfare administration to agree to public hearings on personnel questions—an impossibility in the private sector.[48]

Another factor is that state workers and especially state dependents bear the main burden of the fiscal crisis, which already has forced the state to cut back budgets for welfare and health and education and freeze wages and salaries in many localities. If (as seems likely) parity cannot be maintained between salaries in the state and monopoly sectors, it will be more difficult to keep state workers locked into the system. Then there is the illegality of strikes, the unwillingness of state administrators to bargain in good faith, and the state's easy access to injunctions against picketing of state facilities: These conditions force state employee unions to think in terms of the whole range of political issues—the right to organize, the right to strike, freedom of assembly, freedom of speech, and so on. Thus, for example, the postal workers' strike necessarily forced the workers to organize themselves and to avoid reliance on either the good will of state administrators or the union officials. The first national-level wildcat strike in U.S. history, it may have ushered in a period of worker action independent of trade unions.[49]

But perhaps the main factor in the politicization of state workers is the developing relationship between state workers and state dependents. As we know, in the competitive sector and in

THE FISCAL CRISIS OF THE STATE

the surplus population in general, economic exploitation of the crudest form, racism, and sexism are all inextricably linked. In the narrow material sense, the activities of state workers and clients, to the degree that state workers are struggling for more resources to serve the people, are not antagonistic but complementary. Further alliances between teachers, students, and office and maintenance personnel, between welfare workers and welfare recipients, between public health workers and people who use public health and medical facilities, and between transport workers and the public served by public transit are possible and likely. This trend is strengthened by the fact that more and more state workers are drawn from the working class itself (particularly the lower strata) and thus more readily identify and empathize with their clients. Clearly, unity among those who are directly or indirectly dependent on the state will sharpen awareness of the disparity between taxation and expenditure and deepen the fiscal crisis.

Again we see the intermingling of quantitative and qualitative demands. The surplus population is challenging not only the distribution of the social product but also the social relations they are compelled to enter into—racism, sexism, authoritarianism, bureaucracy. Students engaged in struggles against authoritarianism in the schools must confront their immediate "enemy"—teachers and low-level administrators. City planners whose technical solutions to problems of renewal, relocation, zoning, housing, and so on are frustrated by profit-seeking businessmen also are confronted by community movements who pose a third alternative—planning for, by, and of those who reside in the community. Public health personnel trying to protect their "professional" status are confronted by patients who demand not only technically competent medical care but also human service. Professors struggling to maintain faculty autonomy, open campuses, and their own traditional scholarly prerogatives are confronted by black and other students who want to develop their own curricula and control their own faculties and in general redefine the meaning of traditional education. Of all state workers, the social and welfare employees, whose jobs put them in constant touch with the most impoverished sections of the surplus population, probably have learned most about dealing with their own authoritarianism and professionalism. But even workers struggling to redefine their jobs and seeking ways to help, not control their clients are confronted by welfare rights groups with their own ideas about welfare and the nature of the welfare system—including social work. Finally, it is more difficult for whites and male employees to struggle against racist and sexist institutional structures in the state sector because blacks and other minorities and women typically are "clients to be looked after" not job peers. This is particularly true to the degree that state service workers aspire to professional status (even though bureaucratic organization, political reality, and institutionalized sexism mitigate against the development of autonomous professional organizations and professional work criteria).[50]

However, the fiscal crisis may make it easier for state workers to identify with state clients—to relate to those "below" them as political equals, rather than as professionals or state bureaucrats. State workers are being proletarianized by the imperatives of capitalist development—the socialization of the costs and expenses of production. Already the fiscal crisis is forcing state and local governments to hold the line on education spending and change priorities in this and other spheres of the state economy. A basic shift in budgetary priorities, the growth of the social-industrial complex, and regional planning and regional government will mean that the state will need technicians, not teachers, social workers, and public health workers; systems analysts and engineers and other organization scientists, technicians, and white-collar personnel, not traditional administrators; paraprofessionals, not volunteers and nurses' aides. The main question is whether these changes will bring about more control from the top or will create a greater opportunity for popular control in the workplace. Consider teaching, for example. In the 1920s, school administrators influenced by the principles of "scientific management" supervised every detail of the education process, whereas today principals exercise relatively loose control over the classroom. What will be the consequences if the education-industrial complex is fully realized and education is mechanized? To the degree that the state defines education outputs quantitatively, there will be a loss of teacher control. But to the degree that the schools need better educated specialists, teachers are likely to have more autonomy. To the extent that modernization requires heavy capital outlays in the form of closed-circuit TV, teaching machines, and so on, greater administrative control over the classroom is likely. But to the extent that teachers' training becomes more esoteric, there is likely to be more teacher control.[51] The AFT warns "it is [a] danger that a new educational elite may combine the new technology with new patterns of organization to manipulate teachers and students to its own ends," citing grade-school readers produced by a subsidiary of Xerox Corporation, which reflect establishment lines on issues such as racism and war.[52]

All in all, there seems to be a fighting chance that Third World groups and coalitions of state workers and clients, women's groups, and other militant organizations and movements will converge politically as the fragmented surplus population is gradually transformed into capital (i.e., wage labor) by the social-industrial complex. If this occurs, the surplus population will be compelled to remake itself and develop a new image of itself (potentially as a revolutionary social force)—if only because, as one well-known establishment economist writes, "today, the Federal government has more money than know-how [and] literally lacks the techniques for remaking people and conditions." [53] Last but not least, even with the further development of the complex (which is by no means inevitable), there will still be hundreds of thousands of jobless workers and millions of "marginal" workers in the competitive sector and at the bottom rungs in the monopoly sector—potentially a militant, even radical constituency. In this respect, the only change will be that poverty will not be so concentrated among blacks, other minorities, and women.[54]

Whether or not state workers and clients forge closer alliances in the future and become more radicalized, there will remain the overriding problem of the relationship between these workers and dependents and monopoly sector organized labor. The social-industrial complex will require much more economic and social planning than exists at present—and thus a much higher degree of social integration. But it is hard to see how monopoly capital and the state administration will be able to integrate organized labor with the surplus population. In specific, although monopoly sector labor has been relatively well-off, the monopoly sector has been growing at a relatively slow rate, and big business has been trying to cut costs to the bone. This has led to a revival of the speedup and stretchout, harder bargaining with unions, and wage controls. In turn, the rank and file, particularly younger workers, are demanding better working conditions and challenging traditional managerial prerogatives. (In Europe, where a similar process is in motion, there has been a noticeable shift from national, official, and centrally directed and controlled strikes to short, local, unofficial slowdowns and walkouts.)

Although monopoly sector workers (together with organized labor in construction and other high-paying competitive industries) still hold comparatively conservative opinions on social-political questions, their attitudes on economic issues are relatively progressive.[55] In a nutshell, they are willing to fight hard to keep themselves "one notch" above competitive sector workers. State workers, however, tend to be socially liberal—because they are in daily touch with social problems and the masses of state clients—and economically conservative even in the context of the fiscal crisis—because their

THE SCOPE AND LIMITS OF CAPITALIST REFORM 253

positions are relatively secure (e.g., their pension plans are better organized and offer greater benefits than those of private sector workers) and because the vast majority do not have to live with the terrible fear of being thrown into the competitive sector by labor-saving technological change. In brief, state workers tend to be conservative economically because they are economically privileged.

Moreover, economic strikes in the state sector are unique. Strikes in the private sector are most effective when they stop the flow of profits and hence threaten the existence of a particular firm or capitalist owner. Strikes in the state sector lead either to increases in prices and inflation or higher taxes or to lower real wages for the tax-paying working class—or both. Thus, although private unions frequently court disapproval by inflicting losses on the public in order to increase pressure on business to accept the unions' terms, the only important tactic available to state unions is to inconvenience the public and hope that popular sentiment will favor the union, not strikes. Strikes conducted by state workers therefore always hold a potential for dividing the working class and reinforcing interest-group not class consciousness. Certainly the only sure way for state worker unions to win their demands is to seek alliances both with other workers (outside the state sector also) and with state dependents. It is perhaps too soon to predict the nature of these alliances—the form they can take, the issues on which they can revolve, and their general political thrust. However, one conclusion can be drawn from current practice. Traditional economic struggles mounted by state workers will not win warm support from private workers (i.e., taxpayers) because the narrow economic interests of the two groups are in conflict. Thus, successful alliances are likely to be forged over qualitative issues such as quality and nature of education and control of the schools. For example, a recent Harris Poll showed that a small majority of citizens support teachers' strikes, undoubtedly because such strikes almost invariably are fought partly in the name of "quality education." In fact, the best strategy available to state workers may be to link wage demands to changes in overall budgetary priorities, which now favor monopoly capital and state contractors. If state workers demanded that their material needs be met by reallocating available resources not by increasing taxes—if they challenged more sharply the content and direction of the social-industrial complex—perhaps some of the present divisions between private and state workers would be narrowed.

When state workers strike for higher pay without linking their demands either to tax reforms or new budgetary priorities, a destructive split between public and private workers results. For then state workers are striking not against capital but against private sector workers. This is precisely what occurred in Sweden in early 1971 when state unions struck in order to maintain historic pay differentials between private sector and state workers. From the standpoint of the state workers, the Swedish goverment wanted to sacrifice their standard of living in an attempt to improve the material condition of the relatively low-paid private workers. But from the standpoint of private sector workers, state employees resisted the government's program not to maintain their standard of living but rather to keep and extend their privileges vis-à-vis private workers.

In the final analysis, whether a social-industrial complex really gets off the ground, whether divisions between state and private workers grow or narrow, and whether state worker organizations can forge an alliance with organized labor and state dependents, radicals and revolutionaries will not be able to exploit present opportunities, much less those that might appear in the future, in the absence of a mass socialist movement that cuts across all divisions within the working class. If monopoly capital's ideological and political hegemony is not effectively challenged, if a unified movement is not organized around opposition to monopoly capital's budgetary priorities, the fiscal crisis will continue to divide all those groups and strata that today fight in dismal isolation for a greater share of the budget or for a smaller share of the tax burden. Put another way, in the absence of a political movement that transcends particular interests, divisions between monopoly sector workers, state workers. and the surplus population could very well deepen.

Finally, in the absence of a socialist perspective that puts forth alternatives to every facet of capitalist society and that can help people comprehend every issue from the class nature of budgetary control to the nature of tax exploitation to the process by which the uses of technology and science are decided, unionists, organizers, and activists will continue to function in a relative theoretical vacuum. Precisely because we live at a time when all strata of the working class relate to each other more and more politically (and at a time when ultimate contradiction is the use of political or social means to achieve individual ends), what is needed is a socialist perspective that seeks to redefine needs in collective terms. The fact is that even if the working class socialized the entire share of income going to profits, the fiscal crisis would reappear in a new form—unless both social investment and social consumption and individual consumption and individualist modes of life are redefined. Stokely

Carmichael's saying, "individualism is·a luxury that we can no longer afford," is becoming true in a political as well as economic sense. In the absence of this kind of general historical consciousness, it will not be possible for organizers and activists to come to grips with even direct and immediate budgetary issues, not to speak of questions of authority, bureaucracy, social control, racism, and sexism—or, finally, the question of what will be the new material basis for social existence itself.[56]

# NOTES AND REFERENCES

1. Needless to add, this is precisely what happened during the 1972 Democratic primaries and convention. The McGovern forces—antiwar businessmen, professionals, youth, etc., social-industrial capitalists (e.g., Max Palevsky, Chairman of the Board of Xerox), and representatives of the surplus population (including the working and nonworking poor) completely outmaneuvered the forces of organized labor and the party machine.

2. Had McGovern won the 1972 election, the social-industrial complex would have been rapidly accelerated. Describing his plans for the unemployed, Sylvia Porter wrote that McGovern would spend

> an immediate Federal investment of $10 billion in programs at creating 2.4 million jobs. . . . High on McGovern's list would be jobs in building new and rehabilitated housing, in creating public transportation systems, in building neighborhood health centers and day-care centers, schools and hospitals, in programs for environmental protection. . . . Private industry would be given contracts for these programs just the way private industry is now given contracts for military production [*San Francisco Chronicle*, June 28, 1972].

Like Nixon (see Chapter 4, note 60), the McGovern-Kennedy corporate liberal forces also wanted to underwrite the new complex by subsidizing R & D in such areas as pollution control, air traffic control, health, noise abatement, drug rehabilitation, mass transit, etc Seemingly, the only difference in this regard was that McGovern was prepared to spend much more money than Nixon on R & D and the encouragement of small-scale technology-intensive companies.

3. Glen W. Fisher and Robert P. Fairbanks, *Illinois Municipal Finance: A Political and Economic Analysis* (Urbana, Ill.: 1968), p. 197.

4. Richard Musgrave, *Fiscal Systems* (New Haven, Conn.: 1969), p. 115, Figure 4–7, and pp. 123–124.

5. *Wall Street Journal*, December 21, 1971.

6. *Ibid.*

7. *Business Week*, October 17, 1970, special issue on the 1970s.

8. Ed Spannausand and Paul Gallagher, "Who Pays for Poverty?" *Viet-Report*, Summer 1968, p 23.

THE FISCAL CRISIS OF THE STATE

**9.** "America's Growing Antibusiness Mood," *Business Week,* June 17, 1972, p. 102.

**10.** As yet there is no movement urging that tax loopholes be created for the working class (e.g., depletion allowances for various types of labor). The reason is that this would truly redistribute income As *Business Week* writes,

the tax reform drive next year will no doubt be far less "threatening" to the beneficiaries of existing loopholes than the specter raised by the Mills repealer. Any tax changes will still be strongly shaped by the Treasury and written by the conservative Ways and Means Committee. Congress is not going to enact a tax bill that seriously jeopardizes economic expansion or redistributes income dramatically. The same pressure groups that won tax preferences in the first place will still be there. ["Congress Gets Serious About Tax Reform," *Business Week,* June 10, 1972, p 14.]

**11.** One student of payroll taxes writes, "whether the favorable reception [of social insurance taxes] will continue to characterize the still higher tax projected for future years is difficult to judge" (James R. Ukockis, "Social Security: Development and Financing," *Monthly Review,* Federal Reserve Bank of Kansas City, April 1968, p. 13).

**12.** The highest percentage was 71 percent during the Korean War. It is interesting to note that the poll indicated no variation in response by income group, race, or political affiliation, perhaps because of the uniformity of the aggregate tax rate on all sections of the population.

**13.** In the nineteenth century the federal government frequently ran budgetary surpluses because of the efficiency of the tariff as a source of revenue. This does not conflict with our analysis, but merely significes that federal expenditures were in fact small.

**14.** On balance, there is no reason to believe that the U.S. economy has reached the limits of its fiscal capacity in terms of "harm" to economic incentives. Available evidence (much of it possibly out of date) indicates that personal income taxes have little effect on the total supply of laborpower [George F Break, "Income Taxes and Incentive to Work: An Empirical Study," *American Economic Review,* 47 (September 1957)]. Similarly, there is no evidence that the individual tax has adverse effects on incentives to enter high-risk, high-return occupations and professions [Herbert G. Grubel and David R. Edwards, "Personal Income Taxation and Choice of Profession," *Quarterly Journal of Economics,* 78 (February 1964)]. Nor does it seem to be true that the income tax has a negative effect on business executives' willingness to work [Thomas H. Sanders, *Effects of Taxation on Executives* (Boston: 1951)].

**15.** One of the reasons that corporate and state planners forced to deal with inflation prefer wage controls to managed recessions is that a state-managed slowdown creates underutilized capacity, a decline in government revenues, and thus big short-run budgetary deficits. These "passive deficits" were quite large during the second Eisenhower recession in the late 1950s and during most of fiscal year 1970–1971 [Lynn Turgeon, "The Crisis of Post-Keynesian Economics: A Revisionist Interpretation of Recent Economic History" (unpublished manuscript)].

**16.** A recent Brookings Institution study concluded that the present tax base will not produce sufficient revenue to balance the budget even at full-employment production "In brief, this projection shows that, between fiscal 1972 and 1974, there will be no fiscal dividend. Total federal expenditures under existing programs and those proposed in the 1972 budget will grow by as much as full employment revenues, even after taking into account further reductions in Vietnam

THE SCOPE AND LIMITS OF CAPITALIST REFORM

costs" [Charles Schultz et al., *Setting National Priorities* (Washington, D.C.: The Brookings Institution, 1972), pp. 319–320]. Another study prepared by Murray Wiedenbaum [*The Federal Budget for 1973* (New York: American Enterprise Institute for Public Policy Research, 1972)] comes to more or less the same conclusions. Both agree that the federal government will have to increase taxes to finance any new programs or initiatives.

17. Sei Fujita, "Political Ceiling on Income Taxation," *Public Finance*, 16:2 (1961), 183.

18. George Katona, *The Mass Consumption Society* (New York: 1964), p. 145–146.

19. "America's Growing Antibusiness Mood," op. cit.

20. Because VAT is an indirect tax it conceals the true tax burden and thus reduces popular consciousness of tax exploitation. As might be expected, it is backed by conservative forces—Nixon, Connolly, Commerce Secretary Peterson, and others. Nixon proposed a 3 percent rate applicable the first year of VAT's operation, which would raise about $18 billion. However, it has been estimated that a VAT of 2 percent would be needed to relieve property owners of the property tax completely.

21. Nixon's so-called New Federalism makes it especially important to link up the issues of the tax burden, domestic and overseas expenditure, and corporate priorities—i.e., to develop a perspective of capitalism as a total system His program envisages the redistribution of federal tax dollars to the states and cities. Redistribution is bound to benefit local politicians and to some degree local capital (which will have to be bribed into accepting regionalization). Local politicians are caught between the need to keep taxes on residential properties low in order to retain the support of organized labor and the need to keep taxes on commercial property low in order to avoid alienating the downtown business interests. But the funds for redistribution will not be available in the absence of economic growth, which in turn is partly dependent on more overseas expansion. Thus, we can see the organic relation between Nixon's revenue-sharing proposals and Connolly's militant nationalism.

22. California State Employees Association, *Forum* (October 1970)

23. Douglas Weiford and Wayne Burggraaff, "The Future of Public Employee Unions," in Daniel H. Kruger and Charles T. Schmidt, eds., *Collective Bargaining in the Public Service* (New York: 1969), p. 67.

24. Ronald W. Glass, "Work Stoppages and Teachers: History and Prospect," *Monthly Labor Review*, 90 (August 1967).

25. Lyle E. Schaller, "City Halls Feel the Impact of Unions," *Mayor and Manager*, 10:16–20 (March 1967).

26. Joel Seidman, "Nurses and Collective Bargaining," *Industrial and Labor Relations Review*, 23:3 (April 1970); Darold T. Barnum, "From Private to Public: Labor Relations in Urban Transit," *Industrial and Labor Relations Review*, 25:1 (October 1971).

27. E. Wright Bakke, "Reflections on the Future of Bargaining in the Public Sector," *Monthly Labor Review*, 93:7 (July 1970).

28. Sheila C. White, "Work Stoppages of Government Employees," *Monthly Labor Review*, 92:12 (December 1969)

29. Teachers are under especially severe pressure because the traditional analyses and solutions to economic disruption, social unrest, poverty, international tensions, and so on are ineffectual or wrong—because of the bankruptcy of bourgeois social thought For those engaged in the reproduction of ruling-class ideas and values, this is another source of bewilderment, frustration, and dis-

illusionment. One study suggests that teachers with the highest "professional orientation" tend to have slightly higher "conflict rates" than the typical teacher (information courtesy of Steve Smith).

**30.** W. Richard Scott, "Professional Employees in a Bureaucratic Situation," in Amitai Etzioni, ed., *The Semi-Professions and their Organization* (New York: 1969), p. 131.

**31.** President's National Advisory Commission on Rural Poverty, *The People Left Behind* (Washington, D.C., September 1967), p. ix.

**32.** Bureau of Social Research, Inc., *Welfare Policy and Its Significance for the Recipient Population: A Study of the AFDC Program,* submitted to the Department of Health, Education, and Welfare, December 1969.

**33.** W. Williard Wirtz, Labor News Release No. USDL–7175 (Washington, D.C., 1966).

**34.** Stanley Aronowitz, "Public Workers Are Sold Out," *National Guardian,* February 24, 1968. See also, David Cole et al., "Collective Bargaining in the Public Sector," *Monthly Labor Review,* 92:7 (July 1969).

**35.** *Business Week,* June 10, 1972, p. 58.

**36.** See Ida Klaus, "The Emerging Relationship," in *Collective Bargaining in the Public Service,* op. cit., p. 19.

**37.** Wirtz, op. cit.

**38.** More than 70 cities have adopted grievance arbitration (David G. Shelton, "Compulsory Arbitration in the Public Service," in *Collective Bargaining in the Public Service,* op. cit.).

**39.** However, Hawaii's legislature recently passed collective bargaining legislation giving government workers a limited right to strike. And in a number of European countries (France, Norway, and Sweden among them), a distinction is made between civil servants who are forbidden by law to strike and public workers who are permitted to strike.

**40.** "The Study Commission Reports," in *Collective Bargaining in the Public Service,* op. cit., p. 103.

**41.** Allan Weisenfeld, "The New Jersey Employer-Employee Relations Act of 1968," *The Economic and Business Bulletin,* 21:4 (Summer 1969), 27.

**42.** Charles T. Douds, "The Status of Collective Bargaining of Public Employees in Pennsylvania," *The Economic and Business Review,* 21:4 (Summer 1969), 29.

**43.** The dynamic of the Chicago teachers' strike suggests the pattern that might be followed in future struggles Following a strike in May 1969, the teachers won a monthly salary raise of $100. Implementation depended on the state legislature's approval of additional state aid for the schools. State aid was not increased and the schools were forced to cut the raise to $50 monthly.

**44.** Public Personnel Association, San Francisco Bay Area Chapter, *Report of the Special Committee to Study Collective Bargaining in the Public Service,* October 14, 1960. This study suggests that collective bargaining in the state sector has no effect at all on strikes.

**45.** The most important changes were Executive Order of the Mayor (New York City), 1958; Federal Executive Order 10988 of President Kennedy; and the Wisconsin Employment Relations Law as amended in 1962 ("The Emerging Relationship," in *Collective Bargaining in the Public Service,* op. cit., p. 69).

**46.** Richard S. Rubin, *A Summary of State Collective Bargaining Laws in Public Employment,* Public Employee Relations Report, No. 3, New York State School of Industrial and Labor Relations, 1968, p. i. The remaining states have no statutes on the issue; the question of whether state agencies are legally required to bargain is unresolved.

THE SCOPE AND LIMITS OF CAPITALIST REFORM          259

47. "The Status of Collective Bargaining of Public Employees in Pennsylvania," op. cit., p. 28.

48. In a letter to the Civil Service Commission (April 11, 1971), the union wrote,

> The law requires that all public bodies be accessible to the people; that employees are entitled to representation according to their wishes; and that no decisions or criteria for decisions be set up or made by a public agency where the procedures or the decisions are contrary to constitutionally required due process. Therefore, we believe that it is mandatory for any such negotiations or Committee to meet in public and hear all testimony brought before it, prior to making any decisions.

49. Stanley Aronowitz and Jeremy Brecher, "Notes on the Postal Strike," *Root and Branch* (June 1970).

50. *The Semi-Professions and their Organization*, op. cit., p. vi. In the last analysis, the authority of knowledge and the authority of administrative hierarchy are incompatible (ibid., p. vii).

51. *The Semi-Professions and Their Organization*, op. cit., pp. 45–46.

52. *American Teacher* (September 1969), 3.

53. Henry C. Wallich, "The Defense Budget," *Newsweek*, June 15, 1972, p. 76.

54. This is the establishment's hope. "There is some hope that better health care, education, and vocational training can bring disadvantaged groups into the mainstream of American society so that almost everyone will be employable and no identifiable group will be stuck in marginal jobs" (*Setting National Priorities*, op. cit., p. 184).

55. According to studies cited in *American Teacher*, 54 (April 1970), 9. This is no doubt why the unions and surplus population are able to work together on some limited "economistic" issues. For example, the UAW and the Indiana Welfare Rights Organization joined to defeat legislation that would cut back welfare grants.

56. Perhaps it is fitting to conclude this work with a statement made five years ago by Martin Nicolaus, whose correspondence with the author around that time helped in the formulation of some of the ideas presented here.

> The sharpening of the contradiction between surplus capital and surplus population has been prevented and is being delayed . . . by the fiscal power of the state. Briefly: defense and space spending, on the one hand, provide absorption outlets for surplus capital and maintain effective demand. Welfare spending, on the other hand, serves to quiet the grumblings of the surplus population. . . . Once the central role of fiscal power in preventing the sharpening of this contradiction is grasped, then it seems to me that the question of how capitalism will be destroyed can, in principle, receive a clear answer. *The capitalist system will fall when the fiscal power of the state is exhausted.* ["Paul Sweezy's 'Critical Reassessment of Marx's Theory of the Proletariat—A Commentary," Second Annual Socialist Scholars Conference, September 1967.]

Comment on this statement now would be redundant. This entire work in a sense can be taken as a critique of it.

# BIBLIOGRAPHY

Below is a selected bibliography (English language) of some useful studies pertaining to the political economy of state expenditures and revenues. Excluded is the vast literature on state regulation, fiscal and monetary policy, and welfare economics, including the micro-economics of taxing and spending. More or less adequate bibliographies of studies in these areas can be found in most conventional public finance texts. Most of the readings cited below are organized around particular topics in order in which they appear in this book.

## GENERAL THEORY OF STATE FINANCE
## OR FISCAL POLITICS

Buchanan, James, *Fiscal Theory and Political Economy* (Chapel Hill, N.C.: University of North Carolina Press, 1960).

————, *The Demand and Supply of Public Goods* (Chicago: 1968).

Deutsch, Karl W., "Social Mobilization and Political Development," *American Political Science Review* (September, 1961).

Galbraith, John Kenneth, *The Affluent Society* (Boston: Houghton-Mifflin, 1958).

Goldscheid, Rudolf, "A Sociological Approach to the Problem of Public Finance," in Richard A. Musgrave and Alan T. Peacock, eds., *Classics in the Theory of Public Finance* (New York: St. Martin's, 1958).

Martin, Alison and Lewis, W. Arthur, "Patterns of Public Revenue and Expenditure," *The Manchester School of Economic and Social Sciences* (September, 1956).

Mattick, Paul, *Marx and Keynes: The Limits of the Mixed Economy* (Boston: Sargent, 1969).

Musgrave, Richard A., *Fiscal Systems* (New Haven, Conn.: Yale University Press, 1969).

O'Connor, James, "Ideological and Scientific Elements in the Theory of Government Policy," *Science and Society* (Fall–Winter, 1969).

Olsen, Mancur, *The Logic of Collective Action* (Cambridge, Mass.: Schocken, 1965).

Oshima, Harry T., "Share of Government in GNP for Various Countries," *American Economic Review* (June, 1957).

Peacock, Alan T. and Wiseman, Jack, *The Growth of Public Expenditures in the United Kingdom* (Princeton, N.J.: University of Princeton Press, 1961).

Schumpeter, Joseph, "The. Crisis of the Tax State," *International Economic Papers* (1954).

Wagner, Adolf, "Three Extracts on Public Finance," in Richard A. Musgrave and Alan T. Peacock, eds., *Classics in the Theory of Public Finance* (New York: St. Martin's, 1958).

## HISTORY OF UNITED STATES GOVERNMENT FINANCE

Broude, Henry W., "The Role of the State in American Economic Development, 1820–1890," in Harry N. Scheiber, ed., *United States Economic History: Selected Readings* (New York: Knopf, 1964).

Conkin, Paul K., *The New Deal* (New York: Crowell, 1967).

Doris, Lillian, *The American Way of Taxation: Internal Revenue, 1862–1963* (Englewood Cliffs, N.J.: Prentice-Hall, 1963).

Fabricant, Solomon, *The Trend of Government Activity in the U.S. Since 1900* (New York: Columbia University Press, 1952).

————, *The Rising Trend of Government Employment* (New York: Columbia University Press, 1949).

Ferguson, E. James, *The Power of the Purse: A History of American Public Finance, 1776–1796* (Chapel Hill, N.C.: University of North Carolina Press, 1961).

Firestone, John M., *Federal Receipts and Expenditures During Business Cycles, 1879–1958* (Princeton, N.J.: Princeton University Press, 1960).

Hawley, Ellis W., *The New Deal and the Problem of Monopoly* (Princeton, N.J.: Princeton University Press, 1966).

Kendrick, M. Slade, *A Century and a Half of Federal Expenditures* (New York: 1955).

Kimmel, Lewis H., "Keynesian Theory, Public Opinion, and the New Deal," in Harry N. Scheiber, ed., *United States Economic History: Selected Readings* (New York: Knopf, 1964).

Lewis, Wilfred, Jr., *Federal Fiscal Policy in Postwar Recessions* (Washington, D.C.: The Brookings Institution, 1962).

Sharkansky, Ira, "Government Expenditures and Public Services in the United States," *American Political Science Review* (December, 1967).

Stein, Herbert, *The Fiscal Revolution in America* (Chicago: University of Chicago Press, 1969).

Trescott, Paul B., "Some Historical Aspects of Federal Fiscal Policy, 1790–1956," in Joint Economic Committee, U.S. Congress, *Federal Expenditure Policy for Economic Growth and Stability* (Washington, D.C.: The Brookings Institution, 1957).

Williamson, Jeffrey G., "Public Expenditures and Revenue: An International Comparison," *The Manchester School of Economic and Social Sciences* (January, 1961).

Wilmerding, Lucius, Jr., *The Spending Power: A History of the Efforts of Congress to Control Expenditures* (New Haven, Conn.: Yale University Press, 1943).

## THE POLITICS OF THE BUDGET

Anton, Thomas J., *The Politics of State Expenditures in Illinois* (Urbana, Ill.: University of Illinois Press, 1966).

Bollens, John C, *Special District Governments in the United States* (Berkeley: University of California Press, 1957).

Fenno, Richard F., Jr., *The Power of the Purse: Appropriations Politics in Congress* (Boston: Little, Brown, 1966).

Fisher, Glenn W, *Taxes and Politics: A Study of Illinois Public Finance* (Urbana, Ill.: University of Illinois Press, 1969).

—— and Fairbanks, Robert P., *Illinois Municipal Finance: A Political and Economic Analysis* (Urbana, Ill : University of Illinois Press, 1968).

Haveman, Robert and Margolis, Julius, eds., *Public Expenditures and Policy Analysis* (Chicago: Markham, 1970).

Jacomet, Robert, "The Adaption of Public Finance to the Economic Function of the State," *Public Finance* (1948).

Marchal, Jean, "The State and the Budget," *Public Finance* (1948).

Ott, David J. and Attiat F., *Federal Budget Policy* (Washington, D.C.: The Brookings Institution, 1965).

Schick, Allen, "The Budget Bureau That Was: Thoughts on the Rise, Decline, and Future of a Presidential Agency," *Law and Contemporary Problems* (Summer, 1970).

Schultz, Charles, et al, *Setting National Priorities, 1972* (Washington, D.C.: The Brookings Institution, 1972).

Sharkansky, Ira, *The Politics of Taxing and Spending* (Indianapolis-New York: Bobbs-Merrill, 1969).

Smith, Harold, "The Budget as an Instrument of Legislative Control and Executive Management," *Public Administration Review* (Summer, 1964).

Smithies, Arthur, *The Budgetary Process in the United States* (New York: 1955).

Wildavsky, Aaron, *The Politics of the Budgetary Process* (Boston: Little, Brown, 1964).

## URBAN RENEWAL AND TRANSPORTATION

Abrams, Charles, *The City Is the Frontier* (New York: Harper & Row, 1966).

Anderson, Martin, *The Federal Bulldozer* (Cambridge, Mass.: The M.I.T. University Press, 1964).

Beagle, Dan, Haber, Al, and Wellman, David, "Turf Power and the Taxman: Urban Renewal, Regionalization, and the Limits of Community Control," *Leviathan* (April, 1969).

DeFreitas, Greg, "BART: Rapid Transit and Regional Control," *Pacific Research and World Empire Telegram* (November–December, 1972).

Ives, Ralph, Lloyd, Gary W., and Sawers, Larry, "Mass Transit and the Power Elite," *Review of Radical Political Economics* (Summer, 1972).

Lawrence, David, "The Initial Decision to Build the Supersonic Transport," *American Journal of Economics and Sociology* (October, 1971).

Wheeler, George Shaw, "The Crisis in Transport," *Czechoslovak Economic Papers* (1965).

## MILITARY EXPENDITURES

Baldwin, William, *The Structure of the Defense Market, 1955–1964* (Chapel Hill, N.C.: University of North Carolina Press, 1967).

Barnet, Richard, *The Economy of Death* (New York: Atheneum, 1969).

Cook, Fred, *The Warfare State* (New York: Macmillan, 1966).

Magdoff, Harry, "Militarism and Imperialism," *American Economic Review* (May, 1970).

Melman, Seymour, *Pentagon Capitalism* (New York: McGraw-Hill, 1970).

————, ed., *The War Economy of the United States: Readings in Military Industry and Economy* (New York: St. Martin's Press, 1971).

Reich, Michael and Finkelhor, David, "Capitalism and the Military-Industrial Complex: The Obstacles to Conversion," *Review of Radical Political Economics* (1970).

Rosen, Paul, "Militarism and American Technological and Scientific Progress," *Monthly Review* (March, 1957).

U.S. Congress, Subcommittee on Economy in Government, Joint Economic Committee, *The Economics of Military Procurement* (Washington, D.C.: Government Printing Office, 1969).

## SOCIAL SECURITY AND WELFARE

Ehrenreich, John and Barbara, *The American Health Empire: Power, Profits, and Politics* (New York: 1970).

Pechman, Joseph A., Aaron, Henry J., and Taussig, Michael K., *Social Security: Perspectives for Reform* (Washington, D.C.: The Brookings Institution, 1968).

Piven, Francis Fox and Cloward, Richard A., *Regulating the Poor: The Functions of Public Welfare* (New York: Random House, 1971).

Seligman, Ben, ed., *Poverty as a Public Issue* (New York: The Free Press, 1968).

## STATE ENTERPRISE

Apicella, Vincenzo, "The Development of the Public Sector," *Annals of Public and Co-Operative Economy* (January/March, 1964).

Baum, Warren C., *The French Economy and the State* (Princeton, N.J.: Princeton University Press, 1958).

Boccara, Paul, "Introduction to the Question of State Monopoly Capitalism," *Economic Bulletin,* New Series (January, 1968).

Fabricant, Solomon, *The Trend of Government Activity in the United States Since 1900* (Princeton, N.J.: Princeton University Press, 1950).

Kendrick, John W., "Exploring Productivity Measurement in Government," *Public Administration Review* (June, 1963).

Langer, Edmond, "Nationalizations in Austria," *Annals of Public and Co-Operative Economy* (April/September, 1964).

Lenouda, Pella, "Public Enterprise in Greece," *Public Finance* (1963).

Lytton, Henry D., "Public Sector Productivity in the Truman-Eisenhower Years," *Review of Economics and Statistics* (May, 1961).

Posner, M. V. and Woolf, S. J., *Italian Enterprise* (Cambridge, Mass.: Harvard University Press, 1967).

Robson, W. A., *Nationalized Industry and Public Ownership* (London: Allen & Unwin, 1960).

Sheahan, John, *Promotion and Control of Industry in Postwar France* (Cambridge, Mass.: Harvard University Press, 1963).

Shonfield, Andrew, *Modern Capitalism* (New York: Oxford University Press, 1965).

Strumthal, Adolf, "The Structure of Nationalized Enterprises in France," *Political Science Quarterly* (September, 1952).

## STATE TAXATION AND THE STATE DEBT

Eisenstein, Louis, *The Ideologies of Taxation* (New York: Ronald, 1961).

Gottlieb, Manuel, "The Capital Levy After World War I," *Public Finance* (1952).

———, "Political Economy of the Public Debt," *Public Finance* (1956).

Gurley, John G., "Federal Tax Policy," *National Tax Journal* (September, 1967).

Hellerstein, Jerome R., *Taxes, Loopholes, and Morals* (New York: McGraw-Hill, 1963).

Maxwell, James, *Financing State and Local Governments* (Washington, D.C.: The Brookings Institution, 1965).

Pechman, Joseph, *Federal Tax Policy* (Washington, D.C.: The Brookings Institution, 1966).

———— and Okner, Benjamin, *Individual Income Tax Erosion by Income Classes* (Washington, D.C.: The Brookings Institution, 1972).

Rabinowitz, Alan, *Municipal Bond Finance and Administration* (New York: Wiley, 1965).

## THE RELATIONS OF PRODUCTION IN THE STATE SECTOR

American Assembly, The, *Public Workers and Public Unions* (New Jersey: 1972).

Baird, Robert N. and Landon, John H., "The Effects of Collective Bargaining on Public School Teachers' Salaries," *Industrial and Labor Relations Review* (April, 1972).

Barnum, Donald T., "From Private to Public: Labor Relations in Urban Transit," *Industrial and Labor Relations Review* (October, 1971).

Baumol, William J., "Macroeconomics of Unbalanced Growth: The Anatomy of Urban Crisis," in Robert L. Heinbroner and Arthur M. Ford, eds., *Is Economics Relevant?: A Reader in Political Economics* (Pacific Palisades, Calif.: Goodyear, 1971).

Brown, Michael Barratt, "Against the Conservative Attack on Public Enterprise," *Bulletin of the Institute of Workers Control* (1971).

Kruger, Daniel H. and Schmidt, Charles T., eds., *Collective Bargaining in the Public Service* (New York: Random House, 1969).

Owen, John D., "Toward a Public Employment Wage Theory: Some Econometric Evidence on Teacher Quality," *Industrial and Labor Relations Review* (January, 1972).

Stanley, David T., *Managing Local Government Under Pressure* (Washington. D.C.: The Brookings Institution, 1972).

Sturmthal, Adolf, "Nationalization and Workers' Control in Britain and France," *Journal of Political Economy* (February, 1953).

## REGIONAL GOVERNMENT AND THE SOCIAL-INDUSTRIAL COMPLEX

Cohen, Fred and Weiss, Marc, "Big Business and Urban Stagnation," *Pacific Research and World Empire Telegram* (1970).

Feshbach, Dan and Shipnuck, Les, "Regional Government:

A National Perspective," *Pacific Research and World Empire Telegram* (November–December, 1972).

———, "Bay Area Council: Regional Powerhouse," *Pacific Research and World Empire Telegram* (November–December, 1972).

Gellen, Martin, "The Making of a Pollution-Control Complex," *Ramparts* (May, 1970).

Weiss, Marc, "Housing-Industrial Complex," *Pacific Research and World Empire Telegram* (November–December, 1972).

BIBLIOGRAPHY                                                              267

# INDEX

Abzug, Bella, 245
Ackerman, Frank, 52
Ackley, Gardner C., 50
Advisory Commission on Intergovernmental Relations, 56, 90
Advisory Commission on Public Employee Relations, 247
AFL-CIO, 225, 237, 238, 242
Agency for International Development (AID), 168
Aggregative fiscal policy, 78
Agricultural Adjustment Administration, 68
Agricultural price supports, 81
Aid for Dependent Children (AFDC), 165
Alabama, 88
American Association for Labor Legislation, 139
American Federation of Government Employees, 237
American Federation of State, County, and Municipal Employees (AFSCME), 237, 238
American Federation of Teachers (AFT), 235, 236, 238, 242, 252
American Nurses Association, 238
American Postal Workers Union, 237
Apicella, Vincenzo, 187
Appalachia, 102, 105
Appropriations: Congressional control over, 73; impounding of, 73; lump sum, 74
"Aristocracy of finance," 190, 192
Associations, private, 66
Atomic Energy Panel, 247

Bahl, Roy, 128–129
Balance of payments, 49
Baran, Paul A., 160
Basic research, 114

Baumol, William J., 31, 131
Bay Area Council, 54, 109
Bay Area Rapid Transit (BART), 54, 87, 107, 109
Benham, F. C., 131
"Bipartisan foreign policy," 153
Blacks, 133, 134, 162, 223, 243, 251. *See also* Minorities
Blakkan, Renée, 142–143
Bollens, John, 87
Brookings Institution, 75, 215
Budget and Accounting Act (1920), 74–75
Budgetary: authority, centralization of, 78; changes in policy, 70–71; decisions, 76; expansion, 79; overall planning, 78; priorities, 99; reform, 73
Budgeting and budgets: administrative, 75, 78–79; balanced, 71–72; cash-consolidated, 78; congressional, 74; control of, 10, 41, 53; Federal, Program composition of (Table), 100; and Federal Government, 65–82; financing of, 179–183, 203–215; line-item, 75; local, 85–90; military, 41, 52, 79. *See also* Military-industrial complex; national income, 78; outlays, Trends in (Table), 98; planning, 53, 73; as private profit source, 72; program, 51, 75–76; state and local governments, 82–88
Business Advisory Council, 68, 139
Bureau of the Budget, 65, 68, 74, 75, 76, 78, 80, 81, 182
Bureau of Highways, 67
Bureau of Labor Statistics, 140
Bureau of Old Age and Survivors Insurance, 70
Burkhead, Jesse, 77
*Business Week,* 110, 116, 126–127